Contents

Numbers in brackets refer to similar items appearing in Social Trends 32

Introduction

Article: The role of Social Capital

Table A.1	Membership of selected environmental organisations	19
Figure A.2	Post-war turnout for general elections	20
Figure A.3	Community spirit in neighbourhoods	21
Figure A.4	Trust in neighbours: by age, 2000/01	22
Figure A.5	Satisfactory relatives and friendship networks: by length of residence, 2000/01	23
Table A.6	Characteristics of people with high and low social capital	24

1: Population

Population profile
Table 1.1	Population of the United Kingdom (1.1)	30
Table 1.2	Population: by age and sex (1.3)	31
Figure 1.3	Dependent population: by age	31
Table 1.4	Population aged 65 and over: EU comparison	32
Table 1.5	Population: by ethnic group and age, 2001-02 (1.4)	32
Figure 1.6	Population of working age: by sex and socio-economic classification, 2002 (1.5)	33

Population change
Table 1.7	Population change (1.6)	34
Figure 1.8	Births and deaths (1.7)	34
Table 1.9	Deaths: by age and sex (1.8)	35

Geographical distribution
Map 1.10	Population change, mid-1981 to mid-2001 (1.9)	36
Table 1.11	Inter-regional movements within the United Kingdom, 2001 (1.11)	37

Migration
Table 1.12	Net international migration: by citizenship	37
Figure 1.13	Grants of settlement: by region of origin (1.14)	38
Table 1.14	Asylum applications, including dependants: EU comparison, 2001	38

International perspective
Map 1.15	World population densities: by country, 2001	39
Table 1.16	World demographic indicators (1.16)	39

2: Households and Families

Households and families
Table 2.1	Households: by size (2.1)	42
Table 2.2	Households: by type of household and family (2.2)	42

Figure 2.3	Percentage of all households where heads of household live alone: by age and sex (2.4)	43
Table 2.4	Percentage of children living in different family types (2.16)	43
Table 2.5	Families with dependent children: by ethnic group, 2002 (2.18)	44
Table 2.6	Frequency of adults seeing relatives and friends, 2001	44
Table 2.7	Frequency of adults having contact with their grandchildren, 2001	45

Partnerships

Table 2.8	Proportion of the population: by marital status and sex (2.5)	45
Figure 2.9	Non-married people cohabiting: by sex and age, 2000/01	46
Figure 2.10	Marriages and divorces (2.8)	46
Table 2.11	Marriage and divorce rates: EU comparison, 2001	47
Table 2.12	Average age at marriage and divorce	47
Figure 2.13	Stepfamily couples with dependent children: by family type, 2000/01	48

Family formation

Table 2.14	Conceptions: by outcome	48
Table 2.15	Teenage conceptions: by age at conception and outcome, 2000	49
Figure 2.16	Live births to teenage women: EU comparison, 2001	49
Figure 2.17	Abortion rates: by age (2.11)	50
Figure 2.18	Births outside marriage as a percentage of all live births (2.14)	50
Table 2.19	Average age of mother at childbirth	51
Figure 2.20	Percentage of women childless at age 25, 35 and 45: by year of birth	51
Table 2.21	Maternities with multiple births: by age of mother at childbirth, 2001	52
Figure 2.22	Adoption orders (2.20)	52

3: Education and Training

Early years education

| Figure 3.1 | Children under five in schools as a percentage of all three and four year olds (3.2) | 56 |
| Table 3.2 | Good things about nursery education providers, 2001 | 56 |

Schools

Table 3.3	School pupils: by type of school (3.1)	57
Figure 3.4	Appeals lodged by parents against non-admission of their children to maintained schools	58
Table 3.5	Permanent exclusions from schools: by sex (3.8)	58
Table 3.6	Pupils in maintained schools whose mother tongue is other than English, 2002	59
Table 3.7	Pupils reaching or exceeding expected standards: by key stage and sex, 2002 (3.15)	59
Table 3.8	Knowledge and skills of 15 year olds in three literacy areas: EU comparison, 2000	60
Table 3.9	GCSE attainment: by parents' socio-economic classification, 2000	61

Post compulsory participation

Table 3.10	Participation in education and training of 16, 17 and 18 year olds: by sex, 2001	62
Table 3.11	People working towards a qualification: by age, 2002 (3.14)	62
Table 3.12	Students in further and higher education: by type of course and sex (3.13)	63
Table 3.13	Enrolments on adult education courses: by subject, age and sex, November 2001 (3.27)	64

Post compulsory outcomes

Table 3.14	Achievement at GCE A level or equivalent: by sex (3.18)	65
Table 3.15	NVQ awards: by framework area and level, 2000/01	65
Table 3.16	Destinations of first degree graduates	66
Table 3.17	Highest qualification: by region, 2002	66

Lifelong learning and training

Figure 3.18	Employees receiving job-related training: by sex and age, 2002 (3.25)	67
Figure 3.19	Types of off-the-job training provided, 2001	67
Table 3.20	Learning reported: by disability, 2001	68
Table 3.21	Obstacles to learning: by sex, 2001	68

Educational resources

Table 3.22	Expenditure on education as a percentage of GDP: EU comparison, 1999	69
Figure 3.23	Full-time nursery & primary and secondary school teachers: by sex (3.10)	69
Table 3.24	Non-teaching staff: by type of school (3.5)	70
Table 3.25	Teachers who feel confident in the use of ICT	70
Figure 3.26	Student standard maintenance grant and loan in real terms	71

4: Labour Market

Economic activity

Figure 4.1	Economic activity rates: by sex (4.6)	74
Figure 4.2	Economic activity rates: by sex and age, 2002	75
Table 4.3	Economic activity status of female lone parents: by age of youngest dependent child, 1992 and 2002	75
Table 4.4	Economic activity status of disabled people: by sex, 2002 (4.8)	76
Table 4.5	Reasons for economic inactivity: by sex, 1997 and 2002 (4.11)	76
Table 4.6	Working age households: by household economic status	77

Employment

Figure 4.7	Employment rates: by sex (4.1)	77
Table 4.8	Working age population: by employment status and sex, EU comparison, 2001	78
Map 4.9	Employment rates: by area, 2002 (4.2)	78
Table 4.10	Economic activity: by employment status and sex, 1987 and 2002 (4.3)	79
Table 4.11	Employment rates: by ethnic group, sex and highest qualification, 2001-02 (4.9)	79

Patterns of employment

Table 4.12   Employee jobs: by sex and industry (4.13)   80

Table 4.13   Employees: by sex and occupation, 2002 (4.14)   80

Table 4.14   Employees and self-employed who have second jobs:
by industry of main job, 2002   81

Figure 4.15   Self-employment: by sex, EU comparison, 2001   81

Figure 4.16   Self-employment: by ethnic group, 2001-02 (4.15)   82

Unemployment

Figure 4.17   Unemployment: by sex (4.19)   82

Figure 4.18   Unemployment rates: by region, 2002   83

Table 4.19   Unemployment rates: by sex and age, (4.20)   84

Figure 4.20   Unemployment rates: by ethnic group and age, 2001-02 (4.21)   84

Figure 4.21   Unemployment rates: by previous occupation, 2002   85

Labour market dynamics

Figure 4.22   Length of service of employees, 2002 (4.23)   85

Table 4.23   Reasons full-time employees were for looking for
a new job: by sex and presence of dependent children, 2002   86

Figure 4.24   Ways in which current job was obtained, 2002   86

Table 4.25   People entering employment through the New Deal:
by age and type of employment,
January 1998 to September 2002 (4.25)   87

Working lives

Figure 4.26   Distribution of usual weekly hours of work: by sex, 2002 (4.18)   87

Figure 4.27   Full-time employees who worked more than 50 hours a week:
by occupation, 2002   88

Table 4.28   Overemployment: by age, sex and work pattern, 2002   88

Table 4.29   Underemployment: by age, sex and work pattern, 2002   89

Chapter 5: Income and Wealth

Household income

Figure 5.1   Real household disposable income per head and
gross domestic product per head (5.1)   92

Table 5.2   Composition of household income (5.2)   93

Table 5.3   Sources of gross household income: by household type, 2000/01   94

Table 5.4   Pensioners' gross income: by age and source   95

Figure 5.5   Median individual net income: by family type and sex, 2000/01   95

Earnings

Figure 5.6   Earnings growth of full-time employees in the top and
bottom deciles   96

Figure 5.7   Hourly earnings sex differential   97

Map 5.8   Average gross weekly earnings: by area, April 2002   98

Table 5.9   Distribution of hourly earnings: by industry, spring 2002   98

Table 5.10   Composition of weekly pay of employees:
by sex and type of work, April 2002   99

Table 5.11   Selected taxable fringe benefits received by
employees and company directors:
by gross annual earnings, 2000/01   99

Taxes

Table 5.12	Income tax payable: by annual income, 2002/03 (5.10)	100
Figure 5.13	Indirect taxes as a percentage of disposable income: by income grouping of household, 2000/01	100

Income distribution

Figure 5.14	Distribution of real household disposable income (5.12)	102
Table 5.15	Distribution of equivalised disposable income: by ethnic group of head of household, 2000/01	103
Table 5.16	Number of movements made by individuals within the income distribution between 1991 and 2000	104
Table 5.17	Redistribution of income through taxes and benefits, 2000/01 (5.16)	105

Low incomes

Figure 5.18	Percentage of people whose income is below various fractions of median income (5.17)	106
Table 5.19	Individuals in households with incomes below 60 per cent of median disposable income: by economic activity status	107
Table 5.20	Jobs paid below National Minimum Wage rates: by age, sex and employment status (5.20)	108
Figure 5.21	Individuals living in households below 60 per cent median income: by region, 2000/01	108
Table 5.22	Proportion of individuals experiencing periods of persistent low income, 1991 to 2000 (5.19)	109
Figure 5.23	Proportion of children living in households below 60 per cent of median income	109
Table 5.24	Health and school exclusions of children living in selected family types: by work/benefit status of family, 2000	110

Wealth

Table 5.25	Composition of the net wealth of the household sector (5.23)	111
Table 5.26	Distribution of wealth (5.24)	111
Table 5.27	Savings: by economic status of benefit unit and amount, 2000/01	112

National income and expenditure

Figure 5.28	Annual growth in gross domestic product at constant prices (5.26)	113
Table 5.29	Gross domestic product per head: EU comparison (5.28)	113
Figure 5.30	Gross value added by households, 2000	114
Table 5.31	Expenditure of general government in real terms: by function	114
Table 5.32	Contributions to, and receipts from, the EC budget, 2000	115

6: Expenditure

Household and personal expenditure

Figure 6.1	Household expenditure at constant prices (6.1)	118
Table 6.2	Household expenditure (6.2)	118
Table 6.3	Household expenditure: by economic activity status of household reference person, 2001/02	119
Table 6.4	Household expenditure on selected items: by family type, 2001/02 (6.5)	120

Table 6.5   Expenditure of retired households: by whether
                 or not mainly dependent on state pension, 2001/02 (6.10)   120

Figure 6.6   Household weekly expenditure: by region, 1999-2002 (6.3)   121

Table 6.7   Total weekly household expenditure: on selected
                 items by place of purchase, 2001/02   121

Transactions and credit
Figure 6.8   Volume of retail sales   122

Figure 6.9   Non-cash transactions: by method of payment (6.13)   122

Table 6.10   Plastic card holders: by age, 2001   123

Figure 6.11   Net borrowing by consumers in real terms   123

Figure 6.12   Number of individual insolvencies   124

Prices
Figure 6.13   Retail prices index (6.15)   124

Table 6.14   Percentage change in retail prices index: 2001 (6.16)   125

Table 6.15   Average prices of selected items   125

Figure 6.16   Percentage change in consumer prices: EU comparison, 2001   126

Figure 6.17   Comparative price levels for household expenditure,
                 EU comparison, 2000   126

7: Health

The nation's health
Figure 7.1   Expectation of life at age 65: by sex   130

Table 7.2   Life expectancy at birth: by social class and sex   130

Table 7.3   Infant mortality: by social class   131

Figure 7.4   Notifications of selected infectious diseases (7.7)   132

Table 7.5   New episodes of asthma: by sex and age   132

Figure 7.6   Prevalence of diagnosed diabetes: by sex and age, 1998   133

Table 7.7   New episodes of genital chlamydia: by sex and age   133

Figure 7.8   Prevalence of neurotic disorder among adults: by sex, 2000   134

Figure 7.9   Number of prescription items for anti-depressant drugs   134

Causes of death
Table 7.10   Main causes of child mortality: by sex and age, 1998-2000   135

Figure 7.11   Mortality: by sex and major cause (7.11)   135

Figure 7.12   Death rates from selected cancers: by sex (7.13)   136

Table 7.13   One and five year relative survival rates for major cancers:
                 by sex of patient diagnosed during 1993-95   136

Table 7.14   Drug-related poisoning deaths: by selected type of drug   137

Lifestyle and diet
Table 7.15   Average weekly alcohol consumption: by sex and
                 socio-economic group   138

Table 7.16   Prevalence of cigarette smoking: by sex and socio-economic group 138

Figure 7.17   Prevalence of recent use of cannabis, amphetamines
                 and cocaine, among young adults, EU comparison, 1999   139

Figure 7.18   Incidence of breastfeeding: by age at which mother
                 completed full-time education, 2000   139

Figure 7.19   Consumption of fresh fruit and vegetables:
                 by income group of head of household   140

Figure 7.20   Body mass: by sex, 2001   140
Figure 7.21   Number of emergency contraceptives prescribed   141

Prevention
Table 7.22   Immunisation of children by their second birthday (7.22)   141
Table 7.23   Cervical screening coverage: by age (7.23)   142
Table 7.24   Breast cancer screening coverage: by region, 2000/01 (7.24)   142
Table 7.25   Smoking cessation: by age and sex, 2001/02   143

8: Social Protection

Expenditure
Figure 8.1   Expenditure on social protection benefits in real terms:
               by function, 1990/91 and 2000/01 (8.2)   146
Figure 8.2   Expenditure on social protection benefits per head:
               EU comparison, 1999 (8.1)   146
Figure 8.3   Real growth in social security benefits and gross
               NHS expenditure (8.3)   147
Figure 8.4   Social security benefit expenditure: by recipient group,
               2001/02 (8.4)   147
Table 8.5   Receipt of selected social security benefits: by family type,
               2000/01 (8.5)   148
Figure 8.6   Local authority personal social services expenditure,
               2000/01 (8.8)   149
Figure 8.7   Charitable expenditure on social protection of the
               top 500 charities: by function, 1999/2000   149

Carers and caring
Table 8.8   Places available in residential care homes: by sector (8.10)   150
Figure 8.9   Households visited by home help and home care   150
Table 8.10   Types of help given by informal carers, 2000/01   151
Table 8.11   Health symptoms felt by informal carers:
               by number of hours spent caring, 2000/01   151

Sick and disabled people
Table 8.12   NHS in-patient activity for sick and disabled people (8.13)   152
Table 8.13   NHS hospital waiting lists: by patients' region of residence, 2002   152
Figure 8.14   Total emergency calls and those resulting in a response
               by an ambulance   153
Table 8.15   Health and personal social services staff (8.7)   153
Figure 8.16   NHS general medical practitioner consultations: by age, 2000/01 154
Table 8.17   Satisfaction with NHS hospitals and GPs in their area, 2001   154
Table 8.18   Recipients of benefits for sick and disabled people (8.17)   155

Older people
Table 8.19   Pension provision: by selected employment status,
               sex and age, 2000/01 (8.24)   156
Table 8.20   Distribution of income for pensioners:
               by family type and pension scheme   157

Families and children

Table 8.21 Day care places for children (8.18) 158

Table 8.22 Children looked after by local authorities:
by type of accommodation (8.19) 158

Figure 8.23 Adoptions by date of entry in Adopted Children Register:
by age of child 159

9: Crime and Justice

Offences

Table 9.1 Recorded crime: by type of offence, 2001/02 (9.3) 162

Figure 9.2 Crime committed within last 12 months:
by offence category, 2001/02 162

Table 9.3 Crimes committed within last 12 months: by outcome, 2001/02 163

Figure 9.4 Percentage change in serious crimes recorded by the police:
EU comparison, 1996 and 2000 (9.5) 164

Figure 9.5 Crime: by area type, 2000 164

Table 9.6 Seizures of selected drugs (9.7) 165

Figure 9.7 Thefts of mobile phones: by type of offence, 1999-2000 166

Figure 9.8 Crimes recorded by the police in which firearms were
reported to have been used: by principal weapon 166

Victims

Table 9.9 Victims of vehicle-related thefts and burglary within
the last 12 months: by age of head of household, 2001/02 167

Table 9.10 Worry about crime: by household income, 2001/02 167

Figure 9.11 Beliefs about the change in the national crime rate 168

Figure 9.12 Violent crimes: repeat victimisation, 2001/02 168

Offenders

Table 9.13 Offenders found guilty of, or cautioned for,
indictable offences: by sex, type of offence and age, 2001 (9.11) 169

Table 9.14 Juvenile reconviction within one year: by offence category 169

Table 9.15 Offenders cautioned for indictable offences:
by type of offence (9.12) 170

Table 9.16 Offenders sentenced for indictable offences:
by type of offence and type of sentence, 2001 (9.13) 170

Police and courts action

Figure 9.17 Motoring offences: by action taken 171

Table 9.18 Detection rates for recorded crime:
by type of offence, 2001/02 (9.17) 171

Probation and prisons

Figure 9.19 Prison population 172

Table 9.20 People commencing criminal supervision orders (9.21) 172

Civil justice

Figure 9.21 Writs and summonses issued (9.22) 173

Table 9.22 Domestic violence applications and orders:
by type of court and nature of proceedings, 2001 173

Resources

Figure 9.23	Community legal services: new matters started in selected legal help categories, 2001/02	174
Table 9.24	Police officer strength: by sex, minority ethnic group and rank (9.24)	174

10: Housing

Housing stock and housebuilding

Figure 10.1	Stock of dwellings (10.1)	178
Figure 10.2	Stock of dwellings: by tenure (10.5)	178
Table 10.3	Type of accommodation: by construction date, 2001/02 (10.2)	179
Figure 10.4	Housebuilding completion rates: by sector, 2001/02	179
Figure 10.5	Housebuilding completions: by number of bedrooms (10.4)	180

Tenure and accommodation

Table 10.6	Tenure: by type of accommodation, 2000/01	180
Table 10.7	Socio-economic group of household reference person: by tenure, 2000/01 (10.10)	181
Table 10.8	Households living in the most deprived wards and least deprived wards: by tenure, 2001/02	181
Table 10.9	Tenure: by economic status of household reference person, 2001/02	182
Table 10.10	Age of household reference person: by tenure, 2000/01 (10.7)	182
Table 10.11	Ethnic group of head of household: by tenure, 1999-2002 (10.9)	183
Table 10.12	Household type: by type of accommodation, 2000/01 (10.11)	183

Homelessness

Figure 10.13	Homeless households in temporary accommodation	184
Figure 10.14	Households accepted as homeless by local authorities: by main reason for loss of last settled home (10.13)	184

Housing condition and satisfaction with area

Figure 10.15	Accommodation without central heating: by tenure, 2001/02	185
Table 10.16	Overcrowding and under-occupation: by tenure of household, 2001/02 (10.14)	185
Table 10.17	Satisfaction with area: by tenure, 2001/02 (10.15)	186
Table 10.18	Aspects of their area that householders would like to see improved	186

Housing mobility

Table 10.19	Households resident under one year: previous tenure by current tenure, 2001/02	187
Table 10.20	Main reasons for moving: by post-move tenure, 2001/02 (10.22)	188
Figure 10.21	Sales and transfers of local authority dwellings (10.23)	189

Housing costs and expenditure

Table 10.22	Average dwelling prices: by region and type of accommodation, 2001 (10.24)	189
Figure 10.23	Average dwelling prices: by type of buyer	190

Figure 10.24   Type of mortgage for house purchase (10.26)   190
Figure 10.25   Mortgage loans in arrears and repossessions   191

11: Environment

Environmental concerns and behaviour
Table 11.1   Concern about the environment: by age, 2001   194
Table 11.2   Personal actions taken on a regular basis which may
have a positive environmental impact: by settlement size, 2001   194

Pollution
Table 11.3   Air pollutants: by source, 2000 (11.3)   195
Figure 11.4   Emissions of selected air pollutants (11.4)   195
Figure 11.5   Water pollution incidents: by source, 2001   196
Table 11.6   Chemical quality of rivers and canals: by country (11.14)   196

Global warming
Figure 11.7   Difference in average surface temperature:
comparison with 1961-90 average (11.5)   197
Table 11.8   Emissions of carbon dioxide: EU comparison (11.6)   198
Figure 11.9   Emissions of carbon dioxide: by end user   198
Figure 11.10   Proportion of electricity produced by renewable sources:
EU comparison, 2000   199

Countryside, wildlife and farming
Table 11.11   Agricultural land use   199
Table 11.12   Land in environment schemes   200
Table 11.13   Land changing to residential use: by previous use   200
Figure 11.14   New woodland creation (11.12)   201
Table 11.15   Breeding populations of selected birds   201

The local environment and waste
Table 11.16   Perception of local conditions: by sex, November 2001   202
Table 11.17   Management of municipal waste: by method   202
Map 11.18   Household waste recycling: by area 2000/01   203

Use of resources
Figure 11.19   Environmental impacts of households (11.18)   203
Table 11.20   Average annual rainfall: by region   204
Figure 11.21   Production of primary fuels (11.19)   205
Table 11.22   Oil and gas reserves, 1991 and 2001   205

12: Transport

Overview
Table 12.1   Passenger transport: by mode   208
Table 12.2   Trips per person per year: by sex, main mode
and trip purpose, 1999-2001 (12.2)   209
Table 12.3   Trips per person per year: by real household income
quintile group and trip purpose, 1999-2001   209
Figure 12.4   Goods moved by domestic freight transport:
by mode (12.6)   210

Prices and Expenditure

Table 12.5	Passenger transport prices (12.4)	210
Table 12.6	Household expenditure on transport in real terms (12.5)	211
Figure 12.7	Premium unleaded petrol prices: EU comparison, mid-June 2002	212

Access to transport

Table 12.8	Cars and motorcycles currently licensed and new registrations	212
Figure 12.9	Households with regular use of a car	213
Figure 12.10	Households with access to one or more cars: by type of area, 1989-91 and 1999-2001	213
Table 12.11	Time taken to walk to nearest bus stop: by region, 1999-2001	214

Travel to work and school

Figure 12.12	Mean time taken to travel to work: by sex and area type of residence, 1999-2001	214
Table 12.13	Average time taken to travel to school: by age of child and area type of residence	215

Road

Table 12.14	Average daily flow of motor vehicles: by class of road	215
Figure 12.15	Bus travel	216
Table 12.16	Attitudes to road transport and the environment, 2001	217

Rail

Table 12.17	Rail journeys: by operator (12.14)	217
Table 12.18	National rail fare price index	218

International travel

Table 12.19	International travel: by mode (12.21)	218
Figure 12.20	UK residents visiting abroad: by month, 1991 and 2001	219
Figure 12.21	International passenger movements by air: 1991 and 2001	219

Transport safety

Table 12.22	Passenger death rates: by mode of transport (12.16)	220
Figure 12.23	Casualties from road accidents involving illegal alcohol levels (12.17)	220
Figure 12.24	Road deaths: EU comparison, 2000 (12.18)	221

13: Lifestyles and Social Participation

Time use

Table 13.1	Activities on weekdays at selected times, 2000-01	224
Figure 13.2	Time spent on various activities: by sex, 2000-01	224
Table 13.3	Attitudes to various activities for the home: by sex, 2000-01	225

Social activities

Table 13.4	Volunteering: by type of activity carried out and sex, 2001	226
Table 13.5	Indicators of neighbourliness: by age, 2000/01	226

Leisure time

Table 13.6	Participation in selected sports: by sex, 2000-01 (13.11)	227
Table 13.7	Attendance at cultural events	227

Table 13.8   Reasons for attending the arts: by age, 2001   228

Figure 13.9   Cinema attendance: by age (13.9)   228

Holidays and tourism

Table 13.10   Type of accommodation used on
                holidays in the United Kingdom   229

Table 13.11   Visits to the most popular tourist attractions   229

Table 13.12   Holidays abroad: by destination (13.13)   230

Media and communications

Figure 13.13   Households with selected durable goods   230

Figure 13.14   Households with access to the Internet: by region, 2001/02   231

Table 13.15   Video/DVD rentals and purchases   231

Table 13.16   Television viewing patterns, 2000   232

Figure 13.17   Sales of CDs, LPs, cassettes and singles (13.4)   232

Figure 13.18   Library books issued per person: by type of book (13.6)   233

Figure 13.19   Spending on selected reading materials: by gross
                income quintile group, 2001/02   233

Websites and Contacts   235

References and Further Reading   247

Geographical Areas of the United Kingdom   256

Major Surveys   257

Symbols and Conventions   258

Appendix: Definitions and Terms   259

Articles Published in Previous Editions   293

Index   295

List of Contributors

Authors:	Carl Bird
	Simon Burtenshaw
	Ben Bradford
	Keith Brook
	Jenny Church
	David Gardener
	Steve Howell
	Hannah McConnell
	Conor Shipsey
	Anna Upson
Production Manager:	Kate Myers
Production Team:	Tajbee Ahmed
	John Chrzczonowicz
	Sunita Dedi
	Joseph Goldstein
	Paul Janvier
	Shiva Satkunam
Review Team:	Jill Barelli
	David Harper
	Nina Mill

Acknowledgements

The Editors wish to thank all their colleagues in the contributing Departments and other organisations for their generous support and helpful comments, without whom this publication would not be possible. Our thanks also go to the following for their help in the production of this volume:

Design and Artwork:	Shain Bali, Jonathan Harris, ONS Design
Picture Research:	Frances Riddelle
Tables and Figures:	Spire Origination, Norwich
Maps:	Alistair Dent, ONS Geography
Data:	SARD Data Collection Team
Picture Credits:	Front cover: Sage Music Centre, Gateshead; © Foster and Partners
	Overview chapter: Graham Burns/BTCV
	Chapters 1, 5, 8, 9 and 10: Newcastle Document Services
	Chapters 6 and 13: International Press Unit, Foreign and Commonwealth Office

Introduction

This is the 33rd edition of *Social Trends* – one of the flagship publications from the Office for National Statistics. It draws together statistics from a wide range of government departments and other organisations to paint a broad picture of our society today, and how it has been changing. Each of the 13 chapters focuses on a different social policy area, described in tables, figuress and explanatory text. This year *Social Trends* features an article on social capital, which describes how people's interaction with family, friends and others can benefit themselves, and the wider community.

Social Trends is aimed at a very wide audience: policy makers in the public and private sectors; service providers; people in local government; journalists and other commentators; academics and students; schools and the general public.

The editorial team always welcomes readers' views on how *Social Trends* could be improved. Please write to the Editors at the address shown below with your comments or suggestions.

New material and sources

To preserve topicality, half of the 310 tables and figures in the chapters of *Social Trends 33* are new compared with the previous edition, and draw on the most up-to-date available data.

In all chapters the source of the data is given below each table and figure, and where this is a major survey the name of the survey is also included. A list of contact telephone numbers, including the contact number for each chapter author, and a list of useful website addresses can be found on page 235. A list of further reading, directing readers to other relevant publications, is also given, beginning on page 247. Regional and other sub-national breakdowns of much of the information in *Social Trends* can be found in the ONS's publication *Regional Trends*.

Definitions and terms

The Appendix gives definitions and general background information, particularly on administrative and legal structures and frameworks. Anyone seeking to understand the tables and figures in detail will find it helpful to read the corresponding entries in the Appendix, as well as the footnotes on the tables and figures. An index to this edition starts on page 295.

Revisions to data

The results of the 2001 Census showed that previous estimates of the total UK population were about 1 million too high. This was mainly due to the overestimation of the net flow of international migrants into the United Kingdom. As a result, the ONS published interim revised estimates of the population for the years 1982 to 2000, which are consistent with the 2001 Census findings. In addition, interim 2001-based national population projections were produced by the Government Actuary's Department. Using the new population data, interim revised Labour Force Survey estimates were also published. The interim population and migration data have been incorporated within this volume, and will be updated within the *Social Trends* datasets on the NS website (www.statistics.gov.uk) in late spring 2003 when all the final revised data are available. The labour market data will be updated in summer 2003.

Availability on electronic media

Social Trends 33 is available electronically as an interactive PDF via the National Statistics website, www.statistics.gov.uk/socialtrends.

Contact

Carol Summerfield

Penny Babb

Social Analysis and Reporting Division

Office for National Statistics

Room: B5/03

1 Drummond Gate

London

SW1V 2QQ

Email:
social.trends@ons.gov.uk

Investing in each other and the community: the role of social capital

Paul Haezewindt

In recent years there has been an explosion of interest in the concept of social capital and its impact upon society. Social capital is closely associated with community spirit and cohesion, and while definitions vary, the main aspects of social capital are citizenship, neighbourliness, trust and shared values, community involvement, volunteering, social networks, and civic and political participation.

The Organisation for Economic Co-operation and Development defines social capital as 'networks together with shared norms, values and understandings that facilitate co-operation within or among groups'[1]. Social capital concerns people's networks of friends, neighbours and colleagues and the values and trust that people share which help them work together for collective benefits or shared goals. Social capital has both direct and indirect consequences for a wide range of positive social and economic outcomes in areas such as health, education, crime and well being.

Social capital is difficult to quantify for a number of reasons and no single measure or index exists. Firstly, social capital is made up of many different aspects and therefore studies of social capital tend to focus on a range of indicators rather than a single measure. Secondly, many of the indicators of social capital such as trust in people, and people's values or norms of behaviour, are subjective and intangible, and cannot easily be measured. Finally, there are few longstanding surveys in the United Kingdom which attempt to measure indicators of social capital. However, recently the General Household Survey (GHS) and the Home Office Citizenship Survey have collected data on many of the key aspects of social capital.

Trends over time

The United Kingdom has a long tradition of civic culture with high levels of social trust, and political and civic participation[2]. Indicators of social capital such as civic engagement, social trust, political trust and participation, and perceptions of local neighbourhoods have, however, demonstrated mixed results over recent years.

The United Kingdom has a history of dense civic networks with clubs, unions, leagues, societies, commissions and committees set up for a host of social, political and environmental activities and causes. In general, average membership levels among most kinds of voluntary organisations have risen at least enough to keep pace with population growth since the Second World War[3]. Some types of voluntary organisations, such as environmental organisations, have experienced very high levels of growth in membership. The National Trust had a membership of 3 million in 2002, which is more than ten times the number in 1971 (Table A.1). This represents a significant growth in membership, well above the 5 per cent growth in the United Kingdom population over the same period. There has also been a boom in the formation of new sports clubs. The number of clubs affiliated to the English Football Association rose by 23 per cent in 20 years, from 37,461 clubs in 1975[4] to 46,150 in 1995[5]. However, for certain types of voluntary organisations, particularly women's organisations, membership levels are in decline. Membership of the National

Table A.1

Membership of selected environmental organisations

United Kingdom   Thousands

	1971	1981	1991	1997	1999	2002
National Trust[1]	278	1,046	2,152	2,489	2,643	3,000
Royal Society for the Protection of Birds	98	441	852	1,007	1,004	1,020
Civic Trust[2]	214	..	222	330	..	330
Wildlife Trusts[3]	64	142	233	310	325	413
World Wide Fund for Nature	12	60	227	241	255	320
The National Trust for Scotland	37	105	234	228	236	260
Woodland Trust	..	..	63	60	63	115
Greenpeace	..	30	312	215	176	221
Ramblers Association	22	37	87	123	129	137
Friends of the Earth	1	18	111	114	112	119
Council for the Protection of Rural England	21	29	45	45	49	59

1 Covers England, Wales and Northern Ireland.
2 Latest Civic Trust data is for 2001.
3 Includes the Royal Society for Nature Conservation.
Source: Organisations concerned

Federation of Women's Institutes have fallen by 46 per cent over the last 30 years from 442,000 in 1972 to 240,000 in 2002[6]. Trade unions also experienced a drop in membership from a peak in 1979 of 13.2 million to 7.8 million in 2000[7].

Research indicates that organisational membership and social trust, or trust in other people, are closely linked. Findings from the British Social Attitudes survey (BSA)[8] suggested that those who join in and belong to organisations tend to be more trusting of other people, and vice versa. The survey also suggested that it is the act of belonging to a group, rather than the type of organisation or activity, which makes people more trusting in others. The World Values Survey[9] and the BSA both asked the following question of adults: 'Generally speaking, would you say that most people can be trusted or that you can't be too careful in dealing with people?' A similar question was asked in the 1959 Civic Culture Study[10]. Data from this study and from the World Values Survey show that there was a decline in social trust in Great Britain from the late 1950s to the early 1980s. In 1959[10], 56 per cent of adults agreed that 'most people can be trusted', but by 1981[9] this had fallen to 44 per cent. BSA data indicates that this was followed by a period of stability. Over the next two decades, between 1981 and 2000, the level of social trust remained stable, with 45 per cent of adults agreeing that 'most people can be trusted' in 2000.

The decline in social trust from the late 1950s to the early 1980s was matched by a similar decline in political trust. The BSA asked adults in Great Britain the following question: 'How much do you trust British governments of any party to place the needs of the nation above the interests of their own political party?' The proportion of respondents who 'just about always' or 'most of the time' trusted British governments fell from 39 per cent in 1974[11] to 16 per cent in 2000. Similarly there was a decline in electoral turnout for local, national and European elections, especially in the last decade. The turnout for the 2001 UK general election was 59 per cent[12], which was the lowest turnout for any post-war UK general election (Figure A.2).

Figure **A.2**

Post-war turnout[1] for general elections
United Kingdom

Percentages

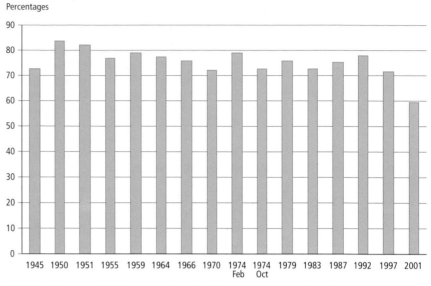

1 The number of votes cast as a percentage of the number of people on the electoral registers in force at the time of the elections.
Source: International Institute for Democracy and Electoral Assistance

However, some other forms of political participation have increased in recent years. According to the BSA, political action increased from the mid-1980s to 2000, with a peak in political involvement in the early 1990s. In 1986, 34 per cent of people had signed a petition, this rose to 53 per cent in 1991 and then fell to 42 per cent in 2000. Eleven per cent of people had contacted an MP in 1986, compared with 17 per cent in 1991 and 16 per cent in 2000. The number of people who had gone on a protest or demonstration steadily increased from 6 per cent in 1986 to 10 per cent in 2000. The Liberty and Livelihood March in September 2002 highlighted active political participation in the United Kingdom, as an estimated 400,000 people marched in protest through the streets of central London. The main focus of the protest concerned opposition to a proposed ban on hunting with dogs in England and Wales, but the march also incorporated other grievances from rural communities.

People's perceptions of their local neighbourhood give an indication of the

Figure **A.3**

Community spirit in neighbourhoods[1]
England & Wales

Percentages

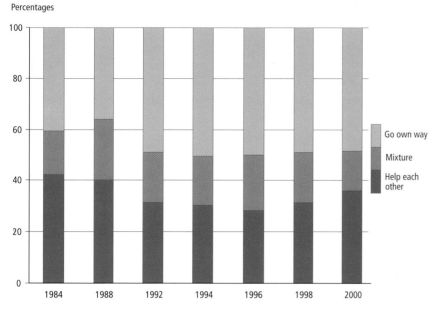

1 Respondents were asked, 'In general, what kind of neighbourhood would you say you live in? Would you say it is a neighbourhood in which people do things together and try and help each other or one in which people mostly go their own way?'
Source: British Crime Survey, Home Office

strength of community spirit and neighbourliness. Since 1984 the British Crime Survey[13] has asked adults in England and Wales the following question: 'In general, what kind of neighbourhood would you say you live in? Would you say it is a neighbourhood in which people do things together and try and help each other or one in which people mostly go their own way?' In 1984 the proportion of respondents who perceived their neighbourhood as one in which people 'go their own way' or one where people 'helped each other' were broadly similar, roughly 40 per cent each (Figure A.3). However, in 1992 there was a sharp increase in the proportion of respondents who perceived that in their neighbourhood people mostly 'go their own way' to 49 per cent. At the same time there was a corresponding fall in the proportion of respondents who thought that most people 'help each other' to 31 per cent. This illustrates a possible decline in community cohesion. Since 1996 the proportion of

neighbourhoods where people are perceived to 'help each other' has risen slowly to 36 per cent by 2000, while those where people are perceived to 'go their own way' remained stable.

Demographic and geographic trends

Within the broader national picture it is possible to find significant variations in the presence or absence of aspects of social capital between both people with different socio-demographic characteristics and people living in different geographical areas. The way in which some people gain benefit and advantage through social capital, while others do not, is of great interest to planners and policy makers. While the relationship between different groups of people and different indicators of social capital is complex, some key characteristics of people demonstrating high or low levels of social capital can be identified.

In 2000/01 the GHS included a module on social capital. Data were collected on indicators of social capital in Great Britain relating to five main areas: civic engagement; neighbourliness; social networks; social support, and people's perceptions of their local area. Many of these indicators were found to have statistically significant relationships with people's demographic characteristics.

Age has a major impact upon indicators of social capital. Young adults aged between 16 and 29 were found to be the least neighbourly (see Table 13.5 on page 226) and least likely to be civically engaged. Compared with adults aged 30 or above, they had lower levels of reciprocity (in terms of doing favours for and receiving favours from neighbours), were less likely to speak to neighbours, and were more likely to trust fewer neighbours. Trust in neighbours rose steadily with age. Seventy five per cent of people aged 70 and above trusted most or many of their neighbours compared with 39 per cent of those aged 16 to 29 (Figure A.4). Young adults, however, had more active social networks, as they were more likely to see and phone friends more frequently than older adults. Adults aged 30 and over, however, were more likely to be involved in their local communities: they were more likely to be involved in local organisations; be better informed about local affairs, and feel more civically engaged than younger adults.

Many indicators of social capital, such as civic engagement and friendship networks do not vary between men and women. However, for indicators that do vary by sex, women are most often characterised as having higher levels of social capital than men. Women have more social support and are more likely to be able to call upon a greater number of people for help in a crisis. Women, in comparison to men, are also more neighbourly as they are more likely to know and speak to more people in the local neighbourhood and are also more likely to trust neighbours. Men, however, have better perceptions of their local area and are more likely to feel safe walking alone after dark in their local area than women. In 2000/01, 31 per cent of women reported that they never went out alone after dark compared with only 8 per cent of men.

There were some variations by socio-economic group. People in the managerial and technical group were most likely to feel civically engaged. People in the managerial and technical, and non-manual groups were also more likely to have higher levels of reciprocity among neighbours. They were also most likely to have satisfactory relatives networks, defined by the GHS as having seen or spoken to relatives at least once a week and having at least one close relative who lived nearby. People in the professional social class were least likely to have a satisfactory relatives network.

Marital status and household type shows a significant relationship with a number of indicators of social capital. Married couples exhibited the highest levels of social capital. They were more likely to be trusting of their neighbours and enjoy high levels of reciprocity with them and were also most likely to have higher levels of social support. Eighty four per cent of married people had three or more people to turn to in a crisis. Divorced or separated people had the lowest level of social support, 72 per cent had three or more people to turn to. This group were also least likely to enjoy living in their local area. Single people were less likely to be civically engaged and be less neighbourly than other groups, but they were more likely to have satisfactory friendship

Figure A.4

Trust in neighbours:[1] by age, 2000/01

Great Britain

Percentages

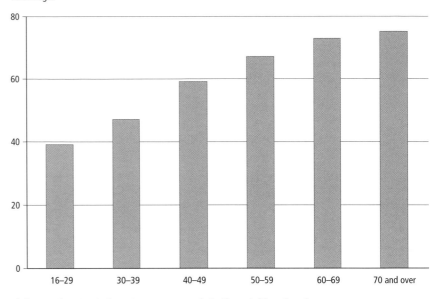

1 Respondent trusted most or many people in the neighbourhood.
Source: General Household Survey, Office for National Statistics

networks. It should be noted, however, that marital status is strongly related to age. For example, 75 per cent of single men and women are aged between 16 and 34, while 84 per cent of married people are aged 35 or above[14]. High proportions of lone parent households were likely to have both satisfactory friendship and relatives networks. Non-related households, such as people in flat-shares, were least likely to know, trust and speak to neighbours, and low proportions also reported having a satisfactory relatives network.

High educational achievement is strongly related to civic engagement, social trust, neighbourliness, social support and how people perceive their local area. People with qualifications were more likely than people without qualifications to be better informed about their local area and more likely to be involved in a local organisation. Despite knowing and speaking to fewer neighbours,

Figure **A.5**

Satisfactory relatives and friendship networks:¹ by length of residence, 2000/01

Great Britain

Percentages

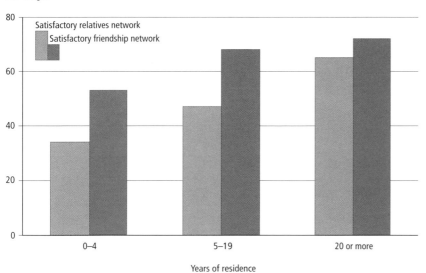

Years of residence

1 Those described as having a 'satisfactory relatives or friendship network' were those people who saw or spoke to relatives or friends at least once a week and had at least one close relative or friend who lived nearby.
Source: General Household Survey, Office for National Statistics

people with qualifications were more likely to be trusting of their neighbours and more likely to do and receive favours from neighbours. Educational achievement is also linked to social support. Eighty six per cent of people with an A level qualification or above had three or more people to turn to in a crisis, compared with 77 per cent of people without any qualifications. Those with qualifications were more likely to have a better perception of their local neighbourhood, and were also more likely to feel safe walking alone after dark in their local area.

Few social capital indicators are found to have statistically significant relationships with factors such as income or employment status in the GHS data set. However, certain relationships do exist. People's employment status appears to affect how people perceive their local area, as those in employment were most likely to feel safer walking alone after dark in their local area than economically inactive people, and the unemployed were least likely to enjoy living in their local area. Data from the ONS Omnibus Survey[15] in 2001

also suggested that employment status had an impact upon volunteering. Those who were employed were more likely than the unemployed to do voluntary work, and the economically inactive were the most likely to be involved. In terms of income, people with higher incomes were more likely to feel safe walking alone after dark in their local area, but were also likely to have the poorest relatives networks. The people most likely to have satisfactory relatives networks were in the middle income ranges, followed by the people on the lower income.

People's level of education, employment status and income are all closely related. People with higher levels of education are more likely to be employed and have higher incomes than people with lower levels of education. Income is closely related with tenure and the type of area in which people live. The level of deprivation in an area has an impact upon indicators of social capital. According to the 2001 Home Office Citizenship Survey, people in the least deprived areas participated much more in civic and social activities, and both formal and informal volunteering, than those people who lived in more deprived areas.

People with higher incomes tend to own their own homes, while those on lower incomes tend to rent, either privately or socially. GHS data indicate that homeowners had higher levels of social capital than people who were either social or private renters. For example, 15 per cent of homeowners had responsibilities with a local organisation, compared with only 8 per cent of renters. There are also differences between private and social renters. One indicator of neighbourliness is the amount of reciprocal help that neighbours give each other. Fifty eight per cent of homeowners, 42 per cent of social renters and only 34 per cent of private renters were found to have high reciprocity. Private renters do, however, enjoy living in their local area more than social renters, although the people most likely to be satisfied living in their local area were homeowners.

Tenure and length of residence are closely related. The majority of private renters stay in a residence for less than five years, while the vast majority of homeowners stay in a residence for over five years. The length of time people have lived in an area is a particularly important factor in terms of the strength and breadth of people's social networks. The longer a person has lived in an area, the deeper roots they have in that community and the more likely they are to be civically engaged, belong to local organisations, look out for and help neighbours, and enjoy living in their local area.

Figure A.5 highlights the relationship between the number of years people have lived in an area and satisfactory relatives and friendship networks. Both the proportions of people with a satisfactory relatives network and those with a satisfactory friendship network steadily increased with the length of residence. The proportion of people with a satisfactory relatives network almost doubled from 34 per cent for those who had lived in their residence for less than five years to 65 per cent for those who had been in their residence for 20 or more years. Satisfactory friendship networks also sharply rose from 53 per cent of those in a residence for under five years up to 72 per cent of those in a residence for twenty or more years. There was a greater increase in the proportion of people with a satisfactory relatives network than a satisfactory friendship network after 20 or more years of residence. The BSA also highlighted the length of residence as an important factor in civic participation. In 2001 20 per cent of people who had lived in a neighbourhood for 6 to 10 years belonged to at least one community organisation. This was double the proportion for people who had lived in an area for less than one year.

Volunteering and people who volunteer are strong indicators of social capital. The ONS Omnibus Survey showed that 32 per cent of adults aged 16 and over had volunteered at least once in the past 12 months and 54 per cent of those who had volunteered had done some form of voluntary activity in the previous four weeks. Volunteers share similar demographic characteristics to those who engage in other activities relating to social capital. ONS Omnibus Survey data indicate that women were involved in more voluntary activities, and volunteer more often, than men. This was despite having less 'free time' than men according to the UK 2000 Time Use

Table **A.6**

Characteristics of people with high and low social capital

High social capital	Low social capital
Lives outside London region	Lives in London region
Aged 30 and above	Aged 29 and below
Women	Men
Married	Single
Highly educated	Little/no education
Higher income	Lower income
Employed	Unemployed
Least deprived area	Most deprived area
Homeowner	Private renter
5+ years of residence	0–4 years of residence

Source: Office for National Statistics from the General Household Survey, 2000/01

Survey[16]. The ONS Omnibus Survey also showed that men and women took part in different types of voluntary activity. Women were much more likely to personally raise or collect money and give practical help, while men were more likely to give non-professional advice and serve on committees (see Table 13.4 on page 226 for more details). Voluntary activity also increased steadily with age. Sixty four per cent of adults aged 70 or over had volunteered in the last four weeks, compared with 46 per cent of adults aged 16 to 29. As well as the benefits to society associated with doing voluntary work and the potential benefits for social capital, the economic value of formal volunteering has been estimated at over £13 million a year[15].

As well as people's socio-demographic and economic circumstances affecting aspects of high and low social capital, where people lived in Britain also had an impact. GHS data indicated that there was a strong correlation between the region in which people lived and indicators of social capital. Government Office Regions are the smallest geographical levels at which GHS data can be analysed. Despite these being large geographical areas, there were marked regional differences for many indicators of social capital. The highest levels of trust in neighbours were found in Scotland and the South West of England. Regions where people had the lowest trust in neighbours were the West Midlands and London. The most consistent finding was that people living in the London region tended to have less positive indicators of social capital in terms of being less neighbourly, having poorer friendship and relatives networks, and being less civically engaged than people in other regions.

Benefits of social capital

The general characteristics of people with high and low levels of social capital are summarised in Table A.6. The characteristics highlighted provide a summary, and are not in any order of significance. People who have high levels of social capital can be expected to benefit from a wider range of opportunities and positive social and economic outcomes than those with lower levels of social capital. Extensive academic research has associated links between social capital and economic achievement, health, education, crime and quality of government.

At the individual level, the economic benefits of high social capital include helping people to find employment. The majority of jobs are found by networking, people use the help and knowledge of friends and 'friends of friends' to find work (see also Figure 4.24 on page 86). Extensive and diverse social networks are linked with lower unemployment, faster career advancement and higher pay[17]. As well as helping out in the job market, having high levels of social capital is also good for your health. Research has shown that people who are more socially connected and have more social support, live longer, recover quicker from illness, suffer less from mental health problems, and engage less in behaviours damaging to health such as smoking.

Social capital and education has a reciprocal relationship, since social capital influences educational attainment and people's level of education also influence aspects of social capital. The physical presence of adults in a family, and especially parents' attention and engagement with a child, are shown to have a big influence on educational achievement, child development and the transition to adult life[18]. A person's peer group and

neighbourhood may also have an influence on education in both a positive and negative way[19]. The influence of others and other aspects of social capital can also help combat crime. In areas of high social capital, people's social norms, values and sanctions act to discourage anti-social or criminal behaviour. People with high levels of social capital are less likely to commit, or be a victim of, crime and are more likely to act to prevent criminal activity[17].

Benefits of high social capital can also be felt on a larger community or national scale. Social capital can benefit business by helping to facilitate the flow of information and lowering transaction costs through increased trust and the use of networks[17]. Rates of crime, and especially violent crime, are closely linked to levels of social trust at a national level, and national differences in educational attainment are also strongly linked to variations in social trust. Research also indicates that high social capital helps to create and maintain democracy and encourage good government. Strong social capital provides people with a framework for organised opposition to non-democratic regimes, and for existing democracies, social capital through organisations and associations helps to 'teach tolerance, promote compromise, stimulate political participation, and train leaders'[20]. As well as an aid to democracy, aspects of social capital are also linked to the quality and effectiveness of government. Better quality, less corrupt and more effective governments are strongly linked with high levels of trust and civic engagement.

Negative outcomes of social capital have also been identified. Negative effects occur when social capital is used as a private rather than a public good, or when people or groups are isolated from certain networks. For example, criminal gangs are often characterised by strong internal social capital, which facilitates their illegal activities to the detriment of society. A cartel is an example of how a group of businesses may join forces to limit competition or fix prices, which would then have a negative impact upon other businesses and consumers. Social capital may also help to divide rather than unite communities. In strongly sectarian societies, high levels of social capital may be found within groups, but very little social capital may be found between them[21]. The civil disturbances in Burnley, Bradford and Oldham in the summer of 2001 were largely attributed to strongly divided and segregated communities. In some instances it could be argued that the stronger the social capital within a group, the greater the hostility to outsiders[22].

Conclusion

Social capital has become a highly visible feature of policy debates, and has begun to influence areas of UK legislation. Recent government schemes have been designed to encourage greater involvement in and commitment to society. From September 2002 citizenship became a compulsory part of the National Curriculum in schools in England. The Millennium Volunteers scheme was set up to encourage 16 to 24 year olds to volunteer in their local community. For older people, the Experience Corps, launched in 2001, aims to attract 250,000 new volunteers aged over 50 by 2004. Through such schemes, the Home Office has set a target of increasing voluntary and community sector activity, including increasing community participation, by 5 per cent between 2001 and 2006[23].

Social capital is a highly complex subject and has a wide range of implications for different groups of people living in different places. People also rely on different types of social capital at different points in their lives. In childhood, for example, children are heavily reliant upon their families' social capital. In adult life, however, social capital plays an important role at times of job search. Many of the aspects of social capital, such as social trust and civic engagement, have long been considered to have important impacts on society. However, the term social capital has given researchers, planners and decision-makers a new common language in which to consider and convey these issues. Research on the multitude of beneficial social and economic outcomes created by high levels of positive social capital has encouraged policy makers to consider how social capital can be created and maintained to benefit people and their communities.

References

1 Cote, S and Healey, T. (2001) The Well Being of Nations. *The Role of Human and Social Capital*. Organisation for Economic Co-operation and Development. Paris

2 Almond, G and Verba, S. (1982) The Civic Culture. In M. Olson (ed.), *The Rise and Decline of Nations*. New Haven Conn.: Yale University Press (cited on p.419 in reference 3)

3 Hall, P. (1999) Social Capital in Britain. *British Journal of Political Science*. Vol 29, 417-461

4 The Centre for Leisure Research (1986) *A Digest of Sports Statistics for the UK*. 2nd edition. Information series no.7. The Sports Council. London December 1986

5 Sport England website (www.sportengland.org/resources/info/basic.htm)

6 National Federation of Women's Institutes

7 Certification Officer's Annual Reports (www.dti.gov.uk/er/emar/trade_tables.pdf)

8 Park, A; Curtice, J; Thomson, K; Jarvis, L and Bromley, C (eds.). (2001) *British Social Attitudes: the 18th Report*. 'Public policy, Social ties'. National Centre for Social Research. London: Sage

9 World Values Survey (cited on p.182 in reference 8)

10 1959 Civic Culture Study (cited on p.182 in reference 8). Wording of the survey question was as follows: 'Some people say that most people can be trusted. Others say you can't be too careful in your dealings with people. How do you feel about it?' (cited on p.431 in reference 3)

11 1974 Political Action Study (cited on p.204 in reference 8)

12 International Institute for Democracy and Electoral Assistance

13 British Crime Survey. Home Office

14 Living in Britain 2000. General Household Survey

15 ONS Omnibus Survey, January and March 2001. Office for National Statistics

16 2000 UK Time Use Survey. Office for National Statistics

17 Aldridge, S; Halpern, D and Fitzpatrick, S. (2002) *Social Capital – A Discussion Paper.* Performance and Innovation Unit

18 Coleman, J. (1988) Social Capital in the Creation of Human Capital. *American Journal of Sociology.* Vol 94, Supplement S95-S120. University of Chicago

19 Sun, Y. (1999) The Contextual Effects of Community Social Capital on Academic Performance. *Social Science Research* (cited on p.22 in reference 17)

20 Paxton, P. (2002) Social Capital and Democracy: An Interdependent Relationship. *American Sociological Review.* Vol. 67, 254-277

21 Mohan, G and Mohan, J. (2002) Placing Social Capital. *Progress in Human Geography.* 26(2), 191-210

22 Halpern, D. (1999) *Social Capital: the New Golden Goose?* Faculty of Social and Political Sciences. Cambridge University. Unpublished Review

23 Active Community Unit, Home Office (www.homeoffice.gov.uk/acu/acu.htm)

Further Reading

Coulthard, M; Walker, A and Morgan, A. (2002) *People's Perceptions of their Neighbourhood and Community Involvement – Results from the Social Capital Module of the General Household Survey 2000.* London: TSO

Johnston, M and Jowell, R. (2001) How robust is British civil society? Chapter 8, in A Park; J Curtice; K Thomson; L Jarvis and C Bromley (eds.) *British Social Attitudes: the 18th Report.* 'Public policy, Social Ties'. National Centre for Social Research. London: Sage

Prime, D; Zimmeck, M and Zurawan, A. (2002) Active Communities: Initial Findings from the 2001 Home Office Citizenship Survey: (www.homeoffice.gov.uk/acu/infindin.pdf)

Chapter 1

Population

Population profile

- The population of the United Kingdom was estimated to be 58.8 million in 2001. (Table 1.1)

- In 2001 there were 30.2 million females compared with 28.6 million males in the United Kingdom, with women outnumbering men from the age of 22. (Table 1.2)

- The number of people aged 65 and over in the United Kingdom has increased by 51 per cent since 1961, to 9.4 million in 2001. By 2025 it is projected that there will be more than 1.6 million more people aged 65 and over than people under 16. (Figure 1.3)

- In the United Kingdom 55 per cent of people of Mixed ethnic origin were aged under 16 in 2001-02, almost three times (19 per cent) the proportion of White people. (Table 1.5)

Population change

- There were 669,000 births and 604,000 deaths registered in the United Kingdom in 2001. The number of deaths is projected to exceed the number of births from 2028. (Figure 1.8)

Geographical distribution

- Between 1981 and 2001 the population of the Milton Keynes Unitary Authority rose by 65 per cent, more rapidly than in any other area of the United Kingdom. (Map 1.10)

Migration

- There were 71,400 application for asylum in the United Kingdom in 2001 (excluding dependants), an 11 per cent drop on the 2000 level. (Page 38)

International perspective

- Over the last 50 years the world population has increased by over 3.6 billion, to exceed 6.1 billion in 2001. (Page 38)

- There is a high infant mortality rate in Africa, at 83 infant deaths per 1,000 live births, while in North America and Europe the rate is less than 10 infant deaths per 1,000 live births. (Table 1.16)

Information on the size and structure of the population is essential in understanding aspects of society, such as the labour market and household composition. Changes in the demographic patterns not only affect social structures, but also the demand for services.

Population profile

The population of the United Kingdom was estimated to be 58.8 million, in 2001 – the majority (84 per cent) lived in England (Table 1.1). These mid-year estimates, based on results from the 2001 Census, indicate that the UK population is 919,000 smaller than was suggested by the estimates for 2000. Most of the difference is due to the difficulty in estimating migration. It is thought that over the last 20 years more people have emigrated than previously estimated, causing the population to grow a little more slowly than expected. Population estimates for 1982 to 2000 have been revised following the 2001 Census; these interim revised estimates are subject to further revision when final revised population estimates are released in late spring 2003.

The number of people living in the United Kingdom has increased by around 8.6 million in the last 50 years, a growth of 17 per cent. The populations of England, Wales and Northern Ireland all grew over this period, while the population of Scotland remained stable. Population projections suggest that the UK population will continue to increase, reaching 63 million in 2025. Longer-term projections suggest that the population will peak around 2040, at almost 64 million, and will then gradually start to fall.

The age structure of the population reflects past trends in births, deaths and migration. The number of people in any age group within the population depends on how many people are born in a particular period and how long they survive. It is also affected by the numbers and ages of migrants moving to and from the country. Further information on the factors affecting population change and the effects of migration can be found later in this chapter on page 34.

More boys than girls are born each year, but there are more women overall in the population; 30.2 million females compared with 28.6 million males in 2001. Women

Table **1.1**

Population[1] of the United Kingdom

Millions

	1951	1991[2]	2001	2011	2021	2025
England	41.2	48.2	49.2	50.9	52.7	53.4
Wales	2.6	2.9	2.9	2.9	3.0	3.0
Scotland	5.1	5.1	5.1	5.0	4.9	4.8
Northern Ireland	1.4	1.6	1.7	1.7	1.8	1.8
United Kingdom	50.2	57.8	58.8	60.5	62.4	63.0

1 Data for 1951 are census enumerated; mid-year estimates for 1991 and 2001; 2001-based projections for 2011 to 2025. See Appendix, Part 1: Population estimates and projections.

2 Estimates for England, Wales and Scotland will be revised in the light of the 2001 Census. The UK figure is an interim population estimate and is subject to further revision.

Source: Office for National Statistics; Government Actuary's Department; General Register Office for Scotland; Northern Ireland Statistics and Research Agency

outnumbered men from the age of 22 in 2001, reflecting the sex differences in life expectancy and migration.

In 2001 there were 11.9 million children aged under 16 in the United Kingdom: 6.1 million boys and 5.8 million girls. Children made up 20 per cent of the population in 2001 compared with 23 per cent in 1961 (Table 1.2). Projections suggest that the proportion of the population who are children will continue to fall to around 18 per cent of the population by 2011.

There were 9.4 million people aged 65 and over in 2001. This represents an increase of 51 per cent since 1961. There were 1.1 million people aged 85 and over in 2001, over three times as many as in 1961. Women accounted for 72 per cent of this age group in 2001. By age 90 and over, women outnumbered men by more than three to one.

Historically the ageing of the population was largely a result of the fall in fertility that began towards the end of the 19th century. Early in the 20th century lower mortality helped to increase the number of people surviving into old age. The effects were greater among younger people, however, off-setting the trend towards the population ageing. More recently, lower fertility rates and

Table **1.2**

Population:[1] by age and sex

United Kingdom

Percentages

	Under 16	16–24	25–34	35–44	45–54	55–64	65–74	75 and over	All ages (=100%) (millions)
Males									
1961	25	14	13	14	14	11	6	3	25.5
1991[2]	21	14	16	14	12	10	8	5	27.9
2001	21	11	14	15	13	11	8	6	28.6
2011	19	12	13	14	14	12	9	7	29.5
2021	19	11	13	12	13	13	10	8	30.3
2026	19	11	13	13	12	13	10	9	30.6
Females									
1961	22	13	12	13	14	12	9	5	27.3
1991[2]	19	12	15	13	11	10	9	9	29.6
2001	19	11	14	15	13	11	9	9	30.2
2011	17	11	13	14	14	12	9	9	31.0
2021	17	10	13	12	13	13	11	10	32.1
2026	17	10	13	13	12	14	11	11	32.5

1 Data for 1961 are census enumerated; mid-year estimates for 1991 and 2001; 2001-based projections for 2011 to 2026. See Appendix, Part 1: Population estimates and projections.

2 Data for 1991 are interim population estimates revised following the 2001 Census and are subject to further revision.

Source: Office for National Statistics; General Register Office for Scotland; Government Actuary's Department; Northern Ireland Statistics and Research Agency

Figure **1.3**

Dependent population: by age[1]

United Kingdom

Millions

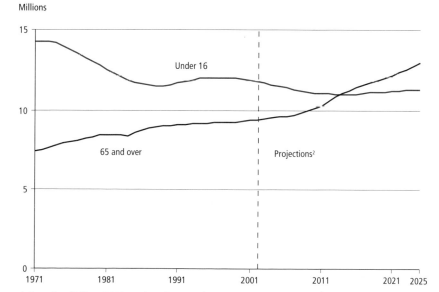

1 Data for 1982 to 2000 are interim population estimates revised following the 2001 Census and are subject to further revision.

2 2001-based projections.

Source: Office for National Statistics; Government Actuary's Department; General Register Office for Scotland; Northern Ireland Statistics and Research Agency

improvements in the rates of mortality for older people have contributed to the ageing trend. In 2001 projected average life expectancy at birth in the United Kingdom was 76 years for males and 80 years for females. Over the last 30 years the projected average life expectancy at birth increased by around 6 years for men and 5 years for women (see page 130 in the Health chapter). The average age of the population is expected to rise from 39.1 years in 2001 to 42.4 in 2026.

Projections suggest that the number of people aged 65 and over will exceed the numbers aged under 16 by 2014 (Figure 1.3). By 2025 there will be more than 1.6 million more people over the age of 65 than people under 16. The increase in the number of pensioners has policy implications, placing greater demands on health, social services and social security arrangements (see Figure 8.1 in the Social Protection chapter). As a response to this, the state pension age (currently 65 for men and 60 for women) will be increased between 2010 and 2020 to 65 for both sexes.

An ageing population is a characteristic shared by the other countries in the European Union (EU). The percentage of the EU population aged 65 and over has increased by a third since 1970. In 2001, 16 per cent of the UK population were aged 65 and over, close to the EU average of 17 per cent (Table 1.4). Italy and Greece had the largest proportion of people age 65 and over in 2001, at 18 per cent. The largest increases since 1970 were in Italy and Spain, rising by 7 percentage points between 1970 and 2001. The proportion of people aged 65 and over in the Irish Republic has remained stable over the last 30 years, at 11 per cent. Projections suggest that the population of the EU will continue to age, although the rate of increase in the United Kingdom will be slower than in the EU overall.

The age structure of the population varies between ethnic groups, reflecting past immigration and fertility patterns. The numbers of people from minority ethnic groups in the United Kingdom increased following the Second World War. There was large scale immigration from countries of the New Commonwealth, such as India, Jamaica and Nigeria, following the *British Nationality Act 1948*. The government encouraged immigration to tackle labour shortages during the 1950s and 1960s, leading to substantial immigration from the Caribbean and the Indian subcontinent. Subsequent legislation curtailed this. Many people of south Asian descent also entered the United Kingdom as refugees from Kenya, Malawi and Uganda in the 1960s and 1970s.

In 2001-02, 4.5 million people in the United Kingdom described themselves as belonging to a minority ethnic group (8 per cent). From 2001 the way in which the different ethnic groups are classified in National Statistics official statistics and surveys has been changed to bring them in line with the 2001 Census. More information about the changes is included in the Appendix, Part 1: Classification of ethnic groups.

Minority ethnic groups tend to have a younger age profile than the White population (Table 1.5). The Mixed group has the youngest age structure – 55 per cent of people of Mixed origin were aged under 16 in 2001-02. This was almost three times the proportion of the White group, where 19 per cent were aged

Table 1.4

Population aged 65 and over: EU comparison

Percentages

	1970	1981	1991	2001
Italy	11	13	15	18
Greece[1]	11	13	14	18
Sweden	14	16	18	17
Belgium	13	14	15	17
Spain	10	11	14	17
Germany	14	16	15	17
Portugal	10	11	14	16
France	13	14	14	16
United Kingdom	13	15	16	16
Austria	14	15	15	16
Finland	9	12	14	15
Denmark	12	15	16	15
Luxembourg	13	14	13	14
Netherlands	10	12	13	14
Irish Republic	11	11	11	11
EU average	12	14	15	17

1 Data for 2001 are 1999-based population projections.
Source: Eurostat

Table 1.5

Population: by ethnic group and age, 2001–02[1]

United Kingdom

Percentages

	Under 16	16–34	35–64	65 and over
White	19	25	40	16
Mixed	55	27	16	2
Asian or Asian British				
Indian	22	33	38	6
Pakistani	35	36	25	4
Bangladeshi	38	38	20	3
Other Asian	22	36	38	4
Black or Black British				
Black Caribbean	25	25	42	9
Black African	33	35	30	2
Other Black[2]	35	34	26	–
Chinese	18	40	38	5
Other	20	37	39	4
All ethnic groups[3]	20	26	39	15

1 Population living in private households 2001-02. See Appendix, Part 1: Classification of ethnic groups, and Part 4: Local LFS.
2 Sample size was too small for a reliable estimate of the 65 and over age group.
3 Includes those who did not state their ethnic group.
Source: Annual Local Area Labour Force Survey, Office for National Statistics

under 16. The Pakistani, Bangladeshi, Other Black and Black African groups also had comparatively high proportions of people aged under 16. This reflects the tendency for these families to have a larger number of children than other groups. In contrast, the White group had the highest proportion of people aged 65 and over. Sixteen per cent of the White group were aged 65 and over, compared with 2 per cent of the Black African group, 2 per cent of those in the Mixed group and 3 per cent of the Bangladeshi group. Progressive ageing of the minority ethnic population is anticipated in the future, but changes will be dependent upon fertility levels, mortality rates and future migration.

The socio-economic status of the population has changed over the last thirty years. The proportion of men of working age in professional and managerial occupations has increased. There have also been increases in the numbers of women in these occupations, albeit more slowly than for men. From 2001 the new National Statistics Socio-economic Classification (NS-SEC) has been used in all official statistics and surveys. This classification is based on occupation, employment status and, for some classes, the size of the organisation. More information about this is included in the Appendix, Part 1: National Statistics Socio-economic Classification.

In spring 2002 men were far more likely than women to be in the 'higher managerial and professional' class (which includes lawyers and engineers), the 'small employers and own account workers' class (which contains the self-employed), and the 'lower supervisory and technical' class (which includes traffic wardens and bakers). Three out of four people in each of these classes were male (Figure 1.6). Women were more likely than men to be in the 'intermediate' class (including receptionists and dental nurses); three quarters of people in this class were female.

These Labour Force Survey (LFS) estimates are not seasonally adjusted and have not been adjusted to take account of the 2001 Census results. The Office for National Statistics is producing reweighted LFS estimates based on the findings of the 2001 Census; these will be available from summer 2003 (see Appendix, Part 4: LFS reweighting).

Figure **1.6**

Population of working age: by sex and socio-economic classification, 2002[1]

United Kingdom

Percentages

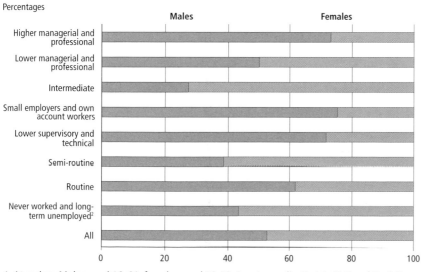

1 At spring. Males aged 16–64, females aged 16–59. See Appendix, Part 1: National Statistics Socio-economic Classification. These estimates for 2002 are not seasonally adjusted and have not been adjusted to take account of the 2001 Census results. See Appendix, Part 4: LFS reweighting.
2 People unemployed for less than 1 year are classified according to their previous occupation. Includes those not classified elsewhere.

Source: Labour Force Survey, Office for National Statistics

Population change

The rate of population change over time depends upon the net natural change – the difference between the number of births and the number of deaths – and the net effect of people migrating to and from the country. Natural change is an important factor in population growth in the United Kingdom, however in recent years net migration has had an increased influence (Table 1.7). Projections suggest that this trend will continue with net migration accounting for 60 per cent of population growth over the next 10 years.

The fastest population growth of the 20th century occurred in the first decade, when the population increased by an average of 385,000 a year. This rapid growth at the start of the century, and again during the 1960s, was due to the high number of births during these decades. There was a substantial fall in the number of births following the 1960s' baby boom, and this contributed to slower population growth between 1971 and 1981.

There were 669,000 births in the United Kingdom in 2001, 38 per cent fewer than 100 years earlier (Figure 1.8). The two World Wars had a major impact on births. There was a fall during the First World War, followed by a post-war baby-boom – the number of births peaked at 1.1 million in 1920. The numbers then decreased and remained low during the 1930s' depression and the Second World War. A second baby-boom then occurred after the War, followed by a further boom during the 1960s. Projections suggest that the number of births will remain reasonably constant over the next 40 years.

The number of women of reproductive age affects the trends in births. For example, the number of births rose during the 1980s as the women born during the baby-boom of the 1960s entered their peak reproductive years. The decrease in the number of births over the 1990s is partly a result of the smaller numbers of women born in the 1970s – there are now fewer women entering their peak reproductive years than in previous decades. However there are also lower fertility rates, particularly among women aged under 30. Further information on births and fertility can be found in the Households and Families chapter, on page 50.

Table 1.7

Population change[1]

United Kingdom

Thousands

	Annual averages					
	Population at start of period	Live births	Deaths	Net natural change	Net migration and other[2]	Overall change
1901–1911	38,237	1,091	624	467	−82	385
1951–1961	50,287	839	593	246	6	252
1971–1981	55,928	736	666	69	−27	42
1991–2000	57,814	738	636	102	114	216
2001–2011	58,837	679	611	68	101	169
2011–2021	60,524	704	617	86	100	186

1 Data are census enumerated for 1901–1911; mid-year estimates for 1951 to 2000; 2001-based projections for 2001 to 2021. Data for 1991 to 2000 are interim population estimates revised following the 2001 Census and are subject to further revision. See Appendix, Part 1: Population estimates and projections.
2 Data for 1981 to 2001 are derived using interim population estimates and are subject to further revision.

Source: Office for National Statistics; Government Actuary's Department; General Register Office for Scotland; Northern Ireland Statistics and Research Agency

Figure 1.8

Births[1,2] and deaths[1]
United Kingdom

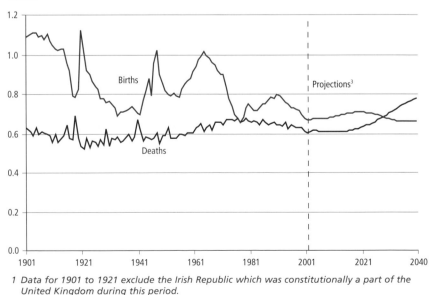

1 Data for 1901 to 1921 exclude the Irish Republic which was constitutionally a part of the United Kingdom during this period.
2 Data from 1981 exclude the non-residents of Northern Ireland.
3 2001-based.

Source: Office for National Statistics; Government Actuary's Department; General Register Office for Scotland; Northern Ireland Statistics and Research Agency

The number of deaths has fluctuated around the 600,000 level over the last century, with 604,000 deaths registered in 2001. It is projected that the number of deaths will begin to increase in the 2020s as those people born during the baby-boom following the Second World War reach advanced ages. Deaths are projected to exceed births from 2028. This has previously occurred only once during the 20th century, when in 1976 the number of deaths exceeded the number of births by 5,000.

Although the number of deaths each year over the last century has remained relatively constant, the death rates have fallen considerably. Rising standards of living, the changing occupational structure and developments in medical technology and practice help to explain the decline in the mortality rates. Between 1971 and 2001, death rates for all males fell by 17 per cent and those for all females by 5 per cent (Table 1.9). Infant mortality rates have seen the biggest decrease over the last 30 years, falling by almost 70 per

cent. Death rates for those aged 55 to 64 have also reduced considerably, falling by almost half for men and by more than a third for women.

Death rates are higher for males than for females in all age groups, resulting in the life expectancy of females being higher than that of males. However the overall crude death rate was higher for females than for males in 2001; the death rate for all females was 10.5 per 1,000 women compared with 10.1 per 1,000 males. This is because the female population has an older age structure than the male population.

Geographical distribution

In 2001 the majority of the UK population lived in England, while Northern Ireland had the smallest population of the four constituent countries (see Table 1.1). The regions of England with the largest populations were the South East and London, at 8.0 million and 7.2 million people respectively.

Table **1.9**

Deaths: by age and sex

United Kingdom

Death rates per 1,000 in each age group

	Under 1[1]	1–15	16–34	35–54	55–64	65–74	75 and over	All ages	All deaths (thousands)
Males									
1971	20.2	0.5	1.0	4.8	20.4	51.1	131.4	12.1	329
1981	12.7	0.4	1.0	4.0	18.1	46.4	122.2	12.0	329
1991[2]	8.3	0.3	0.9	3.1	14.2	38.7	110.7	11.3	314
2001	6.0	0.2	1.0	2.8	10.4	28.8	96.7	10.1	288
2011[3]	4.2	0.2	0.8	2.6	10.0	24.3	86.5	10.1	296
2021[3]	3.6	0.1	0.8	2.4	8.7	23.0	79.3	10.7	324
Females									
1971	15.5	0.4	0.5	3.1	10.3	26.6	96.6	11.0	317
1981	9.5	0.3	0.4	2.5	9.8	24.7	90.2	11.4	329
1991[2]	6.3	0.2	0.4	1.9	8.4	22.3	84.1	11.2	332
2001	5.0	0.1	0.4	1.8	6.4	17.9	81.7	10.5	316
2011[3]	3.7	0.1	0.4	1.7	6.1	15.8	78.9	10.1	312
2021[3]	3.1	0.1	0.3	1.6	5.0	14.6	69.5	9.7	312

1 Rate per 1,000 live births.
2 Data for 1991 are based on interim population estimates revised following the 2001 Census and are subject to further revision.
3 2001-based projections.
Source: Office for National Statistics; Government Actuary's Department; General Register Office for Scotland; Northern Ireland Statistics and Research Agency

Population change between 1981 and 2001 in the United Kingdom has produced changes in the geographical distribution of the population (Map 1.10). Over this period the largest population increase was in the Milton Keynes Unitary Authority (UA), with a rise of 65 per cent. The biggest declines in population between 1981 and 2001 were in Glasgow City, where the population fell by 19 per cent, and in Inverclyde and the Shetland Islands, both with a fall of 17 per cent.

Regional populations are affected by people relocating within the United Kingdom, as well as births, deaths and by international migration flows. During the last century there has been a movement of people from the coal, ship building and steel industry areas in the north of England, Scotland and Wales to the south of England and the Midlands where the light industries and service industries are based.

During 2001, Wales, Scotland and Northern Ireland gained 9,000, 6,000 and 2,000 people, respectively, from migration within the United Kingdom, while England experienced a net loss of 16,000 people (Table 1.11). At a regional level, the greatest fall in population occurred in London where 84,000 more people left the area than moved into it. Of those people leaving London for elsewhere in the United Kingdom, a third moved into the neighbouring South East region and a quarter moved into the East of England. The South West experienced the highest net gain of all the regions due to internal migration (32,000 people). Of those moving to the South West, a third came from the South East.

Young adults are the most mobile age group. Many people in their twenties leave their parental home to study, seek employment or set up their own home. In 2000, London experienced the largest net increase of people aged 15 to 24 due to migration within the United Kingdom (18,000 people). The West Midlands experienced the biggest net loss of people in this age group, of over 4,000. However, London experienced the largest net losses among all other age groups, particularly those aged under 15 and those aged 35 to 44. The regions with the highest net gains in the 35 to 44 age group were the South East and South West. Information about some of the

Map **1.10**

Population change, mid-1981 to mid-2001[1]

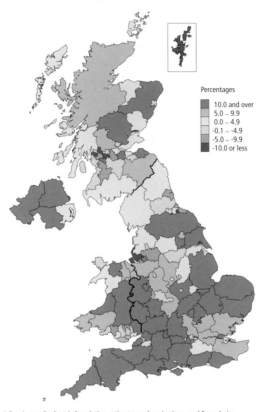

Percentages
- 10.0 and over
- 5.0 – 9.9
- 0.0 – 4.9
- -0.1 – -4.9
- -5.0 – -9.9
- -10.0 or less

1 See Appendix, Part 1: Population estimates and projections, and Boundaries
Source: Office for National Statistics; Statistical Directorate, Welsh Assembly Government; General Register Office for Scotland; Northern Ireland Statistics and Research Agency

reasons why people move home can be found in Table 10.20 in the Housing chapter.

Migration

The pattern of people entering and leaving the United Kingdom has changed over the last 30 years. There was a net loss of people from the United Kingdom during the 1970s; between 1975 and 1979 the net loss totalled 106,000. In 1981 approximately 79,000 more people emigrated from the United Kingdom than migrated into the country. Since then there has been an overall increase in net migration to the United Kingdom and it is now a significant factor in population growth. Interim revised figures estimated that 126,000 more people migrated to, rather than from, the United Kingdom in 2001, an increase of more than a quarter on the 2000 level (Table 1.12). These figures are to be revised in spring 2003.

Nationals of the European Economic Area (EU and Norway, Iceland and Liechtenstein) have

Table **1.11**

Inter-regional movements[1] within the United Kingdom, 2001

United Kingdom   Thousands

	United Kingdom	England	North East	North West	Yorkshire & the Humber	East Midlands	West Midlands	East	London	South East	South West	Wales	Scotland	Northern Ireland
							Origin							
Destination														
United Kingdom	.	120	43	110	96	96	102	127	244	216	111	51	50	11
England	104	.	37	89	86	88	87	117	228	195	95	49	46	9
North East	40	35	.	6	8	3	2	3	4	5	2	1	4	–
North West	106	88	6	.	18	9	12	8	12	14	8	9	8	2
Yorkshire & the Humber	96	88	9	19	.	16	8	9	10	12	6	3	5	1
East Midlands	115	108	4	10	18	.	16	19	14	21	8	3	3	1
West Midlands	95	84	3	12	7	14	.	8	12	16	12	8	3	1
East	147	139	3	7	8	13	7	.	62	28	10	3	4	1
London	160	146	5	13	10	10	12	29	.	52	16	5	7	1
South East	224	207	4	13	10	14	14	28	91	.	33	8	7	1
South West	143	129	2	9	6	9	16	14	23	49	.	10	4	1
Wales	60	58	1	11	3	3	10	4	6	10	11	.	2	–
Scotland	56	53	5	8	6	4	4	5	8	9	5	2	.	2
Northern Ireland	13	10	–	2	1	1	1	1	2	2	1	–	3	.

1 Based on patients re-registering with NHS doctors in other parts of the United Kingdom. Moves where the origin and destination lie within the same region do not appear in the table.

Source: Office for National Statistics; General Register Office for Scotland; Northern Ireland Statistics and Research Agency

Table **1.12**

Net international migration: by citizenship[1]

United Kingdom   Thousands

	1992	1996	2000	2001
British	−72	−72	−66	−56
European Union	−1	17	–	4
Old Commonwealth	1	10	22	26
New Commonwealth	31	28	63	64
Other	–	32	80	87
All	−42	14	100	126

1 These are interim estimates and are subject to revision following the rebasing of the population estimates using the 2001 Census. See also Appendix, Part 1: International migration estimates, and Citizenship.

Source: International Passenger Survey, Office for National Statistics; Home Office; Irish Central Statistical Office

the right to live in the United Kingdom if they are working or if they are otherwise able to support themselves financially. Most other overseas nationals who want to live permanently in the United Kingdom require Home Office acceptance for settlement. The number of people granted settlement in the United Kingdom fell by 15 per cent between 2000 and 2001, to 107,000. This decrease was primarily due to falls in asylum-related settlement grants. These rose sharply in 1999 and 2000 due to a change in the rules reducing the qualifying periods for people granted asylum and exceptional leave to remain, and effectively increasing the number of people eligible for settlement. Forty one per cent of grants of settlement in 2001 were granted to Asian nationals, and a further 29 per cent to African nationals (Figure 1.13 - see overleaf). The fall in grants in 2001 was mainly due to a fall in acceptances to African nationals – these fell by 29 per cent from 2000.

The number of people seeking asylum varies considerably from year to year. In the late 1980s, applications for asylum (based on the principal applicant) started to rise sharply from around 4,000 a year during 1985 to 1988, to 44,800 in 1991, and reached a record 80,300 in 2000. There were 71,400 applications in 2001, an 11 per cent drop on the 2000 level. Quarterly figures for 2002 show that the number of asylum applications has begun to rise again.

The countries from which people arrive to claim asylum vary with world events. The conflict in Afghanistan led to an increase in Afghan asylum applications in 2001, from 5,600 applications in 2000 to 9,000 in 2001. Large numbers of asylum seekers in 2001 also came from Iraq, Somalia and Turkey, areas that have seen escalations in internal conflict.

The total number of asylum applications, including dependants, to EU countries has remained relatively steady since 1999. As well as the United Kingdom, Belgium, Finland, the Irish Republic, Italy and the Netherlands each recorded a fall in applications between 2000 and 2001. Applications to Belgium and Italy, for example, almost halved, while applications to Austria increased by 65 per cent and to France by 22 per cent. In 2001 the United Kingdom received more asylum applications than any other EU country, closely followed by Germany (Table 1.14). However when the relative size of the countries' populations are taken in to account, by looking at the number of asylum seekers per 1,000 population, the United Kingdom ranks joint seventh with Luxembourg. Austria has the highest rate at 3.7 asylum seekers per 1,000 population, while Portugal has the lowest of less than 0.1 per 1,000 population.

International perspective

In 2001 the world's population exceeded 6.1 billion people, an increase of over 3.6 billion in the previous 50 years. World population growth was at its highest between 1965 and 1970, when the annual growth rate was 2 per cent. Since 1970 the world population has been growing at a slower rate and between 2000 and 2005 it is estimated to be growing at a rate of 1.2 per cent, or 77 million people per year. India and China account for a third of this annual growth: India for 21 per cent and China for 12 per cent.

Figure **1.13**

Grants of settlement: by region of origin

United Kingdom

Thousands

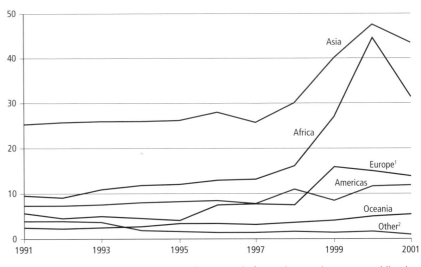

1 European Economic Area (EEA) nationals may apply for settlement, but are not obliged to do so. The figures do not represent the total number of Europeans eligible to stay indefinitely in the UK. Data on EEA nationals granted settlement have not been recorded since 1998.
2 Includes British Overseas citizens, those whose nationality was unknown and, up to 1993, acceptances where the nationality was not separately identified; from 1994 these nationalities have been included in the relevant geographical area.

Source: Home Office

Table **1.14**

Asylum applications, including dependants: EU comparison, 2001

	Number of asylum seekers[1]	Asylum seekers per 1,000 population
Austria	30,100	3.7
Belgium[2]	28,000	2.7
Irish Republic	10,300	2.7
Sweden	23,500	2.6
Denmark	12,400	2.3
Netherlands	32,600	2.0
Luxembourg	700	1.5
United Kingdom[2]	92,000	1.5
Germany	88,300	1.1
France[2]	53,900	0.9
Greece	5,500	0.5
Finland	1,700	0.3
Spain	9,200	0.2
Italy	9,600	0.2
Portugal	200	–
All applications to EU	397,900	1.1

1 Figures have been rounded to the nearest 100.
2 Figures have been adjusted to include an estimated number of dependants.
Source: Home Office

Map **1.15**

World population densities: by country, 2001

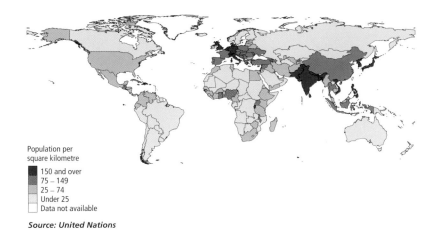

Population per
square kilometre

- 150 and over
- 75 – 149
- 25 – 74
- Under 25
- Data not available

Source: United Nations

Table **1.16**

World demographic indicators

	Population (millions) 2001	Percentage in urban areas 2001	Infant mortality rate[1]	Total fertility rate[2]	Life expectancy at birth (years) Males	Life expectancy at birth (years) Females
Asia	3,721	38	53	2.5	66	69
Africa	813	38	83	5.0	51	52
Europe	726	74	9	1.3	70	78
Latin America & Caribbean	527	76	32	2.5	67	74
North America	317	78	7	1.9	75	81
Oceania	31	74	24	2.4	72	77
World	6,134	48	55	2.7	64	68

1 Per 1,000 live births.
2 Total fertility rate is the number of children that would be born to a woman if current patterns of fertility persisted throughout her childbearing life.

Source: Department for Economic and Social Affairs, United Nations

By 2050, the world population is expected to be between 7.9 billion and 10.9 billion. China, with a population of 1.3 billion in 2000, is currently the country with the largest population, although India is expected to have overtaken it by 2050.

Globally the number of people aged 60 and over is expected to triple by 2050, from 606 million in 2000 to around 2 billion. In 2000, 10 per cent of the world's population were aged 60 and over; by 2050 this is projected to reach 21 per cent.

Population density varies considerably throughout the world. In 2001, the Western Sahara had the lowest density, at one person per square kilometre, while Macau, in China, had the highest, at over 24,100 people per square kilometre, followed by Hong Kong at 6,400 and Singapore at 6,300 (Map 1.15). In contrast, the population density of the United Kingdom was 240 people per square kilometre.

In 2001 almost half of the world's population lived in urban areas. However there is wide variability between regions: less than 40 per cent of people in Asia and Africa lived in urban areas compared with 78 per cent of those in North America (Table 1.16). There is a high infant mortality rate in Africa, at 83 infant deaths per 1,000 live births, while the rate in North America and Europe is considerably lower at less than 10 infant deaths per 1,000 live births. The total fertility rate is also higher in Africa, at 5.0 children per woman, while Europe has a total fertility rate of 1.3. There is also wide variability in life expectancy; those children born in Africa that survive childhood can expect to live to about 50 years old, while those born in North America or Europe can expect to live 20 or more years longer.

Low fertility means that international migration has a significant impact upon population growth in many developed countries. Data from the United Nations suggest that without migration, the population of the more developed regions, as a whole, would start declining in 2003 rather than 2025. International migration is projected to remain high during the 21st century, with the more developed regions of the world expected to continue to be net receivers, and an average gain of about 1.9 million migrants per year over the next 50 years.

Chapter 2

Households and families

Households and families

- There were 24.4 million households in Great Britain in 2002, an increase of almost a third since 1971. (Table 2.1)

- In spring 2002 a fifth of dependent children in Great Britain lived in lone parent families, almost twice the proportion as 1981. (Table 2.4)

- In 2001, almost nine in ten people aged 60 and over in Great Britain were grandparents. (Page 45)

Partnerships

- A quarter of non-married adults aged 16 to 59 in Great Britain were cohabiting in 2000/01. (Page 45)

- In 2000 there were 306,000 marriages in the United Kingdom; this was the first year that marriages had increased since 1992. (Figure 2.10)

- The average age at first marriage in England and Wales has increased by around five years since 1961, to 30.5 years for men and 28.2 years for women in 2000. (Table 2.12)

Family formation

- The United Kingdom had the highest rate of live births to teenage girls in the European Union in 2000, with a rate of 29 live births per 1,000 girls aged 15 to 19. (Figure 2.16)

- In 2001, three quarters of births outside marriage in England and Wales were jointly registered by both parents and, of these births, three in four were to parents living at the same address. (Page 50)

- In England and Wales, the average age of women at the birth of their first child increased by one and a half years over the last decade, to reach 27.1 years in 2000. (Table 2.19)

- In 2001, 145 in every 10,000 maternities in the United Kingdom resulted in the birth of twins, while 4 in every 10,000 maternities led to triplets or more. (Table 2.21)

- There were just under 6,000 adoptions in England and Wales in 2001, an increase of over 1,600 adoptions (39 per cent) since 1999. (Figure 2.22)

The types of households and families that people live in today are increasingly diverse, reflecting changes in relationship formation and dissolution. People live in a variety of household types over their lifetimes. They may leave their parental home, form partnerships, marry, and have children. Some people experience separation, divorce, lone parenthood and the formation of new partnerships, leading to new households and second families. More people now spend time living on their own, whether before or instead of marriage or cohabitation, or because of divorce or the breakdown of a relationship.

Households and families

There were 24.4 million households in Great Britain in 2002. The number of households has grown at a faster rate than the population. The population of Great Britain has increased by 5 per cent over the last 30 years, while the number of households increased by 31 per cent (Table 2.1) (see also Table 1.1 in the Population chapter). These Labour Force Survey (LFS) estimates, and others used in this chapter, for 2002 are not seasonally adjusted and have not been adjusted to take account of the 2001 Census results. The Office for National Statistics is producing reweighted LFS estimates based on the findings of the 2001 Census; these will be available from summer 2003 (see Appendix, Part 4: LFS reweighting).

Trends towards smaller households have contributed to the increase in the number of households. Although the majority (58 per cent) of households are headed by a couple, there has been an increase in one person households: in 1971 they accounted for 18 per cent of households, and this had risen to 29 per cent by 2002. Conversely there has been a fall in large households: the percentage of households made up of five or more people halved between 1971 and 2002, falling from 14 per cent to 7 per cent. The average household size was around 4.6 people for the first half of the 20th century, but had fallen below 3.0 people by 1971. Since then it has reduced further to 2.4 people per household in 2002.

Household composition has become more varied in recent decades. There has been a decline in the 'traditional' family household – a couple family with dependent children – and an increase in the number of lone-parent

Table **2.1**

Households:[1] by size

Great Britain   Percentages

	1971	1981	1991	2002[2]
One person	18	22	27	29
Two people	32	32	34	35
Three people	19	17	16	16
Four people	17	18	16	14
Five people	8	7	5	5
Six or more people	6	4	2	2
All households (=100%)				
(millions)	18.6	20.2	22.4	24.4
Average household size				
(number of people)	2.9	2.7	2.5	2.4

1 See Appendix, Part 2: Households. These estimates for 2002 are not seasonally adjusted and have not been adjusted to take account of the 2001 Census results. See Appendix, Part 4: LFS reweighting.
2 At spring 2002.
Source: Census, Labour Force Survey, Office for National Statistics

Table **2.2**

Households:[1] by type of household and family

Great Britain   Percentages

	1971	1981	1991	2002[2]
One person				
Under state pension age	6	8	11	15
Over state pension age	12	14	16	14
Two or more unrelated adults	4	5	3	3
One family households				
Couple[3]				
No children	27	26	28	29
1–2 dependent children[4]	26	25	20	19
3 or more dependent children[4]	9	6	5	4
Non-dependent children only	8	8	8	6
Lone parent[3]				
Dependent children[4]	3	5	6	6
Non-dependent children only	4	4	4	3
Multi-family households	1	1	1	1
All households (=100%) (millions)	18.6	20.2	22.4	24.4

1 See Appendix, Part 2: Households and Families. These estimates for 2002 are not seasonally adjusted and have not been adjusted to take account of the 2001 Census results. See Appendix, Part 4: LFS reweighting.
2 At spring 2002.
3 Other individuals who were not family members may also be included.
4 May also include non-dependent children.
Source: Census, Labour Force Survey, Office for National Statistics

Figure **2.3**

Percentage of all households where heads of household live alone: by age and sex

England

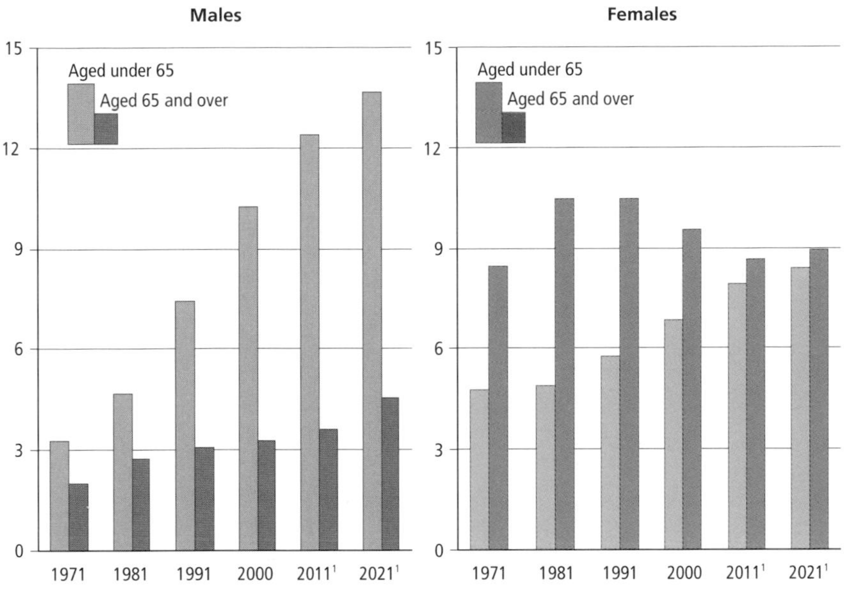

Percentages

1 1996-based household projections.
Source: Office of the Deputy Prime Minister

Table **2.4**

Percentage of children[1] living in different family types

Great Britain
Percentages

	1981	1992[2]	2002[2]
Couple families			
1 child	18	18	17
2 children	41	39	37
3 or more children	29	27	24
Lone mother families			
1 child	3	4	6
2 children	4	5	7
3 or more children	3	4	6
Lone father families			
1 child	1	1	1
2 or more children	1	1	1
All children[3]	100	100	100

1 See Appendix, Part 2: Families. These estimates for 2002 are not seasonally adjusted and have not been adjusted to take account of the 2001 Census results. See Appendix, Part 4: LFS reweighting.
2 At spring.
3 Excludes cases where the dependent child is a family unit, for example, a foster child.
Source: General Household Survey and Labour Force Survey, Office for National Statistics

households and people living alone. The proportion of households comprising a couple with dependent children fell from a third in 1971 to just under a quarter in spring 2002 (Table 2.2). Between 1971 and 1991 the proportion of lone-parent households with dependent children doubled, from 3 to 6 per cent. The proportion then remained at around this level up to 2002.

One of the most notable changes in household composition over the last 30 years has been the increase in the proportion of one person households. The number of such households in England more than doubled from 3.0 million in 1971 to 6.2 million in 2001. In the 1970s women aged 65 and over made up the largest proportion of one person households, accounting for 8 per cent of all households in England in 1971; by 2000 this has risen to almost 10 per cent (Figure 2.3). There is now an increasing trend for younger people, particularly men, to live on their own. The largest increase in the proportion of households containing people living alone has been among men aged under 65, more than tripling from 3 per cent of households in 1971 to 10 per cent by 2000. Projections suggest that this trend will continue and that by 2021, 14 per cent of households will contain men under the age of 65 living alone. These increases reflect the decline in marriage, the increase in the age at which people first marry and the rise in separation and divorce.

There have been changes in the family types in which children live. Over the last 20 years, there has been an overall decrease in the percentage of dependent children living in couple families and an increase in those living in lone parent families. In spring 2002 around a fifth of dependent children in Great Britain lived in lone-parent families, almost twice the proportion in 1981 (Table 2.4). However despite this increase, most children still live in the traditional family household headed by a couple – 78 per cent lived in such a family in spring 2002.

A large part of the increase in lone parents up to the mid-1980s was due to divorce, more recently the number of single lone mothers has grown at a faster rate, because of a growth in the proportion of births outside marriage. Lone mothers headed the majority of lone-parent families in spring 2002; 10 per cent of lone-parent families were headed by lone fathers.

Household size and composition vary across ethnic groups. Demographic structures, cultural traditions and economic characteristics of the ethnic groups in the United Kingdom underlie many of these differences. In spring 2002, of families with dependent children, three fifths of those headed by a person of Mixed origin and just over half headed by a person of Black Caribbean origin were lone-parent families, compared with a quarter headed by a White person and a tenth headed by an Indian person (Table 2.5).

There are large differences between ethnic groups in their views about ideal family size. These differences in attitude are reflected in patterns in actual household size. Pakistani and Bangladeshi households tend to be larger than those of other ethnic groups. Asian households may contain three generations, with grandparents living with a married couple and their children. The average size of Bangladeshi households in spring 2002 was 4.7 people per household and for Pakistani households the average was 4.2 people. In comparison, the average sizes of Black Caribbean, Mixed origin and White households were each around 2.3 people.

Increased mobility means that people are less likely to live in the same area throughout their lifetime and now tend to live further from their relatives than previously (see page 187 of the Housing chapter). Despite these changes, families continue to play an important role in people's lives and regular contact with close relatives living elsewhere is common. In 2001 the British Social Attitudes survey asked adults aged 18 and over how often they saw close relatives they did not live with. More than half of adults saw their mother once a week or more, and over two fifths saw their father as frequently (Table 2.6). People were less likely to see their siblings as regularly as their other relatives. This can be partly explained by the tendency for adult siblings to live further from one another than from their other relatives.

The decrease in family size means that in the future, people will have fewer aunts, uncles and cousins. At the same time the ageing of the population means there will be more older

Table 2.5

Families with dependent children:[1] by ethnic group,[2] 2002[3]

United Kingdom		Percentages
	Couples	Lone parents
White	77	23
Mixed	39	61
Asian or Asian British		
Indian	91	9
Pakistani	85	15
Bangladeshi	89	–
Other Asian	90	–
All Asian groups	89	11
Black or Black British		
Black Caribbean	46	54
Black African	54	46
Other Black	–	–
All Black groups	49	51
Chinese	79	–
Other ethnic group	80	20
All families[4]	77	23

1 May also include non-dependent children. Excludes cases where head of family is a child, for example, a foster child. These estimates for 2002 are not seasonally adjusted and have not been adjusted to take account of the 2001 Census results. See Appendix, Part 4: LFS reweighting.
2 Ethnic group of head of family unit. See Appendix, Part 1: Classification of ethnic groups.
3 At spring.
4 Includes those families whose head did not state their ethnic group.
Source: Labour Force Survey, Office for National Statistics

Table 2.6

Frequency[1] of adults seeing relatives and friends, 2001

Great Britain					Percentages
	Mother	Father	Sibling	Adult child	Best friend[2]
Daily	8	4	2	12	9
At least several times a week	19	14	10	17	21
At least once a week	24	24	18	22	28
At least once a month	17	16	16	14	18
Several times a year	19	19	25	10	16
Less often	7	11	15	2	4
Never	3	9	7	2	–
All[3]	100	100	100	100	100

1 By people aged 18 and over. Those without the relative and those who live with the relative were excluded.
2 Best friend is the respondent's own definition.
3 Includes respondents who did not answer.
Source: British Social Attitudes Survey, National Centre for Social Research

Table **2.7**

Frequency of adults having contact with their grandchildren,[1] 2001

Great Britain   Percentages

	See their grandchildren	Other types of contact[2]
At least once a week	61	60
At least every month	17	12
Only in school holidays or once every three months	10	3
Less often	10	9
Never	2	16
All	100	100

1 Those without grandchildren and those who live with their grandchildren were excluded.
2 Contact by letter, telephone, fax or e-mail.
Source: Omnibus Survey, Office for National Statistics; London School of Hygiene and Tropical Medicine

Table **2.8**

Proportion of the population: by marital status and sex[1]

Great Britain   Percentages

	1971	1981	1991	2000
Males				
Single	24	27	31	34
Married	71	66	60	54
Widowed	4	4	4	4
Divorced	1	3	6	8
All males	100	100	100	100
Females				
Single	19	21	23	26
Married	65	61	56	52
Widowed	15	15	14	13
Divorced	1	4	7	9
All females	100	100	100	100

1 Adults aged 16 and over.
Source: Office for National Statistics; General Register Office for Scotland

generation relatives, increasing the proportion of people who have grandparents and great-grandparents – sometimes called the bean-pole effect. Changes in family relationships have implications for the role of grandparents within the family. The increased participation of women in the labour market and the rise in relationship breakdown has meant that some grandparents may be required to help to care for their grandchildren.

Of the adults aged 24 and over who responded to the September and October 2001 ONS Omnibus survey module, analysed by researchers at the London School of Hygiene and Tropical Medicine, 43 per cent had grandchildren. Almost nine in ten respondents aged 60 and over were grandparents. Sixty one per cent of all grandparents in Great Britain saw their grandchildren at least once a week (Table 2.7). Only 10 per cent saw their grandchildren less than once every three months, while 2 per cent never saw them. In addition 60 per cent of grandparents had contact with their grandchildren by telephone, letter, fax or e-mail at least once a week, though 16 per cent never had contact with their grandchildren in these ways.

Partnerships

The pattern of partnership formation has changed over the last 30 years. Although the majority of men and women still marry, the proportion of the population who are married has fallen. In 1971, 71 per cent of men and 65 per cent of women in Great Britain were married; by 2000 this had fallen to 54 per cent of men and 52 per cent of women (Table 2.8). Over the same period the proportion of the population who were divorced increased and was eight times greater for men and nine times greater for women, to reach almost a tenth of each group. There has also been an increase in the proportion of the population who are single. In 1971 a quarter of men and a fifth of women were single; this rose to a third of men and a quarter of women in 2000.

While the proportions of men and women who are married have declined, the proportions that are cohabiting have increased. In Great Britain a quarter of non-married adults aged 16 to 59 were cohabiting in 2000/01. The longest time series on cohabitation exists for non-married women aged 18 to 49. Between 1979 and 2000/01 the proportion who were cohabiting almost tripled, from 11 to 30 per cent. The prevalence of cohabitation is highest among men aged 30 to 34 and women aged 25 to 29 (Figure 2.9).

Cohabitation is not necessarily a replacement for marriage – for some couples it is a transitional stage, eventually leading to marriage, in the same way that long engagements were customary in the past. Combined data from the 1998/99 and 2000/01 General Household Surveys show that around a third of people aged 16 to 59 cohabited with their future partner before their first marriage. Almost two thirds of people who were in their 30s when they married for the first time had cohabited with their partner compared with a third of those aged 20 to 29.

Although most cohabiting couples expect to marry, not all unions lead to marriage. In 2000/01, 14 per cent of adults aged 16 to 59 reported at least one cohabiting union that did not lead to marriage. This was more likely among those aged 30 to 34, with almost a quarter reporting such a union, compared with one in twenty adults aged 50 to 54.

In 1950 there were 408,000 marriages in the United Kingdom (Figure 2.10). The number of marriages grew during the mid- to late-1960s to reach a peak of 480,000 in 1972. This growth was partly a result of the babies born in the post-war boom reaching marriageable ages and partly that people were marrying younger. The total number of marriages then began to decline, reaching a low of 301,000 marriages in 1999. In 2000 there were 306,000 marriages, a 2 per cent increase from 1999. This was the first year that marriages had increased since 1992. The number of first marriages peaked in 1970 at almost 390,000, and since has decreased to less than half this number to reach 180,000 in 2000.

The number of divorces in Great Britain doubled between 1961 and 1969. Divorce was also permitted in Northern Ireland after 1969. By 1972, the number of divorces in the United Kingdom had doubled again. This latter increase was partly a result of the *Divorce Reform Act 1969* in England and Wales, which came into effect in 1971. The Act introduced a single ground for divorce – irretrievable

Figure **2.9**

Non-married[1] people[2] cohabiting: by sex and age, 2000/01
Great Britain

Percentages

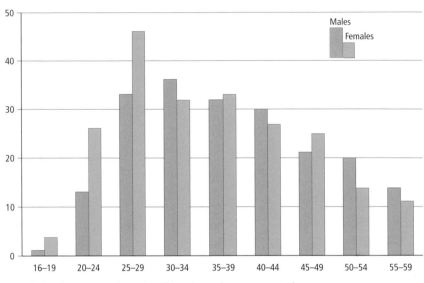

1 Includes those respondents describing themselves as separated.
2 Males and females aged 16-59.
Source: General Household Survey, Office for National Statistics

Figure **2.10**

Marriages and divorces
United Kingdom

Thousands

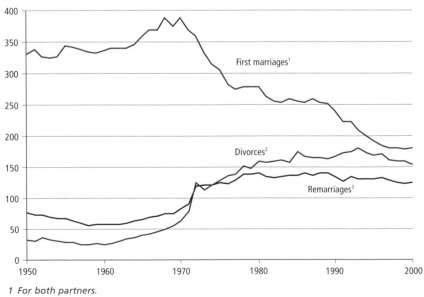

1 For both partners.
2 Includes annulments. Data for 1950 to 1970 for Great Britain only.
3 For one or both partners.
Source: Office for National Statistics; General Register Office for Scotland; Northern Ireland Statistics and Research Agency

Table **2.11**

Marriage and divorce rates: EU comparison, 2001

Rates per 1,000 population

	Marriages[1]	Divorces[2]
Denmark	6.6	2.7
Portugal	5.7	1.8
Greece	5.4	0.9
Spain	5.2	1.0
United Kingdom	5.1	2.6
France	5.1	2.0
Irish Republic	5.1	0.7
Netherlands	5.1	2.3
Italy	4.9	0.7
Finland	4.8	2.6
Germany	4.7	2.4
Luxembourg	4.5	2.3
Austria	4.2	2.5
Belgium	4.2	2.9
Sweden	4.0	2.4
EU average	5.1	1.9

1 2000 data for UK, Italy and EU average.
2 2000 data for UK, Austria, Germany, Spain, Italy, Irish Republic and EU average. 1999 data for France.
Source: Eurostat

Table **2.12**

Average age at marriage and divorce

England & Wales

Mean age (years)

	First marriage		Divorce	
	Males	Females	Males	Females
1961	25.6	23.1	..	..
1971	24.6	22.6	39.4	36.8
1981	25.4	23.1	37.7	35.2
1991	27.5	25.5	38.6	36.0
2000	30.5	28.2	41.3	38.8

Source: Office for National Statistics

breakdown – which could be established by proving one or more certain facts: adultery; desertion; separation either with or without consent; or unreasonable behaviour. Although there was a drop in the number of divorces in 1973 in the United Kingdom, the number increased again in 1974 and peaked in 1993 at 180,000. The number of divorces then fell to 155,000 in 2000 before increasing slightly to around 157,000 in 2001. This was the first time there had been a rise since 1996.

Following divorce, people often form new relationships and may remarry. Remarriages, for one or both partners, increased by about a third between 1971 and 1972 following the introduction of the *Divorce Reform Act 1969*, and peaked at 141,000 in 1988. In 2000 there were 126,000 remarriages, accounting for two fifths of all marriages.

There is a trend for falling marriage rates and increased marital breakdown across Europe. This trend started in northern Europe, but has since spread throughout western and most of southern Europe. The majority of countries are now reporting a drop in the number of marriages. However, there is some variation across the European Union (EU). Denmark had the highest marriage rate at 6.6 marriages per 1,000 people in 2001, while Sweden had the lowest rate of 4.0 (Table 2.11). The marriage rate in the United Kingdom in 2000 was around the EU average at 5.1 per 1,000 people.

There are differing divorce rates across the EU mainly due to religious, social, cultural and legal differences. In 2001 countries in northern and western Europe typically had the highest divorce rates, while the Irish Republic and countries in southern Europe had the lowest divorce rates. Belgium had the highest divorce rate, at 2.9 divorces per 1,000 people in 2001, while Italy and the Irish Republic had the lowest rates, at 0.7 per 1,000 people each in 2000. The rate in the United Kingdom, at 2.6 in 2000, was above the EU average of 1.9 per 1,000 people.

The age at which people get married for the first time has continued to increase. In 1961 the average age at first marriage in England and Wales was 25.6 years for men and 23.1 years for women; by 2000 this had risen to 30.5 and 28.2 years, respectively (Table 2.12).

Generally, women marry men older than themselves and in 2000 the average age gap was just over two years. The age at first marriage has risen in all EU countries over the last 40 years and the average age at first marriage for the EU as a whole has risen by almost 4 years since 1961. Differences exist between the countries. In 2000 the country with the youngest newly-weds was Portugal, while Sweden had the oldest. The growth in pre-marital cohabitation partly explains the trend for later marriage, but other factors, such as increased and longer participation in further and higher education coupled with women's participation in the labour market, have also contributed.

The age at which people get divorced has also increased, from 39.4 years for men and 36.8 years for women in England and Wales in 1971, to 41.3 and 38.8 years, respectively, in 2000. This increase is related to the growing trend for postponing marriage, as the length of marriage for couples divorcing has changed little since 1963 – the first year for which this information is available. The median duration of marriage for couples divorcing in 2000 was 11 years while in 1963 it was just under 12 years.

Stepfamilies are formed when people with children form new partnerships and remarry or cohabit with new partners. In 2000/01 stepfamilies accounted for 8 per cent of families with dependent children whose head was aged under 60 in Great Britain. The majority (88 per cent) of these consisted of a couple with one or more children from the previous relationship of the female partner only (Figure 2.13). This occurs because there is a tendency for children to stay with their mother following the break up of a partnership.

Family formation

There were around 767,000 conceptions in England and Wales in 2000, a fall of 10 per cent from 1991 (Table 2.14). Just over three quarters of conceptions in 2000 led to a maternity. The percentage leading to abortion has almost doubled from 12 per cent in 1971 to 23 per cent in 2000. Abortion is more common when the conception takes place outside marriage. Around a third of conceptions outside marriage are terminated by an abortion, compared with one tenth of conceptions within marriage. In

Figure **2.13**

Stepfamily couples[1] with dependent children:[2] by family type, 2000/01

Great Britain

Percentages

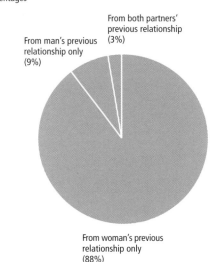

From man's previous relationship only (9%)

From both partners' previous relationship (3%)

From woman's previous relationship only (88%)

1 Family head aged 16–59.
2 One or more children.
Source: General Household Survey, Office for National Statistics

Table **2.14**

Conceptions:[1] by outcome

England & Wales   Percentages

	1971	1981	1991	2000
Conceptions leading to				
Maternities	88	83	81	77
Legal abortions[2]	12	17	19	23
All conceptions (=100%) (thousands)	836	752	854	767

1 See Appendix, Part 2: Conceptions.
2 Legal terminations under the 1967 Abortion Act.
Source: Office for National Statistics

Table **2.15**

Teenage conceptions:[1] by age at conception and outcome, 2000

England & Wales

	Number of conceptions		Rates per 1,000 women	
	Leading to maternities	Leading to abortions	Leading to maternities	Leading to abortions
Age at conception				
Under 14	161	237	0.5	0.7
14	790	1,100	2.4	3.4
15	2,779	3,048	8.6	9.4
All aged under 16	3,730	4,385	3.8	4.5
16	7,299	5,854	23.5	18.9
17	12,061	8,020	38.7	25.7
18	16,529	9,651	54.5	31.8
19	19,619	10,517	64.2	34.4
All aged under 20	59,238	38,427	38.1	24.7

1 See Appendix, Part 2: Conceptions.
Source: Office for National Statistics

Figure **2.16**

Live births to teenage women:[1] EU comparison, 2001[2]

Live births per 1,000 women

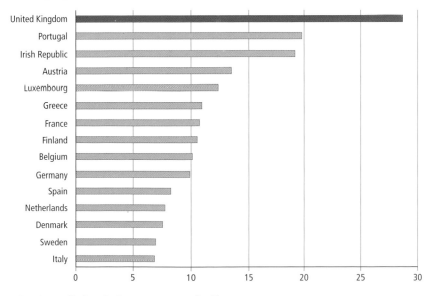

1 See Appendix, Part 2: Average teenage fertility rate.
2 2000 data for France, United Kingdom and Germany. 1999 data for Spain, Greece and Italy.
  1996 data for Belgium.
Source: Council of Europe

2000, just over half of conceptions were outside marriage while in 1971 just over a fifth were. Compared with 30 years ago fewer conceptions occurring outside marriage now lead to a birth inside marriage; this reflects the increased acceptance of lone parents and births to unmarried women.

There were almost 98,000 conceptions to teenage girls, aged under 20, in England and Wales in 2000 – 61 per cent of these led to a maternity and 39 per cent to abortions (Table 2.15). There were 8,000 conceptions among girls under the age of 16, less than a tenth of the total number of conceptions to teenagers. Of these conceptions almost 400 were to girls under the age of 14, 160 of which led to maternities.

Throughout most of western Europe, teenage birth rates have fallen rapidly since the 1970s, but in the United Kingdom the rates have remained at the early 1980s level or above. The United Kingdom, with an average live birth rate of 29 live births per 1,000 girls aged 15 to 19 in 2000, had the highest rate of live births to teenage girls in the EU (Figure 2.16). This was more than two fifths higher than Portugal, the country with the next highest rate. Italy and Sweden had the lowest rates at 7 live births per 1,000 girls aged 15 to 19, and Denmark and the Netherlands had rates of almost 8 live births per 1,000 young women.

Trends in abortion rates vary according to the age of the woman. Women under 16 and those aged 35 and over have lower abortion rates than those in other age groups. In 2001 the abortion rate among women under 16 years of age was 3.7 per 1,000 women and for women aged 35 and over the rate was 6.4 per 1,000 women (Figure 2.17 - see overleaf). Following the introduction of the *Abortion Act 1967* the abortion rates have risen particularly rapidly for young women aged 16 to 24. For women aged 20 to 24 the rate was more than four times higher in 2001 than in 1969, increasing from 7.0 abortions per 1,000 women in this age group to 30.6 abortions per 1,000 women. Abortion rates among women aged 16 to 19 rose almost as quickly over this period, increasing from 6.1 abortions per 1,000 women in this age group to 26.1 abortions per 1,000 women.

During the early 1990s the abortion rate among young women fell slightly, but then rose again between 1995 and 1996. This increase is thought to have been the result of a pill scare. In 1995 the Committee on Safety of Medicines warned that several brands of the contraceptive pill carried an increased risk of thrombosis. This warning is believed to have contributed to an increase in conceptions and a related increase in abortions in 1996, particularly among young women as they were more likely to have been using the pill. Following this pill scare the abortion rates did not fall back to the 1995 level, but have continued to rise. There have been subsequent warnings about the links between the contraceptive pill and thrombosis.

Changes in fertility patterns influence the size of families and affect the age structure of the population. At the start of the 20th century there were about 115 live births per 1,000 women aged 15 to 44 in the United Kingdom. Fertility rates have fluctuated over the last century, aside from brief peaks after both World Wars, they rose in the 1960s but then dropped rapidly from the late 1960s to the late 1970s. They recovered slightly and remained steady during the 1980s, but have since gradually declined. In 2001 there were 55 births per 1,000 women of childbearing age.

With the exception of the periods immediately after the two World Wars, few births occurred outside marriage during the first 60 years of the 20th century. During the 1960s and 1970s this proportion rose. In 2001 most children were born to married couples, but around 40 per cent of live births in the United Kingdom occurred outside marriage (Figure 2.18). Most of the increase in the number of births outside marriage since the late 1980s has been to cohabiting couples, that is parents living at the same address. In 2001, more than three quarters of births outside marriage in England and Wales were jointly registered by both parents. Three in four of these births were to parents living at the same address.

Despite the high rate of teenage pregnancy in the United Kingdom, there is an overall trend towards later childbearing. In England and Wales the average age of mothers at childbirth has increased by three years since 1971, rising

Figure **2.17**

Abortion rates:[1] **by age**

England & Wales

Rates per 1,000 women

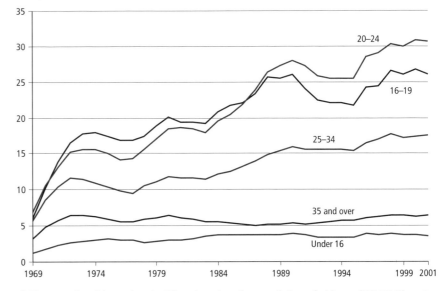

1 The rates for girls aged under 16 are based on the population of girls aged 13–15. The rates for females aged 35 and over are based on the population of females aged 35–49.
Source: Office for National Statistics

Figure **2.18**

Births outside marriage as a percentage of all live births

United Kingdom

Percentages

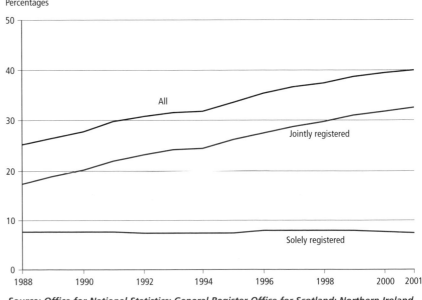

Source: Office for National Statistics; General Register Office for Scotland; Northern Ireland Statistics and Research Agency

Table **2.19**

Average age of mother at childbirth

England & Wales				Mean age (years)
	1971	1981	1991	2000
All births				
All live births	26.2	26.8	27.7	29.1
All first births	..	..	25.7	27.1
Births inside marriage				
All births inside marriage	26.4	27.3	28.9	30.8
First births inside marriage	24.0	25.4	27.5	29.6
Births outside marriage				
All births outside marriage	23.8	23.5	24.8	26.5

Source: Office for National Statistics

Figure **2.20**

Percentage of women childless at age 25, 35 and 45:[1] by year of birth
England & Wales

Percentages

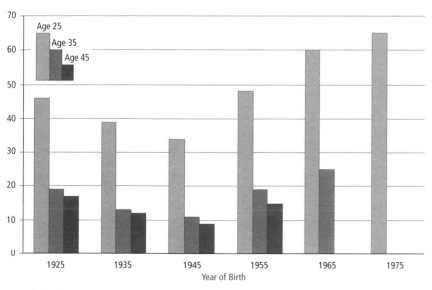

1 Includes births at ages over 45. Data for women aged 35 born in 1975 and for those aged 45 born since 1965 are not available.

Source: Office for National Statistics

from 26.2 years to 29.1 years in 2000 (Table 2.19). Over the last decade the average age of women at the birth of their first child has risen by one and a half years, to reach 27.1 in 2000.

Information on the average age at first birth over the last 30 years is only available for married women. The average age of women giving birth for the first time inside marriage has increased by almost six years since 1971. Births outside marriage tend to take place at a younger age than those inside marriage. In 2000 women giving birth outside marriage were more than four years younger than their married counterparts. The average age of fathers at childbirth has also risen, from 27.2 years in 1971 to 31.7 years in 2001 for births registered by both parents.

Linked to the trend for delaying childbirth is the growth in the number of women remaining childless. Nine per cent of women born in 1945 were still childless at the age of 45; this increased to 15 per cent of those born in 1955 (Figure 2.20). It is expected that this trend will continue and that a growing proportion of women born after 1955 will be childless at age 45.

While some women might choose not to have children, others may be unable to due to fertility problems. In addition, those women who choose to postpone motherhood to later in life can experience increased difficulty in conceiving. Some women use infertility treatments to help them conceive. In vitro fertilisation (IVF) became available in the United Kingdom in 1978 and since then the total number of treatment cycles carried out has increased dramatically, peaking in 1998/99 at over 35,000. In 2000/01 the number of treatment cycles was lower at around 25,000. However, the success rate of IVF has risen from 9 per cent of treatment cycles leading to a live birth in 1986, to 22 per cent in 2000/01.

The greater use of fertility treatment is an important factor in the increased rate of multiple births. In 2001, 145 in every 10,000 maternities resulted in the birth of twins, while 4 in every 10,000 maternities led to triplets or more (Table 2.21 - see overleaf). The rates are higher for older women – among women aged over 40, twins accounted for 194 in every 10,000 maternities, and triplets for 11 in every 10,000 maternities. In comparison, for women aged under 20, twins accounted for 61 in every 10,000 maternities and triplets for less than 1 in every 10,000 maternities. To decrease the likelihood of multiple births following fertility treatment, the Human Fertilisation and Embryology Authority recently revised its guidelines to reduce the number of embryos used in IVF from three to two.

Families may also be formed or extended by the adoption of children. Since the early 1970s, the number of adoptions in England and Wales has decreased from almost 21,500 in 1971 to just under 6,000 in 2001. However this was an increase of over 1,600 adoptions (39 per cent) since 1999 (Figure 2.22). There was a rapid decline in the number of children available for adoption following the introduction of legal abortion in the *Abortion Act 1967* and after the implementation of the *Children Act 1975*. This required court dealings with adoption applications for children of divorced parents to be dismissed where a legal custody order was in the child's best interests.

The increased use of contraception and a change in attitudes to lone parents have also contributed to this fall. Despite these changes, children born outside marriage have formed the majority of children adopted since 1971, and accounted for 70 per cent of children adopted in 2001. Fewer babies are available for adoption than in the past – the proportion of all children adopted in Great Britain who were aged under 1 decreased from 26 per cent in 1981 to 4 per cent in 2001. In comparison the proportion of children adopted who were between the ages of 1 and 4 increased during the same period from 20 per cent to 44 per cent. Nearly a third of children adopted in 2001 were aged 5 to 9 and a fifth were aged 10 or over.

Table 2.21

Maternities with multiple births: by age of mother at childbirth, 2001

United Kingdom		Rate per 10,000 maternities
	Maternities with twins only	Maternities with triplets and over
Under 20	61.2	0.6
20–24	91.6	1.2
25–29	127.9	2.3
30–34	179.7	5.3
35–39	205.4	6.2
40 and over	194.0	11.2
All	144.8	3.7

Source: Office for National Statistics; General Register Office for Scotland; Northern Ireland Statistics and Research Agency

Figure 2.22

Adoption orders

England & Wales

Thousands

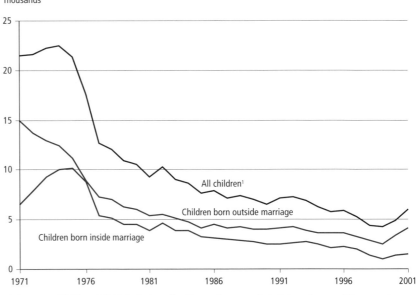

1 Between 1985 and 1990 includes adoptions where marital status of parent(s) was unknown.
Source: Office for National Statistics

Chapter 3

Education and training

Early years education

- In 1970/71, 21 per cent of three and four year olds in the United Kingdom attended schools; by 1999/2000 this had tripled to 63 per cent, and remained at this level up to 2001/02. (Figure 3.1)

Schools

- In 2001/02 there were 34,500 schools in the United Kingdom, accommodating over 10 million pupils. (Page 57)

- The rates for appeals lodged by parents against non-admission to secondary schools in England have increased by one and a half times since 1993/94, from 42 per 1,000 new admissions to 103 per 1,000 new admissions in 2000/01. (Figure 3.4)

- In 2000 the United Kingdom ranked second in the European Union for mathematics and science, and third for reading. (Table 3.8)

Post compulsory participation

- In 2000/01 there were four times as many female further education students in the United Kingdom as in 1970/71, but only twice as many male students. (Table 3.12)

Post compulsory outcomes

- In 2000/01 nearly 400,000 NVQs and a further 29,000 SVQs were awarded in the United Kingdom. (Table 3.15)

- In 2001, 67 per cent of first degree graduates (whose first destinations were known) went into employment, compared with 53 per cent in 1991. (Table 3.16)

Adult training and learning

- In England and Wales in 2001 participation in learning among those with a work limiting disability was lower than for those with no disability (56 per cent compared with 80 per cent). (Table 3.20)

Educational resources

- The number of non-teaching staff in England who provide additional learning support within the classroom has increased by 83 per cent since 1996, to over 167,000 in 2002. (Table 3.24)

- The percentage of teachers in England who felt confident in the use of ICT in their subject increased from 63 per cent in 1998 to 76 per cent in 2002. (Table 3.25)

For many education begins with early learning and participation in pre-school education and continues beyond compulsory schooling. The number going into further and higher education has increased over the last 30 years. Over the last five years the proportion of adults taking part in learning has increased, whereas the number of employees taking part in job-related training has remained fairly constant.

Early years education

Over the last 30 years there has been a major expansion in pre-school education with an increased emphasis on children beginning their compulsory education with a basic foundation in literacy and numeracy. In 1970/71, 21 per cent of three and four year olds in the United Kingdom attended schools; by 1999/2000 this had tripled to 63 per cent, and then remained at this level (Figure 3.1). In 2000/01, 28 per cent of three and four year olds in the United Kingdom were enrolled in non-school education settings in the private and voluntary sector, such as local playgroups and day nurseries. Table 8.21 in Chapter 8: Social Protection gives more information on these, and other, day care places for children.

Currently in England, all four year olds are entitled to a free part-time pre-school (or nursery education) place. By September 2004, all three year olds will also be guaranteed the same entitlement. These early years of education in England for children aged three to five are recognised as a distinct phase of education – the foundation stage. The associated early learning goals aim to develop keys skills such as speaking, listening, concentration, learning to work and play with others and early literacy and numeracy. The foundation stage intends to prepare children for learning at key stage 1 and is consistent with the National Curriculum (see Appendix, Part 3: The National Curriculum).

In 2001, a survey on the use of early years services asked parents of three and four year olds in England who used nursery education in the week prior to interview, 'What, if anything, is particularly good about the nursery education provider?' (Table 3.2). In response, 38 per cent said that the standard of teaching was good and the same proportion said that teachers and carers related well to

Figure **3.1**

Children under five[1] in schools as a percentage of all three and four year olds
United Kingdom

Percentages

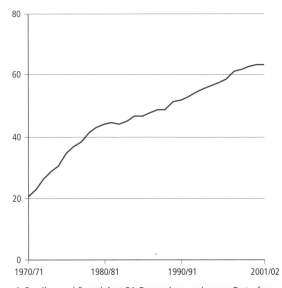

1 Pupils aged 3 and 4 at 31 December each year. Data for 2001/02 for Wales and Scotland relate to 2000/01.
Source: Department for Education and Skills; National Assembly for Wales; Scottish Executive; Northern Ireland Department of Education

Table **3.2**

Good things[1] about nursery education providers,[2] 2001
England

Percentages

	Total
Teaching/teaching methods/education standards good	38
Teachers/carers relate well to children	38
Child likes going there	31
Small, friendly school/place	28
Teachers/carers communicate well with parents	25
Good standard of care	22
Variety of activities available	19
Child learns a lot there	19
Child gets a lot of individual attention	17
Good discipline	15
Close to home/convenient	15
Child learns useful life/social skills	14
Good facilities/equipment	14
Nothing particularly good	5

1 Parents of three and four year old children who used a nursery education provider in the week prior to interview were asked, 'What, if anything, is particularly good about the nursery education provider?' Parents could give more than one answer.
2 See Appendix, Part 3: Stages of education – Foundation stage.
Source: National Centre for Social Research, for the Department for Education and Skills

the children. High proportions of parents also mentioned that their child liked going there, and that the provider was small and friendly. Very few parents, just 5 per cent, said that there was nothing particularly good about their nursery education provider. The survey also looked at parents' perceptions of what their children learnt at their nursery education provider. Parents were most likely to agree that the provider helped their child learn to work and play with other children (94 per cent). Three quarters of parents agreed that their provider had helped their child learn to read and write.

Schools

The number of children of school age in the United Kingdom has fluctuated due to factors such as the raising of the school-leaving age and changes in the birth rate. The declining birth rates during the late 1970s led to a fall in pupil numbers in the 1980s and early 1990s. Pupil numbers increased to 2000/01, but saw a decline in the last year – numbers are still below the peak level of the 1970s.

In 2001/02 there were 34,500 schools in the United Kingdom, accommodating over 10 million pupils (Table 3.3). Public sector schools (not including special schools) were attended by over 9 million or 92 per cent of all pupils. Six per cent of pupils attended one of the 2,409 non-maintained schools, and 1 per cent attended one of the 1,483 special schools. There were 340 pupil referral units (PRUs), catering for 10,000 pupils in 2001/02. PRUs provide suitable alternative education on a temporary basis for pupils who may not be able to attend a mainstream school.

There have been changes in the structure of secondary education. Prior to the introduction of comprehensive schools in England and Wales, children were required to take the '11 plus', which determined whether they would attend a grammar or secondary modern school. In England and Wales, the '11 plus' had largely been abolished by the late 1960s when comprehensive schools replaced grammar and secondary modern schools. Comprehensive schools were introduced with the aim of providing equality of opportunity for children of all abilities. In 2001/02, 86 per cent of pupils in secondary schools in the United Kingdom attended comprehensive schools, while only 5 per cent went to grammar schools and 3 per cent attended secondary modern schools. These figures compare with 37 per cent, 19 per cent and 33 per cent, respectively, in 1970/71. All publicly funded secondary schools in Scotland and Wales are comprehensive. In Northern Ireland, secondary education is largely organised on selective lines; in 2001/02, 40 per cent of pupils attended grammar schools.

A local education authority (LEA) may decide to make a statement of need when it concludes that special educational provision is necessary to meet a pupil's needs and that these cannot reasonably be provided for within the resources available to the school. In 2001/02 there were 292,400 full- and part-time pupils with statements of special educational needs in the United Kingdom, representing 3 per cent of all pupils. Sixty three per cent of pupils with statements attended mainstream schools. Not all special educational needs students have statements of need, in 2001/02, nearly 90 per cent of pupils in maintained primary and secondary schools with special

Table **3.3**

School pupils:[1] by type of school[2]

United Kingdom						Thousands
	1970/71	1980/81	1990/91	1994/95	2000/01	2001/02
Public sector schools						
Nursery & primary	5,952	5,260	5,060	5,341	5,450	5,395
Secondary						
Comprehensive	1,313	3,730	2,925	3,093	3,340	3,390
Grammar	673	149	156	184	205	209
Modern	1,164	233	94	90	117	103
Other	403	434	298	289	260	247
All public sector schools	9,507	9,806	8,533	8,996	9,367	9,344
Non-maintained schools	621	619	613	600	626	635
Special schools	103	148	114	117	113	112
Pupil referral units	.	.	.	.	10	10
All schools	10,230	10,572	9,260	9,714	10,116	10,102

1 Headcounts.

2 See Appendix, Part 3: Main categories of educational establishments and Stages of education.

Source: Department for Education and Skills; National Assembly for Wales; Scottish Executive; Northern Ireland Department of Education

needs did not have statements. Special educational needs' assessments do not always lead to a statement.

In England and Wales parents have the right to express a preference for a school for their child at all stages of their child's education. If their choice is not met, they may appeal against the decision to a panel made up of representatives that are independent of the school's governing body and the LEA which maintains the school. Appeals lodged by parents against non-admission to secondary schools in England have increased by one and a half times since 1993/94, from 42 per 1,000 new admissions to 103 per 1,000 new admissions in 2000/01 (Figure 3.4). The rates of appeal to primary school non-admissions peaked at 57 per 1,000 new admissions in 1996/97, and have since declined to 47 per 1,000 in 2000/01 – rates are still 25 per cent higher than in 1993/94. The success of appeals to secondary schools has been stable with around a third of appeals decided in favour of the parents each year since 1993/94. For primary schools the success rate has declined from a half in 1993/94 to just over a third in 2000/01.

There has been growing awareness and concern over the number of children outside the education system. Some have been excluded from schools, while others truant. In 2000/01, almost 10,000 children in Great Britain were permanently excluded from schools (Table 3.5). This was 10 per cent higher than in the previous year, but still lower than in 1998/99, when just over 11,000 children were permanently excluded. The number of boys permanently excluded outnumbered girls by nearly five to one in 2000/01. The highest exclusion rates in England in 2000/01 were among Black Other and Black Caribbean pupils, with around 39 in every 10,000 pupils of compulsory school age being excluded compared with only 3 in every 10,000 Indian pupils. Exclusions were most common among those aged 13 and 14; pupils of these ages accounted for half of all permanent exclusions.

In 2002 there were over 630,000 (9 per cent) pupils in primary and secondary schools in England whose mother tongue was not English (Table 3.6). The figure was slightly higher for primary schools than secondary schools. In 2002 differences between the regions ranged from 48 per cent of pupils in primary and 44

Figure 3.4

Appeals lodged by parents against non-admission of their children to maintained schools

England

Rate per 1,000 new admissions

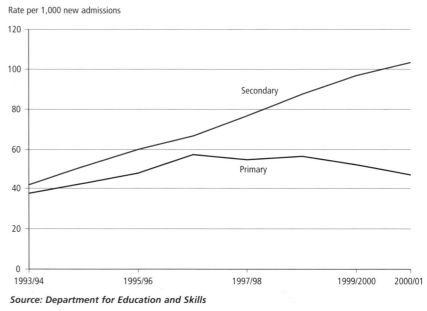

Source: Department for Education and Skills

Table 3.5

Permanent exclusions from schools:[1] by sex

Great Britain			Thousands
	Males	Females	Percentage excluded[2]
1995/96[3]	10.8	2.2	0.16
1996/97[3]	10.9	2.2	0.16
1997/98[3]	10.7	2.1	0.16
1998/99	9.1	1.9	0.12
1999/00	7.6	1.4	0.10
2000/01	8.2	1.7	0.11

1 Maintained primary, secondary and special schools. Figures for England include independent special schools.
2 The number of permanent exclusions expressed as a percentage of the number (headcount) of full- and part-time pupils of all ages (excluding dually registered pupils in special schools) in January each year.
3 England and Wales only.
Source: Department for Education and Skills; National Assembly for Wales; Scottish Executive

Table **3.6**

Pupils in maintained schools whose mother tongue is other than English,[1] 2002

Percentages

	Primary	Secondary
England	10	9
North East	3	2
North West	6	5
Yorkshire & the Humber	8	7
East Midlands	8	6
West Midlands	12	10
East	5	6
London	33	30
Inner	48	44
Outer	25	24
South East	4	4
South West	2	2

1 The number of pupils whose mother tongue is known, or believed, to be other than English expressed as a percentage of the number of pupils of compulsory school age and above.
Source: Department for Education and Skills

Table **3.7**

Pupils reaching or exceeding expected standards:[1] by key stage and sex, 2002

England

Percentages

	Teacher assessment		Tests	
	Males	Females	Males	Females
Key stage 1				
English	81	89	.	.
Reading	81	88	81	88
Writing	79	88	82	90
Mathematics	87	90	89	92
Science	88	91	.	.
Key stage 2				
English	67	78	70	79
Mathematics	74	75	73	73
Science	82	83	86	87
Key stage 3				
English	59	75	58	75
Mathematics	69	72	67	68
Science	66	69	66	67

1 See Appendix, Part 3: The National Curriculum.
Source: Department for Education and Skills

per cent of pupils in secondary schools in Inner London, to around 2 per cent of pupils in maintained primary and secondary schools in the South West.

Between 1989 and 1996 the National Curriculum was introduced in England and Wales with the aim of ensuring that children receive a comparable and balanced programme of study throughout their compulsory schooling. The subjects taught to children between the ages of 5 and 16 in state schools are to a large extent determined by the National Curriculum, which has four key stages. School pupils in England and Wales are formally assessed at three key stages before GCSE level – at the ages of 7, 11 and 14. The assessment at all three key stages covers the core subjects of English (and Welsh in Wales), mathematics and science. The purpose of these tests is to help inform teachers and parents about the progress of individual pupils and to give a measure of the performance of schools. There are two forms of assessment: tests and teacher assessment. In Wales at key stage 1 there is only teacher assessment. Pupils' attainment is shown as a level on the National Curriculum scale. Typically, a 7 year old is expected to achieve level two at key stage 1, an 11 year old level four at key stage 2, and a 14 year old between levels five and six (level five in Wales) at key stage 3.

In 2002, the proportion of boys in England reaching the required standard for English at all key stages was lower than for girls, particularly at key stages 2 and 3 (Table 3.7). However, similar proportions of boys and girls reached the expected level in tests and teacher assessments for mathematics and science. The proportion of pupils achieving the expected level declined with age for both sexes (the same was also true in Wales). At key stage 1, for example, 81 per cent of boys and 89 per cent of girls in England achieved the expected level in English teacher assessments. By key stage 3, this had fallen to 75 per cent of girls and 59 per cent of boys. In teacher assessments for science, 91 per cent of girls and 88 per cent of boys at key stage 1 reached the expected level, compared with 69 and 66 per cent respectively at key stage 3.

Patterns of achievement at key stages 1 to 3 in Wales in 2002 were similar to those in England. In Wales it is compulsory for schools to teach

Welsh but taking a key stage test is optional. In 2000/01, 16 per cent of primary school children were fluent in Welsh, compared with 13 per cent in 1986/87. In secondary schools 14 per cent of pupils in year groups 7 to 11 (ages 11 to 15-16), were taught Welsh as a first language. This figure has increased virtually every year since 1977/78 when the figure was 9 per cent. Eighty five per cent of pupils were taught Welsh as a second language in 2000/01, and represents a major growth in this area – in 1977/78 the comparable figure was 36 per cent.

Northern Ireland has its own common curriculum, which is similar but not identical to the National Curriculum in England and Wales. A similar system of key stage assessment also exists in Northern Ireland, however, key stage 1 is assessed at age 8, and there is only teacher assessment at key stages 1 and 2. In Northern Ireland in 2001, there was also a difference in the proportion of boys and girls achieving the required standard in key stage 1 teacher assessments, particularly in English, and the proportion of pupils achieving the expected level generally declined with age.

There is no statutory National Curriculum in Scotland. National guidelines for pupils aged 5 to 14 set out the ground to be covered and the ways that pupils' learning should be assessed and reported. Progress is measured by attainment of six levels based on the expectation of the performance of the majority of pupils on completion of certain stages between the ages of 5 and 14. Results in Scotland cannot be compared to those in the rest of the United Kingdom. The proportion of pupils achieving the expected levels was lower in older age groups. In the primary year 3 group (children aged 7/8), 95 per cent of pupils attained the required standard or above in mathematics, while 87 per cent did so in reading and 83 per cent in writing. By the secondary year 2 group (children aged 13/14), less than half of pupils had attained the required standard in writing in 2000/01, whilst for reading and mathematics the percentage

of pupils attaining the required standard was 51 per and 56 per cent respectively. In secondary year 2, reading had become the subject in which most pupils reached the required standard, whereas it was mathematics in primary year 3.

In 2000 the Programme for International Student Assessment (PISA), for the Organisation for Economic Co-operation and Development (OECD), measured the knowledge and skills of 15 year olds across 32 countries in three literacy areas: reading, mathematics and science. The scale for each literacy area of PISA was devised so that across all participating countries around two thirds of the 265,000 students who took part achieved between 400 and 600 points, the average score was 500 points. In the United Kingdom, as in all participating countries, girls did better than

Table 3.8

Knowledge and skills of 15 year olds in three literacy areas:[1] EU comparison,[2] 2000

Mean scores (OECD = 500)

	Reading	Mathematics	Science
Finland	546	536	538
Irish Republic	527	503	513
United Kingdom	523	529	532
Sweden	516	510	512
Austria	507	515	519
Belgium	507	520	496
France	505	517	500
Denmark	497	514	481
Spain	493	476	491
Italy	487	457	478
Germany	484	490	487
Greece	474	447	461
Portugal	470	454	459
Luxembourg	441	446	443
OECD average	500	500	500

1 See Appendix, Part 3: Programme for International Student Assessment.
2 The response rate of schools in the Netherlands was too low to allow accurate estimates of literacy.
Source: Organisation for Economic Co-operation and Development

boys on the reading scale. In the United Kingdom, for mathematics, boys did better than girls, as in half of all countries, while for science boys did better than girls in the United Kingdom but across all countries differences between the sexes for science averaged out.

Table 3.8 shows the scores in each literacy area for the countries within the EU in 2000. Of these countries, Finland achieved the highest scores for each of the three literacy areas. Compared with other EU countries, the United Kingdom ranked second for both mathematics and science, and third for reading, while the mean student scores were lowest in Luxembourg, Portugal and Greece. Luxembourg scored below 450 in all three literacy areas. These rankings change when the mean scores for each of the 32 countries that took part in PISA are considered. Among all

participating countries, the mean student scores for reading literacy remained highest in Finland (546), while Japan and Korea scored highest in mathematics (557) and science (552) respectively. The United Kingdom came seventh for reading, eighth for mathematics and fourth for science. Only Mexico recorded mean scores below those for Luxembourg, scoring 422 for reading and science, and 387 for mathematics.

In England, Wales and Northern Ireland, young people aged 15 and 16 sit GCSEs, while Standard Grades are taken in Scotland. In 2000/01, 51 per cent of pupils in the United Kingdom gained five or more GCSEs (or their equivalent) at grades A* to C, compared with 46 per cent in 1995/96. Pass rates have risen over the last few years for both sexes but girls continue to outperform boys. In 2000/01, 57 per cent of girls gained five or more GCSEs, compared with 46 per cent of boys.

The socio-economic status and educational attainment of parents can have a significant impact on the GCSE attainment of their children. For example, more pupils whose parents are classified as being in the professional groups achieve five or more GCSEs at grades A* to C than those in the routine groups. In England and Wales, three quarters of pupils whose parents were in the higher professional group achieved five or more GCSEs at grades A* to C in 2000 (Table 3.9). Of those pupils whose parents were in the routine group, less than a third achieved the same level.

Young people whose parents have higher qualifications are also much more likely to achieve five or more GCSEs grades A* to C (or the GNVQ equivalent) than those whose parents have lower qualifications. Seventy two per cent of young people whose parents were qualified to degree level and 56 per cent whose parents highest qualification was a GCE A Level achieved five or more GCSEs A* to C in 2000, compared with 39 per cent of young people whose parents were not qualified to at least GCE A level.

Table 3.9

GCSE attainment:[1] by parents' socio-economic classification,[2] 2000

England & Wales					Percentages
	5 or more GCSE grades A*–C	1–4 GCSE grades A*–C[3]	5 or more GCSE grades D–G	1–4 GCSE grades D–G	None reported
Higher professional	74	17	6	1	2
Lower professional	61	22	13	2	2
Intermediate	51	26	18	3	3
Lower supervisory	36	31	24	4	4
Routine	29	34	26	5	7
Other/not classified[4]	24	29	26	8	13

1 For pupils in year 11. Includes equivalent GNVQ qualifications achieved in year 11.
2 See Appendix, Part 1: National Statistics Socio-Economic Classification.
3 Consists of those with 1–4 GCSE grades A*–C and any number of other grades.
4 Includes a high percentage of respondents who had neither parent in a full-time job.
Source: Youth Cohort Study, Department for Education and Skills

Post compulsory participation

At age 16 young people are faced with the choice of whether to remain in education, go into training or seek employment. Over the last decade young people have become more likely to continue with their education.

In 2001, just over three out of four 16 to 18 year olds in England were in education or training, an increase from just over seven out of ten in 1991. Over half of 16 to 18 year olds were in full-time education in 2001. As would be expected, those aged 16 were more likely to be in education or training than those aged 18. In 2001 at ages 16 and 17, females were more likely to be in full-time education than males, while at 18 the difference was much smaller (Table 3.10).

Not everyone working towards a qualification beyond the age of 16 will have worked their way continuously through the various levels of education. Table 3.11 shows that of people of working age who were studying towards a qualification in the United Kingdom in spring 2002, just over half were aged between 16 and 24, while a fifth were aged 40 and over. These Labour Force Survey (LFS) estimates, and others used in the chapter, are not seasonally adjusted and have not been adjusted to take account of the recent Census 2001 results. ONS are working toward producing reweighted LFS estimates based on the findings of the 2001 Census, which will be available from summer 2003. See Appendix, Part 4: LFS reweighting.

Age composition varies according to qualification being undertaken. For example, in spring 2002, while the majority, 70 per cent, of those studying towards a GCE A level or equivalent were in the 16 to 19 age group, 21 per cent were aged 25 and over. Similar percentages were seen among those studying towards a GCSE or equivalent. In contrast, among those taking higher education qualifications below degree level, 65 per cent were aged 25 and over, and among those studying for degrees or higher (or equivalent), 44 per cent were aged 25 and over.

There were 5.0 million students in further education in the United Kingdom in 2000/01, 58 per cent of whom were female (Table 3.12). In 2000/01 there were four times as many female students in further education as in 1970/71, but only twice as many male students.

Table 3.10

Participation in education and training of 16, 17 and 18 year olds: by sex, 2001

England

Percentages

	Aged 16		Aged 17		Aged 18	
	Males	Females	Males	Females	Males	Females
Full-time education[1]	67	75	55	62	35	39
of which						
in schools	33	36	26	30	3	3
Government supported training (GST)	8	6	11	8	10	7
Employer funded training (EFT)	4	2	6	4	10	7
Other education and training[2]	6	6	7	7	7	8
Total in education and training[3]	84	89	78	81	61	60
Not in any education and training	16	11	22	19	39	40
Population (=100%) (thousands)	324.9	307.0	313.8	296.4	316.5	297.7

1 Including all schools and those in publicly funded institutions of further and higher education.
2 Includes part-time education not funded by employers or through GST; also full- or part-time education in independent institutions.
3 The total of all full-time education and GST (less GST in full-time education) plus EFT and Other education and training.
Source: Department for Education and Skills

Table 3.11

People working towards a qualification:[1] by age, 2002[2]

United Kingdom

Percentages

	Degree or higher or equivalent	Higher education[3]	GCE A level or equivalent	GCSE or equivalent	Other qualification[4]	All studying
16–19	14	15	70	67	11	32
20–24	41	19	8	7	11	19
25–29	13	13	5	3	14	10
30–39	19	27	9	12	28	19
40–49	9	19	6	7	22	13
50–59/64[5]	4	7	2	4	14	7
All aged 16–59/64[5]	100	100	100	100	100	100

1 For those working towards more than one qualification, the highest is recorded. See Appendix, Part 3: Qualifications.
2 At spring. These estimates are not seasonally adjusted and have not been adjusted to take account of the recent Census 2001 results. See Appendix, Part 4: LFS reweighting.
3 Below degree level but including NVQ level 4.
4 Includes those who did not state which qualifications.
5 Of working age population, defined as males aged 16–64 and females aged 16–59.
Source: Department for Education and Skills, from the Labour Force Survey

Table **3.12**

Students[1] in further and higher education: by type of course and sex

United Kingdom

Thousands

	Males				Females			
	1970/71	1980/81	1990/91	2001/02[2]	1970/71	1980/81	1990/91	2001/02[2]
Further education[3]								
Full-time	116	154	219	543	95	196	261	543
Part-time	891	697	768	1,528	630	624	986	2,376
All further education	1,007	851	987	2,071	725	820	1,247	2,918
Higher education[3]								
Undergraduate								
Full-time	241	277	345	519	173	196	319	620
Part-time	127	176	193	257	19	71	148	380
Postgraduate								
Full-time	33	41	50	86	10	21	34	86
Part-time	15	32	50	140	3	13	36	151
All higher education[4]	416	526	638	1,003	205	301	537	1,238

1 Home and overseas students.
2 Further education data for 2001/02 are not available so figures for 2000/01 have been shown.
3 See Appendix, Part 3: Stages of education – Further education and Higher education.
4 Figures for 2001/02 include a number of higher education students for which details are not available by level.
Source: Department for Education and Skills; National Assembly for Wales; Scottish Executive; Northern Ireland Department for Employment and Learning

Part-time study dominates the sector with 78 per cent of students studying part-time. The same number of males and females study full-time, but females are more likely than males to study part-time, 81 per cent and 74 per cent respectively among those undertaking further education.

There have also been substantial increases in the number of students in higher education in the United Kingdom. In 2001/02 there were 2.2 million students in higher education, 55 per cent of whom were female. The number of enrolments has increased for both sexes over the last 30 years. For women, there were six times as many enrolments in higher education in 2001/02 than in 1970/71. For men, enrolments increased by two and a half times over the same period.

In the United Kingdom, students from minority ethnic groups accounted for 13 per cent of all accepted home applicants to undergraduate higher education courses in 2001/02, whereas minority ethnic groups

Table **3.13**

Enrolments on adult education courses:[1] by subject, age and sex, November 2001

England

Percentages

	Males			Females			
	Under 19	19 to 59	60 and over	Under 19	19 to 59	60 and over	Total
All academic courses[1]	13	5	3	13	5	2	4
All vocational courses[1]	23	37	23	22	33	14	29
All other courses[1]	64	58	74	65	62	84	66
of which							
Practical crafts/skills	14	16	28	15	19	32	22
Physical education/sport/fitness	21	13	11	24	20	25	19
Languages	4	8	9	5	5	5	6
Office/business	3	5	8	2	4	5	4
Humanities	2	3	6	3	3	6	4
Independent living/ communication skills	1	2	2	1	1	1	1
Role education (excludes independent living)	1	1	1	1	1	1	1
Other	16	10	10	13	9	9	9
Total (=100%) (thousands)	12.9	174.7	76.1	23.2	546.9	192.0	1,025.8

1 See Appendix, Part 3: Adult education.
Source: Department for Education and Skills

accounted for only 8 per cent of the population (see Table 1.5 in Chapter 1: Population). Students of Indian origin continued to make up the largest proportion of non-White undergraduates – 4.8 per cent of all undergraduates in 2001/02, compared with 3.8 per cent in 1990/91. Students of Black African and Pakistani origins have increased the most since 1990/91 – by 1.3 and 1.1 percentage points respectively.

Many adults continue their education, either for enjoyment or to develop new skills. In November 2001 over 1 million adults in England were enrolled on adult education courses (Table 3.13). Enrolment rates are generally higher for women than for men. In 2001, three out of four people enrolled on adult education courses were women.

A third of all enrolments on adult education courses were on academic and vocational courses which lead to some form of qualification. Other courses are offered in a range of subjects, the most popular being practical crafts/skills and physical education/sport/fitness which together account for around two fifths of all enrolments. Of those enrolled on adult education courses the proportion enrolled on academic courses is highest among those aged under 19, whereas for 'All other courses' aged 60 and over the proportion is highest.

Post compulsory outcomes

The GCE A Level (or equivalent) is usually taken after GCSEs (or equivalent) and a further two years of study in a sixth form or equivalent (one year in Scotland). There has

Table **3.14**

Achievement at GCE A level[1] or equivalent: by sex

United Kingdom   Percentages

	Males		Females	
	2 or more A levels[2]	1 A level[3]	2 or more A levels[2]	1 A level[3]
1995/96	27	7	33	9
1996/97	27	7	33	8
1997/98	30	6	37	7
1998/99	30	6	37	7
1999/2000	31	6	39	7
2000/01[1]	33	4	42	5

1 2 AS levels count as 1 A level pass. Data for 2000/01 are not on the same basis as earlier years. See Appendix, Part 3: Qualifications.
2 Equivalent to 3 or more Highers.
3 Equivalent to 1 or 2 Highers. Includes those with 1.5 A levels.
Source: Department for Education and Skills; National Assembly for Wales; Scottish Executive; Northern Ireland Department of Education

Table **3.15**

NVQ awards:[1] by framework area and level, 2000/01

United Kingdom   Thousands

	Level 1	Level 2	Level 3	Level 4 & 5	Total
Providing business services	5.8	57.9	34.7	11.3	109.7
Providing goods and services	24.1	68.5	14.7	..	107.5
Providing health, social & protective services	..	28.0	23.3	2.0	53.8
Engineering	1.4	23.5	14.7	..	39.7
Constructing	8.3	21.0	7.7	..	37.2
Manufacturing	5.6	18.3	1.7	..	25.6
Tending plants, animals and land	2.6	6.0	1.4	..	10.0
Other	1.4	8.2	4.5	1.2	15.3
Total[2]	49.6	231.2	102.8	15.3	398.8

1 Missing figures were less than 1,000. See Appendix, Part 3: Qualifications.
2 A further 29,000 Scottish Vocational Qualifications were awarded in 2000/01.
Source: National Information System for Vocational Qualifications, from the Department for Education and Skills

been an increase in the proportion of pupils in the United Kingdom gaining two or more GCE A levels (or equivalent) from 30 per cent in 1995/96 to 37 per cent in 2000/01. The proportion of young women who achieve this has increased by around a quarter since 1995/96 to 42 per cent in 2000/01 (Table 3.14). For young men over the same period, the increase was around a fifth to reach 33 per cent in 2000/01. Results varied regionally within England from 30 per cent in the North East to 43 per cent in the South East.

An alternative to the more traditional and academic GCE A levels are National Vocational Qualifications (NVQs). These were introduced in 1987. By September 2001, over 3.5 million NVQs and Scottish Vocational Qualifications (SVQs) had been awarded in the United Kingdom. NVQs can be gained in a variety of areas. In 2000/01 nearly 400,000 NVQs and a further 29,000 SVQs were awarded in the United Kingdom (Table 3.15). Over a quarter of NVQs were in areas providing business services (such as management studies), a further quarter were in areas providing goods and services (such as catering and tourism). Over 15,000 NVQ awards were in other areas such as transporting, extracting and providing natural resources, and communicating. The level 2 qualification (equivalent to five GCSEs grades A* to C) was the most common level of award gained, accounting for 58 per cent of NVQs in 2000/01. Over 15,000 students (4 per cent) gained levels 4 and 5 which are equivalent to a first or higher degree. Among those gaining this level, 74 per cent studied business services.

In 2000/01, 470,300 qualifications were obtained by higher education students in the United Kingdom, and more than half of these were first degrees. Nine per cent of students gained a first class honours degree in 2000/01, and 44 per cent obtained an upper second class honours degree. Fifty eight per cent of female students gained a first class or an upper second class honours degree in 2000/01, compared with 50 per cent of male students.

In 2001, 67 per cent of first degree graduates whose first destinations were known went into employment compared with 53 per cent in 1991 (Table 3.16). In 1991 the number of unemployed in the population as a whole (see Figure 4.17 on page 82) had begun to increase from a low of just under 2 million in 1990. Around 20 per cent of first degree graduates continued their education and training in 2001, a proportion which has changed little since 1986. Six per cent were assumed to be unemployed in 2001, a decrease from 12 per cent in 1991. Of those first degree graduates whose first destination was known to be employment in 2001, 17 per cent of posts gained were classified as managers and administrators, 27 per cent as professional occupations, 22 per cent as associate professional and technical occupations and 17 per cent as clerical and secretarial occupations (see Appendix, Part 4: Standard Occupational Classification).

Table **3.16**

Destinations of first degree graduates

United Kingdom   Percentages

	1981[1]	1986	1991	1996	1999	2001[2]
UK/Overseas employment	52	63	53	65	67	67
Education and training	26	22	24	21	21	20
Not available for employment, study or training	2	..	..	5	5	6
Assumed to be unemployed	13	8	11	8	5	6
Others[3]	7	7	12	2	1	1
All known destinations[3] (=100%) (thousands)	80.9	97.2	118.1	179.2	188.2	183.0
Total (thousands)	92.4	112.4	135.9	225.4	235.7	224.2

1 For 1981 coverage is 'traditional' UK universities and former polytechnics in England and Wales.
2 From 2000 the coverage for first destinations excluded non-EU overseas domiciled students.
3 See Appendix, Part 3: Stages of education – Higher education.
Source: Department for Education and Skills; Higher Education Statistics Agency

Table **3.17**

Highest qualification:[1] by region, 2002[2]

Percentages

	Degree or equivalent	Higher education qualification[3]	GCE A level or equivalent	GCSE grades A*–C or equivalent	Other qualifications	No qualifications	All
United Kingdom	16	8	24	22	13	16	100
England	16	8	24	22	14	15	100
North East	10	8	27	23	13	18	100
North West	13	8	24	25	12	18	100
Yorkshire & the Humber	13	7	26	22	14	18	100
East Midlands	13	7	25	23	14	17	100
West Midlands	13	8	23	23	14	19	100
East	15	7	24	25	15	14	100
London	25	6	19	17	19	14	100
South East	19	9	24	23	13	11	100
South West	15	9	26	24	14	11	100
Wales	12	9	24	23	11	19	100
Scotland	16	12	30	17	9	16	100
Northern Ireland	14	8	25	22	7	24	100

1 Males aged 16–64, females aged 16–59. See Appendix, Part 3: Qualifications.
2 At spring. These estimates are not seasonally adjusted and have not been adjusted to take account of the recent Census 2001 results. See Appendix, Part 4: LFS reweighting.
3 Below degree level.
Source: Department for Education and Skills, from the Labour Force Survey

Figure **3.18**

Employees[1] receiving job-related training:[2] by sex and age, 2002[3]
United Kingdom

Percentages

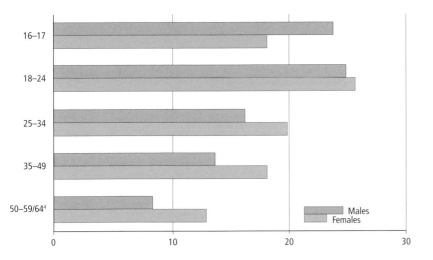

1 Employees are those in employment excluding the self-employed, unpaid family workers and those on government programmes.
2 Percentage who received job-related training in the four weeks before interview.
3 At spring 2002. These estimates are not seasonally adjusted and have not been adjusted to take account of the recent Census 2001 results. See Appendix, Part 4: LFS reweighting.
4 Males aged 50–64, females aged 50–59.
Source: Department for Education and Skills from the Labour Force Survey

Figure **3.19**

Types of off-the-job training provided,[1] 2001
England

Percentages

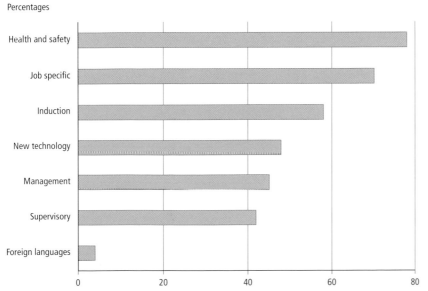

1 Based on all employers with 5 or more employees providing off-the-job training at the location in the last 12 months.
Source: Learning and Training at Work, IFF Research Limited for the Department for Education and Skills

Table 3.17 shows the highest qualifications held by the working age population in the United Kingdom in spring 2002. Sixteen per cent of the population of working age were educated to degree level, while the same proportion had no qualifications. The proportion with a degree ranged from a quarter in London to a tenth in the North East. Only London and the South East had figures above the UK average. Northern Ireland had the highest percentage of people with no qualifications, nearly a quarter, whereas the South East and South West had the lowest proportions at around a tenth. In spring 2002, those in the banking, finance and insurance industry, and in public administration, education and health were most likely to have some form of higher education qualification at 39 and 46 per cent, respectively. In contrast, those in agriculture and fishing were most likely to have no qualifications (24 per cent).

Adult training and learning

Learning throughout the working life is becoming increasingly necessary because of the pace of change within the labour market; training is seen by a large number of employers as an essential investment for the future. Many people receive training in the workplace. In spring 2002, 16 per cent of employees of working age in the United Kingdom had received some job-related training in the four weeks prior to interview in the LFS. Figure 3.18 shows those who received job-related training by age and sex. Young people aged 18 to 24 were the most likely to have received job-related training, with the incidence generally decreasing as the age of the employees increases.

Training within the workplace can take place on- and off-the-job. In England, the Learning and Training at Work 2001 survey asked those employers who had provided off-the-job training which types of training had been provided. Training in health and safety was the type of off-the-job training provided by most employers, by 78 per cent in 2001 (Figure 3.19). Job-specific training was also common, provided by 70 per cent of employers, while only 4 per cent of employers provided training in foreign languages. The proportion of employers providing each type of off-the-job training has declined since 2000. The most notable decline was in training in new technology which decreased by 12 percentage points, from 60 per cent in 2000 to 48 per cent in 2001. The figure was 57 per cent in 1999.

On-the-job training was carried out by 78 per cent of employers in England in 2001. A variety of training methods were used by employers. It was most commonly provided by a line manager or supervisor (75 per cent), by other experienced staff in the organisation (66 per cent), or by a training officer or specialist staff (36 per cent).

Training and learning can also take place outside the work environment. The National Adult Learning Survey explores participation in a wide range of learning activities and is used to evaluate the effectiveness of adult learning policies. Between 1997 and 2001 the proportion of non-learners (aged 16 to 69 and outside continuous full-time education) in England and Wales decreased from 26 to 24 per cent, in line with the 2002 national learning target for the adult population.

Inequalities in reported learning participation exist within the population. Participation in learning was lower among people with a disability than the average. In 2001 it was particularly low among those with a work limiting disability in comparison to people with no disability (Table 3.20). Differences between these groups were marked in relation to vocational learning against non-vocational learning. Of adults with a work limiting disability, only 43 per cent took part in vocational learning, compared with 73 per cent with no disability.

Other groups with low levels of learners include those with no qualifications and those outside the labour market. Since 1997 participation in learning (for those aged 16 to 69) increased among people looking after the family (from 47 to 52 per cent) and the retired (from 43 to 48 per cent), while it declined among the unemployed (from 72 to 68 per cent).

The most common reason for non-involvement in learning in 2001 for both sexes was that they prefer to spend time doing other things (Table 3.21). Men were more likely than women to give this reason, or to say that they did not have time due to work or found it hard to get time off work. Women were more likely to mention that it was hard to pay

Table 3.20

Learning reported:[1] by disability, 2001

England & Wales   Percentages

	Work limiting disability	Other long term disability	No disability	All
Taught	37	56	62	59
Self-directed	40	55	63	60
Vocational	43	58	73	68
Non-vocational	24	31	23	25
Any	56	71	80	76

1 All respondents aged 16–69.
Source: National Adult Learning Survey, National Centre for Social Research for the Department for Education and Skills

Table 3.21

Obstacles to learning:[1] by sex, 2001

England & Wales   Percentages

	Males	Females	All
Prefer to spend time doing other things	38	30	34
Lack of time due to work	34	24	29
Hard to pay course fees	22	29	26
Do not know about local learning opportunities	25	23	24
Lack of time due to family	16	27	22
Hard to get time off work to learn	23	14	19
Nervous about going back to classroom	12	22	17
Do not have qualifications to get on course	14	17	15
Worried about keeping up with course	10	19	15
Would only do learning if someone paid fees	15	13	14

1 Top ten obstacles. Percentages sum to more than 100 because respondents could mention more than one obstacle. All respondents aged 16–69.
Source: National Adult Learning Survey, National Centre for Social Research for the Department for Education and Skills

Table 3.22

Expenditure on education[1] as a percentage of GDP: EU comparison, 1999

Percentages

	Primary and secondary education	Higher education	All levels[2]
Denmark	4.8	2.4	8.1
Sweden	5.1	2.1	7.7
Austria	4.1	1.7	6.3
Finland	3.8	2.1	6.2
France	4.2	1.1	6.0
Portugal	4.2	1.0	5.7
Belgium	3.5	1.5	5.5
Netherlands	3.1	1.3	4.8
United Kingdom	3.3	1.1	4.7
Germany	3.0	1.1	4.7
Italy	3.2	0.8	4.5
Spain	3.3	0.9	4.5
Irish Republic	3.1	1.2	4.3
Greece	2.4	1.1	3.6
Luxembourg	..	..	..

1 Direct expenditure for institutions and public subsidies to students eg for tuition fees and living costs.
2 Includes expenditure for early childhood education and other miscellaneous expenditure.
Source: Education at a Glance 2002, Organisation for Economic Co-operation and Development

Figure 3.23

Full-time nursery & primary and secondary school teachers:[1] by sex
United Kingdom

Thousands

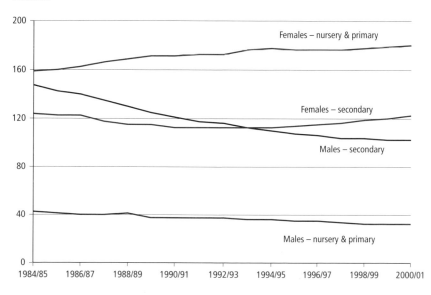

1 Qualified teachers only.
Source: Department for Education and Skills; Scottish Executive; Northern Ireland Department of Education

course fees, that they lacked time due to family commitments, that they were nervous about getting back in the classroom, or that they were worried about keeping up with the course. Around a quarter of both sexes said that they did not know about local learning opportunities.

Those who had done no learning in the last three years were asked what would encourage them to do some learning. The two most commonly mentioned incentives among those aged 16 to 69 were funding and advice on learning, given by 25 and 19 per cent of respondents, respectively. Nearly half (47 per cent) said that nothing would have encouraged them to do any learning. Those who were non-learners but said they would like to take part in some learning were further asked what subject they would have liked to study. The most common subject was keyboard and computing skills (30 per cent), followed by training for professions or trades (20 per cent) and leisure activities (19 per cent).

Educational resources

Spending on education varies across the EU. In 1999, in terms of expenditure on education as a percentage of GDP the United Kingdom was towards the middle of the ranking for EU countries (Table 3.22). Denmark spent the most on education at all level as a proportion of GDP at 8.1 per cent and Greece spent the least at 3.6 per cent. In the United Kingdom, along with Italy, the Netherlands and Sweden, public expenditure on education increased between 1995 and 1999, despite falling public budgets in real terms.

In 2000/01, total managed expenditure (TME) on education services in the United Kingdom was £44.1 billion, including £2.3 billion directly on under fives, £26.8 billion on schools, £5.7 billion on further education and £6.0 billion on higher education. This total represented 4.6 per cent of GDP (based on the National Accounts aggregate of TME).

Within nursery and primary, and secondary public sector mainstream schools in the United Kingdom the numbers of full-time qualified teachers decreased by 34,000 to 438,000 between 1984/85 and 2000/01. Figure 3.23 shows that the number of full-time female teachers in these schools increased by 7 per cent over the period to 303,000, while the number of male teachers declined by 29 per cent to 135,000. Overall, women represented the majority of full-time teachers – in nursery and primary schools 85 per cent of full-time teachers were female in 2000/01, while for secondary schools it is more balanced with females comprising 54 per cent of teachers. In addition, in the United Kingdom there were 22,800 full-time equivalent teachers in nursery and primary schools and 17,300 in secondary schools in 2000/01.

Evidence from the Office for Standards in Education shows that the presence of a teaching assistant in the classroom can improve the quality of teaching. An evaluation of the impact of teaching assistants in primary schools found that teachers value teaching assistants' support and appreciate the benefits of having another adult in the classroom. The number of non-teaching staff in England who provide additional learning support within the classroom has increased by 83 per cent since 1996 to over 167,000 in 2002 (Table 3.24). An increase in the number of non-teaching staff occurred in all types of school, with primary schools accounting for nearly three fifths of these staff in 2002.

Society is becoming increasingly dependent on technological knowledge and skills, as is the labour market. Students with little exposure to information and communications technology (ICT) in schools may face difficulties in making the transition to the modern labour market. Computers have been widespread as resources for learning in schools since the 1980s, and ICT has been part of the National Curriculum since 1990.

Results from the 1998 to 2002 ICT surveys of schools in England show that there has been a considerable increase in the percentage of schools connected to the Internet. In 2002 almost 100 per cent of all maintained schools in England were connected to the Internet, an increase from 28 per cent in 1998. There was an average of 8.8 pupils per computer (used mainly for teaching and learning) in 2002 compared with 13.8 in 1998.

Table 3.24

Non-teaching staff:[1] by type of school

England   Thousands

	1996	2000	2001	2002
Nursery	2.1	2.3	2.4	2.6
Primary[2]	50.6	68.7	83.1	96.9
Secondary[2]	23.1	31.8	37.3	45.1
Special[3]	15.2	18.1	19.2	21.8
Pupil referral units	0.3	0.7	0.7	0.9
Total non-teaching staff	91.4	121.5	142.7	167.3

1 Includes both full-time and the full-time equivalent of part-time non-teaching staff. Includes teaching assistants, technicians and other non-teaching staff.
2 Includes middle schools as deemed. See Appendix, Part 3: Stages of education.
3 Includes non-maintained special schools, special and general hospital schools.
Source: Department for Education and Skills

Table 3.25

Teachers' who feel confident in the use of ICT[1]

England   Percentages

	1998	1999	2000	2001	2002
Primary[2]	65	68	67	76	76
Secondary[2]	61	66	65	70	75
Special	63	68	73	77	74
All schools	63	67	66	73	76

1 Within the curriculum.
2 Includes middle schools as deemed. See Appendix, Part 3: Stages of education.
Source: Annual Survey of Information and Communications Technology in Schools, Department for Education and Skills

With the increased use of computers in schools, staff training and confidence in the use of ICT is important. The percentage of teachers who felt confident in the use of ICT in their subject increased from 63 per cent in 1998 to 76 per cent in 2002 (Table 3.25). Between 1998 and 2000 the percentage of teachers who felt confident in the use of ICT increased the greatest among secondary teachers. In 2002, 90 per cent of teachers had received some training in the use of ICT equipment and 87 per cent had updated their training in the past two years.

Financial support for students in higher education has changed considerably in recent years. Figure 3.26 shows that between 1980/81 and 1983/84 there was a fall of 8 per cent in the overall value in real terms (after allowing for inflation) of student grants. The value then remained at around £3,300 to 1989/90. In 1990/91, student loans were introduced and the value of the grant plus loan for higher education students was £3,715. The non income-assessed mortgage-style student loans were introduced to provide extra resources towards living expenses and to partially replace grants. The main grant rates were frozen at their 1990/91 value until 1994/95 when the shift from grant to loan was accelerated by reducing the level of grant rates and increasing loan rates. Broad parity between the main rates of grant and loans was achieved in the academic year 1996/97. In 1997/98, the overall value of grants and loans was 5 per cent higher than in 1980/81 (see also Appendix, Part 3: Student support).

New student support arrangements in higher education came into effect in August 1998. For the first year of the new scheme (1998/99), eligible new entrants received support through both grants (around a quarter of the support available) and loans (around three quarters of the support available). From 1999/2000 students received support mainly through loans which are partly income-assessed. Grants are no longer available except for some limited allowances to assist with special needs. The amount available through loans has increased to compensate for the reduction in grants. Repayment of these loans will be on an income-contingent basis. In 2001/02 the maximum amounts available for all those receiving student support through the full-year loan, and where applicable, the basic mandatory grants, were 2 per cent higher in real terms than the maximum rates for those students in 1991/92. From 1998/99, new entrants to higher education courses were, with certain specified exceptions, expected to contribute to the cost of their tuition (up to £1,075 per year in 2001/02) depending on family income.

Figure **3.26**

Student standard maintenance grant and loan[1] in real terms[2]

England & Wales[3]

£ thousand at 2001/02 prices

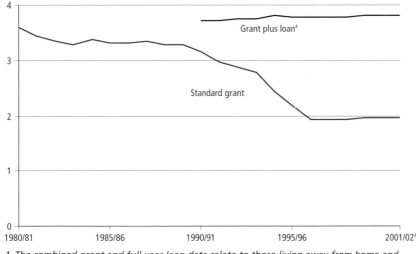

1 The combined grant and full year loan data relate to those living away from home and studying outside London.

2 Adjusted to 2001/02 prices using the September retail prices index (excluding mortgage interest payments).

3 The rate of maintenance grant is applicable to students normally domiciled in England and Wales. Student loans are available to students domiciled in the United Kingdom.

4 Grants where applicable. New student support scheme funding arrangements in higher education came into effect on 12 August 1998. See Appendix, Part 3: Student support.

Source: Department for Education and Skills; Office for National Statistics

Chapter 4

Labour market

Economic activity

- In the United Kingdom, male economic activity has decreased since 1984 while female economic activity has increased. The gap between economic activity rates for men and women has halved, from 22 percentage points in 1984 to 11 percentage points in spring 2002. (Figure 4.1)

- In 2002 the economic activity rate for female lone parents in the United Kingdom was 57 per cent, an increase of 9 percentage points since spring 1992. (Table 4.3)

- Just over half of people with long-term or work-limiting disability in the United Kingdom were economically active in spring 2002. (Table 4.4)

Employment

- In spring 2002 there were 27.7 million people in employment in the United Kingdom, the highest number since records began. (Table 4.10)

- In spring 2002, 3.1 million people in the United Kingdom were self-employed, the majority (74 per cent) were men. (Table 4.10)

Patterns of employment

- The largest increase in male and female jobs in the United Kingdom over the last 20 years has been in financial and business services, which accounted for about one in five of both male and female jobs in 2002. (Table 4.12)

- Around a fifth of Pakistani and Chinese people in employment in the United Kingdom were self-employed in 2001-02, compared with just over one in ten White people. (Figure 4.16)

Unemployment

- In 2001 unemployment in the United Kingdom reached 1.4 million, its lowest level since the ILO measure of unemployment was introduced in 1984. However, there was a small increase between spring 2001 and spring 2002 to 1.5 million. (Figure 4.17)

- Overall, Bangladeshi, Pakistani and people from the Other Black group had the highest unemployment rates in the United Kingdom in 2001-02, at 21 per cent, 16 per cent and 16 per cent respectively. (Figure 4.20)

Labour market dynamics

- In spring 2002 almost one in three employees in the United Kingdom had been in the same job for more than 10 years. (Figure 4.22)

Working lives

- Around 25 per cent of employed men and 11 per cent of employed women were working more than 50 hours a week in spring 2002. (Figure 4.27)

Most people spend a large part of their lives in the labour force, and so their experience of the world of work has an important impact on their lives and attitudes. The proportion of time spent in the labour force has been falling as young people are remaining longer in education and older people, due to the increase in longevity, are spending more years in retirement. More women than ever before are in paid employment, and employment in service industries continues to increase while employment in manufacturing continues to fall.

Economic activity

People are considered to be economically active, or in the labour force, if they are aged 16 and over and are either in work or actively looking for work.

In the United Kingdom, the economic activity rates by sex show a decrease in the proportion of economically active men and an increase in the proportion of economically active women over the long term (Figure 4.1). As the economically active include those who are unemployed (on the International Labour Organisation (ILO) definition – see Glossary on page 83), the rates are less affected than employment rates by economic cycle trends. Male economic activity rates show a generally downward trend, falling from 89 per cent in 1984 to 84 per cent in 2002. The female economic activity rate, on the other hand, has risen, from 67 per cent in 1984 to 73 per cent in 2002. The gap between economic activity rates for men and women has halved from 22 percentage points in 1984 to 11 percentage points in 2002.

Economic activity rates in the United Kingdom differ with age. In 2002, it was highest for 25-34 year old men at 93 per cent, while for women it was highest for 35-49 year olds at 78 per cent (Figure 4.2). People over the state retirement age (65 for men and 60 for women) can also be economically active, although the rates are low: 8 per cent of men over 65 and 9 per cent of women over 60. Over the past 30 years there has been a decline in the economic activity rate for men over 50 as more move into economic inactivity.

Young people's labour market activity is influenced by their participation in full-time education. For those aged 16-17 and 18-24 in

Figure **4.1**

Economic activity rates:[1,2] by sex

United Kingdom

Percentages

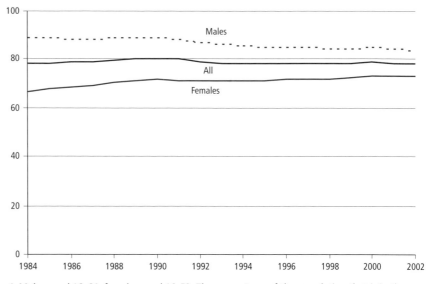

1 Males aged 16–64, females aged 16–59. The percentage of the population that is in the labour force.
2 Data are seasonally adjusted, at spring.
Source: Labour Force Survey, Office for National Statistics

Labour Force Survey (LFS) data

The results from the 2001 Census, published in September 2002, showed that previous estimates of the total United Kingdom population were around one million too high. As a result, ONS published interim revised estimates of the population for the years 1982 to 2001 which are consistent with the 2001 Census findings. Interim national LFS estimates consistent with the latest population data have now been produced.

Initial analysis work conducted by the ONS has shown that revisions to the LFS census-adjusted data have a greater impact on levels data than on rates. Generally, revisions to rates are within sampling variability, while those for levels are not. This chapter uses adjusted data where possible, however where adjusted data are not available only rates have been used. For more information, see Appendix, Part 4: Labour Force Survey (LFS) reweighting.

Figure 4.2

Economic activity rates: by sex and age, 2002[1]

United Kingdom

Percentages

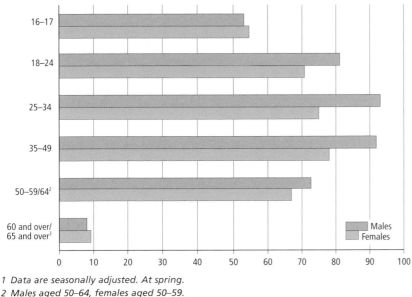

1 Data are seasonally adjusted. At spring.
2 Males aged 50–64, females aged 50–59.
3 Males aged 64 and over, females aged 60 and over.
Source: Labour Force Survey, Office for National Statistics

Table 4.3

Economic activity status of female lone parents:[1] by age of youngest dependent child, 1992 and 2002

United Kingdom

Percentages

	Age of youngest dependent child				
	Under 5	5–10	11–15	16–18[2]	All
1992					
Working full-time	8	18	35	39	18
Working part-time	13	26	26	24	20
Unemployed[3]	8	12	6	..	9
Economically active	29	55	67	72	48
Looking after family/home	65	35	19	..	43
Other inactive	6	10	14	17	9
2002					
Working full-time	12	23	33	45	23
Working part-time	22	32	31	29	28
Unemployed[3]	5	8	7	..	6
Economically active	39	62	70	80	57
Looking after family/home	52	25	15	..	31
Other inactive	9	13	15	16	12

1 Females aged 16–59. At spring each year. These estimates are not seasonally adjusted and have not been adjusted to take account of the recent Census 2001 results. See Appendix, Part 4: LFS reweighting.
2 Those in full-time education.
3 See Appendix, Part 4: Unemployment.
Source: Labour Force Survey, Office for National Statistics

full-time education, 45 per cent and 46 per cent respectively were economically active, compared with 78 per cent and 86 per cent of those not in full time education.

The presence of a dependent child in the family still has a major effect on the economic activity of women. Fifty six per cent of women whose youngest child was under 5 were economically active in spring 2002. This rose with the age of the youngest child so that for those whose youngest dependent child was aged 11 to 15 it reached 79 per cent, 3 percentage points higher than women with no dependent children. Among women with pre-school children, most were either economically inactive (44 per cent) or working part-time (36 per cent). Overall, 42 per cent of women of working age had dependent children.

The presence of dependent children has a dramatic effect on the economic activity rates of lone parents. Over the past decade, more lone mothers have become economically active, although the rate is still lower than for the female working age population as a whole (57 per cent, compared with 73 per cent). The gap is decreasing, as female lone parents' economic activity has risen by 9 percentage points since 1992 (Table 4.3). The increase has been largest for those with pre-school aged children, reflecting the general trend for women to return to the labour market sooner after the birth of their children. Economic activity also increases with the age of the youngest child from 39 per cent for those with a child under 5, to 80 per cent for those whose youngest dependent child is aged 16 to 18.

In spring 2002, 12 per cent of all lone parents were male. Their economic activity rate is higher than female lone parents, 77 per cent compared with 57 per cent, and is only 7 percentage points lower than the economic activity rate for all men of working age.

Disability also has an impact on an individual's participation in the labour market. In spring 2002 one in five people of working age in the United Kingdom had a long-term disability, of whom just over half were economically active. This compares with an economic activity rate for the whole working age population of 79 per cent. Disabled men are more likely than disabled women to be in employment (Table 4.4) though the gap between the employment rates is smaller (just over 3 percentage points) than for the population as a whole (11 percentage points). Disabled men are also more likely to be unemployed than disabled women, at 5 per cent compared with 3 per cent respectively.

The unemployment rate among disabled people was much higher than those for the non-disabled (9 per cent compared with 5 per cent). Unemployed disabled people were also more likely to have been unemployed for at least a year, and to be economically inactive than non-disabled people.

People can be economically inactive for a number of reasons: some do not want a job, while others want a job but are either not available for, or are not seeking, work. In spring 2002 there were nearly 8 million people of working age classified as economically inactive in the United Kingdom (Table 4.5). The number of economically inactive people and the reasons for their inactivity have changed little between 1997 and 2002. The majority did not want a job while just over a quarter wanted a job but were not seeking work. The most common reasons differed according to sex: for women, 'looking after the family/home' was the most common reason, whereas for men it was being 'long term sick or disabled'. Over the longer term, there has been an increase in the number of economically inactive men and a decrease in economically inactive women.

There are now more people in employment than at any other time in the post-war period, and most working age households in the United Kingdom are work-rich – that is, where at least one person is of working age and all people of working age are in employment. Work-rich households as a proportion of all working age households has risen from 50 per cent in spring 1992 to 58 per cent in spring 2002 (Table 4.6).

In spring 2002, around 16 per cent of working age households were workless, little changed over the past 10 years. However, among lone parent households with dependent children, the proportion who are workless is much higher, at 44 per cent in spring 2002, although this is 10 percentage points lower than in 1992.

Table 4.4

Economic activity status of disabled[1] people: by sex, 2002[2]

United Kingdom   Percentages

	Males	Females	All
In employment			
Working full time	43	24	34
Working part time	6	21	13
All in employment	49	46	48
Unemployed[3]			
Less than one year	3	3	3
One year or more	2	1	1
All unemployed	5	3	5
Unemployment rate[3]	10	7	9
Economically inactive	45	51	48

1 Males aged 16–64 and females aged 16–59 with current long term disability. See Appendix, Part 4: Disabled people.
2 At spring. These estimates are not seasonally adjusted and have not been adjusted to take account of the recent Census 2001 results. See Appendix, Part 4: LFS reweighting.
3 See Appendix, Part 4: Unemployment.
Source: Labour Force Survey, Office for National Statistics

Table 4.5

Reasons for economic inactivity:[1] by sex, 1997 and 2002

United Kingdom   Percentages

	1997			2002		
	Males	Females	All	Males	Females	All
Does not want a job	67	70	69	68	72	71
Wants a job but not seeking in last four weeks						
Looking after family/home	2	14	10	2	12	8
Long term sick or disabled	14	6	9	15	6	10
Student	5	3	3	4	3	3
Discouraged worker[2]	2	1	1	1	0	0
Other	6	5	5	6	4	5
All wanting a job but not seeking work	29	27	28	28	25	26
Wants a job and seeking work but not available to start[3]	3	2	3	3	2	2
All reasons (=100%) (millions)	2.8	4.8	7.6	3.0	4.7	7.7

1 At spring each year, seasonally adjusted. Males aged 16–64, females aged 16–59.
2 People who believed no jobs were available.
3 Not available for work in the next two weeks. Includes those who did not state whether or not they were available.
Source: Labour Force Survey, Office for National Statistics

Table **4.6**

Working age households:[1,2] by household economic status

United Kingdom   Percentages

	1992	1997	2000	2001	2002
Households with all in employment[3]	50	55	57	58	58
Workless households	17	18	16	16	16
Working-age people living in workless households	13	13	12	12	12
Children in workless households	19	18	16	15	16
Workless lone parent households with dependent children[4]	54	50	45	44	44

1 Percentages have been adjusted to include estimates for households with unknown economic activity. Percentages based on all working age households, at spring each year.
2 These estimates are not seasonally adjusted and have not been adjusted to take account of the recent Census 2001 results. See Appendix, Part 4: LFS reweighting.
3 As a percentage of working age households.
4 Percentage of all lone parent households.
Source: Labour Force Survey, Office for National Statistics

Figure **4.7**

Employment rates:[1] by sex

United Kingdom

Percentages

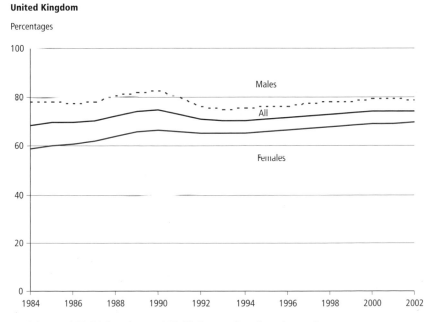

1 Males aged 16–64, females aged 16–59. Seasonally adjusted, at spring.
Source: Labour Force Survey, Office for National Statistics

The proportion of working age people living in households with no one in employment has changed little in the past ten years. The proportion of children in workless households has been falling since the mid-1990s and remained stable between 2000 and 2002. The changes in all these proportions can be attributed partly to changes in economic activity and partly to changes in household size and structure over time.

Employment

The proportion of the working age population in employment has varied between 70 and 75 per cent for most of the period from 1959 (when current records began) to 2002. Although there have been business cycle effects in evidence, over the period as a whole there is no sign of a long-run change in employment rates.

However, trends in the overall rate mask large differences for men and women. Since the mid-1960s, the trend in employment rates for men has been gradually downwards. Each time a dip in the economic cycle has resulted in a faster fall, the following recovery has not been sufficient to restore rates to their pre-recession levels. There is some evidence that the downward trend has now stabilised with a gradual rise between 1993 and 2002 which appears not simply to be an economic cycle effect (Figure 4.7).

For women the picture is very different, as the long term employment rates among women have been rising. As with men, the proportion of women in employment has followed the economic cycle, but for them such effects have generally been less marked. For example between 1990 and 1993 the female employment rate fell less sharply than the male rate and recovered more quickly thereafter. However, since 1993 it has risen at virtually the same rate as the male employment rate. As with economic activity rates (see Figure 4.1) the difference in the employment rates of males and females is narrowing, from 19 percentage points in 1984 to 9 percentage points in 2002.

In March 2000, the Lisbon European Council agreed an aim to achieve an overall European Union (EU) employment rate as close as possible to 70 per cent by 2010 and, for women, an employment rate of more than 60 per cent. In 2001, the overall employment rate in the EU was 64 per cent and the United Kingdom was one of only four out of the fifteen member states with employment rates above the 2010 overall target. In 2001, the United Kingdom had one of the highest employment rates across the EU, after Denmark, Sweden and the Netherlands (Table 4.8). The range in employment rates across the EU differed greatly between men and women. For men, the Netherlands had the highest employment rate – 15 percentage points higher than Italy, the country with the lowest rate. The range of employment rates for women was more than double that of men, from 73 per cent in Sweden to 41 per cent in Greece and Italy.

Within the United Kingdom, employment rates vary across the country (Map 4.9). Many inner city areas and former industrial areas had the lowest rates in spring 2002 – for example, 59 per cent in Inverclyde and 60 per cent in Glasgow City, Hartlepool and Neath Port Talbot. Conversely, some of the highest employment rates were in Scotland and Central and Southern England. The highest rates of all were in Bracknell Forest and Milton Keynes (both over 86 per cent), with Midlothian being the highest in Scotland (also 86 per cent). Within Wales, the Vale of Glamorgan had the highest employment rate (80 per cent).

In spring 2002, there were 27.7 million people in employment in the United Kingdom (Table 4.10). This is the highest number of people in employment since the series began in 1959 – although the highest employment rate was recorded in 1974, it only represented 24.4 million people. Comparing the labour market in spring 2002 with that in spring 1987, the number of people in employment has risen by nearly 3 million, as more people are working and fewer people are unemployed. Twenty five per cent of employees were working part-time in spring 2002, and 82 per cent of part-time workers were women. The number of part-time workers has increased by almost a third since 1987.

Employment rates vary between people of different ethnic groups in the United Kingdom, for a variety of cultural reasons, as well as because of differing age structures. Having qualifications, and the level of those qualifications, has an important influence on

78

Table **4.8**

Working age population:[1] by employment status and sex, EU comparison, 2001

Percentages

	In employment		Unemployed		Economically active	
	Males	Females	Males	Females	Males	Females
Netherlands	83	65	2	3	84	67
Denmark	80	71	4	5	83	75
United Kingdom	78	65	5	4	83	68
Portugal	77	61	3	5	79	65
Sweden	76	73	5	4	80	76
Irish Republic	76	54	4	4	79	56
Austria	76	60	4	4	79	62
Luxembourg	75	51	2	2	76	52
Germany	73	59	8	8	79	64
Spain	72	43	7	15	78	50
Finland	72	67	10	11	80	75
Greece	71	41	7	16	76	49
France	70	56	7	11	75	62
Belgium	69	51	6	7	73	55
Italy	68	41	8	13	74	47
EU average	73	55	7	9	78	60

1 People aged 15–64, except for the United Kingdom where data refer to those aged 16–64.

Source: Labour Force Surveys, Eurostat

Map **4.9**

Employment rates:[1] by area,[2] 2002[3]

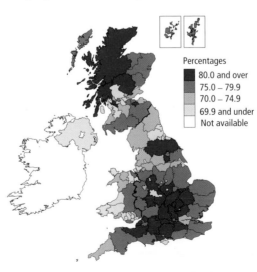

Percentages
- 80.0 and over
- 75.0 – 79.9
- 70.0 – 74.9
- 69.9 and under
- Not available

1 Total employed as a percentage of all people of working age.
2 Counties and unitary authorities, except for Northern Ireland.
3 At spring. These estimates are not seasonally adjusted and have not been adjusted to take account of the recent Census 2001 results. See Appendix, Part 4: LFS reweighting.
Source: Labour Force Survey, Office for National Statistics

Table **4.10**

Economic activity: by employment status and sex, 1987 and 2002[1]

United Kingdom
Millions

	1987			2002		
	Males	Females	All	Males	Females	All
Economically active						
In employment						
Full-time employees	11.1	5.5	16.7	11.4	6.7	18.1
Part-time employees	0.5	4.2	4.7	1.1	5.1	6.2
Self-employed	2.3	0.7	3.0	2.3	0.8	3.1
Others in employment[2]	0.3	0.2	0.5	0.1	0.1	0.2
All in employment	14.3	10.7	24.9	14.9	12.8	27.7
Unemployed[3]	1.8	1.2	3.0	0.9	0.6	1.5
All economically active	16.1	11.9	28.0	15.8	13.4	29.2

1 At spring each year. Seasonally adjusted.
2 Those on government employment and training schemes and unpaid family workers.
3 See Appendix, Part 4: Unemployment.
Source: Labour Force Survey, Office for National Statistics

employment rates. Table 4.11 explores the degree to which the presence of qualifications accounts for differences in employment rates between the various ethnic groups.

In each ethnic group, and for both men and women, employment rates are higher among those with higher qualifications. In 2001-02 employment rates among men from minority ethnic groups with higher qualifications ranged from 91 per cent for Indians to 76 per cent for Bangladeshis, compared with 90 per cent for White men. For Black African men and men from the Mixed group, the difference in employment rates between those with higher and those with no qualifications is particularly marked, with differences of 48 percentage points and 46 percentage points, compared with 31 percentage points overall. Among employment rates for men from minority ethnic groups overall, Indians have the highest employment rate (73 per cent) and Bangladeshis have the lowest (55 per cent), compared with 80 per cent for White men.

Table **4.11**

Employment rates:[1] by ethnic group, sex, and highest qualification, 2001–02[2]

United Kingdom
Percentages

	Males				Females			
	Higher qualification	Other qualification	No qualifications	All aged 16–64	Higher qualification	Other qualification	No qualifications	All aged 16–59
White	90	82	58	80	85	72	48	71
Mixed	89	66	43	68	66	56	33	55
Asian or Asian British								
Indian	91	67	60	73	80	56	36	58
Pakistani	82	60	53	61	64	29	7	24
Bangladeshi	76	53	51	55	..	27	..	17
Other Asian	83	64	46	67	80	46	..	52
Black or Black British								
Black Caribbean	85	68	50	67	84	63	45	65
Black African	79	56	31	61	75	48	15	49
Other Black	..	63	..	58	..	55	..	57
Chinese	84	57	68	66	74	47	38	54
Other	78	60	41	62	65	45	28	48
All ethnic groups	89	81	58	79	84	70	45	69

1 The percentage of the working age population in employment.
2 See Appendix, Part 4: Annual Local Area Labour Force Survey.
Source: Annual Local Area Labour Force Survey, Office for National Statistics

For women from minority ethnic groups with higher qualifications, Black Caribbeans had the highest employment rate, at 84 per cent, followed by Indian women and those from the Other Asian group, both at 80 per cent, compared with 85 percentage points for White women. Overall the lowest employment rates for women of working age are among the Pakistani and Bangladeshi communities, at 24 per cent and 17 per cent respectively. These low employment rates are reflected in the high economic inactivity rate among these women. Among Pakistani and Black African women in particular, the presence of qualifications makes a great difference to whether or not they are in employment than it does for other women. Seventy five per cent of Black African women and 64 per cent of Pakistani women with a higher qualification were in employment, compared with 15 per cent and 7 per cent of those with no qualification.

Patterns of employment

The United Kingdom economy experienced structural change in the post-war period, with a decline in the manufacturing sector and an increase in service industries. In 1982, almost one in three male employee jobs were in manufacturing but this fell to just over one in five in 2002 (Table 4.12). The proportion of female employee jobs in the manufacturing sector also fell, from under one in five to less than one in ten. The largest increase in both male and female jobs over the period has been in financial and business services, which accounted for about one in five of both male and female jobs in spring 2002. The total number of jobs done by men is now virtually the same as the number done by women – 13.0 million compared with 12.7 million – whereas in 1982 there were 2.7 million more male than female employee jobs. Note that this table is based on jobs rather than people – one person may have more than one job, and jobs may vary in the number of hours' work they involve.

The pattern of occupations followed by men and women are quite different (Table 4.13). About a quarter of women employees are in administrative and secretarial work, while men are most likely to be employed as managers and senior officials or in skilled trades. These occupations are among the least likely to be followed by women. Conversely women are

Table 4.12

Employee jobs[1] by sex and industry

United Kingdom   Percentages

	Males			Females		
	1982	1992	2002	1982	1992	2002
Manufacturing	30	24	21	17	11	8
Distribution, hotels, catering and repairs	17	20	22	26	26	26
Financial and business services	12	16	20	13	17	19
Transport and communication	10	10	9	2	2	3
Construction	8	8	8	2	2	1
Agriculture	2	2	1	1	1	1
Energy and water supply	4	2	1	1	1	0
Other services	16	18	19	39	41	41
All employee jobs (=100%) (millions)	12.7	11.6	13.0	10.0	11.6	12.7

1 Data are at June each year.
Source: Short-term Turnover and Employment Survey, Office for National Statistics

Table 4.13

Employees: by sex, and occupation, 2002[1]

United Kingdom   Percentages

	Males	Females
Managers and senior officials	18	9
Professional occupations	13	10
Associate professional and technical	14	14
Administrative and secretarial	6	24
Skilled trades	16	2
Personal service	2	13
Sales and customer service	5	13
Process, plant and machine operatives	13	3
Elementary occupations	13	13

1 At spring. These estimates are not seasonally adjusted and have not been adjusted to take account of the recent Census 2001 results. See Appendix, Part 4: LFS reweighting.
Source: Labour Force Survey, Office for National Statistics

Table **4.14**

Employees and self-employed who have second jobs: by industry[1] of main job, 2002[2]

United Kingdom   Percentages

	Same industry group as main job	Different industry group from main job	All in second jobs
Public administration, education and health	3.9	3.0	6.9
Agriculture, forestry and fishing	..	3.5	4.5
Banking, finance and insurance	1.2	2.4	3.6
Distribution, hotels and restaurants	1.2	2.3	3.5
Transport and communication	..	2.1	2.4
Manufacturing	0.3	2.1	2.4
Construction	..	1.7	2.0
Other services	1.6	4.0	5.6

1 Energy and water industry sample too small for reliable estimates.
2 At spring. These estimates are not seasonally adjusted and have not been adjusted to take account of the recent Census 2001 results. See Appendix, Part 4: LFS reweighting.
Source: Labour Force Survey, Office for National Statistics

Figure **4.15**

Self-employed:[1] by sex, EU comparison, 2001

Percentages

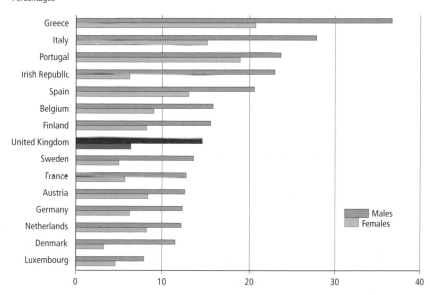

1 As a percentage of the working age population. People aged 15–64, except for the United Kingdom where data refer to those aged 16–64.
Source: Labour Force Surveys, Eurostat

more likely than men to be employed in the personal services and in sales and customer services. Only the associate professional and technical and the elementary (mainly routine) occupations are equally likely to be followed by both men and women: about one in eight were employed in each of these occupations.

According to Labour Force Survey (LFS) estimates, around 4 per cent of those in employment in the United Kingdom had a second job in spring 2002. People in the public administration, education and health group were the most likely to have a second job (Table 4.14). They were also the most likely to have a second job in the same industry as their main one, although overall most of those who have a second job are employed in a different industry to their main one. People working in the construction industry as their main job are the least likely to have a second job (2 per cent). A higher proportion of women have second jobs: 5 per cent of employed women have a second job, compared with 3 per cent of men. Just over a quarter of people in second jobs are self-employed in their main job.

Of course, not all people in employment work as employees. About 3 million people in spring 2002 were self-employed and the majority of these (74 per cent) were men (see Table 4.10). Since the mid-1980s the percentage of people in employment who were self-employed has remained stable and was 11 per cent in spring 2002. Eurostat estimates that 11 per cent of people in employment in the United Kingdom in 2001 were self employed (15 per cent for men and 6 per cent for women), below the EU average of 14 per cent. In all EU countries the proportion of self-employed men is higher than women (Figure 4.15). The range of self-employment rates across the EU is broad, from 37 per cent for men in Greece to 3 per cent for women in Denmark.

Evidence from the LFS in spring 2000 indicated that the main reason people in the United Kingdom became self-employed was that they wanted to be independent (31 per cent of respondents). It was the most important reason for both men and women. Over one fifth said they were self-employed because of the nature of their occupation.

Figure 4.16 shows that people from certain ethnic groups are more likely to be self-employed than others. Around a fifth of Pakistani and Chinese people in employment were self-employed in 2001-02, compared with around a tenth of White people and even fewer Black African and Black Caribbean people.

People also vary considerably in the type of self-employed work they undertake. Overall, around a fifth of self-employed people work in the construction industry, and similar proportions work in distribution, hotels and restaurants and in banking, finance and insurance.

Unemployment

The number of unemployed people is linked to the economic cycle, albeit with a time lag. Broadly speaking, as the country experiences economic growth so the number of jobs grow and unemployment falls, though any mismatches between the skill needs of the new jobs and the skills of those available for work may slow this process. Conversely as the economy slows and goes into recession so unemployment tends to rise. The latest peak occurred in 1993, when it reached just under 3 million (Figure 4.17). This recession had a much greater effect on unemployment among men than among women. In 2001 the number of people unemployed fell to its lowest level since the introduction of the ILO measure of unemployment in 1984. Since spring 2001, however, unemployment has increased slightly to 1.5 million people.

The measure of unemployment shown in Figure 4.17 is based on LFS estimates of the number of people without a job who are seeking work. It is based on internationally agreed definitions and is the official measure of unemployment. An alternative indicator of unemployment is the claimant count. This is a count of the number of people claiming unemployment-related benefits. While there is significant overlap between ILO unemployment and the claimant count, not all people who claim unemployment-related benefits are ILO unemployed and not all people who are ILO unemployed claim unemployment-related benefits. For example, ILO unemployment includes women who are often not entitled to claim benefits because

Figure **4.16**

Self-employment:[1,2] by ethnic group, 2001–02
United Kingdom

Percentages

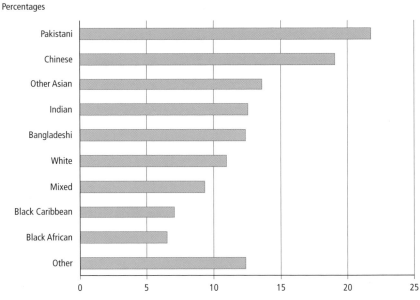

1 Percentage of all in employment who were self-empoyed.
2 See Appendix, Part 4: Annual Local Area Labour Force Survey.
Source: Annual Local Area Labour Force Survey, Office for National Statistics

Figure 4.17

Unemployment:[1] by sex
United Kingdom

Millions

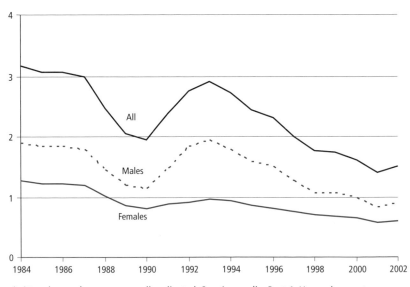

1 At spring each year, seasonally adjusted. See Appendix, Part 4: Unemployment.
Source: Labour Force Survey, Office for National Statistics

Glossary of terms

Employees (Labour Force Survey measure) – a measure, obtained from household surveys, of people aged 16 and over who regard themselves as paid employees. People with two or more jobs are counted only once.

Self-employed – a measure, obtained from household surveys, of people aged 16 and over who regard themselves as self-employed, i.e. who in their main employment work on their own account, whether or not they have employees.

In employment – a measure, obtained from household surveys and censuses, of employees, self-employed people, participants in government employment and training programmes, and people doing unpaid family work.

Government employment and training programmes – a measure, obtained from household surveys, of those who said they were participants on Youth Training, Training for Work, Employment Action or Community Industry or a programme organised by the Learning and Skills Council (LSC) in England and the National Council for Education and Training for Wales (ELWa), together with LECs in Scotland.

Unemployment – an International Labour Organisation (ILO) recommended measure, used in household surveys such as the Labour Force Survey, which counts as unemployed those aged 16 and over who are without a job, are available to start work in the next two weeks, who have been seeking a job in the last four weeks or are waiting to start a job already obtained.

Economically active (labour force) – those **in employment** plus those **unemployed**.

Unemployment rate – the percentage of the **economically active** who are **unemployed**.

Economically inactive – people who are neither in employment nor unemployed. For example, all people under 16, those looking after a home or retired, or those permanently unable to work.

Economic activity rate – the percentage of the population in a given age group which is economically active.

Working age household – a household that includes at least one person of working age.

Workless household – a household that includes at least one person of working age where no-one is in employment.

Figure **4.18**

Unemployment rates:[1] by region, 2002[2]

Percentages

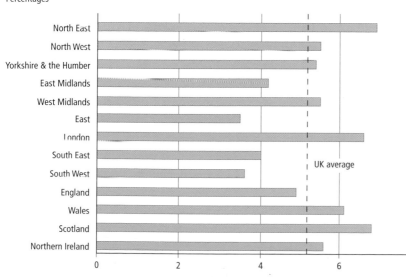

1 See Appendix, Part 4: Unemployment.
2 At spring. The estimates are not seasonally adjusted and have not been adjusted to take account of the recent Census 2001 results. See Appendix, Part 4: LFS reweighting.
Source: Labour Force Survey, Office for National Statistics

their partner is also a claimant. Similarly some people claim Job Seekers' Allowance but carry out a small amount of part-time work and so would not be counted as ILO unemployed. A key strength of the claimant count is that it can provide small area estimates at a lower level of geographic disaggregation than is possible from the LFS, and it is also more timely.

The ILO and claimant count measures both tend to move in the same direction. In times of economic downturn, the claimant count tends to rise faster than the ILO measure so that at the trough of the last recession, in 1993, the two measures were very close together. However, in times of economic upturn the claimant count tends to fall faster than the ILO measure. This is because economically inactive people become more optimistic about their employment prospects, start looking for work and hence become (ILO) unemployed.

Unemployment is not equally distributed across the UK labour force (Figure 4.18). Age, qualifications, sex, ethnicity and location all have an impact on whether or not people

Table **4.19**

Unemployment rates:[1] by sex and age

United Kingdom   Percentages

	1993	1994	1995	1996	1997	1998	1999	2000	2001	2002
Males										
16–17	20.5	20.7	20.9	22.7	21.0	19.9	23.4	22.3	20.3	22.0
18–24	21.3	19.4	18.0	17.4	15.2	13.5	13.1	12.3	11.4	12.2
25–49	10.5	9.7	8.6	8.2	6.8	5.5	5.4	4.7	4.2	4.5
50 and over	11.3	10.4	8.6	8.0	6.6	5.5	5.3	5.0	3.7	3.9
All aged 16 and over	12.5	11.5	10.2	9.7	8.2	6.9	6.8	6.2	5.4	5.8
Females										
16–17	17.7	19.1	17.7	17.3	17.9	17.4	16.8	19.5	15.8	18.3
18–24	13.6	12.6	12.4	11.1	10.6	10.3	10.2	9.5	8.8	8.4
25–49	6.8	6.6	6.2	5.8	5.0	4.7	4.5	4.1	3.8	3.8
50 and over	5.3	5.1	4.1	3.8	3.8	3.1	3.0	2.9	2.0	2.7
All aged 16 and over	7.9	7.6	7.0	6.5	5.9	5.5	5.3	5.0	4.4	4.6

1 At spring each year. Seasonally adjusted. See Appendix, Part 4: Unemployment.
Source: Labour Force Survey, Office for National Statistics

become unemployed and on the length of time people spend out of work. In spring 2002 the North East had the highest unemployment rate of the English regions at 6.9 per cent, while the lowest rates were 3.5 per cent in the East and 3.6 per cent in the South West. Among the constituent countries of the United Kingdom, Scotland had the highest rate at 6.8 per cent, followed by Wales (6.1 per cent), Northern Ireland (5.6 per cent) and England (4.9 per cent).

A higher proportion of men than women are unemployed and a higher proportion of young people than older people are unemployed. Unemployment rates peaked in 1993 and since then have declined across almost all age groups. The largest decline was for those aged 18 to 24, with a fall of 9.1 percentage points for men and 5.2 percentage points for women (Table 4.19). For those aged 16 to 17, unemployment rates have fluctuated over the past decade between around 20 and 23 per cent for young men and around 16 to 20 per cent for young women. The lowest unemployment rates in spring 2002 were among men and women over 50, at 3.9 per cent of men and 2.7 per cent of women.

Figure **4.20**

Unemployment rates:[1] by ethnic group and age,[2] 2001–02
United Kingdom

Percentages

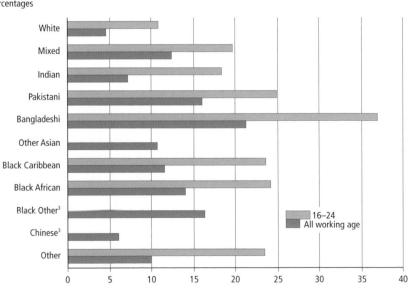

1 See Appendix, Part 4: Unemployment and Annual Local Area Labour Force Survey.
2 Males up to the age of 64, females up to the age of 59.
3 16–24 year olds, sample size too small for reliable estimates.
Source: Annual Local Area Labour Force Survey, Office for National Statistics

Figure **4.21**

Unemployment rates:[1,2] by previous occupation,[3] 2002

United Kingdom

Percentages

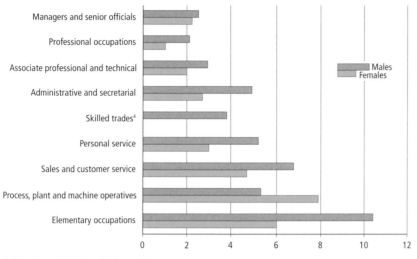

1 See Appendix, Part 4: Unemployment.

2 These estimates are not seasonally adjusted and have not been adjusted to take account of the recent Census 2001 results. See Appendix, Part 4: LFS reweighting.

3 Bases for rates are calculated by adding those currently employed in each occupational group to those who are now unemployed but whose last job was in that occupational group.

4 Sample size for females too small for reliable estimate.

Source: Labour Force Survey, Office for National Statistics

Figure **4.22**

Length of service of employees, 2002[1,2]

United Kingdom

Percentages

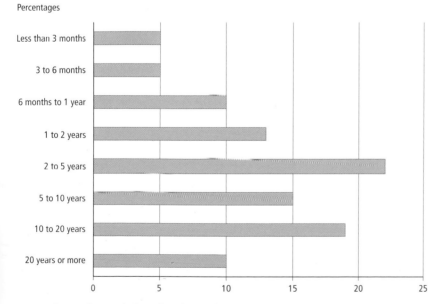

1 At spring; males aged 16–64, females aged 16–59.

2 These estimates are not seasonally adjusted and have not been adjusted to take account of the recent Census 2001 results. See Appendix, Part 4: LFS reweighting.

Source: Labour Force Survey, Office for National Statistics

People from minority ethnic groups had higher unemployment rates than those in the White group in 2001-02 (Figure 4.20) and young people (aged 16 to 24) had higher unemployment rates than the working age population across all ethnic groups. Overall the Bangladeshi, group had the highest unemployment rate, at 21 per cent. Unemployment among young people aged 16-24 ranged from 37 per cent among young Bangladeshi people to 11 per cent of young White people.

Levels of educational attainment and occupation can affect unemployment rates. The rate among those with no qualifications in spring 2002 was 11 per cent, four times that of those with higher qualifications and twice the United Kingdom average. Unemployment rates also vary according to an individual's previous occupation. Those occupations associated with higher levels of qualifications, such as the professionals and managerial and senior officials, experienced the lowest levels of unemployment for both men and women (Figure 4.21). In spring 2002 the highest unemployment rate was for men previously in elementary occupations (those that involve mainly routine tasks and do not require formal qualifications) at 10 per cent. For women, those previously working as process, plant and machine operatives had the highest unemployment rates, at nearly 8 per cent.

Labour market dynamics

Figure 4.22 gives some indication of how long people stay in a job. In spring 2002, one in ten employees of working age had been in their current job for less than six months, and a similar proportion had been in the same job for over 20 years. Most people – four out of five – had been in the same job for a year or more.

Research using the LFS by Gregg and Wadsworth indicates that in the late 1990s, when someone started a new job it lasted typically about 15 months, but that the average job in progress lasted around 5.5 years. This is because most employees eventually find a long-term job match. Average job tenure has remained relatively stable since 1975. However, this masks sharp contrasts between the sexes. Job tenure has risen among women with children, partly as a result of the increased provision and use of maternity leave. However, it has fallen for men and for women without dependent children. The largest fall in job tenure has been among men aged 50 and over.

One major determinant of workers' mobility is whether or not they achieve promotion. The British Household Panel Survey provides longitudinal information about how the labour market position of a fixed sample of individuals changes from year to year. Evidence from the first five waves of this survey, covering the period 1991-95, shows that promotion plays a substantial role in workers' mobility, accounting for about 36 per cent of position changes each year. The promotion rates of younger workers are higher than those of older workers, but the gender differences are small. This research finds that men and women who are married, have a full-time job, are employed in large establishments and in high-level occupations are more likely to achieve promotion.

Most people who want to move jobs are dissatisfied with aspects of their current job (Table 4.23). In spring 2002, about 6 per cent of both male and female full-time employees in the United Kingdom were looking for a new job. For a third of men and almost a quarter of women, unsatisfactory pay in their current job was a trigger for looking for another one. Similar proportions of men and women without dependent children were looking for a new job because they were filling in time before finding another, they wanted shorter hours or the journey was unsatisfactory. A slightly higher proportion of women without dependent children were looking for a new job than those with dependent children. One in ten men working part-time was looking for a new job with three in ten filling in time before finding another job.

People have different ways of finding work. Figure 4.24 shows that men are most likely to have obtained their current job by hearing from someone who worked at their current workplace (31 per cent), whereas women are most likely to have obtained their job by replying to an advertisement (32 per cent). An individual's method of job search also differs according to their occupation. Replying to an advertisement is the most common method for most occupations, but people employed in

Table **4.23**

Reasons[1] full-time employees were looking for a new job: by sex and presence of dependent children, 2002[2]

United Kingdom
Percentages

	Males	Females With dependent children	Females Without dependent children	All
Pay unsatisfactory in present job	32	28	21	23
Present job may come to an end	16	14	16	16
In present job to fill time before finding another	8	..	10	9
Wants shorter hours than in present job	8	..	6	7
Journey unsatisfactory in present job	7	..	7	7
Other aspects of present job unsatisfactory	37	45	41	41
Percentage of full-time employees looking for a new job	6.1	5.1	6.3	5.9

1 More than one reason could be given.
2 At spring. These estimates are not seasonally adjusted and have not been adjusted to take account of the recent Census 2001 results. See Appendix, Part 4: LFS reweighting.
Source: Labour Force Survey, Office for National Statistics

Figure **4.24**

Ways in which current job was obtained, 2002[1]
United Kingdom
Percentages

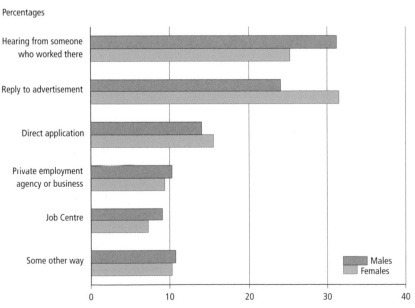

1 At spring. These estimates are not seasonally adjusted and have not been adjusted to take account of the recent Census 2001 results. See Appendix, Part 4: LFS reweighting.
Source: Labour Force Survey, Office for National Statistics

Table **4.25**

People entering employment through the New Deal: by age and type of employment, January 1998 to September 2002

Great Britain

Percentages

	18–24	25 and over	All aged 18 and over
Sustained employment			
Unsubsidised	73	64	71
Subsidised	6	16	8
All sustained employment	79	80	79
Other employment			
Unsubsidised	20	15	20
Subsidised	1	2	2
All other employment	21	20	21
All entering employment			
(=100%) (thousands)	398	126	525
Those entering sustained employment as a percentage of all leavers	40	21	33

Source: Department for Work and Pensions

Figure **4.26**

Distribution of usual weekly hours[1] of work: by sex, 2002[2]

United Kingdom

Thousands

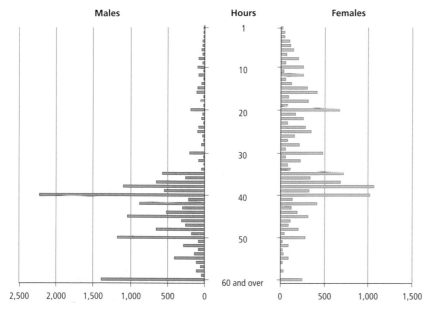

1 *Figures based on valid hours.*
2 *At spring. These estimates are not seasonally adjusted and have not been adjusted to take account of the recent Census 2001 results. See Appendix, Part 4: LFS reweighting.*
Source: Labour Force Survey, Office for National Statistics

skilled trades, process plant and machine operatives and elementary occupations are most likely to use their contacts (hearing from someone who worked there).

Participation in the Government's New Deal scheme is mandatory for 18-24 year olds who have claimed Jobseeker's Allowance continuously for six months. Initially there is a Gateway period which includes intensive careers advice and guidance and help with jobsearch skills. The aim is to find unsubsidised jobs for as many as possible. Those who do not find a job then move onto one of a number of options: subsidised employment; work experience with a voluntary organisation or on an environmental task force, both with training; or full-time education. For those reaching the end of their option without keeping or finding work, there is a follow-through period of support and further training if needed. The New Deal scheme also covers other groups, including, people with disabilities, the long term unemployed, those over 50 and lone parents.

Of those young people in Great Britain leaving the New Deal during the period January 1998 to September 2002, 40 per cent went into sustained employment (lasting 13 weeks or more) (Table 4.25). Among those aged 25 and over, a lower proportion moved into sustained employment (21 per cent).

Working lives

Table 4.10 showed that there were 6.2 million people working part-time in the United Kingdom in spring 2002, of whom 5.1 million were women. However, to distinguish only between 'full-time' and 'part-time' masks a wide variety of patterns of working hours which people experience. Figure 4.26 shows the distribution of usual weekly hours of work, including regular paid and unpaid overtime, for both men and women in spring 2002.

The most common length of working week for men was 40 hours followed by 60 hours and over, and then 50 hours, and for women the most common length was only slightly shorter at 38 hours but the second most common was 40 hours. However, note that there is a tendency for LFS respondents' reported hours to be bunched around 5 hour marks and so the distribution of hours worked has to be treated with some caution. However the figure clearly illustrates that women are more likely to work fewer hours than men, but it also shows the wide range of working hours which they undertake. Over 1.8 million women worked 15 hours or less, and a further 1.6 million worked between 16 and 20 hours. Men were more likely than women to work in excess of 60 hours per week – nearly 1.4 million did so, compared with 0.25 million women.

Around 25 per cent of working men and 11 per cent, respectively, of working women were working more than 50 hours a week in the United Kingdom in spring 2002. For men, those working as managers and senior officials were most likely to be working over 50 hours a week (38 per cent) followed by those working as process, plant and machine operatives (30 per cent) (Figure 4.27). For women, those in professional occupations were most likely to work more than 50 hours a week (33 per cent) and the majority of these were in the teaching profession, this was followed by female managers and senior officials (18 per cent). For both men and women, those in the administrative and secretarial occupations (8 and 2 per cent, respectively) were least likely to work over 50 hours a week.

People working in certain industries were also more likely to work over 50 hours a week. The largest proportions of people working over 50 hours are employed in agriculture (33 per cent), transport and communications (29 per cent) and construction (26 per cent), with the smallest proportion employed in manufacturing (17 per cent). The differences between the hours worked in different occupations and industries also reflects the mix of part-time and full-time workers, as well as any difference in the standard working week. Self-employed people work, on average, longer hours than full-time employees.

In spring 2002 almost a fifth of workers of working age in the United Kingdom were dissatisfied with the number of hours that they worked. In each age category a higher proportion of women than men were overemployed (those who want to work fewer hours and would accept an equivalent pay cut). The proportions of full time workers who are overemployed increased with age, from 4 per cent for 16 to 17 year olds, to 17 per cent of those between 50 and state pension age (Table 4.28). Managers and senior officials and

Figure 4.27

Full-time employees[1] who worked more than 50 hours a week: by occupation, 2002[2]

United Kingdom

Percentages

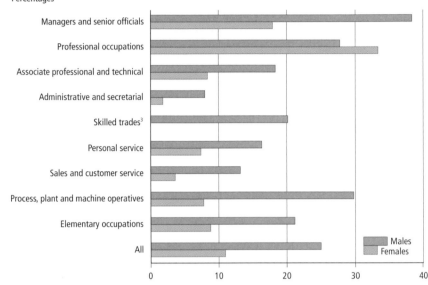

1 Percentages are based on totals that exclude those who either did not know or did not state how many hours they worked.
2 At spring. The estimates are not seasonally adjusted and have not been adjusted to take account of the recent Census 2001 results. See Appendix, Part 4: LFS reweighting.
3 Sample size for females too small for reliable estimate.
Source: Labour Force Survey, Office for National Statistics

Table 4.28

Overemployment:[1] by age, sex and work pattern, 2002[2]

United Kingdom

Percentages

	16–17	18–24	25–34	35–49	50–59/64[3]
Full-time					
Males	..	5	7	11	16
Females	..	6	15	18	20
All wanting fewer					
hours for less pay	4	5	10	14	17

1 All in employment who want to work fewer hours for less pay.
2 At spring. These estimates are not seasonally adjusted and have not been adjusted to take account of the recent Census 2001 results. See Appendix, Part 4: LFS reweighting.
3 Males aged up to 64, females aged up to 59.
Source: Labour Force Survey, Office for National Statistics

Table 4.29

Underemployment:[1] by age, sex and work pattern, 2002[2]

United Kingdom   Percentages

	16–17	18–24	25–34	35–49	50–59/ 64[3]
Full-time					
Males	..	8	6	4	3
Females	..	7	5	3	3
All wanting more hours	8	8	5	4	3
Part-time					
Males	25	30	38	38	20
Females	23	26	18	18	11
All wanting more hours	24	27	21	19	13

1 All in employment who want to work more hours.

2 At spring. These estimates are not seasonally adjusted and have not been adjusted to take account of the recent Census 2001 results. See Appendix, Part 4: LFS reweighting.

3 Males aged up to 64, females aged up to 59.

Source: Labour Force Survey, Office for National Statistics

professionals were those most likely to be overemployed, while those in the elementary occupations were least likely to be overemployed.

Conversely, there are people who are under employed (those wanting to work more hours). Higher proportions of men than women were underemployed, particularly those working part-time (Table 4.29). However, as those working part-time are predominately women (see Table 4.10) there were greater numbers of women who were underemployed than men. The difference in proportions was highest among those part-time workers aged 25 to 49 (38 per cent of men compared with 18 per cent of women).

DESCRIPTIO

SALARY

Chapter 5

Income and wealth

Household income

- Household disposable income per head in the United Kingdom, adjusted for inflation, grew by 6.5 per cent between 2000 and 2001, compared with growth in GDP per head of 1.9 per cent. (Figure 5.1)

- Social security benefits form the main source of income for lone parent households. (Table 5.3)

- In 2000/01, the median net income of women in Great Britain was 56 per cent of that of men, taken over all family types. (Figure 5.5)

Earnings

- Over the period 1987 to 2002, earnings in Great Britain generally grew faster for the top 10 per cent of the earnings distribution than for the bottom 10 per cent. (Figure 5.6)

- In 2002 the average hourly earnings of women working full-time in Great Britain were 81 per cent of those of men, compared with 63 per cent in 1970. (Figure 5.7)

Taxes

- The Inland Revenue estimates that there will be 29.4 million taxpayers in 2002/03 in the United Kingdom, over half the adult population. (Table 5.12)

Income distribution

- Around 20 per cent of those adults in the top quintile group of income in Great Britain in 1991 remained in that group throughout the period 1991 to 2000. (Table 5.16)

Low incomes

- Children are disproportionately present in low-income households: 21 per cent of children (2.7 million) were living in households with below 60 per cent of median income (before deduction of housing costs) in Great Britain in 2000/01. (Figure 5.23)

Wealth

- The holdings by UK households in life assurance and pension funds and in securities and shares fell steeply in value in real terms between 2000 and 2001, by 14 per cent and 33 per cent respectively, reflecting the fall in stock market values. (Table 5.25)

National income and expenditure

- The long term average annual growth rate in GDP per head in the United Kingdom was 2.6 per cent between 1948 and 2001, somewhat higher than the growth of 2.0 per cent between 2000 and 2001. (Figure 5.28)

Although most of *Social Trends* is concerned with people's social well-being, their economic well-being is also important since it often influences the extent to which they are able to participate fully in society. People's income is usually regarded as the best proxy for their economic well-being, in that it determines how much they are able to spend and save. Income levels depend on the level of activity within the economy as a whole – the national income – and on the way in which national income is distributed. Wealth, on the other hand, represents the ownership of assets valued at a point in time.

Household income

The most commonly used measure of economic activity is gross domestic product (GDP), sometimes also referred to as the amount of 'value added' generated within the economy of a country. The total income generated is divided between individuals, companies and other organisations (for example in the form of profits retained for investment), and government (in the form of taxes on production). Analysis of the trends in GDP may be found in the final section of this chapter.

Household income is derived not only directly from economic activity in the form of wages and salaries and self-employment income but also through transfers such as social security benefits. It is then subject to a number of deductions such as income tax, local taxes, and contributions towards pensions and national insurance. The amount of income remaining is referred to as household disposable income – the amount people have available to spend or save – and it is this measure which is commonly used to describe people's 'economic well-being'.

Household disposable income per head, adjusted for inflation, increased one and a quarter times between 1971 and 2001 (Figure 5.1). During the 1970s and early 1980s growth was somewhat erratic, and in some years there were small year-on-year falls, such as in 1974, 1976, 1977, 1981 and 1982. However, since then there has been growth each year, with the exception of 1998 when there was a very slight fall when adjusted for inflation. Over the period since 1971, a comparison of the patterns of growth of household disposable income and GDP per head shows that there

Figure **5.1**

Real household disposable income per head[1] and gross domestic product per head[2]

United Kingdom

Index (1971=100)

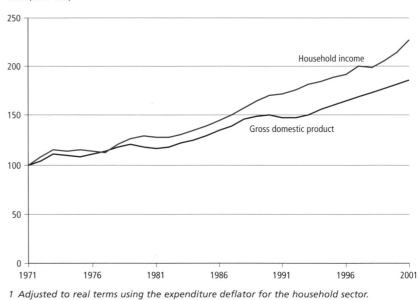

1 Adjusted to real terms using the expenditure deflator for the household sector. See Appendix, Part 5: Household sector.
2 Adjusted to real terms using the GDP deflator.
Source: Office for National Statistics

has been a small shift between the shares of households and organisations in GDP in favour of households. Between 2000 and 2001, real household disposable income per head grew by 6.5 per cent compared with GDP per head growth of 1.9 per cent.

Table 5.2 illustrates how the shares of the various components of household income have changed since 1987. This shows a fall in the proportion derived from wages and salaries from 52 per cent to 47 per cent in 1996, but since then a gradual rise to 50 per cent in 2000 and 2001. The proportion of income derived from social benefits has remained at around 20 per cent throughout the period.

Taxes on income as a proportion of household income have remained stable over this period at around 11 per cent, and social contributions (that is, employees' national insurance

Table **5.2**

Composition of household income

United Kingdom						Percentages
	1987	1991	1996	1999	2000	2001
Source of income						
Wages and salaries[1]	52	50	47	49	50	50
Operating income[2]	11	11	12	12	12	12
Property income gross	15	16	14	14	14	14
Social benefits[3]	19	19	21	21	20	21
Other current transfers[4]	3	4	5	4	4	4
Total household income						
(=100%) (£ billion at 2001 prices)[5]	632	725	809	885	932	985
Taxes etc as a percentage of						
total household income						
Taxes on income	11	11	10	11	12	12
Social contributions[2]	9	8	8	8	8	8
Other current taxes	2	2	2	2	2	2
Other current transfers	2	3	4	3	3	3
Total household disposable income						
(£ billion at 2001 prices)[5]	427	496	562	609	636	678

1 Excludes employers' social contributions.
2 Includes self-employment income for sole-traders and rental income.
3 Comprises pensions and benefits.
4 Mostly other government grants, but including transfers from abroad and non-profit making bodies.
5 Adjusted to 2001 prices using the expenditure deflator for the household sector.
Source: Office for National Statistics

contributions) have also remained stable at 8 per cent of household income. More information on taxes may be found in the Taxes section of this chapter beginning on page 100.

The data in Figure 5.1 and Table 5.2 are derived from the UK national accounts (see Appendix, Part 5: Household sector). In the national accounts, households are combined with the non-profit making institutions such as universities, charities and clubs, and it is not at present possible to separate the two sectors. Non-profit making bodies receive income mainly in the form of property income (that is, investment income) and of other current receipts. Thus if it were possible to separate the two sectors, receipts of these two types of income by households alone would be lower than that shown in Table 5.2.

The household sector also includes people living in institutions such as nursing homes, as well as people living in private households. In most of the remainder of this chapter, the tables and figures are derived directly from surveys of households (such as the Family Resources Survey, the Family Expenditure Survey (from April 2001, the Expenditure and Food Survey), the Labour Force Survey, and the British Household Panel Survey) and surveys of businesses (such as the New Earnings Survey). Data from these surveys cover the population living in households and some cover certain parts of the population living in institutions, but all exclude non-profit making institutions. They can be used to analyse the distribution of household income between different sub-groups of the population, such as pensioners.

Survey sources differ from the national accounts not only in their population coverage but also in the way that household income is defined. One of the main differences is that the national accounts include the value of national insurance contributions made on behalf of employees by their employer as part of total household income, whereas survey sources do not. Also, receipts of investment income are usually expressed net of repayments of loans in the national accounts. However, for the first time in *Social Trends*, household income in Table 5.2 has been re-defined to exclude employers' national insurance contributions and to include gross receipts of investment income. This means that the data are not comparable with those in previous editions, but they are more consistent with the definition of income used for most income surveys.

Survey sources are also subject to under-reporting and non-response bias. In the case of household income surveys, investment income is commonly underestimated, as is income from self-employment. All these factors mean that the survey data on income used in the rest of this chapter are not entirely consistent with the national accounts household sector data.

The main sources of household income identified in Table 5.2 differ considerably in their importance between different types of households, particularly according to their family and employment circumstances. Social security benefits and private pensions form the

Table **5.3**

Sources of gross household income: by household type, 2000/01

Great Britain   Percentages

	Wages and salaries	Self-employment income	Investment income	Tax credits	Retirement pensions	Private pensions	Disability benefits	Other benefits	Other income
One adult above pensionable age, no children	3	2	7	0	46	26	5	10	2
Two adults one or both over pensionable age, no children	18	4	8	0	30	31	5	3	1
Two adults below pensionable age									
No children	78	10	2	0	0	5	2	2	1
One or more children	75	13	2	1	–	1	1	6	2
One adult below pensionable age									
No children	75	8	3	0	0	3	3	7	2
One or more children	33	3	1	7	–	1	2	43	10
Other households	69	15	2	–	2	4	2	3	3
All households	64	10	3	1	6	7	2	5	2

Source: Family Resources Survey, Department for Work and Pensions

main sources of income for households where one or both members are over pensionable age (Table 5.3). Pensioner households also derive higher proportions of income than other households from investments, reflecting the fact that they have been able to build up savings throughout their working lives. Social security benefits form the main source of income for lone parent households overall, though for lone parents with one child only, wages and salaries are almost as important as benefits and tax credits. 'Other income' sources are also important for lone parent households – these include child support payments from the absent parent. For other types of household, 80 per cent or more of their income is derived from their participation in the labour market.

Income composition also varies according to ethnic group. Black and Indian households derive higher than average proportions of income from wages and salaries and lower than average proportions from pensions, reflecting at least in part the younger age structure of the minority ethnic populations compared with the White population – see Table 1.5 in Chapter 1. Pakistani/Bangladeshi households derive almost equal proportions of their income from wages and salaries and from self-employment income. Black and

Pakistani/Bangladeshi households also derive above average proportions of income from social security benefits other than pensions.

Although the largest source of income for pensioner families in Great Britain is social security benefits, which include the state retirement pension, the average levels and sources of income vary with age and with marital status (Table 5.4). Single pensioners aged 75 years and over received two thirds of their gross income from social security benefits in 2000/01 compared with two fifths for couples aged under 75. Occupational pensions are more important for couples than for single pensioners – they accounted for just under a third of the gross income of couples compared with around a fifth for single pensioners.

The average income of pensioner families grew in real terms, that is adjusted for inflation, by 17 per cent between 1994/95 and 2000/01, an average annual growth rate of 2.8 per cent. Growth was higher for older pensioners than for younger ones – 22 per cent for both couple and single pensioners over 75, compared with 15 per cent for couples and 18 per cent for single pensioners under 75. Over the same period average earnings grew by 9 per cent in real terms (that is, deflated by the all items RPI). Thus not only

Table 5.4

Pensioners'[1] gross income: by age and source

United Kingdom

Percentages

	Couples[2]			Single		
	1994/95	1997/98	2000/01	1994/95	1997/98	2000/01
Under 75						
Benefits	42	41	40	58	58	57
Occupational pensions	28	30	31	23	24	23
Investments	16	16	15	12	10	11
Earnings	13	12	14	7	7	8
Other	–	1	1	1	1	1
All gross income (=100%)						
(£ per week at 2000/01 prices[3])	328	352	376	165	174	194
75 and over						
Benefits	54	52	49	69	69	66
Occupational pensions	29	29	32	17	20	21
Investments	14	14	15	11	9	10
Earnings	3	5	4	2	1	1
Other	–	–	1	1	1	1
All gross income (=100%)						
(£ per week at 2000/01 prices[3])	264	282	323	142	150	173

1 Pensioner units.
2 Classified by age of head of unit. The head of a couple is defined as the man.
3 Adjusted to 2000/01 prices using the retail prices index less local taxes.
Source: Pensioners' Income series, Department for Work and Pensions

Figure 5.5

Median individual net income:[1] by family type and sex, 2000/01

Great Britain

£ per week

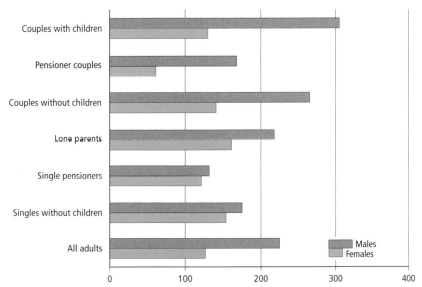

1 See Appendix, Part 5: Individual income.
Source: Individual Income, Department for Work and Pensions

did average pensioner incomes grow in real terms between 1994/95 and 2000/01, but they grew at a faster rate than earnings. However, changes in average income do not just reflect the changes experienced by individual pensioners but also reflect changes in the composition of the pensioner group, for example as new retirees with higher incomes join the group.

The information presented in this section so far has been in terms of household or family income, since these are generally considered to be the units across which resources are shared. Thus total household income can be taken as representing the (potential) standard of living of each of its members. The assumption of equal sharing of resources between each member of the household is very difficult to test. Using certain assumptions it is possible to use household survey data to derive estimates of the income accruing to individuals, but it is not possible to infer their living standards.

Figure 5.5 shows the results of such an exercise and compares the median net incomes of men and women by family type. (See Appendix,

Part 5: Individual income for details of how these estimates were derived, and Box on page 101 for explanation of the median. Note also that, as explained further in the Appendix, the term net income is used in place of disposable income for this series because the term disposable income has a different definition from that used elsewhere in this chapter.) Men's incomes exceeded those of women in 2000/01, irrespective of the type of family in which they were living. Taken over all family types the median net income of women was 56 per cent of that of men. However, the gap was largest for pensioner couples and couples with children, where the median net income of women was 37 per cent and 43 per cent of men respectively. Among pensioner couples this is the result mainly of historic factors leading to lower entitlements amongst wives both for state and occupational pensions, whereas among couples with children it is a result of the propensity of women to work part-time or to leave the labour force entirely while bringing up children. The gap was smallest for single people without children and single pensioners.

Earnings

Income from employment is the most important component of household income overall (Tables 5.2 and 5.3). When there is rapid earnings growth across the economy as a whole, this may indicate that the labour market is under-supplied with employees in the right numbers and with the right skills to meet the level of demand within the economy. In addition, a rapid rise may indicate that wage settlements are higher than the rate of economic growth can sustain and thus create inflationary pressures. Slower earnings growth may be a reflection of reduced demand within the economy and may presage a fall in GDP and an increase in unemployment. The relationship between earnings and prices is also of importance. If earnings rise faster than prices, this means that employees' pay is increasing faster than the prices they have to pay for goods and services and that therefore, all things being equal, their purchasing power will rise and they will feel 'better off'.

The pattern of annual change in earnings at the top and bottom of the earnings distribution between 1987 and 2002 is

Figure **5.6**

Earnings growth of full-time employees[1] in the top and bottom deciles
Great Britain

Percentages

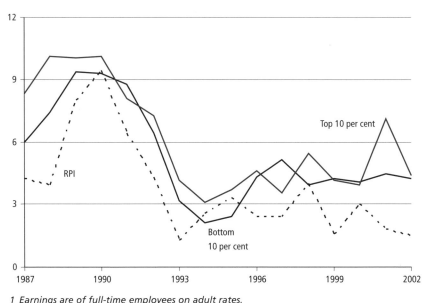

1 Earnings are of full-time employees on adult rates.
Source: New Earnings Survey, Office for National Statistics

illustrated in Figure 5.6. Weekly earnings of the top 10 per cent (or decile group – see Box on page 101) of full-time employees on adult rates in Great Britain generally grew faster than earnings of the bottom 10 per cent, indicating a widening in the dispersion of earnings. Exceptions were 1991, 1997, 1999 and 2000 when the position was reversed and earnings grew faster at the bottom of the distribution than at the top. The particularly high growth in earnings for the top decile group in 2001 is largely attributed to exceptional bonuses among senior managers and professionals, notably in the financial sector.

Figure 5.7

Hourly earnings sex differential[1]

Great Britain

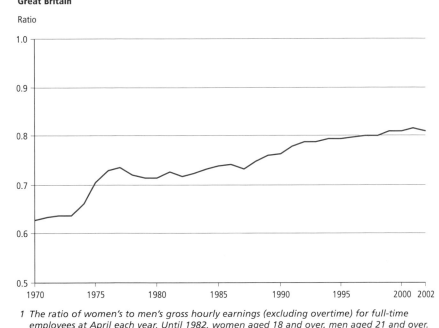

1 The ratio of women's to men's gross hourly earnings (excluding overtime) for full-time employees at April each year. Until 1982, women aged 18 and over, men aged 21 and over. From 1983 onwards for employees on adult rates whose pay for the survey period was not affected by absence.
Source: New Earnings Survey, Office for National Statistics

Throughout the period shown in the figure, earnings growth at the top of the earnings distribution outpaced the growth in prices as measured by the retail prices index (RPI), sometimes substantially so, for example in 1987 and 1988 and in 2001. This was generally true at the bottom of the earnings distribution too. However, there were some years when prices grew faster than average earnings of the bottom 10 per cent – for example 1994 and 1995 – meaning that in those years not only did the dispersion of earnings widen but average earnings at the bottom of the distribution fell in real terms.

A wide variety of factors influence the level of earnings which an employee receives such as their skills and experience, their occupation, the economic sector in which they work, the hours they work, and so on. The area of the country in which they work and their gender may also have an impact. The remainder of this section explores some of these factors.

However, it should be borne in mind that they are all very much interlinked, and no attempt is made here to disentangle the effect that any single factor may have.

Government legislation may also have an effect on wages. The *Equal Pay Act 1970* and subsequent revisions, together with the *Sex Discrimination Act 1975,* established the principle of equal pay for work which can be established to be of equal value to that done by a member of the opposite sex, employed by the same employer, under common terms and conditions of employment. The impact of this legislation, together with other important factors such as the opening up of higher paid work to women, has been to narrow the differential between the hourly earnings of men and women (excluding overtime). There was a sharp narrowing of the differential in the mid-1970s, followed by a more gradual erosion in the next 25 years or so (Figure 5.7).

In 1970, the hourly earnings of women working full-time in Great Britain were 63 per cent of those of men, whereas in 2002 they had risen to 81 per cent. The differential appears to have levelled out, having remained at 81 or 82 per cent over the last four years. Because even those women working full-time tend not to work as many hours as men, the gap for weekly earnings is wider particularly when overtime earnings are included. In 2002, women working full-time earned 75 per cent of the weekly earnings of men (including overtime).

Although average weekly and hourly pay provide a useful comparison between the earnings of men and women, they do not necessarily indicate differences in rates of pay for comparable jobs. Such averages reflect the different employment characteristics of men and women, such as the proportions in different occupations and their length of time in jobs. The fact that women are more likely than men to be in non-manual occupations raises their overall average pay relative to that of men: the average hourly earnings of non-manual women is higher than that of men in manual work. However, among both manual and non-manual workers, women are concentrated in lower paid occupations which reduces their relative pay.

Average gross weekly earnings for full-time employees in Great Britain in 2002 were highest in a central band of England running roughly from Bristol in the west to Hampshire and West Sussex (Map 5.8). Within this geographic band, gross earnings were the highest in London at £624 per week, followed by Bracknell Forest Unitary Authority at £613 per week. A number of isolated pockets of high earnings also exist elsewhere: for example, in Aberdeen City where the North Sea industries have a substantial influence, earnings averaged £505 per week. The lowest earnings were to be found in parts of Wales such as Conwy, in Devon and Cornwall, and in parts of Scotland.

Wage rates can vary considerably between industrial sectors. Agriculture has traditionally been a relatively low-paid sector in the United Kingdom and this is still the case, with 40 per cent of employees on wage rates of less than £6 per hour in spring 2002 (Table 5.9). However, the hotel and restaurant sector is the lowest paid industry, with 68 per cent earning less than £6 per hour and the wholesale and retail trade is also relatively low paid with 44 per cent earning less than £6 per hour. At the other end of the scale, 45 per cent of those in financial intermediation earned £12 or more per hour. Averaged over all industries, about a quarter of employees earned less than £6 per hour.

Wage rates also vary according to occupation. In April 2001, treasurers and company financial managers, earning an average of £1,180 per week, topped the earnings league for full-time employees. Aircraft flight deck officers and medical practitioners also had average weekly earnings exceeding £1,000. The lowest paid of all full-time adult employees were kitchen porters, bar staff, and retail cash desk and check-out operators, all with average earnings below £200 per week, less than a fifth of the earnings of the highest paid occupational group.

For many employees, overtime and other additions can supplement basic weekly pay. Overtime is particularly important to men in manual occupations, accounting on average for 12 per cent of total weekly earnings in the United Kingdom in 2002 compared with only 2 per cent for men in non-manual occupations (Table 5.10). Overtime was a much less

Map 5.8

Average gross weekly earnings: by area[1], April 2002

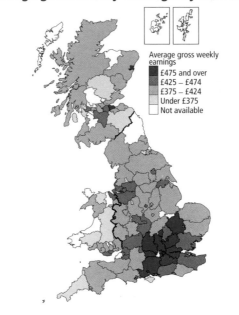

Average gross weekly earnings
- █ £475 and over
- ▓ £425 – £474
- ▒ £375 – £424
- ░ Under £375
- □ Not available

1 Counties and unitary authorities, for England. Unitary authorities for Scotland and Wales.
Source: New Earnings Survey, Office for National Statistics

Table 5.9

Distribution of hourly[1] earnings: by industry, spring 2002

United Kingdom   Percentages

	Less than £4	£4 but less than £6	£6 but less than £8	£8 but less than £10	£10 but less than £12	£12 and over
Hotels and restaurants	4	64	17	7	4	6
Wholesale and retail trade	1	43	22	12	7	16
Agriculture, hunting, forestry and fishing	–	39	37	14	4	5
Health and social work	1	26	22	14	12	25
Real estate, renting and business activities	1	22	19	13	9	36
Construction	–	9	25	23	15	27
Education	1	22	20	12	9	36
Manufacturing	–	15	23	20	14	29
Transport, storage and communication	–	13	29	21	12	25
Public administration and defence	–	9	22	17	16	36
Financial intermediation	–	6	20	17	12	45
Mining, quarrying, electricity, gas and water supplies	–	5	14	19	20	41
Other services	1	31	22	13	9	23
All industries[2]	1	23	22	15	11	29

1 Both full- and part-time employees, including overtime payments, whose gross hourly earnings were less than £100.
2 Includes those whose workplace is abroad and those who did not state their industry.
Source: New Earnings Survey, Office for National Statistics

Table 5.10

Composition of weekly pay of employees:[1] by sex and type of work, April 2002

United Kingdom
Percentages

	Overtime	Bonuses and commissions	Shift premia	Average gross weekly earnings (£)
Males				
Manual	11.8	3.3	3.0	366.6
Non-manual	2.3	4.6	0.7	608.7
Females				
Manual	5.5	2.4	2.7	250.3
Non-manual	1.5	2.4	0.9	404.0
All employees	4.1	3.6	1.2	462.6

1 As a percentage of average gross weekly earnings.
Source: New Earnings Survey, Office for National Statistics

important component of weekly pay for women in manual work compared with men, and again was relatively unimportant for those in non-manual occupations. Bonuses and commissions were important components of pay for men in non-manual work. Payments for shift work were less important than overtime and bonuses/commissions overall, but showed a similar pattern to overtime between sexes and types of work.

For some workers, the value of income 'in kind' forms an important part of their overall remuneration package. Such benefits may include a company car, free fuel, or private medical insurance. Information is available from the Inland Revenue on those benefits whose value to the recipient is liable to taxation. In 2000/01, the average value of taxable benefits was £2,720 per recipient, but increased with income (Table 5.11). The average value of a company car was £3,480 per recipient.

Table 5.11

Selected taxable fringe benefits received by employees[1] and company directors: by gross annual earnings, 2000/01[2]

United Kingdom

	Company car		Free fuel		Private medical insurance		Any benefit or expenses payment	
	Number of recipients (thousands)	Average value[3] (£)	Number of recipients (thousands)	Average value[4] (£)	Number of recipients (thousands)	Average value[5] (£)	Number of recipients[6] (thousands)	Average value[6] (£)
Employees[1]								
Below £25,000	480	2,360	220	1,690	770	320	1,760	1,220
£25,000 but under £35,000	350	3,030	160	2,000	430	390	760	2,220
£35,000 but under £45,000	210	3,490	90	2,090	250	450	380	2,980
£45,000 or more	260	4,600	130	2,370	370	580	480	4,570
Directors								
Below £25,000	90	3,570	60	2,150	40	780	210	3,970
£25,000 but under £35,000	60	3,940	50	2,370	30	750	90	5,370
£35,000 but under £45,000	40	4,410	40	2,440	40	750	60	6,540
£45,000 or more	120	6,240	100	2,790	110	930	160	10,940
All employees[1] and directors	1,610	3,480	850	2,130	2,040	460	3,900	2,720

1 Employees with gross earnings of at least £8,500 a year, but excluding directors. Except for 'Any benefit or expenses payment', as some benefits and expenses are taxable regardless of income.
2 Estimates for 2000/01 are based on projections from the 1999/2000 survey.
3 The taxable value of company cars is based on the list price of the car subject to reductions for age and business mileage.
4 The taxable value of free fuel is based on a scale charge which depends on both the car engine size and the type of fuel.
5 The cost to the employer of providing the benefit.
6 Includes other benefits not shown separately. Some recipients receive more than one type of benefit.
Source: Survey of Expenses and Benefits, Inland Revenue

Taxes

Table 5.2 showed that in 2001, 12 per cent of household income was paid out in taxes on income and 8 per cent in social contributions. Since every taxpayer is entitled to a personal allowance, which in 2002/03 is £4,615, those with income below this do not pay any tax. People aged over 65 may be entitled to further allowances. The income tax regime for 2002/03 includes three different rates of tax. Taxable income of up to £1,920 (that is, after the deduction of allowances and any other tax relief to which the individual may be entitled) is charged at 10 per cent. Taxable income above £1,920 but less than £29,900 is charged at 22 per cent, while income above this level is charged at 40 per cent. Special rates apply to savings income.

The Inland Revenue estimates that in 2002/03 there will be around 29.4 million taxpayers in the United Kingdom, over half the adult population (Table 5.12). Because of the progressive nature of the income tax system, the amount of tax payable increases both in cash terms and as a proportion of income as income increases, averaging £150 per year for taxpayers with taxable incomes between £5,000 and £7,499 and £76,600 for those with incomes of £100,000 and above.

National insurance (NI) contributions are paid according to an individual's earnings rather than their total income, and for employees, payments are made both by the individual and by their employer. Employees' contributions tend to be slightly smaller as a proportion of earnings for those on higher weekly earnings compared with those on lower earnings because there is a ceiling on contributions: in 2002/03 contributions are levied only on the first £585 of weekly earnings.

In addition to direct taxes such as income tax, households also pay indirect taxes through their expenditure. Indirect taxes include value added tax (VAT) and customs and excise duties and are included in the prices of consumer goods and services. These taxes are specific to particular commodities: for example, in 2002/03 VAT was payable on most consumer goods at 17.5 per cent of their value, though not on most foods nor on books and newspapers, and at a reduced rate on heating and lighting. Customs and excise duties on the

Table 5.12

Income tax payable: by annual income, 2002/03[1]

United Kingdom

	Number of taxpayers (millions)	Total tax payable (£ million)	Average rate of tax payable (percentages)	Average amount of tax payable (£)
£4,615–£4,999	0.4	10	–	20
£5,000–£7,499	3.1	480	2	150
£7,500–£9,999	3.6	1,890	6	530
£10,000–£14,999	6.3	7,850	10	1,240
£15,000–£19,999	5.1	11,170	13	2,200
£20,000–£29,999	6.0	21,680	15	3,620
£30,000–£49,999	3.4	22,590	18	6,680
£50,000–£99,999	1.1	19,830	26	17,320
£100,000 and over	0.4	27,650	34	76,600
All incomes	29.4	113,150	17	3,850

1 Based on projections in line with the November 2002 Pre-Budget Report.
Source: Inland Revenue

Figure 5.13

Indirect taxes as a percentage of disposable income: by income grouping[1] of household, 2000/01

United Kingdom

Percentages

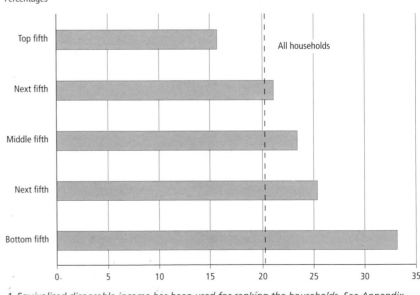

1 Equivalised disposable income has been used for ranking the households. See Appendix, Part 5: Equivalisation scales.
Source: Office for National Statistics

other hand tend to vary by the volume rather than value of goods purchased. Because high income households are more likely to devote a larger proportion of their income to investments or repaying loans, and low income households may be funding their expenditure through taking out loans or drawing down savings, the proportion of income paid in indirect taxes tends to be higher for those on low incomes than for those on high incomes (Figure 5.13).

A further means of raising revenue from households is through local taxes, comprising council tax in Great Britain and domestic rates in Northern Ireland. These taxes are raised by local authorities to part-fund the services they provide. For both council tax and domestic rates, the amount payable by a household depends on the value of the property they occupy. However, for those on low incomes, assistance is available in the form of council tax benefits (rates rebates in Northern Ireland). In 2000/01, estimates from the Family Expenditure Survey indicate that local taxes as a percentage of gross income varied within Great Britain between 2.3 per cent in London and 3.5 per cent in Scotland and the North West. Net domestic rates in Northern Ireland, which are based on a quite different valuation system, represented 1.8 per cent of household gross income.

Income distribution

We have already seen how the various components of income differ in importance for different household types and how the levels of earnings vary between individuals. The result is an uneven distribution of total income between households, though the inequality is reduced to some extent by the deduction of taxes and social contributions and their redistribution to households in the form of social security benefits and other payments from government. The analysis of income distribution is therefore usually based on household disposable income, that is total income less payments of income tax and social contributions. However, in the analysis of Households Below Average Income carried out by the Department for Work and Pensions on which most of the items in this and the next section are based, disposable income is presented both before and after the further deduction of housing costs. It can be argued that the costs of housing faced by different households at a given time may or may not reflect the true value of the housing that they actually enjoy. For example, the housing costs faced by someone renting a property in London may be much higher than they would have to pay for a property of similar quality outside London. Equally, a retired person living in a property which they own outright will

Equivalisation – in analysing the distribution of income, household disposable income is usually adjusted to take account of the size and composition of the household. This is in recognition of the fact that, for example, to achieve the same standard of living a household of five would require a higher income than would a single person. This process is known as equivalisation (see Appendix, Part 5: Equivalisation scales).

Quintile and decile groups – the main method of analysing income distribution used in this chapter is to rank units (households, individuals or adults) by a given income measure, and then to divide the ranked units into groups of equal size. Groups containing 20 per cent of units are referred to as 'quintile groups' or 'fifths'. Thus the 'bottom quintile group' is the 20 per cent of units with the lowest incomes. Similarly, groups containing 10 per cent of units are referred to as 'decile groups' or tenths.

Percentiles – an alternative method used in the chapter is to present the income level above or below which a certain proportion of units fall. Thus the ninetieth percentile is the income level above which only 10 per cent of units fall when ranked by a given income measure. The median is then the midpoint of the distribution above and below which 50 per cent of units fall.

enjoy the same level of housing as their younger neighbour in an identical property but owned with a mortgage, but their housing costs will be very different. Thus estimates are presented on both bases to take into account variations in housing costs that do not correspond to comparable variations in the quality of housing. Neither is given pre-eminence over the other. For more details, see Appendix, Part 5: Households Below Average Income.

During the 1970s there was relatively little change in the distribution of disposable income among households (Figure 5.14). However, the 1980s were characterised by a large increase in inequality: between 1981 and 1989 average (median) income rose by 27 per cent when adjusted for inflation, whereas income at the ninetieth percentile rose by 38 per cent and that at the tenth percentile rose by only 7 per cent. During the first half of the 1990s, the income distribution appeared to stabilise, but in the most recent period there appears to have been a further small increase in inequality.

The Institute for Fiscal Studies has investigated some of the possible explanations for the changes in inequality seen over the last two decades, and in particular why the trends are different over the economic cycles of the 1980s and 1990s. They found that wage growth played a part: inequality tends to rise during periods of rapid wage growth because the poorest households are the most likely to contain non-working individuals. The economic recovery in the 1980s was characterised by large increases in wages in each of the years from 1984 to 1988 matching the period when inequality increased rapidly. In contrast wage growth was very slow to return in the recovery of the early to mid-1990s – a time of stable or falling inequality. Growth in self-employment income and in unemployment were also found to be associated with periods of increased inequality. It would appear that demographic factors such as the growth in one person households make a relatively unimportant contribution compared with labour market

Figure 5.14

Distribution of real[1] household disposable income[2]
United Kingdom

£ per week

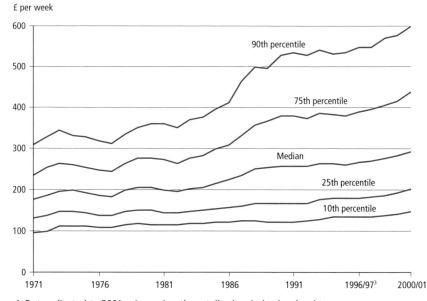

1 Data adjusted to 2001 prices using the retail prices index less local taxes.
2 Equivalised household disposable income before housing costs. See Appendix, Part 5: Households Below Average Income, and Equivalisation scales.
3 Data from 1993/94 onwards are for financial years; data for 1994/95 onwards exclude Northern Ireland.

Source: Institute for Fiscal Studies

Table **5.15**

Distribution of equivalised disposable income:[1] by ethnic group of head of household, 2000/01

Great Britain
Percentages

	Bottom quintile	Second quintile	Third quintile	Fourth quintile	Top quintile	All (=100%) (millions)
Before deduction of housing costs						
White	19	20	20	21	20	52.7
Black Caribbean	24	22	20	17	18	0.7
Black Non-Caribbean	34	22	14	16	14	0.5
Indian	29	17	20	15	19	1.0
Pakistani/Bangladeshi	64	21	8	2	5	1.0
Other	30	17	14	16	23	1.0
After deduction of housing costs						
White	18	20	21	21	20	52.7
Black Caribbean	27	22	18	17	16	0.7
Black Non-Caribbean	46	16	11	12	14	0.5
Indian	26	23	19	14	18	1.0
Pakistani/Bangladeshi	60	24	9	3	4	1.0
Other	34	18	12	14	22	1.0

1 See Appendix, Part 5: Households Below Average Income, and Equivalisation scales.
Source: Households Below Average Income, Department for Work and Pensions

changes. However, they have found that changes in the tax and benefit system have an impact in accordance with what economic theory would suggest: the income tax cuts of the 1970s and early 1980s worked to increase income inequality while direct tax rises in the early 1980s and 1990s – together with the increases in means-tested benefits in the late 1990s – produced the opposite effect.

People in households headed by a member of a minority ethnic group were more likely than those where the head was White to be in the bottom quintile group of disposable income in 2000/01 (Table 5.15). This pattern was particularly marked for the Pakistani/ Bangladeshi group, with around three out of five individuals in these families having household incomes in the bottom quintile of

the income distribution. The section on low incomes which begins on page 105 examines the characteristics of those at the lower end of the income distribution in more depth.

The Department for Work and Pensions' Households Below Average Income analysis, from which Table 5.15 is derived, provides an annual cross-sectional snapshot of the distribution of income based on the Family Resources Survey. The British Household Panel Survey (BHPS) complements this by providing longitudinal information about how the incomes of a fixed sample of individuals change from year to year. This enables us to track how people move through the income distribution over time, and to identify the factors associated with changes in their position in the distribution.

Table **5.16**

Number of movements made by individuals within the income distribution[1] between 1991 and 2000

Great Britain

Percentages

	1991 income grouping					
	Bottom fifth	Next fifth	Middle fifth	Next fifth	Top fifth	All individuals
Number of movements between quintile groups						
None	10	2	2	2	20	7
One	4	6	7	8	7	6
Two	19	12	10	11	15	13
Three	13	16	12	14	11	13
Four	17	16	19	18	15	17
Five	15	18	19	22	15	18
Six	11	17	15	13	9	13
Seven	8	8	12	9	6	9
Eight	3	4	3	3	3	3
Moved every year	1	1	1	1	–	1
Total (all individuals)	100	100	100	100	100	100

1 Equivalised household disposable income before deduction of housing costs has been used for ranking the individuals. See Appendix, Part 5: Equivalisation scales, and Households Below Average Income.

Source: Department for Work and Pensions from British Household Panel Survey, Institute for Social and Economic Research

Around 20 per cent of those adults in the top quintile group of gross income in 1991 remained in the same group throughout the period 1991 to 2000 (Table 5.16). A much lower proportion of people (10 per cent) remained in the bottom quintile group throughout the nine year period. The majority of people (over 90 per cent) moved between quintile groups at least once over the period. There is more movement in and out of the three middle quintile groups, simply because it is possible to move out of these groups through either an increase or a decrease in income. Movement out of the top group generally only occurs if income falls – an individual will remain in the group however great an increase in income is experienced. The converse is true at the bottom of the distribution. Nevertheless, the table shows that there is a considerable degree of turnover within each income group.

As discussed earlier in this chapter, households initially receive income from various sources such as employment, occupational pensions, investments, and transfers from other households. The state then intervenes both to raise taxes and national insurance contributions from individuals and to redistribute the revenue thus raised in the form of cash benefits to households, and in the provision of services which are free or provided at a subsidised price at the point of use. Some households will pay more in tax than they receive in benefits, while others will benefit more than they are taxed. Overall, this process results in a redistribution of income from households with higher incomes to those on lower incomes.

The average taxes paid and benefits received by each quintile group in 2000/01 are set out in Table 5.17. The distribution of 'original' income – before any state intervention – is highly

Table **5.17**

Redistribution of income through taxes and benefits,[1] 2000/01

United Kingdom   £ per year

	Quintile group of households[2]					
	Bottom quintile	Next quintile	Middle quintile	Next quintile	Top quintile	All house-holds
Average per household						
Wages and salaries	1,920	6,100	14,560	24,050	39,900	17,300
Imputed income from benefits						
in kind	10	30	140	380	1,220	350
Self-employment income	370	810	1,100	1,960	8,420	2,530
Occupational pensions, annuities	470	1,400	1,980	2,300	2,950	1,820
Investment income	200	340	580	1,010	3,070	1,040
Other income	120	140	220	250	200	190
Total original income	3,090	8,820	18,570	29,950	55,740	23,230
plus Benefits in cash						
Contributory	2,400	2,780	1,830	1,120	750	1,780
Non-contributory	2,930	2,690	1,690	920	360	1,720
Gross income	8,420	14,290	22,080	32,000	56,850	26,730
less Income tax[3] and NIC[4]	430	1,410	3,320	6,010	12,230	4,680
less Local taxes[5] (net)	560	670	810	920	1,070	810
Disposable income	7,440	12,200	17,960	25,060	43,550	21,240
less Indirect taxes	2,470	3,100	4,220	5,290	6,850	4,390
Post-tax income	4,970	9,100	13,730	19,770	36,690	16,850
plus Benefits in kind						
Education	1,970	1,410	1,480	1,180	710	1,350
National Health Service	2,510	2,520	2,140	1,840	1,610	2,130
Housing subsidy	80	70	40	10	10	40
Travel subsidies	50	50	50	50	60	50
School meals and welfare milk	80	30	10	–	–	20
Final income	9,670	13,190	17,460	22,870	39,080	20,460

1 See Appendix, Part 5: Redistribution of income.
2 Equivalised disposable income has been used for ranking the households. See Appendix, Part 5: Equivalisation scales.
3 After tax relief at source on life assurance premiums.
4 Employees' National Insurance Contributions.
5 Council tax net of council tax benefits, rates and water charges. Rates net of rebates in Northern Ireland.
Source: Office for National Statistics

unequal, with the average income of the top quintile group about 18 times greater than that of the bottom quintile group. Payment of cash benefits reduces this disparity so that the ratio of gross income in the top group compared with the bottom is 7:1, and deduction of direct and local taxes reduces the ratio further to around 6:1. Based on people's expenditure patterns it is then possible to calculate an estimated payment of indirect taxes such as VAT and excise duties, which are deducted to produce a measure of post-tax income. Finally, an estimate is made for the value of the benefit they receive from government expenditure on services such as education and health. (It is not possible to estimate the benefit to households of some items of government expenditure, for example defence and road-building.) Addition of these estimates gives a household's final income. The ratio of average final income in the top quintile group to that in the bottom quintile group is 4:1. In this analysis, around 56 per cent of general government expenditure is allocated to households in the form of benefits.

Low incomes

Being disadvantaged, and thus 'excluded' from many of the opportunities available to the average citizen, has often been seen as synonymous with having a low income. While low income is clearly central to poverty and social exclusion, it is now widely accepted that there is a wide range of other factors which are important. People can experience poverty of education, of training, of health, and of environment, as well as poverty in purely cash terms. Nevertheless, the prevalence of low income remains an important indicator of social exclusion. Information on many of the other aspects may be found in other chapters of Social Trends.

The definition of 'low' income has always been a source of debate and to some extent has to be arbitrary. Only in countries at a very low level of economic development is it sensible to take an absolutist, 'basic needs' approach, which costs the bare essentials to maintain human life and uses this as the yardstick against which incomes are measured. All other approaches are to a greater or lesser extent relative: 'low' income is defined in terms of what is generally considered adequate to maintain an acceptable standard of living given the norms of a particular society at a particular time. With such approaches, it is possible and indeed perfectly acceptable for 'low' income to differ both temporally and spatially. So for example, while in one country the possession of sufficient income to pay for central heating might be considered a necessity, this might not have been the case in the same country a generation ago and nor might it be so for a different country today.

In this section, the threshold generally adopted to define low income is 60 per cent of median equivalised household disposable income. This is one of a set of indicators in the *Opportunity For All* report used to monitor the Government's strategy to tackle poverty and social exclusion. It has also been agreed by the Statistical Programme Committee of the European Union as the basis for making international comparisons of numbers of people on low incomes.

The Institute for Fiscal Studies estimates that in 2000/01, 17 per cent of the population in Great Britain lived in households with income below this level (Figure 5.18). This proportion was fairly static during the 1960s, 1970s and early 1980s, fluctuating between 10 and 15 per cent. It then rose steeply from 1985 to reach a peak of 21 per cent in 1992. During the 1990s the proportion declined in most years, with the exception of 1996/97, though it remained well above the pre-1985 level. This pattern is also reflected in the proportion of people with incomes less than 50 per cent of the median.

There is a clear relationship between work and income, illustrated in Table 5.19. Overall, 17 per cent of the population were living in low-income households in 2000/01, compared with only 2 per cent of those living in families where all adults were in full-time work (income measured before deducting housing costs). In contrast, 64 per cent of people in families where the head or spouse were unemployed had low incomes. This proportion has fallen since the 1991/92 estimate of 71 per cent. About a quarter of people in families

Figure 5.18

Percentage of people whose income is below various fractions of median income[1]

United Kingdom

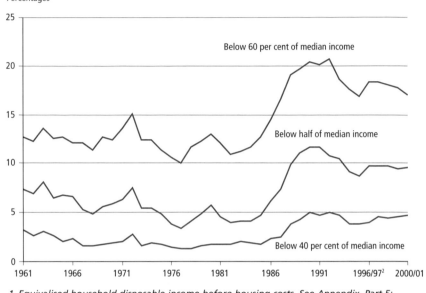

Percentages

1 Equivalised household disposable income before housing costs. See Appendix, Part 5: *Households Below Average Income*, and *Equivalisation scales*.
2 Data from 1993/94 onwards are for financial years; data for 1994/95 onwards exclude Northern Ireland.
Source: Institute for Fiscal Studies

where the head or spouse were aged 60 or over had low incomes in 2000/01. The pattern according to economic status was similar in 1981, though as we have already seen from Figure 5.18 the overall risk of low income was lower at that time.

When income is measured after the deduction of housing costs, the proportions of individuals with low incomes are generally higher than before the deduction of housing costs, whatever their economic status. This is principally because housing costs for low-income households are large in relation to their income as a whole. This relationship applies not only to the results in Table 5.19 but those in Figures 5.21 and 5.23.

The existence of income from employment is not always sufficient to lift a household out of low income. For people in some occupations

Table **5.19**

Individuals in households with incomes below 60 per cent of median disposable income:[1] by economic activity status

Great Britain[2]

Percentages

	1981	1991/92	1996/97	1999/00	2000/01
Income before deduction of housing costs					
Head or spouse unemployed	52	71	62	62	64
Head or spouse aged 60 or over	19	31	24	24	24
One or more in part-time work	24	26	25	25	22
Self-employed[3]	13	19	19	21	19
One in full-time work, one not working	8	12	15	14	14
One in full-time, one in part-time work	2	3	3	3	3
Single or couple, all in full-time work	1	2	2	2	2
Other[4]	36	51	42	42	42
All	13	21	18	18	17
Income after deduction of housing costs					
Head or spouse unemployed	57	76	78	76	77
Head or spouse aged 60 or over	23	36	30	29	28
One or more in part-time work	27	32	32	33	29
Self-employed[3]	15	24	22	24	25
One in full-time work, one not working	9	17	20	20	20
One in full-time work, one in part-time work	3	5	4	5	5
Single or couple, all in full-time work	1	2	3	4	4
Other[4]	45	62	64	63	61
All	15	25	25	23	23

1 Equivalised household disposable income. See Appendix, Part 5: Households Below Average Income, and Equivalisation scales.
2 Data for 1981 and 1991/92 are based on the Family Expenditure Survey which covers the United Kingdom. Data for 1996/97 and 1998/99 are based on the Family Resources Survey which covers Great Britain only.
3 Those in benefit units which contain one or more adults who are normally self-employed for 31 or more hours a week.
4 Includes long-term sick and disabled people and non-working single-parents.
Source: Households Below Average Income series, Department for Work and Pensions

and industries, wage rates may be so low that their household income may still be insufficient for them to support a family adequately. The aim of Working Families' Tax Credit, which replaced Family Credit from 5 October 1999, is to guarantee a minimum income to working families with children.

The national minimum wage (NMW), which came into force in April 1999, is another measure to combat the phenomenon of the 'working poor'. The NMW has had an impact on the earnings distribution. In spring 1998, before the introduction of the NMW, about 6 per cent of jobs of employees aged 22 and over were paid at less than the rates at which it was first introduced in 1999 (Table 5.20 - see overleaf). The proportion then fell to about 2 per cent in spring 1999 and fell further to 1 per cent in spring 2002. However, the likelihood of

being paid less than the NMW varies according to age, employment status and sex. Overall, women were more than twice as likely as men to have a job with hourly pay below the NMW in spring 2002, but the group most at risk were males working part-time, followed by female part-timers. Young people aged between 18 and 21 are also more likely than those aged over 21 to be paid at rates below the NMW. Note that these estimates cannot be used as a measure of non-compliance because it is not possible to discern from the data sources whether an individual is eligible for minimum wage rates.

The population of each region within the United Kingdom differs in age structure, labour market conditions and other social characteristics, which in turn result in varying proportions of people living on low incomes.

Figure 5.21 shows that the highest proportion of people living in low-income households was to be found in the North East region in 2000/01, and the lowest proportion was in the South East region, whether income is measured before or after the deduction of housing costs. However, these proportions mask what can be very large differences between localities within regions.

For some people, for example students and those unemployed for only a brief period, the experience of low income may be a relatively transient one, whereas for others it may be a more-or-less permanent state through their life times. The British Household Panel Survey (BHPS) provides longitudinal data which allow income mobility and the persistence of low income to be analysed. Table 5.22 shows that although around half of individuals had had some experience of living in households with income below 60 per cent of the median over the period 1991 to 2000, only 2 per cent were on low incomes throughout the period. This finding corroborates academic research that has examined different types of low-income trajectories and found that a considerable proportion of the population were 'blipping' in and out of low income or experiencing repeated spells of low income.

The Government's *Opportunity For All* indicators use alternative definitions of 'persistence' of low incomes to that used in Table 5.22, taking those individuals with incomes below 60 per cent and those below 70 per cent of the median in at least three out of four years. Based on the first of these definitions and again using BHPS data, over the period 1997-2000 16 per cent of children experienced persistent low income compared with 17 per cent of pensioners and only 7 per cent of working age adults. Between 1991 and 2000 there are indications of a decrease in the risk of persistent low incomes for children.

Children are disproportionately present in low-income households: 21 per cent of children (2.7 million) were living in households with below 60 per cent of median income (before deduction of housing costs) in Great Britain in 2000/01 (Figure 5.23). This proportion rose steeply between 1979 and 1981 from 12 per cent to 18 per cent and continued to rise to reach a peak of 27 per cent in 1992/93. It fell

Table **5.20**

Jobs paid below National Minimum Wage rates:[1] by age, sex and employment status[2]

United Kingdom | | | | | Percentages

	1998[3]	1999	2000	2001	2002
Age					
18 to 21	7.3	2.3	2.2	2.1	2.5
22 and over	5.9	2.2	0.9	0.9	1.2
Male employees					
Full-time	2.1	0.9	0.3	0.3	0.5
Part-time	15.8	7.3	4.0	4.6	4.1
All male employees	3.3	1.5	0.7	0.7	0.8
Female employees					
Full-time	3.9	1.2	–	–	0.7
Part-time	15.2	4.9	2.3	2.4	3.4
All female employees	9.1	2.9	1.3	1.3	1.9

1 Prior to 2001, figures are for jobs paid less than £3.00 per hour (for those aged 18-21) or £3.60 (for those aged 22 and over). In 2001 the hourly rate for the lower age group is £3.20, with £3.70 for those aged 22 and over, and in 2002 the rates are £3.50 and £4.10 respectively.
2 At spring.
3 Figures for 1998 are before the National Minimum Wage was introduced.
Source: Office for National Statistics

Figure **5.21**

Individuals living in households below 60 per cent median income: by region, 2000/01

Great Britain

Percentages

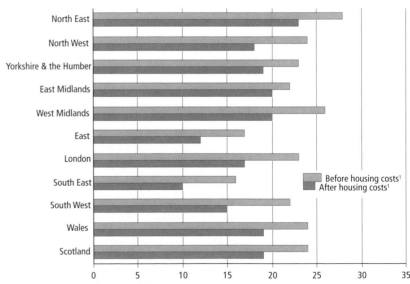

1 Equivalised household disposable income. See Appendix, Part 5: Households Below Average Income, and Equivalisation scales.
Source: Households Below Average Income series, Department for Work and Pensions

Table **5.22**

Proportion of individuals experiencing periods of persistent low income,[1] 1991 to 2000

Great Britain   Percentages

	Below 60% median income	Below 70% median income
Number of years spent below specified income threshold		
At least one year	49	59
At least 5 years	15	25
At least 7 years	8	16
All 10 years	2	5

1 Equivalised household disposable income before housing costs. See Appendix, Part 5: Households Below Average Income, and Equivalisation scales.

Source: Department for Work and Pensions from British Household Panel Survey, Institute for Economic and Social Research

Figure **5.23**

Proportion of children living in households below 60 per cent of median income[1]

United Kingdom

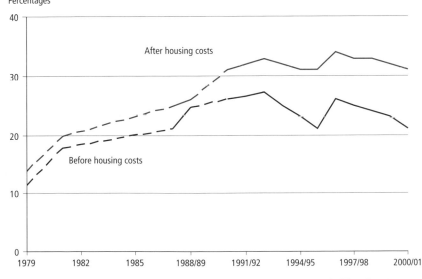

1 Equivalised household disposable income. See Appendix, Part 5: Households Below Average Income, and Equivalisation scales. Data are not available for 1980 and 1982 to 1986/87. Data from 1979 to 1993/94 are for United Kingdom from the Family Expenditure Survey and a two-year moving average has been used from 1987/88 to 1993/94; from 1994/95 onwards data are for Great Britain from the Family Resources Survey.

Source: Households Below Average Income series, Department for Work and Pensions

back during the first half of the 1990s but then rose again to 26 per cent in 1996/97 since when the pattern has been very similar to that of the early 1990s. If housing costs are deducted from income, the pattern of annual change during the 1990s is much the same, but at a level around 10 percentage points higher, resulting in nearly 4 million children living in low-income households in 2000/01 on this basis.

Children living in workless families have a much higher risk of low income than those in families with one or more adults in full-time work. Around half of children living in workless lone parent families and around two thirds of children living in workless couple families in 2000/01 were living in households with below 60 per cent of median income (before deduction of housing costs). If housing costs are deducted, these proportions rose to three quarters for children in both workless couple and lone parent families. Other risk factors include being part of a large family, being in a family headed by someone from a minority ethnic group, particularly where the head is of Pakistani or Bangladeshi origin.

Children living in low-income families may experience disadvantage in terms both of their health and education. Table 5.24 (overleaf) shows that in 2000, 30 per cent of lone parent families in Great Britain where the adult worked less than 16 hours a week or not at all and 21 per cent of lone parent families that were eligible for but not receiving Working Families' Tax Credit contained one or more children with a long-standing illness or disability. For couple families, the proportions ranged from 27 per cent to 37 per cent. The proportion of these lone parent households with children having a Special Educational Need ranged between 11 and 21 per cent and the corresponding proportion for couple families ranged between 14 and 24 per cent. Exclusions from school were more common within lone parent and couple households working less than 16 hours a week or not at all than for other work/benefit status groups. However, the survey also indicates that permanent exclusions were very rare among all work/benefit status groups – less than one per cent in each group had one or more children permanently excluded from school.

Table **5.24**

Health and school exclusions of children living in selected family types:[1] by work/benefit status of family, 2000

Great Britain
Percentages

	Lone parent families			Couple families		
	Working less than 16 hours or none[2]	Working Families Tax Credit recipient	Eligible for but not receiving Working Families Tax Credit	Working less than 16 hours or none[2]	Working Families Tax Credit recipient	Eligible for but not receiving Working Families Tax Credit
Containing children with long-standing illness or disability						
None	70	74	79	63	67	73
One or more	30	26	21	37	32	27
Containing children identified at school as having a Special Educational Need						
None	79	86	90	76	81	87
One or more	21	14	11	24	19	14
Containing children who have been excluded from school						
None	93	96	96	89	95	97
One or more	8	4	4	11	4	3

1 Excludes families where one or both parents are self-employed.
2 Respondent (and any partner) not working 16 or more hours per week and therefore not eligible for WFTC.
Source: Families and Children Study 2000, Department for Work and Pensions

Wealth

Although the terms 'wealthy' and 'high income' are often used interchangeably, in fact they relate to quite distinct concepts. 'Income' represents a flow of resources over a period, received either in cash or in kind. 'Wealth' on the other hand describes the ownership of assets valued at a particular point in time. These assets may provide the owner with a flow of income, for example interest payments on a building society account, or they may not, for example the ownership of works of art – unless of course the asset is sold. However, not all assets can be sold and their value realised. In particular, an individual's stake in an occupational pension scheme often cannot be 'cashed in'. The distinction is therefore usually made between 'marketable wealth' which the owner can sell if they so desire, and 'non-marketable wealth'. Wealth may be accumulated either by the acquisition of new assets, or by the increase in value of existing assets.

The wealth of the household sector in the United Kingdom, net of any loans outstanding on the purchase of assets such as housing, has

shown strong growth in recent years increasing by an average of 4.1 per cent per year between 1987 and 2001 after adjusting for inflation (Table 5.25). Non-financial assets such as the value of residential dwellings formed the most important component of the wealth of the household sector in 2001, though the largest category of liability is loans secured on dwellings. Growth in the value of the stock of non-financial assets was 6.8 per cent between 2000 and 2001, reflecting the buoyant state of the housing market. The second most important component of household sector wealth in 2001 was holdings in life assurance and pension funds. The strong growth in this component of wealth over the last 15 years or so has resulted both from increases in the contributions paid into occupational pension schemes as well as increased take-up of personal pension provision. Table 8.19 in Chapter 8: Social Protection shows how pension provision for those of working age varies between age groups and type of work.

Stocks and shares also grew in importance between 1987 and 2001. However, both holdings in life assurance and pension funds

Table **5.25**

Composition of the net wealth[1] of the household sector

United Kingdom   £ billion at 2001[2] prices

	1987	1991	1996	2000	2001
Non-financial assets	1,660	1,803	1,603	2,398	2,562
Financial assets					
Life assurance and pension funds	637	778	1,168	1,667	1,468
Securities and shares	261	323	447	762	576
Currency and deposits	410	487	536	644	692
Other assets	68	82	79	88	93
Total assets	3,036	3,473	3,832	5,559	5,391
Financial liabilities					
Loans secured on dwellings	299	404	442	538	591
Other loans	92	108	102	148	165
Other liabilities	51	56	54	59	59
Total liabilities	442	568	598	744	815
Total net wealth	2,594	2,905	3,235	4,815	4,573

1 See Appendix, Part 5: Net wealth of the household sector.
2 Adjusted to 2001 prices using the expenditure deflator for the household sector.
Source: Office for National Statistics

and in securities and shares fell steeply in value in real terms between 2000 and 2001, by 14 per cent and 33 per cent respectively, reflecting the fall in stock market values. These falls were the main contributors to a reduction in the net wealth of the household sector of 5 per cent between 2000 and 2001.

Wealth is considerably less evenly distributed than income. Life cycle effects mean that this will almost always be so: people build up assets during the course of their working lives and then draw them down during the years of retirement with the residue passing to others at their death. It is estimated that the most wealthy 1 per cent of individuals owned between a sixth and a quarter of the total wealth of the household sector in the last decade (Table 5.26). In contrast, half the population shared between them only 6 per cent of total wealth in 2000. If the value of housing is omitted from the wealth estimates, the resulting distribution is even more skewed indicating that this form of wealth is rather more evenly distributed than the remainder.

This analysis of the aggregate data available on the distribution of wealth is borne out by information available from the Family

Table **5.26**

Distribution of wealth[1]

United Kingdom   Percentages

	1976	1981	1986	1991	1996	1999	2000
Marketable wealth							
Percentage of wealth owned by:[2]							
Most wealthy 1%	21	18	18	17	20	23	22
Most wealthy 5%	38	36	36	35	40	43	42
Most wealthy 10%	50	50	50	47	52	54	54
Most wealthy 25%	71	73	73	71	74	74	74
Most wealthy 50%	92	92	90	92	93	94	94
Total marketable wealth (£ billion)	280	565	955	1,711	2,092	2,861	2,968
Marketable wealth less value of dwellings							
Percentage of wealth owned by:[2]							
Most wealthy 1%	29	26	25	29	26	34	32
Most wealthy 5%	47	45	46	51	49	59	57
Most wealthy 10%	57	56	58	64	63	72	72
Most wealthy 25%	73	74	75	80	81	87	88
Most wealthy 50%	88	87	89	93	94	97	99

1 See Appendix, Part 5: Distribution of personal wealth. Estimates for individual years should be treated with caution as they are affected by sampling error and the particular pattern of deaths in that year.
2 Adults aged 18 and over.
Source: Inland Revenue

Resources Survey based on individuals' own estimates of their savings. In 2000/01, about a third of households in Great Britain reported having no savings at all (Table 5.27). Savings patterns vary with economic status. Couples where one or both partner were aged 60 or over are the most likely to have substantial savings – about a fifth had savings of £20,000 or more, nearly twice the proportion in the population as a whole. This is perhaps not surprising since they may have had the opportunity to build up their savings over their working lives. Families where the head or their spouse is unemployed or sick/disabled were the least likely to have any savings.

The term 'financial exclusion' has been coined to describe those people who do not use financial services at all. Data from the Family Resources Survey indicate that in 2000/01, 8 per cent of individuals did not have any kind of current account (including Post Office account) or investments such as savings accounts or premium bonds. This proportion rose to 21 per cent of individuals living in households with an income below 60 per cent of the median (before deduction of housing costs). Since the options for operating a household budget without mainstream financial services are more expensive and often unregulated, this is of policy concern.

National income and expenditure

Gross domestic product (GDP) measures the level of income generated by economic activity in the United Kingdom in accordance with international conventions. Figure 5.1 at the beginning of this chapter showed that, when adjusted for inflation, the trend in GDP per head since 1971 has generally been one of steady growth. However, within this long-term trend the United Kingdom is nevertheless subject to cycles of weaker and stronger growth, usually referred to as the economic or business cycle.

Table **5.27**

Savings: by economic status of benefit unit and amount, 2000/01

Great Britain   Percentages

	No savings	Less than £1,500	£1,500 but less than £10,000	£10,000 but less than £20,000	£20,000 or more	All households (millions=100%)
Self-employed	21	25	28	10	15	1.9
Single or couple, both in full-time work	29	30	26	7	7	7.7
Couple, one in full-time work, one in part-time work	17	26	32	11	13	2.5
Couple, one in full-time work, one not working	25	24	26	10	15	2.3
One or more in part-time work	40	24	16	7	14	2.3
Head or spouse aged 60 or over	27	17	25	10	21	7.3
Head or spouse unemployed	73	19	5	1	2	1.0
Head or spouse sick or disabled	70	16	7	2	4	1.7
Other benefit units	64	17	10	2	7	1.4
All benefit units	34	23	23	8	12	28.1

Source: Family Resources Survey, Department for Work and Pensions

Figure **5.28**

Annual growth in gross domestic product at constant prices[1]
United Kingdom

Percentages

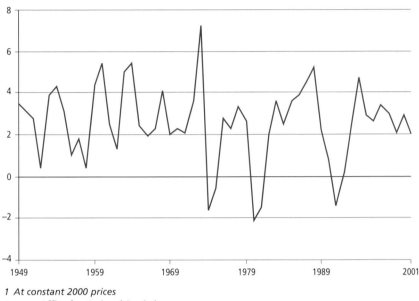

1 At constant 2000 prices
Source: Office for National Statistics

Table **5.29**

Gross domestic product[1] per head: EU comparison

Index (EU=100)

	1991	1996	2000
Luxembourg[2]	161	169	197
Denmark	110	121	119
Irish Republic	77	94	116
Austria	109	112	114
Netherlands[2]	104	109	113
Belgium	107	111	107
Germany	107	108	105
Italy	106	104	105
Finland	94	97	104
Sweden[2]	106	102	101
France	110	101	101
United Kingdom	97	100	100
Spain[2]	81	79	82
Portugal[2]	65	71	73
Greece	61	67	68

1 Gross domestic product at current market prices using current purchasing power standard
and compiled on the basis of the European System of Accounts 1995.
2 Figure for 1991 is an estimate.
Source: Eurostat

The year on year growth rates for GDP, adjusted to remove the effects of inflation, shown in Figure 5.28 suggest that the UK's economy contracted in the mid-1970s, at the time of the OPEC oil crisis, and again in the early 1980s and early 1990s. However, growth has exceeded 4 per cent per year ten times in the post-war period, most recently in 1994. The long-term average annual growth rate was 2.6 per cent between 1948 and 2001, somewhat higher than the growth of 2.0 per cent between 2000 and 2001. In 1995, the base year for these figures, two thirds of gross value added was from the services sector, compared to a quarter from the production sector. Agriculture accounted for less than 2 per cent, and construction for about 5 per cent.

A comparison of GDP per head across the countries of the European Union (EU) in 2000 shows that Luxembourg, where the financial sector dominates the economy, had the highest level of economic activity, nearly twice the EU average (Table 5.29). The gap between Luxembourg and the rest of the EU has grown during the 1990s. At the other end of the scale, Portugal and Greece had GDP per head about a quarter and a third below the EU average respectively, though in both countries it has grown relative to the EU average during the 1990s. Other countries were clustered more closely around the EU average in 2000, with the United Kingdom, France, Finland, Germany, Italy and Sweden all lying within 5 percentage points of the average. The most dramatic increase between 1991 and 2000 in GDP per head was for the Irish Republic, which rose from 77 per cent of the EU average in 1991 to 16 per cent above the average in 2000. These estimates have been converted to a common basis making adjustments for the relative purchasing power of national currencies.

One of the features of GDP as conventionally calculated is that it does not measure and place a monetary value on the outputs produced by households where these are unpaid – for example, unpaid childcare, house maintenance, food preparation and transport services. Experimental estimates have been made by the Office for National Statistics of gross value added for a range of household services, and these are illustrated in Figure 5.30. Details of the methodology may be found in the Appendix, Part 5: Household Satellite Account.

Housing and tenant services (which represents the value of clean, warm, furnished accommodation provided by owner–occupied households as well as the provision of furnishings and maintenance by tenants) forms the largest contribution to the value added by households, followed by informal childcare. Nutrition represents the value of meals and hot drinks prepared in the home and clothing, a very minor contribution to household value added, represents the value of clothes made or repaired at home. In total, value added by informal household production is estimated at £693 billion in 2000, compared with GDP as conventionally measured (less adjustments to avoid double-counting) of £892 billion.

Government receives income primarily through transfers from individuals, companies and other organisations in the form of taxes, national insurance contributions and other payments, though they may also engage in economic activity from which income is derived. This revenue is then spent on the

Figure 5.30

Gross value added by households,[1] 2000

United Kingdom

£ billion

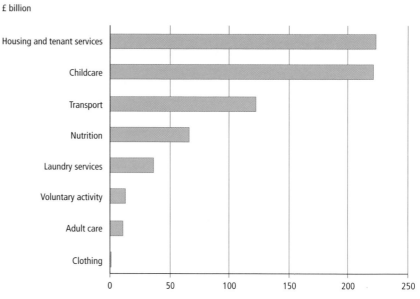

1 See Appendix, Part 5: Household Satellite Account.
Source: UK Household Satellite Account, Office for National Statistics

Table 5.31

Expenditure of general government in real terms:[1] by function

United Kingdom

£ billion at 2001 prices[1]

	1987	1991	1996	1998	1999	2000	2001
Social protection	108	122	145	143	145	148	159
Health	36	41	48	50	54	56	61
Education	34	35	40	41	43	43	47
Defence	34	34	27	27	26	29	28
Public order and safety	13	17	18	19	19	20	19
General public services	8	13	16	17	18	19	19
Housing and community amenities	11	12	7	6	5	4	5
Recreation, culture and religion	4	6	5	5	5	5	5
Other economic affairs and environmental protection[2]	27	29	32	26	25	28	31
Gross debt interest	32	24	32	33	27	27	24
All expenditure	308	332	370	365	366	379	398

1 Adjusted to 2001 prices using the GDP market prices deflator.
2 Includes expenditure on transport and communication, agriculture, forestry and fishing, mining, manufacture, construction, fuel and energy and services.
Source: Office for National Statistics

provision of goods and services such as health care and education, on servicing government debt, and on transfer payments such as social security benefits. The sum of all such expenditure and transfer payments net of requited receipts is known as general government expenditure (GGE) and it is this measure which until recently has been used to analyse trends in public expenditure. The present Government's main measure of public expenditure is however total managed expenditure: one of the main differences between this aggregate and GGE is that it excludes privatisation proceeds.

Although the way in which public expenditure is allocated to different purposes depends on government policy priorities, significant shifts in expenditure patterns tend only to be discernible over a relatively long time period. Over the last fifteen years, by far the most important category of expenditure in the United Kingdom both in cash terms and as a percentage of total expenditure has been social protection – for example, social security benefits (Table 5.31). Government expenditure on social protection rose by nearly 50 per cent in real terms between 1987 and 2001, and accounted for 40 per cent of expenditure in 2001 compared with 35 per cent in 1987. Expenditure on health and education also rose in real terms during the 1990s but expenditure on defence and on housing and community amenities both fell.

As well as expenditure for purely domestic purposes, total managed expenditure also includes the contributions made by the United Kingdom to the EC budget. In 2000, the United Kingdom contributed €13.9 billion (£8.5 billion) and had receipts amounting to €7.7 billion (£4.7 billion) (Table 5.32). Germany was the largest net contributor, with contributions exceeding receipts by €11.7 billion. The table shows that Finland, the Irish Republic, Portugal, Greece and Spain were net recipients from the EC budget in 2000.

Of total EC expenditure in 2001, just under half was budgeted to be spent in support of agriculture in the form of Agricultural Guarantee. Although still substantial, this proportion has fallen by 15 percentage points since 1981, while structural funds expenditure has risen in importance. Structural funds aim to reduce regional disparities and thus to achieve a more even social and economic balance across the EU. The areas within the United Kingdom currently eligible for EU Structural Funds include Cornwall, West Wales and the Valleys, South Yorkshire and Merseyside.

Table **5.32**

Contributions to and receipts[1] from the EC budget,[2] 2000

€ billion

	Contributions	Receipts	Indicative net receipts
Germany	21.8	10.1	−11.7
United Kingdom	13.9	7.7	−6.2
Netherlands	5.5	2.2	−3.3
France	14.5	12.1	−2.4
Sweden	2.6	1.2	−1.5
Belgium	3.4	1.9	−1.5
Austria	2.1	1.4	−0.7
Italy	11.0	10.7	−0.3
Luxembourg	0.2	0.1	−0.1
Denmark	1.7	1.6	−0.1
Finland	1.2	1.4	0.1
Irish Republic	1.1	2.6	1.5
Portugal	1.3	3.2	1.9
Greece	1.3	5.5	4.1
Spain	6.4	10.8	4.3

1 Excludes gains from spending on administration or other institutions.
2 See Appendix, Part 5: Contributions to and receipts from the EC budget.
Source: European Commission and European Court of Auditors

Chapter 6

Expenditure

Household and personal expenditure

- Total UK household expenditure in real terms grew at an annual rate of 4.1 per cent in 2001 which was comparable with growth rates in recent years. (Figure 6.1)

- In 2001/02, UK households with the household reference person in full-time employment spent an average of nearly £520 per week, 34 per cent more than households with the head in part-time employment and more than double for households where the head was unemployed. (Table 6.3)

- For UK retired households mainly dependent on state pension in 2001/02, households with two adults had an average weekly expenditure on transport more than four times than those comprising a single adult. (Table 6.5)

- Nearly a quarter of all adults in Great Britain had used the Internet by July 2002 to order goods or services including travel, tickets for events, books, magazines, music and CDs. (Page 121)

Transactions and credit

- Following a slowdown in the use of cash machines in 2000, reflecting a public reaction to the possibility of charges being introduced for withdrawing cash, the use of UK cash machines recovered in 2001 dispensing £128 billion, nearly half of all cash withdrawn. (Page 122)

- In Great Britain, nine out of ten adults aged 16 and over owned at least one plastic card in 2001 while 86 per cent owned a debit card and 62 per cent a credit/charge card. (Table 6.10)

- UK household borrowing, excluding lending secured on dwellings, increased over the year and reached the highest level ever recorded in the fourth quarter of 2001 before falling slightly in the first two quarters of 2002. (Figure 6.11)

- During 2001, nearly 30,000 individuals in England and Wales became insolvent, of these 79 per cent were declared bankrupt by a court and 21 per cent made a voluntary agreement with their creditors. (Figure 6.12)

Prices

- Inflation measured by the retail prices index was consistently below 2 per cent in the United Kingdom between January and September 2002 but increased in later months to 2.6 per cent in November 2002. (Figure 6.13)

- A visitor from the United Kingdom would have found only two EU countries, Sweden and Denmark, more expensive than the United Kingdom in 2000. (Figure 6.17)

The amount households spend on goods and services provides an indication of their standard of living and material wellbeing. How people choose to spend their income has changed over time; this reflects changes in society and consumer preferences and the growth in choices available to the consumer. Patterns of expenditure also vary within society; the region in which people live, their age, sex and income are just some of the factors that influence levels and patterns of spending.

Household and personal expenditure

The level of spending by households on goods and services has a major impact on the economic well being of a country and on society in general. At constant prices, which allows for inflation, annual household expenditure in the United Kingdom has more than doubled over the last 30 years (Figure 6.1). This represents an average increase in expenditure of 2.9 per cent each year. There were periods, most notably in the mid-1970s and early 1990s, when household expenditure fell as a result of general economic downturns. However, in spite of the economic and other world wide uncertainties which occurred in 2001, household expenditure grew at an annual rate of 4.1 per cent.

The changes in household spending since 1971 are shown in Table 6.2 in terms of indices at constant prices. Over the past 30 years, the categories with the greatest growth have been household expenditure abroad and communication. Spending on these two categories in 2001 were nearly seven and eight times their 1971 levels respectively. However, actual spending in 2001 for both of these categories was relatively small compared with spending on housing, water and fuel, and on transport. Alcohol and tobacco was the only category where household expenditure fell over the 30 year period, although it has remained level since 1991 and may be subject to under-reporting.

Figure 6.1

Household expenditure at constant prices[1]

United Kingdom

£ billion

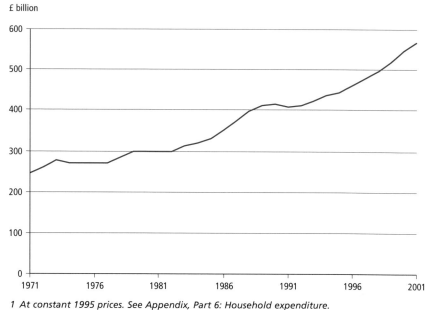

1 At constant 1995 prices. See Appendix, Part 6: Household expenditure.
Source: Office for National Statistics

Table 6.2

Household expenditure[1,2]

United Kingdom   Indices[3] (1971=100)

	Indices at constant prices[3]					£ billion (current prices)
	1971	1981	1991	2000	2001	2001
Housing, water and fuel	100	117	137	151	152	112.7
Transport	100	127	181	235	248	91.8
Recreation and culture	100	160	279	527	571	76.8
Miscellaneous	100	119	230	280	280	75.5
Restaurant and hotels	100	126	167	191	189	70.7
Food and non-alcoholic drink	100	104	117	136	137	60.3
Clothing and footwear	100	120	187	313	350	37.4
Household goods and services	100	116	159	243	256	37.2
Alcohol and tobacco	100	99	92	92	92	25.4
Communication	100	191	306	697	786	13.8
Education	100	160	199	280	274	10.0
Health	100	124	182	175	180	9.5
Less expenditure by foreign tourists, etc	100	152	187	238	203	−12.9
Household expenditure abroad	100	193	298	649	669	22.9
All household expenditure	100	121	167	223	232	631.0

1 See Appendix, Part 6: Household expenditure.
2 Reclassified to COICOP (see Appendix, Part 6: Classification of Individual Consumption by Purpose).
3 At constant 1995 prices.
Source: Office for National Statistics

Table **6.3**

Household expenditure:[1] by economic activity status of household reference person, 2001/02

United Kingdom

£ per week[2]

	Employees		Self-employed	ILO unemployed	Economically inactive		All households
	Full-time	Part-time			Retired	Other	
Transport	79.20	57.20	88.00	24.00	23.50	37.40	57.70
Recreation and culture	70.70	53.60	69.90	34.50	29.20	37.60	54.00
Food and non-alcoholic drink	46.90	41.20	51.70	33.90	32.10	38.10	41.70
Housing, water and fuel	41.20	42.50	41.60	28.10	26.30	30.40	35.90
Restaurants and hotels	45.80	31.00	49.50	18.50	13.30	24.30	33.50
Miscellaneous goods and services	39.50	28.20	42.70	14.90	18.80	18.90	30.60
Household goods and services	37.10	32.20	45.20	14.20	18.20	24.30	30.40
Clothing and footwear	30.40	23.60	28.70	15.40	10.20	17.50	22.70
Alcohol and tobacco	14.00	10.60	13.50	11.20	5.90	11.90	11.40
Communication	12.70	11.70	14.40	8.50	5.60	8.50	10.40
Education	7.60	7.70	15.60	0.60	0.40	2.00	5.50
Health	5.80	3.40	4.50	1.20	3.90	2.40	4.50
Other expenditure items	85.50	43.60	111.30	20.40	22.60	25.60	59.50
All household expenditure	516.50	386.50	576.80	225.30	209.90	279.00	397.70

1 See Appendix, Part 6: Household expenditure.
2 Expenditure rounded to the nearest 10 pence.
Source: Expenditure and Food Survey, Office for National Statistics

The greatest increases in spending between 2000 and 2001 were on clothing and footwear and on communication which increased by 12 per cent and 13 per cent respectively. This was followed by spending on recreation and culture which increased by 8 per cent. Over the same period there was a marked decrease in spending by foreign tourists (15 per cent).

The broad categories of household expenditure which have been used in Table 6.2 are based on a new international classification (see Appendix, Part 6: Classification of individual consumption by purpose). The data are therefore inconsistent with those published in previous editions of Social Trends. Where relevant this new classification has also been used in the remaining tables in this section.

Average weekly household expenditure varies according to a number of household characteristics, such as the economic activity status of the household reference person. This classification has been introduced in the 2001/02 Expenditure and Food Survey (EFS) to replace the head of household (see Appendix, Part 6: Household reference person). On this basis, average weekly household expenditure is highest for households where the household reference person is self-employed (Table 6.3).

For households where the household reference person is in employment, spending is a third higher for those in full-time work compared with those working part-time. Retired households have the lowest expenditure of all the groups shown with their expenditure only 36 per cent of that of self-employed households.

There is less variability by economic activity status for some essential items such as food and non-alcoholic drink. In contrast, there were marked differences in spending on other items with retired households spending only a quarter of the amount spent by the self-employed households on both transport and restaurants and hotels.

On average, households with children spend more than those without children, and couple households spend more than single adult households. This is partly a reflection of the number of people in the household and its income. However, this pattern differs for some less essential items. For example, average weekly spending on restaurant meals and holidays abroad was greater for couples or single adults with no children than for those with children (Table 6.4). Among households without children, average expenditure of couple households was almost double that of single adult households. However, expenditure on holidays abroad by couples with no children was over three times the level of expenditure by single adults.

Retired households also spent different levels according to whether there were one or two adults and whether the household was mainly dependent on state pensions (Table 6.5). Among households mainly dependent on state pensions, those with two adults had an average weekly expenditure of £193, nearly double the expenditure of £101 for those comprising a single adult. For households mainly dependent on sources of income other than state pensions and benefits, the average weekly expenditure of a two adult household was £303 which is about one and a half times that of comparable single pensioner households. However, the pattern varies across the different spending categories.

There is a much smaller difference in spending on housing, water and fuel between single and two adult households for both groups. In addition, communication spending, although relatively low, is between £4.20 and £6.20 per week for all four groups. Conversely, single adult households reliant on the state pension have low transport costs of less than £5 per week which is a quarter of the amount spent by two adult state pension households. This may be mainly due to many single state pension households not owning a car and

Table 6.4

Household expenditure[1] on selected items: by family type,[2] 2001/02

United Kingdom £ per week[3]

	Couples		Singles	
	Dependent children	No children	Dependent children	No children
Restaurant meals	12.70	14.70	5.00	7.00
Take away meals	5.90	3.70	3.70	2.10
Confectionery	1.00	0.20	1.00	0.10
Ice cream	0.40	0.10	0.20	0.00
Holiday abroad	17.20	21.50	5.90	6.90
National Lottery and scratchcards	2.50	2.90	1.10	1.30
Newspapers	1.60	2.00	0.70	1.10
Cinema and theatre	1.70	1.30	0.90	1.10
All household expenditure	552.20	477.80	266.20	257.10

1 See Appendix, Part 6: Household expenditure.
2 Excludes retired families.
3 Expenditure rounded to the nearest 10 pence.
Source: Expenditure and Food Survey, Office for National Statistics

Table 6.5

Expenditure of retired households:[1] by whether or not mainly dependent on state pension, 2001/02

United Kingdom £ per week[2]

	1 adult		2 adults		
	State pension[3]	Other	State pension[3]	Other	All retired households
Food and non-alcoholic drink	20.60	23.10	36.80	43.00	32.10
Recreation and culture	11.40	24.40	28.00	45.90	29.20
Housing, water and fuel	19.00	27.80	26.50	29.70	26.30
Transport	4.50	18.80	20.50	41.60	23.50
Miscellaneous goods and services	8.30	21.30	15.20	24.70	18.80
Household goods and services	9.90	18.00	14.50	27.70	18.20
Restaurants and hotels	5.40	9.50	10.80	21.20	13.30
Clothing and footwear	5.20	7.70	8.20	16.10	10.20
Alcohol and tobacco	3.20	4.20	6.30	8.10	5.90
Communication	4.20	5.30	4.60	6.20	5.60
Health	1.70	3.20	3.70	6.30	3.90
Education	0.00	0.90	0.00	0.40	0.40
Other expenditure items	7.60	26.80	18.30	31.90	22.60
All household expenditure	101.00	191.00	193.40	302.90	209.90

1 Households where the household reference person is over state retirement age and is retired. See also Appendix, Part 6: Retired households, and Household expenditure.
2 Expenditure rounded to the nearest 10 pence.
3 At least three quarters of the total household income is derived from state pensions and other benefits.
Source: Expenditure and Food Survey, Office for National Statistics

Figure **6.6**

Household weekly expenditure:[1] by region, 1999–2002

United Kingdom

£ per week

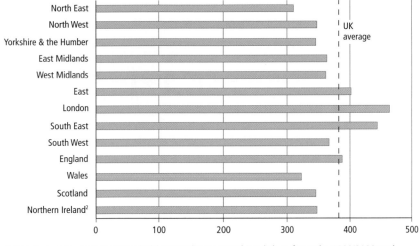

1 See Appendix, Part 6: Household expenditure. Combined data from the 1999/2000 and 2000/01 FES and 2001/02 EFS Surveys.

2 Northern Ireland data are calculated from an enhanced sample but the United Kingdom figures are calculated from the main FES/EFS samples. The data from the FES/EFS include expenditure by children; the Northern Ireland data relate to adults only.

Source: Family Expenditure Survey and Expenditure and Food Survey, Office for National Statistics; Northern Ireland Statistics and Research Agency

Table **6.7**

Household expenditure: on selected items by place of purchase, 2001/02

United Kingdom

Percentages

	Large supermarket chains	All other outlets
Potato products[1]	86	14
Fresh vegetables	84	16
Bread	76	24
Chocolate and confectionery products	60	40
Toiletries (disposable)	57	43
Milk	56	44
Petrol	29	71
Magazines and periodicals	26	74
Electrical consumables	22	78
Cosmetics and related accessories	17	83
Children's clothing	14	86
Newspapers	10	90

1 Includes crisps, savoury snacks, instant and frozen potato products.

Source: Expenditure and Food Survey, Office for National Statistics

having a greater dependency on public transport, which is subsidised for the retired in many areas. The Family Expenditure Survey (FES) reported that in 2000/01 only 15 per cent of single state pension households owned a car compared with 56 per cent of two adult state pension households.

Household expenditure also varied among the different regions of England and between the four countries within the United Kingdom. Due to sample size limitations, Figure 6.6 uses combined data from the 1999/2000 and 2000/01 FES and the 2001/02 EFS, to give an average for the three years. Average household expenditure was lowest in the North East of England and highest in London and the South East. One of the reasons for these regional differences is the variation in the cost of housing; this was a weekly household average of £47.90 in the North East, £90.80 in London and £76.80 in the South East. Wales, Scotland and Northern Ireland all had weekly household spending below that for England and spending differences are again partly due to housing costs. Average weekly household expenditure on housing was £34.70 in Northern Ireland, £46.10 in Wales and £53.80 in Scotland in comparison to £65.30 in England.

In recent years, supermarkets have expanded their range of goods to include items such as clothing, household goods and petrol. In 2001/02, over three quarters of expenditure on potato products, fresh vegetables and bread was at large supermarket chains (Table 6.7). On the other hand, only 10 per cent of spending on newspapers was at large supermarket chains. Of all household expenditure on petrol, 71 per cent was made at traditional forecourts and 29 per cent at large supermarket chains.

A more recent change in purchasing patterns has been the development of shopping through the Internet. The EFS reported that in the second quarter of 2002, 45 per cent of UK households had Internet access at home. The ONS Omnibus survey in July 2002 showed that nearly a quarter of all adults in Great Britain had ordered tickets, goods or services from the Internet. This represented 46 per cent of all those who had ever accessed the Internet for personal use.

The most popular purchases made by adults who had purchased goods or services on the Internet, in the three months prior to interview, were for travel (39 per cent), tickets for events (26 per cent), books or magazines (25 per cent) and music or CDs (20 per cent). Reasons for not making Internet purchases included security concerns and a preference for shopping in person.

Transactions and credit

The volume of retail sales in Great Britain has increased steadily over the last decade (Figure 6.8) and this continued in 2001 when the annual average increased by 6 per cent in comparison to 2000. Retail sales follow a strong seasonal pattern and peak in December of each year. The weekly average in December 2001 was just over a third higher than the average for the year as a whole. This was followed by the lowest period of sales for the year – the weekly average for the first quarter of 2002 was 30 per cent lower than the average for December 2001.

The manner in which transactions are undertaken has changed dramatically in the United Kingdom in the last ten years with a growth in the use of debit and credit cards, increased use of automated payments such as direct debits and standing orders, and a steady decline in personal cheques (Figure 6.9). This increase in automated payments is likely to continue in the next few years, partly as the Government switches to the payment of state benefit by automated means. There was a slowdown in the use of cash machines in 2000, which reflected a public reaction to the possibility of charges being introduced by some financial institutions for non-customers to withdraw money from their cash points. This contributed to a growth in the use of debit cards for cash-back at many retail outlets. The use of cash machines recovered in 2001 to dispense £128 billion in 2.2 billion transactions, providing nearly half of all cash withdrawn. Cash is still the norm for small transactions as nearly three quarters of all personal payments are made by cash. A cashless society is unlikely to become a reality in the medium to longer term.

Figure **6.8**

Volume of retail sales

Great Britain

Index (1995=100)

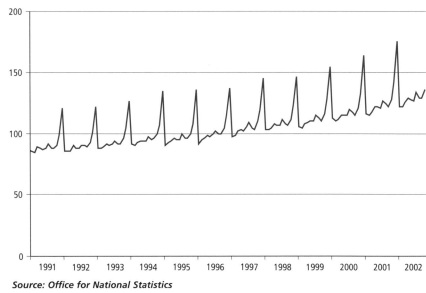

Source: Office for National Statistics

Figure **6.9**

Non-cash transactions:[1] by method of payment

United Kingdom

Billions

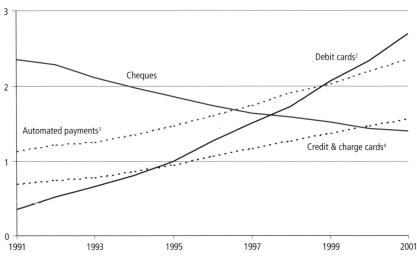

1 Figures are for payments only, cheque encashments and cash withdrawals from ATMs and branch counters using credit/charge and debit cards are not included.
2 Visa Debit and Switch cards in all years; includes Electron cards from 1996 and Solo cards from 1997.
3 Includes direct debits, standing orders, direct credits, inter-branch automated items.
4 Visa, Mastercards, travel/entertainment cards and store cards.
Source: Association for Payment Clearing Services

Table **6.10**

Plastic card holders:[1] by age, 2001

Great Britain
Percentages

	16–24	25–34	35–44	45–54	55–64	65 and over	All adults 16 and over
Any credit/charge card	31	61	70	71	68	65	62
Debit card	79	87	87	90	88	84	86
Store/retailer card	19	34	43	42	37	34	35
Cheque guarantee card	36	72	79	82	79	75	71
ATM card[2]	89	91	87	90	88	84	88
Any plastic card	90	94	92	93	90	84	90

1 Percentage of all adults in age group holding each type of card.
2 Cards used in ATM for cash withdrawals and other bank services. Includes single function ATM cards and multi-function debit cards, but excludes credit/charge cards, most of which can be used to access ATMs.

Source: Association for Payment Clearing Services

Figure **6.11**

Net borrowing[1] by consumers in real terms[2]

United Kingdom

£ billion at 2001 prices[3]

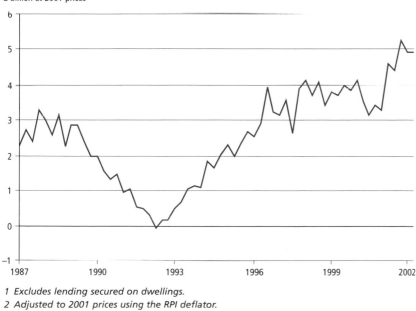

1 Excludes lending secured on dwellings.
2 Adjusted to 2001 prices using the RPI deflator.
3 Quarterly data, seasonally adjusted.

Source: Bank of England; Office for National Statistics

There were seven and a half times as many debit card transactions in 2001 than in 1991 and since 1999 this has been the most common form of non-cash payment. Debit cards are increasingly being used as an alternative to cash payments. During 2001 the average value per transaction for debit cards was £35, compared with £56 for credit cards. The average transaction for cheques was however much higher at £167 which may partly be due to cheques being the most popular way for cardholders to settle credit card bills.

Nine out of ten adults (aged 16 and over) in Great Britain held at least one plastic card in 2001 (Table 6.10). Ownership of debit and automated teller machine (ATM) cards were both nearly 90 per cent, while 71 per cent had a cheque guarantee card and 62 per cent a credit/charge card. Ownership of store/retailer cards was nearly half these rates, at 35 per cent. With the exception of debit and ATM cards, ownership rates of many plastic cards were much lower for young people aged 16-24. The ownership rate of plastic cards for this age group was only about half of the rate for the 25 and older age groups.

The high retail sales recorded during 2001 have been matched by high levels of borrowing. Annual net borrowing in the United Kingdom, in real terms, was at the highest level ever in 2001, at £17.6 billion. Net borrowing, at 2001 prices and seasonally adjusted, fell from the fourth quarter of 1987 to a low point in the second quarter of 1992 (Figure 6.11). It increased again up to 1996 and then fluctuated but generally remained level at the end of the 1990s. Although there was some economic uncertainty during 2001, borrowing increased over the year to reach the highest level ever recorded in the fourth quarter before falling slightly in the first two quarters of 2002.

High levels of borrowing can result in individuals being unable to meet their debt repayments and becoming insolvent. Where a court is satisfied that there is no prospect of the debt being paid, an individual can be declared bankrupt. However, in many cases, a voluntary arrangement is agreed between the debtor and their creditors. Following a sharp increase in the total number of individual insolvencies in England and Wales in the early 1990s, the number decreased steadily to around 24,400 in 1997 but then increased each year to reach 29,800 in 2001 (Figure 6.12). Nearly two thirds of individual bankruptcies were self-employed people in 1991, the rest comprising employees, the unemployed, directors of companies and those of unknown occupation. This pattern has been largely reversed over the last ten years and in 2001 the number of self-employed individuals who were declared bankrupt was only about 40 per cent of the total number of bankruptcies. Where possible, the courts encourage a voluntary arrangement to be agreed and Figure 6.12 shows that these increased between 1998 and 2000 before dropping to 21 per cent of all insolvencies in 2001.

Prices

How people and households choose to spend their money is affected by the price of goods and services that they want to buy. Monthly changes in the retail prices index (RPI) are used to measure the rate of inflation in the United Kingdom. The RPI monitors the cost of a representative shopping basket of over 650 selected goods and services which are bought by a typical household. The majority of prices are collected from retail outlets in 147 different locations throughout the United Kingdom, with prices for around 100 goods and services collected centrally by the ONS.

A small number of changes are made each year to the basket of goods to ensure that the RPI is still representative. Changes to the basket of goods in 2002 involved the removal of 19 items, including canned salmon, pipe tobacco and personal stereo radio cassette players. Twenty six new items were added such as frozen prawns, fabric roller blinds and DVD players. The changes in recent years reflect increasing household expenditure on electronic leisure goods, telecommunications, DIY and leisure activities.

Monthly levels of inflation have varied considerably over the last 40 years and exceeded 20 per cent during some periods in 1975, 1976 and 1980 (Figure 6.13). Inflation rates were generally below 5 per cent throughout most of the 1960s and again during the 1990s, and this continued into 2001. Between January and September 2002 monthly

Figure **6.12**

Number of individual insolvencies

England & Wales

Thousands

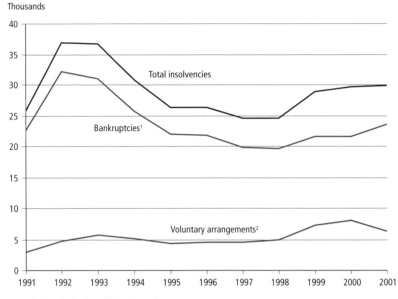

1 Individuals declared bankrupt by a court.
2 Individuals who make a voluntary agreement with their creditors.
Source: Department of Trade and Industry

Figure **6.13**

Retail prices index[1]

United Kingdom

Percentage change over 12 months

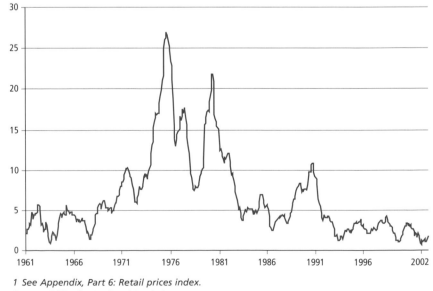

1 See Appendix, Part 6: Retail prices index.
Source: Office for National Statistics

Table **6.14**

Percentage change in retail prices index: 2001[1]

United Kingdom	Percentage change
Leisure services	6.0
Tobacco	5.4
Catering	4.0
Food	3.3
Personal goods and services	3.2
Fares and other travel costs	3.2
Housing	3.1
Alcoholic drink	2.1
Household services	1.1
Household goods	0.9
Fuel and light	0.8
Motoring expenditure	−0.6
Leisure goods	−2.1
Clothing and footwear	−4.3

1 Annual average percentage change on the previous year.
Source: Office for National Statistics

Table **6.15**

Average prices of selected items

United Kingdom		£ (current prices)	
	1991	1996	2001
Food items			
Cheddar cheese, per kg	3.44	4.59	5.10
Size 2 Eggs (65–75g), per dozen	1.18	1.58	1.72
Coffee – pure, instant, per 100g	1.30	1.89	1.81
Cod fillets, per kg	6.30	4.55	8.66
Best beef mince, per kg	3.55	3.42	4.22
Pasteurised milk, per pint	0.32	0.36	0.37
Corned beef, 340g can	1.00	0.95	0.97
White loaf, sliced, 800g	0.53	0.55	0.51
Granulated sugar, per kg	0.66	0.76	0.57
Non-food items			
Cigarettes, 20 king size filter	1.86	2.73	4.12
Unleaded petrol ordinary, per litre	0.45	0.57	0.76
Draught lager, per pint	1.37	1.73	2.03

Source: Office for National Statistics

inflation rates were consistently below 2 per cent and as low as 1 per cent in February and June. Inflation rates have, however, increased in recent months and were 2.1 per cent in October and 2.6 per cent in November 2002.

Table 6.14 shows the annual percentage change for the main components of the RPI in the United Kingdom between 2000 and 2001. The greatest change occurred in prices for leisure services, which increased by 6.0 per cent, while those for tobacco and catering increased by 5.4 per cent and 4.0 per cent, respectively. Three categories decreased in price with the largest reduction being for clothing and footwear at over 4 per cent.

The prices for individual items can change considerably over time. While most non-food items and services normally increase in price, many food items can fluctuate up or down due to production and supply levels which can be affected by weather conditions, stock levels, local or international agricultural policies, disruptions to supplies and, in recent years, health concerns. Table 6.15 shows the prices in 1991 and 2001 for selected items. Prices are also given for 1996 and these demonstrate that food prices can fluctuate. For example, coffee and sugar prices both increased between 1991 and 1996, but then fell in 2001. Over the ten years to 2001 most of the food items increased in price, with the increase in cheese and eggs being nearly 50 per cent. Three food items reduced in price, with sugar having the largest fall. The selected non-food items of cigarettes, unleaded petrol and draught lager, have all increased in price over the ten year period and are traditionally subject to high taxes. Tobacco and petrol duty rates have more than doubled between 1991 and 2001 to £1.85 per 20 cigarettes and nearly 49 pence per litre of unleaded petrol.

The European Union (EU) and European Central Bank (ECB) use the Harmonised Index of Consumer Prices (HICP) to compare inflation in each member state. The index is constructed using the same principles as the RPI but differs in a number of ways including the coverage of goods and services. For example, airfares and purchase of boats are included in the HICP but not in the RPI. Full details are given in the Appendix, Part 6: Harmonised Index of Consumer Prices.

The HICP is one of the key criteria used by the ECB to measure price stability within the Euro area. Within the EU, the United Kingdom had the lowest rate of inflation in 2001 at 1.2 per cent which was nearly half of the EU average of 2.3 per cent (Figure 6.16). France was 0.5 percentages points below the EU average at 1.8 per cent. Six countries were clustered around the EU average, including Germany and Italy. Rates in excess of 3 per cent occurred in four countries: Greece, the Irish Republic, Portugal and the Netherlands. Of these, the Netherlands had the highest average inflation rate; at 5.1 per cent it was more than double the EU average.

The international spending power of the pound depends on the relative price levels of goods and services and the exchange rates between countries. Comparative Price Levels (CPL) (see Appendix, Part 6: Comparative price levels) can be used to indicate whether another country will appear cheaper or more expensive to a UK visitor in a given year. Figure 6.17 gives CPLs for EU member states relative to the United Kingdom. Twelve EU states, and all ten candidate countries which have applied to join the EU in 2004, would have appeared cheaper to UK visitors in 2000. In four EU countries including Spain, the most popular holiday destination for UK residents (see Table 13.12 on page 230), prices would have appeared at least 20 per cent lower than in the UK; in Portugal prices were 37 per cent lower. A further six countries were grouped around the EU average, and would have seemed about 15 per cent cheaper. Only two countries, Sweden and Denmark, would have appeared more expensive to UK visitors in 2000.

Figure **6.16**

Percentage change in consumer prices:[1] EU comparison, 2001

Percentage change over 12 months

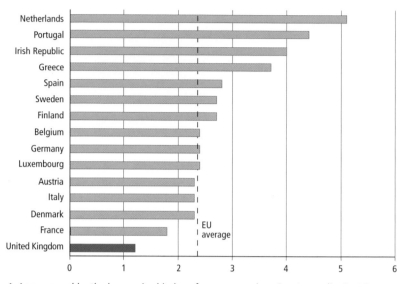

1 As measured by the harmonised index of consumer prices. See Appendix, Part 6: Harmonised Index of Consumer Prices.
Source: Office for National Statistics; Eurostat

Figure **6.17**

Comparative price levels[1] for household expenditure, EU comparison, 2000

Indices (UK=100)

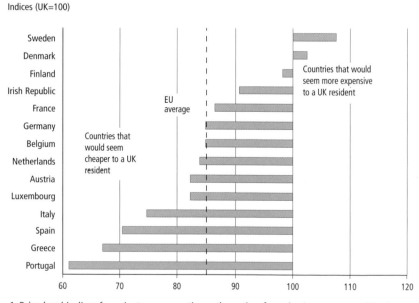

1 Price level indices for private consumption – the ratio of purchasing power parities to exchange rates.
Source: Eurostat

No. 33: 2003 edition

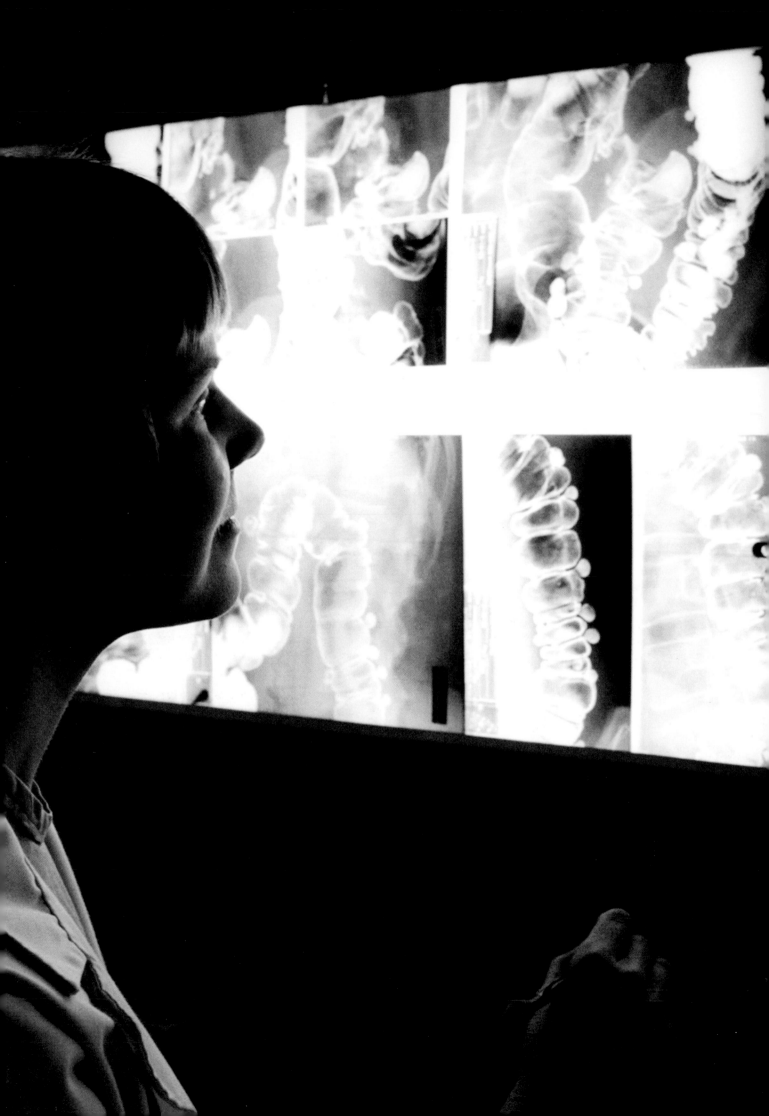

Chapter 7

Health

The nation's health

- Between 1996 and 2001 the rates of newly diagnosed cases of asthma in England and Wales declined from 46.4 to 29.3 per 100,000 females, and from 41.2 to 25.9 per 100,000 males. (Table 7.5)

- In 2001, chlamydia was the most common sexually transmitted infection diagnosed in genito-urinary clinics in England and Wales, with over 70,000 cases, a 10 per cent increase on 2000 and more than double the 30,000 cases diagnosed in 1995. (Table 7.7)

- Between 1991 and 2001 the number of prescription items for anti-depressant drugs dispensed in England more than doubled, from 9 million items in 1991 to 24 million in 2001. (Figure 7.9)

Causes of death

- In the period 1998 to 2000, cancers were the most common cause of death among girls aged 5 to 15 in England and Wales, accounting for 23 per cent of the total. Accidents were the most common cause of death among boys in this age group, representing 27 per cent of the total. (Table 7.10)

- Between 1993 and 2000 the number of drug-related poisoning deaths in England and Wales increased by a third to 3,000. (Table 7.14)

Lifestyle and diet

- In 2000, 39 per cent of men in the unskilled manual group in Great Britain reported being regular cigarette smokers compared with only 17 per cent in the professional group. Similarly, among women the proportions were 35 per cent and 14 per cent. (Table 7.16)

- In 1999, England and Wales and the Irish Republic had the highest proportions of young people using cannabis, amphetamines and cocaine in the EU. Cannabis was the most commonly used drug with 18 per cent of those aged 16 to 34 in England and Wales reporting that they had used it during the previous 12 months. (Figure 7.17)

- In 2001, over one in five males and females aged 16 and over in England were classified as obese, and a further half of men and third of women were classified as overweight. (Figure 7.20)

Prevention

- Concerns by some parents over the safety of the MMR (measles, mumps, rubella) combined vaccine have led to a fall in the number of children in the United Kingdom immunised against MMR by their second birthday, from 91 per cent in 1997/98 to 88 per cent in 2000/01. (Table 7.22)

- Results from the NHS smoking cessation services in England show that in 2001/02, of the 227,300 smokers who set a quit date, 119,800 reported that they had successfully quit at the four-week follow-up stage. (Table 7.25)

Over the past century there have been progressive improvements in the health of the nation. These can be attributed to improved nutrition and housing, advances in medicine and technology, and the development of health services which are freely available to all. There do, however, remain some significant health inequalities between different groups in our society. Factors influencing these include income, and its bearing on the quality of diet and housing that are affordable, as well as access to health services. Government health strategies throughout the United Kingdom focus on reducing avoidable ill health and inequalities, with particular emphasis on cancer, heart disease and mental health.

The nation's health

One of the most striking indications of how the nation's health has improved over the past century is the increase in life expectancy at birth. In 1901, males born in the United Kingdom could expect to live to around 45 years of age and females to around 49. During the next 70 years life expectancy at birth increased substantially, reaching 69 years for males and over 75 years for females in 1971. Since then there has been a more gradual increase, so that by 2001 life expectancy at birth had risen to over 75 years for males and over 80 years for females.

Life expectancy for adults has also been increasing over the past century. Among those aged 65 there were different patterns for men and women (Figure 7.1). In 1901 men aged 65 could expect to live for a further ten and a half years and women for a further eleven and a half years. By 1971 life expectancy for men of this age had risen by just under 2 years, followed by a sharper rise of a further three and a half years to reach almost 16 years in 2001. In contrast, for women aged 65 there was a more steady increase in life expectancy from the 1920s. In 2001 a woman of this age could expect to live for a further 19 years compared with 16 years in 1971.

Although life expectancy at birth has increased over the past 30 years among all social classes, there remain inequalities (Table 7.2). Given current mortality rates, males born in 1997-99 in England and Wales to parents in the professional group could expect to live, if they remained in that social class, to the age of 78.5

Figure **7.1**

Expectation of life[1] at age 65: by sex

United Kingdom

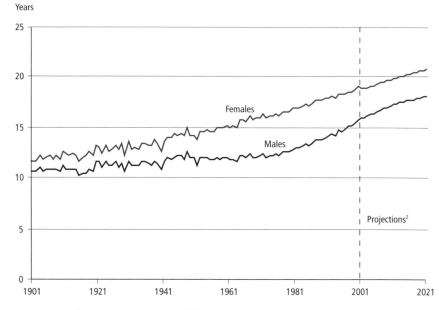

1 See Appendix, Part 7: Expectation of life. The average number of years which a 65 year old person could be expected to live if the rates of mortality at each age were those experienced in that calendar year.
2 2001-based projections.
Source: Government Actuary's Department

Table **7.2**

Life expectancy at birth: by social class and sex

England & Wales   Years

	1972 –76	1977 –81	1982 –86	1987 –91	1992 –96	1997 –99
Males						
Professional	72.0	74.7	75.1	76.7	77.7	78.5
Managerial and technical	71.7	72.4	73.8	74.4	75.8	77.5
Skilled non-manual	69.5	70.8	72.2	73.5	75.0	76.2
Skilled manual	69.8	70.0	71.4	72.4	73.5	74.7
Semi-skilled manual	68.4	68.8	70.6	70.4	72.6	72.7
Unskilled manual	66.5	67.0	67.7	67.9	68.2	71.1
All males	69.2	70.0	71.4	72.3	73.9	75.0
Females						
Professional	79.2	79.9	80.4	80.9	83.4	82.8
Managerial and technical	77.0	78.1	78.5	80.0	81.1	81.5
Skilled non-manual	78.0	78.1	78.6	79.4	80.4	81.2
Skilled manual	75.1	76.1	77.1	77.6	78.8	79.2
Semi-skilled manual	75.0	76.1	77.3	77.0	77.7	78.5
Unskilled manual	73.9	74.9	75.3	76.2	77.0	77.1
All females	75.1	76.3	77.1	77.9	79.3	79.7

Source: Longitudinal Study, Office for National Statistics

years. This was over 7 years longer than males born to parents in the unskilled manual group. Between 1972–76 and 1992–96 the gap between these social classes widened from 5.5 years to 9.5 years. The gap between these two groups then narrowed again to 7.4 years in 1997–99.

There was a similar difference across the social classes for females, with those born to parents in the professional group in 1997–99 having a life expectancy 5.7 years longer than those born to parents in the unskilled manual group. Only females in the unskilled manual group had a lower life expectancy than males in the professional group, and then only since 1987–91.

One of the major factors contributing to increased life expectancy over the past century

has been the huge fall in infant mortality. In 1921, 84.0 children per 1,000 live births in the United Kingdom died before the age of one; by 2001 the rate was 5.4. This decline in infant mortality can be largely attributed to improvements in children's diet, improvements in sanitation and hygiene, better antenatal and postnatal care and the development of vaccines and immunisation programmes. Between 1991 and 2001 there was a decrease in the infant mortality rates for babies born inside and those born outside marriage (Table 7.3). For those born inside marriage the rate fell from 6.3 to 4.6 per 1,000 live births, while for jointly registered births outside marriage the rate fell from 8.8 to 6.1 per 1,000 live births. In 2001 the rate for babies born outside marriage where the birth was solely registered was higher, at 7.6 per 1,000 live births, than for those born inside marriage.

Despite the decline in infant mortality, notable socio-economic inequalities still exist. In England and Wales in 2001, the infant mortality rate among babies born inside marriage whose fathers were in the unskilled manual class was 7.2 per 1,000 live births, twice the rate of 3.6 for those whose fathers were in the professional class. For babies born outside marriage where the birth was jointly registered by both parents, there was a similar trend, with an infant mortality rate of 7.5 per 1,000 live births for babies whose fathers were in the unskilled manual class compared with a rate of 4.5 for those whose fathers were in the professional class.

Although over the past 20 years, diseases such as measles, tuberculosis (TB) and whooping cough have become far less common, their occurrence still fluctuates as a result of epidemics. This volatility can be seen in the trend in the number of notifications of measles over the last ten years (Figure 7.4 - see overleaf). Between 1993 and 1994 notifications of measles in the United Kingdom almost doubled from 12,000 to 23,500. Notifications then fell sharply to 9,000 in 1995, since when there has been a progressive fall, so that by 2001 there were around 2,700 notifications. In the past decade there was a downward trend in the incidence of whooping cough, although there were fluctuations, and in 2001 there were around 1,600 cases compared with 6,300 cases in 1991.

Table 7.3

Infant mortality:[1] by social class[2]

England & Wales — Rates per 1,000 live births[3]

	Inside marriage		Outside marriage[4]	
	1991	2001	1991	2001
Professional	5.1	3.6	4.2	4.5
Managerial and technical	5.3	3.6	6.6	4.0
Skilled non-manual	6.1	4.5	8.5	5.3
Skilled manual	6.2	5.0	7.7	5.8
Semi-skilled manual	7.1	6.2	9.6	6.7
Unskilled manual	8.2	7.2	11.0	7.5
Other	11.6	6.7	21.2	10.8
All	6.3	4.6	8.8	6.1

1 Deaths within one year of birth.
2 Based on father's occupation at death registration.
3 Figures for live births are a 10 per cent sample coded for father's occupation.
4 Jointly registered by both parents.
Source: Office for National Statistics

In contrast, the incidence of TB in the United Kingdom has increased by nearly a fifth over the past decade, and since 1997 it has been more common than either measles or whooping cough. In 2001 there were around 7,200 cases compared with around 6,100 in 1991. The rise has been particularly noticeable in London, and among young men.

Asthma is a disease of the lungs in which the airways are unusually sensitive to a wide range of stimuli, including inhaled irritants and allergens. In England and Wales, overall incidence rates of new diagnoses of asthma were higher in females than in males in 2001. Incidence in women in all age groups from 15 to 74 years was higher than for men, although incidence was higher in boys under 15 than in girls (Table 7.5). In the last five years there has been a decline in the number of new cases of asthma diagnosed in both sexes. Between 1998 and 2001 the overall incidence rate fell among females from 41.4 to 29.3 per 100,000, and among males from 36.1 to 25.9. Among both sexes, new attacks are far more common during childhood, particularly between the ages of 1 and 4 years.

It is estimated that in 1998 there were 1.2 million people in England and Wales with a diagnosis of diabetes. Diabetes is a serious illness that increases the risk of heart disease, stroke, kidney disease and blindness. People with untreated diabetes have an abnormally high blood glucose level due to a lack of, or insensitivity, to the hormone insulin. The three main types of treatment for diabetes are regular injection of insulin, use of an oral (hypoglycaemic) drug to stimulate its production or sensitivity to it, or dietary control alone to restrict the intake of glucose.

In contrast to the recent trends in new cases of asthma, the diagnosis of diabetes has been increasing in recent years. Between 1994 and 1998 the overall age-standardised prevalence of diagnosed diabetes in England and Wales increased by 18 per cent among males, from 18.9 to 22.3 per 1,000, and by 20 per cent among females, from 13.7 to 16.4 per 1,000. Diabetes is more common among older people – the age specific rates in 1998 in England and Wales peaked in the 75 to 84 year age group

Figure 7.4

Notifications of selected infectious diseases

United Kingdom

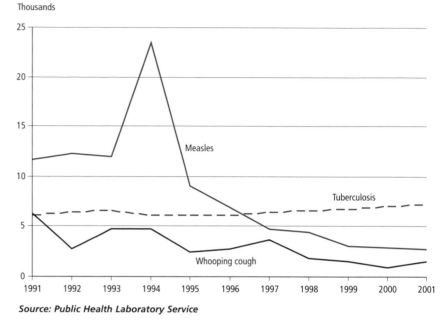

Source: Public Health Laboratory Service

Table 7.5

New episodes[1] of asthma: by sex and age

England & Wales   Rates per 100,000 population

	1996	1998	2000	2001
Males				
Under 1	106.9	74.6	48.5	42.3
1–4	151.9	113.6	90.2	74.8
5–14	78.8	71.2	56.1	49.9
15–24	40.0	33.1	26.0	23.1
25–44	23.6	25.5	22.2	18.4
45–64	22.0	20.7	17.9	16.4
65–74	29.0	25.7	21.5	19.8
75 and over	22.7	18.7	15.6	21.1
All ages	41.2	36.1	29.4	25.9
Females				
Under 1	56.9	37.0	29.6	31.0
1–4	111.9	93.5	56.6	56.4
5–14	65.0	58.5	42.1	32.9
15–24	56.8	53.2	43.4	37.6
25–44	39.9	34.6	31.9	28.2
45–64	34.5	33.3	26.6	24.3
65–74	36.6	34.8	27.6	25.2
75 and over	28.4	22.5	20.7	20.5
All ages	46.4	41.4	33.0	29.3

1 *Mean weekly incidence. A diagnosis for the first time or a previously diagnosed asthmatic person having a new attack.*
Source: The Royal College of General Practitioners

Figure **7.6**

Prevalence of diagnosed diabetes: by sex and age, 1998

England & Wales

Rates per 1,000 population

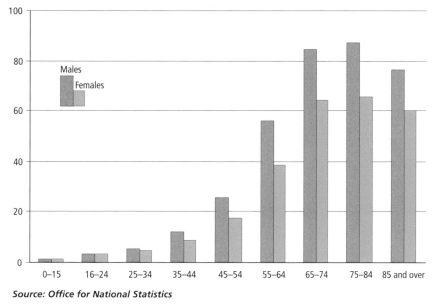

Source: Office for National Statistics

Table **7.7**

New episodes of genital chlamydia: by sex and age

England & Wales

Numbers

	1995	1997	1999	2001
Males				
0–15	45	50	74	85
16–19	1,181	1,866	2,969	4,148
20–24	4,462	5,480	7,534	10,978
25–34	5,922	7,209	8,741	10,862
35–44	1,306	1,694	2,371	3,324
45–64	323	369	613	831
65 and over	32	27	35	39
All ages[1]	13,276	16,706	22,546	30,290
Females				
0–15	394	519	711	950
16–19	4,896	7,478	10,262	13,256
20–24	6,516	8,306	10,788	14,695
25–34	4,382	5,702	6,856	8,714
35–44	704	1,005	1,273	1,861
45–64	140	210	256	350
65 and over	19	17	9	25
All ages[1]	17,086	23,323	30,443	39,888

1 Includes those cases where age is unknown.
Source: Public Health Laboratory Service

at a rate of 87 per 1,000 males and 66 per 1,000 females (Figure 7.6).

The prevalence of diseases that can be sexually transmitted has also been increasing in recent years, especially among young people. In 2001, genital chlamydia was the most common sexually transmitted infection diagnosed in genito-urinary clinics in England and Wales, with a total of just under 70,200 cases, a 10 per cent increase compared with 2000 and more than double the 30,400 cases diagnosed in 1995 (Table 7.7). Between 1995 and 2001 the increase was greatest among those aged under the age of 25. Among young women the number of cases diagnosed rose from 11,800 to 28,900; for young men it increased from 5,700 to 15,200.

In 2001 uncomplicated gonorrhoea was the second most common sexually transmitted infection with 15,800 diagnosed cases among males in England and Wales and 6,800 among females. These figures represent increases of 8 per cent and 6 per cent for males and females, respectively, compared with 2000. Between 2000 and 2001 diagnosis of primary and secondary syphilis showed the largest proportionate increase, rising by 140 per cent to 604 cases among males and by 33 per cent to 100 cases among females.

Since 1995 the overall number of HIV diagnoses in the United Kingdom has risen each year, with over 4,400 cases recorded in 2001. In 1999, sex between men and women overtook sex between men as the most common route of transmission. Between 2000 and 2001 there was an increase of 27 per cent in the number of diagnosed infections attributed to this route, of which over 80 per cent were estimated to have occurred abroad.

Dealing with mental health problems is one of the main priorities set out in the Government's NHS Plan published in July 2000. Fundamental to this is the modernisation of mental health services in the United Kingdom. In 2000/01 there were two million attendances at NHS outpatient facilities for psychiatric specialities in England, 285,000 of which were new attendances. In 2000 the Survey of Psychiatric Morbidity of people aged 16 to 74 years living in private households in Great Britain found that about one in six had a neurotic disorder

(Figure 7.8). Neurotic disorders are characterised by a variety of symptoms such as fatigue and sleep problems, concentration difficulties, irritability, worry, panic and obsessions, which are present to such a degree that they cause problems with daily activities and distress. The survey revealed that a higher proportion of women than men suffered from some form of neurotic disorder. Women were also more likely than men to have significant levels of both anxiety and depression. Similar rates were recorded for both sexes for depression, anxiety and panic disorders.

While a third of all those responding to the survey were unemployed or economically inactive, nearly three quarters of those reporting a neurotic disorder were in these groups. Those with a mental disorder were far more likely than those with no disorder to be living in rented accommodation (38 per cent compared with 24 per cent). About half of those with a mental disorder were living in accommodation rented from a housing association or local authority.

Over the past decade the number of prescription items for anti-depressant drugs dispensed in England has more than doubled, from 9 million items in 1991 to 24 million in 2001 (Figure 7.9). The cost of anti-depressant drugs dispensed in the community in England was £342 million in 2001, representing 5.6 per cent of the net ingredient cost of all prescription medicines dispensed and 67 per cent of the net ingredient cost of all mental health drugs dispensed in the community.

Reducing mental health problems is a priority in the health strategies of all of the constituent governments in the United Kingdom. In July 1999 the Government set a target to reduce the death rate from suicide in England by a fifth by 2010, from an age standardised rate of 9.1 per 100,000 in 1996. In September 2002 the Department of Health launched the National Suicide Prevention Strategy. Over the past 20 to 30 years, suicide rates have fallen in older men and women, but risen in young men. In the United Kingdom in 2001, suicide rates in each age group were around three to four times higher in men than women, with the highest rate, of 24 per 100,000 population, in men aged 25 to 44 years. The highest rate for women occurred among those aged 45 to 64, at 7 per 100,000 population.

Figure **7.8**

Prevalence of neurotic disorder among adults:[1] by sex, 2000

Great Britain

Percentages

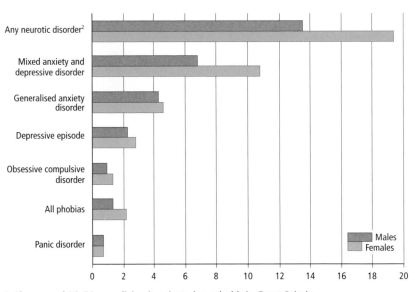

1 Those aged 16–74 years living in private households in Great Britain.
2 People may have more than one type of neurotic disorder so the percentage with any disorder is not the sum of those with specific disorders.
Source: Psychiatric Morbidity Survey, Office for National Statistics

Figure **7.9**

Number of prescription items for anti-depressant drugs[1]

England

Millions

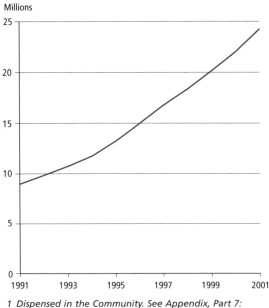

1 Dispensed in the Community. See Appendix, Part 7: Prescription Cost Analysis System. Anti-depressants are defined as those drugs within the British National Formulary (BNF) section 4.3, anti-depressant drugs.
Source: Department of Health

Table **7.10**

Main causes of child mortality: by sex and age, 1998–2000

England & Wales
Percentages

	Males		Females	
	1–4	5–15	1–4	5–15
Infections	10	4	9	6
Cancers	15	24	13	23
Nervous system and sense organs	13	15	13	16
Circulatory system	6	5	8	5
Respiratory system	11	6	9	8
Congenital anomalies	13	6	16	8
Accident[1]	16	27	15	17
Other[2]	17	13	16	16
All deaths (=100%) (numbers)	1,153	1,773	855	1,239

1 See Appendix, Part 7: Accidental deaths.
2 Includes undetermined injury whether accidentally or purposely inflicted, homicide, mental disorders and suicide.

Source: Office for National Statistics

Figure **7.11**

Mortality:[1] by sex and major cause[2]

England & Wales

Rates per million population

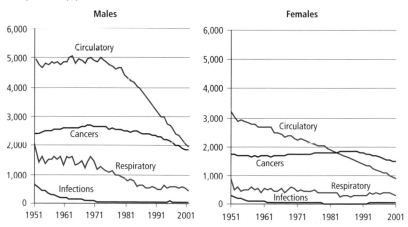

1 People aged 15–74. Data have been age standardised using the European standard population. See Appendix, Part 7: Standardised rates, and International Classification of Diseases. Data for 1982 to 2000 are based on interim population estimates revised following the 2001 Census and are subject to further revision.
2 Data for 1984 to 1992 are not comparable to previous or subsequent years due to changes in the rules used to select the underlying cause of death in England and Wales.

Source: Office for National Statistics

Causes of death

Death rates for children in the United Kingdom fell dramatically during the 20th century, largely due to the huge decrease in infant mortality (see also Table 7.3). In 1998-2000 cancers were the most common cause of death among girls aged 5 to 15 in England and Wales, accounting for 23 per cent of the total in this age group (Table 7.10). They were the second most common cause among boys in this age group, accounting for 24 per cent of deaths. Since the 1980s there have been notable improvements in cancer survival among children aged 5 to 14, largely due to better medical treatment. Between 1985 and 2000 cancer mortality rates in this age group fell by a third, even though the incidence of cancers changed little.

In 1998-2000 accidents were the most common cause of death among boys aged 5 to 15, representing 27 per cent of the total. At 17 per cent, this was the second most common cause of death among girls in this age group. Most of these deaths were caused by transport accidents, accounting for 61 per cent of accidental deaths among boys and 73 per cent among girls.

Infections were a more common cause of death in children aged 1 to 4 years than in older children, causing around a tenth of total deaths in both boys and girls. Deaths caused by cancers and accidents each accounted for around a sixth of deaths among both boys and girls in this age group.

Over the past 50 years, there has been a decrease in mortality rates in all of the major causes of death in England and Wales (Figure 7.11). Cancers are now the most common cause of death in women and the second most common in men, with only slightly fewer deaths in men than from circulatory disease (which includes heart disease and stroke). Death rates from cancer among men peaked at 2,700 per million in the late 1960s. By 2001 the rate had declined to just under 1,900 per million. Cancer death rates for women have been consistently lower than those for men since the early part of the last century. The rates in women did not peak until the mid-1980s, after which they fell from 1,800 per million to 1,500 per million in 2001. However, as a result of greater falls in deaths from other illnesses, the proportion of deaths caused by cancer has risen, so that in 2001 cancers in England and Wales were responsible for 28 per cent of male deaths and 24 per cent of female deaths, compared with 16 per cent among both males and females in 1951.

Female death rates from circulatory diseases have shown a consistent decline since the early 1950s. Among males, this has only been the case since the early 1980s when the rates fell by 54 per cent from 4,300 per million in 1981 to 2,000 per million in 2001. The trend among females during this period was similar, with a fall from 1,900 per million in 1981 to 900 per million in 2001.

Although death rates from infections such as TB and measles, and respiratory diseases such as pneumonia, are much lower than those for cancer and circulatory disease, over the past 10 to 20 years they have not followed the same trends. Death rates from respiratory diseases among men fell from around 800 per million in 1981 to 500 per million in 1991. The rates then fluctuated between 500 and 600 per million. Among women death rates from respiratory diseases rose from around 300 to 400 per million between 1991 and 2000. The fall in death rates from respiratory diseases in both males and females between 2000 and 2001 was largely due to changes in the coding classification.

Since the mid-1970s the greatest decline in death rates from any form of cancer has been in lung cancer among men (Figure 7.12). Between 1976 and 2001 the rate in England and Wales fell from 108 to 57 deaths per 100,000. This reduction can be closely linked to the decline in the prevalence of cigarette smoking among men. In contrast, the lung cancer death rate among women has risen since the 1970s, and is now at half that of men.

Breast cancer is the most common cause of cancer death among women in England and Wales. Death rates from this form of cancer increased slightly between 1976 and 1989, from 39 to 42 deaths per 100,000, since when they have fallen to 31 deaths per 100,000 in 2001.

Colorectal cancer is the third most common cause of cancer death among both men and

Figure **7.12**

Death rates from selected cancers:[1] by sex
England & Wales

Rates per 100,000 population

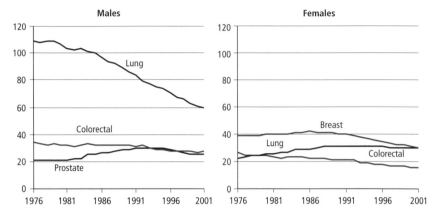

1 People aged 15–74. Data have been age standardised using the European standard population. See Appendix, Part 7: Standardised rates, and International Classification of Diseases. Data for 1982 to 2000 are based on interim population estimates revised following the 2001 Census and are subject to further revision.

Source: Office for National Statistics

Table **7.13**

One and five year relative survival rates for major cancers: by sex of patient diagnosed during 1993–95

England   Percentages

	One year	Five year	Number of cases
Males			
Lung	21	6	52,064
Prostate	84	60	46,010
Colon	66	44	21,287
Females			
Breast	93	76	78,780
Lung	22	6	27,119
Colon	64	43	22,003

Source: Office for National Statistics

women. Between 1991 and 2001 death rates from this form of cancer declined by 21 per cent among men and 29 per cent among women. For prostate cancer, which only affects men, the death rate peaked at 30 deaths per 100,000 in 1992. It has since been showing a steady, gradual decrease, levelling off at around 27 deaths per 100,000 since 1999.

Cancer patient survival is a key indicator of the effectiveness of cancer control in the population. Effective treatments for some cancers, such as chemotherapy for childhood leukaemia, have led to dramatically improved survival during the last 20 years. Early detection through the national cancer screening programmes can also lead to improved chances of survival.

Survival rates from lung cancer are very low compared with the other most common cancers. For those diagnosed with lung cancer in the period 1993 to 1995, the one year survival rate (the proportion of new cases

surviving for at least one year after diagnosis) for both men and women was just over 20 per cent (Table 7.13). Five year survival rates based on the same period of diagnosis were only 6 per cent for both sexes. In contrast five year survival rates for colon cancer were almost 45 per cent for both males and females.

Survival rates for breast and cervical cancers – the two major types of cancer where screening or testing are available – have increased in recent years. This is partly because screening detects cases earlier than they might otherwise have been diagnosed. These patients then appear to live longer after diagnosis even though their lifespan may not be extended. Of those cases diagnosed in the period 1993 to 1995, the five year survival rate for prostate cancer was 60 per cent, and for female breast cancer it was 76 per cent.

Between 1993 and 2000 the number of drug-related poisoning deaths in England and Wales increased by a third (Table 7.14). During this period there was a substantial difference in the patterns for male and female deaths. Male deaths from drug-related poisoning rose by 50 per cent, while deaths among females rose by only 3 per cent. In 2000, heroin and/or morphine were mentioned in 926 deaths; more than any other drug. This was five times the number of deaths mentioning heroin and/or morphine in 1993. In contrast, deaths mentioning over-the-counter substances, such as paracetamol, decreased during the same period. In 2000, paracetamol-related deaths fell to 455, their lowest figure to date, having risen by 21 per cent between 1993 and 1997. This may be associated with legislation introduced in 1998 which limited the maximum amount of paracetamol allowed in a pack.

Lifestyle and diet

The way we choose to live can have a direct impact on our health. The consumption of alcohol in excessive amounts can lead to ill health, and an increased likelihood of problems such as high blood pressure, cancer and cirrhosis of the liver. The current Department of Health advice on alcohol is that consumption of between three and four units a day for men and two to three units a day for women should not lead to significant health risks. Consistently drinking more is not advised because of the progressive health risks.

Table 7.14

Drug-related poisoning deaths: by selected type of drug[1]

England & Wales   Numbers

	1993	1995	1998	1999	2000
Heroin and morphine[2]	187	357	646	754	926
Paracetamol[3]	463	526	523	473	455
Antidepressants	461	489	510	493	449
Methadone	232	310	364	298	238
Temazepam	173	138	111	82	73
Cocaine	12	19	66	88	80
Barbiturates	44	46	35	26	17
MDMA/Ecstasy	8	10	16	26	36
Cannabis	14	17	5	8	11
All drug-related deaths[4]	2,252	2,563	2,922	2,943	2,968

1 Where more than one drug is mentioned on the death certificate the death is included in the figures for each drug. In these cases it is not possible to determine which drug was primarily responsible for the death.

2 As heroin breaks down in the body into morphine, the latter may be detected at post mortem and recorded on the death certificate.

3 Includes deaths with any mention of paracetamol or any compounds containing paracetamol.

4 Includes deaths related to all other drugs.

Source: Office for National Statistics

Between 1998 and 2000 there was an overall, but slight, increase in average weekly alcohol consumption among both men and women in Great Britain (Table 7.15).

Among men, average weekly consumption rose from 17.1 to 17.4 units, while there was a slightly greater increase from 6.5 to 7.1 units among women. On average men consumed more than twice as much as women.

There was little variation by socio-economic group in the average weekly consumption by men in 2000. Among women, the amount of alcohol consumed varied far more between the professional and unskilled manual groups than it did among men, with women in the professional group consuming double the amount of those in the unskilled manual group. Among the unskilled manual group men consumed four times as much as women, while in the professional group men only drank twice as much as women.

While those in the non-manual groups are the most likely to drink, it is those in the unskilled manual group who are most likely to smoke. In 2000 the prevalence of cigarette smoking by socio-economic group varied markedly, and among women the pattern was the opposite to that in alcohol consumption (Table 7.16). Among men in the unskilled manual group, 39 per cent reported being regular cigarette smokers compared with only 17 per cent in the professional group. Similarly, among women, the proportion of regular smokers in the unskilled manual group (35 per cent) was two and a half times that in the professional group (14 per cent).

Over the past 30 years, the reduction in lung cancer deaths in men (see Figure 7.12) can be closely linked to the fall in the proportion of the population who smoke. In 1974, 51 per cent of men and 41 per cent of women in Great Britain reported that they were regular cigarette smokers. By 2000 these proportions had fallen to 29 per cent and 25 per cent respectively, with the falls being faster among men, and among older age groups.

The misuse of drugs, such as heroin, cocaine and amphetamines, is a serious social and health problem. Data from the European Monitoring Centre for Drugs and Drug Addiction show that within the European Union (EU) in 1999, England and Wales and the

Table 7.15

Average weekly alcohol consumption: by sex and socio-economic group[1]

Great Britain   Units of alcohol[2]

	Males		Females	
	1998	2000	1998	2000
Professional	16.2	17.9	7.4	8.6
Employers and managers	16.8	18.0	7.9	7.9
Intermediate non-manual	15.4	18.1	6.7	7.9
Junior non-manual	19.4	16.3	6.2	6.6
Skilled manual	16.1	17.3	5.9	6.9
Semi-skilled manual	16.5	16.2	5.7	5.9
Unskilled manual	17.1	17.1	4.7	4.3
All aged 16 and over	17.1	17.4	6.5	7.1

1 Socio-economic group of the household reference person (excluding those in the Armed Forces and full-time students). See Appendix, Part 10: Household reference person.
2 See Appendix, Part 7: Alcohol consumption.
Source: General Household Survey, Office for National Statistics

Table 7.16

Prevalence of cigarette smoking: by sex and socio-economic group[1]

Great Britain   Percentages

	Males		Females	
	1998	2000	1998	2000
Professional	16	17	14	14
Employers and managers	22	23	21	20
Intermediate/junior non-manual	25	27	24	26
Skilled manual	34	33	30	26
Semi-skilled manual	39	36	33	32
Unskilled manual	44	39	31	35
All non-manual	22	23	22	22
All manual	36	34	31	29
All aged 16 and over	30	29	26	25

1 Socio-economic group of the household reference person (excluding those in the Armed Forces and full-time students). See Appendix, Part 10: Household reference person.
Source: General Household Survey, Office for National Statistics

Figure **7.17**

Prevalence of recent[1] use of cannabis, amphetamines and cocaine, among young adults,[2] EU comparison,[3] 1999[4]

Percentages

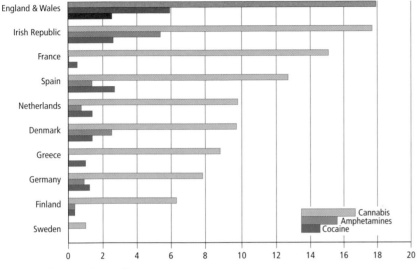

1 During the past 12 months.
2 EMCDDA standard age range for 'young adults' is 15–34. Data for England and Wales and Denmark are for ages 16–34 and Germany 18–39.
3 Data for other EU countries are not available.
4 Data for Netherlands are 1997/98, data for Germany (former West Germany) are 1997, data for Denmark are 2000.
Source: European Monitoring Centre for Drugs and Drug Addiction

Figure **7.18**

Incidence of breastfeeding: by age at which mother completed full-time education, 2000

United Kingdom

Percentages

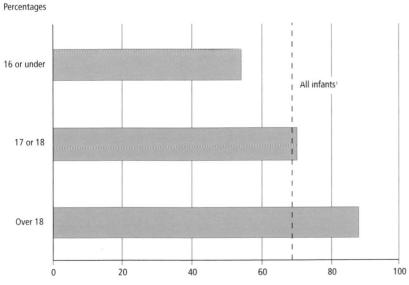

1 Includes cases where the age at which mother completed full-time education was not known.
Source: Infant Feeding Survey, Department of Health

Irish Republic had the highest proportions of young people using cannabis, amphetamines and cocaine (Figure 7.17). Cannabis was the most commonly used of these drugs. In England and Wales, 18 per cent of those aged 16 to 34 had reported using it during the previous 12 months. This compared with around 10 per cent of 15 to 34 year olds in the Netherlands where its use has been decriminalised. Cannabis use increased markedly during the 1990s in most EU countries, particularly among young people, although in recent years its use may have levelled off in some countries.

Good nutrition is important from birth, and studies have shown that breastfeeding gives health benefits to both mother and child. Data from the 2000 Infant Feeding Survey show that a mother's educational level, age and social class are all strongly associated with the incidence of breastfeeding. Only 54 per cent of mothers in the United Kingdom who completed their full-time education by the age of 16 breastfed their babies, compared with 88 per cent of mothers who were over 18 when they completed their full-time education (Figure 7.18).

The incidence of breastfeeding in the United Kingdom has increased since 1990. While mothers in Social Classes I and II (based on husband's or partner's occupation) continued to have the highest breastfeeding rates, the greatest increases were in other social classes, with a significant increase in the incidence of breastfeeding in Social Class V, from 50 per cent in 1995 to 57 per cent in 2000.

The Department of Health recommends that a healthy diet should include at least five portions of a variety of fresh fruit or vegetables (excluding potatoes) a day. To encourage healthy eating from childhood, the National School Fruit Scheme is being introduced in England to provide children aged four to six with free fruit. By the end of 2002 over 500,000 children aged four to six were receiving free fruit each school day. The scheme will be available across England by 2004.

The National Food Survey has been used to monitor the changing pattern of food consumption in Great Britain over the past 25 years. The consumption of fresh vegetables has declined in both the highest and lowest income groups (see Appendix, Part 7: Weekly income of head of household) (Figure 7.19). In 2000, although the lowest income group continued to eat more fresh vegetables than the higher income group (1,595 grams per person per week compared with 1,422 grams), this was due to higher potato consumption (873 grams per person per week compared with 544 grams), as similar amounts of green vegetables were eaten. The overall lower fresh potato consumption over this period can be linked to the increased use of processed and convenience food and an increase in pasta and rice consumption. Between 1975 and 2000 consumption of fresh fruit rose in both income groups. In the lowest income group it rose from 618 grams to 710 grams per person per week and in the higher income group from 758 grams to 968 grams per person per week.

Obesity is a major risk factor linked to heart disease, diabetes and premature death. The body mass index (BMI) (see Appendix 7, Part 7: Body Mass Index) is a common measure for assessing an individual's weight relative to their height, and a BMI score of over 30 is taken as the definition of obesity. In recent years the proportion of the population who are obese or overweight has been rising. In 2001, over a fifth of males and a similar proportion of females aged 16 and over in England were classified as obese (Figure 7.20). A further half of men and third of women were classified as overweight. Obesity levels tend to rise with age, peaking in both sexes in the 55 to 64 year age group. In 2001, 27 per cent of males and 31 per cent of females in this age group were classified as obese. Among those aged 75 years and over, the proportions fell to 18 per cent and 21 per cent respectively.

A small proportion of the population are underweight, with 4 per cent of males and 6 per cent of females being defined as such in 2001. Those aged 16 to 24 years are far more likely than any other age group to be underweight, with around one in six of both males and females being so in 2001. Almost half of this age group are of 'desirable' weight. This remains the case among women aged 25 to 34 years, however, among men of this age group the proportion who are of 'desirable' weight falls to just over a third.

Figure **7.19**

Consumption of fresh fruit and vegetables:[1] by income group[2] of head of household
Great Britain

Grams per person per week

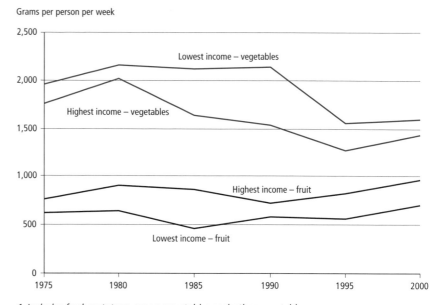

1 Includes fresh potatoes, green vegetables and other vegetables.
2 See Appendix, Part 7: Weekly income of head of household.
Source: National Food Survey, Department for Environment, Food & Rural Affairs

Figure **7.20**

Body mass:[1] by sex, 2001
England

Percentages

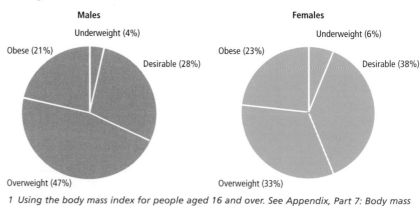

1 Using the body mass index for people aged 16 and over. See Appendix, Part 7: Body mass index.
Source: Health Survey for England, Department of Health

Figure **7.21**

Number of emergency contraceptives prescribed

England

Thousands

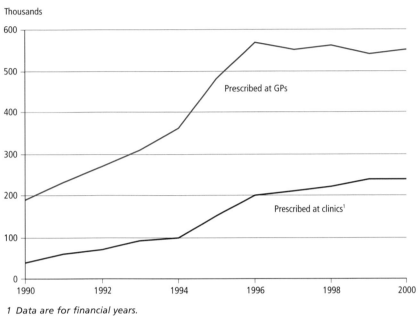

1 Data are for financial years.
Source: Department of Health

Table **7.22**

Immunisation of children[1] by their second birthday[2]

United Kingdom   Percentages

	1981[3]	1991/92	1994/95	1998/99	1999/00	2000/01
Tetanus	83	94	93	96	95	95
Diphtheria	83	94	95	95	95	95
Poliomyelitis	82	94	95	95	95	95
Whooping cough	45	88	95	94	94	94
Measles, mumps, rubella[4]	54	90	91	89	88	88

1 See Appendix, Part 7: Immunisation.
2 Data for Scotland are for calendar years.
3 Data exclude Scotland.
4 Includes measles-only vaccine for 1981. Combined vaccine was not available prior to 1988.
Source: Department of Health; National Assembly for Wales; National Health Service in Scotland; Department of Health, Social Services and Public Safety, Northern Ireland

The Government's public health strategy aims to ensure that effective sexual health services are available to those who need them. A key part of the strategy is the availability of contraceptive advice and treatment from general practitioners (GPs) and family planning clinics. Emergency or 'morning after' contraceptives prevent pregnancy after unprotected sexual intercourse and are available to women on prescription from GPs or clinics. Since 2001 they have also been available without prescription from pharmacists. Between 1990 and 1996 the number of emergency contraceptives prescribed in England more than tripled, after which the number levelled off at just under 800,000 a year, with around two thirds of these being prescribed by GPs (Figure 7.21). In 2001 the total number of emergency contraceptives prescribed fell to 630,000, reflecting their availability without prescription from pharmacists.

Prevention

Over the past 50 years a key factor in the reduction of infectious diseases and the associated morbidity and mortality has been the development of childhood vaccination programmes. The percentage of children in the United Kingdom immunised against tetanus, diphtheria, poliomyelitis, pertussis (whooping cough) and measles, mumps and rubella is shown in Table 7.22. Current government immunisation targets are for 95 per cent of children to be immunised against these diseases by the age of two.

Immunisation against whooping cough was introduced in the 1950s, and this led to a sharp decline in deaths and notifications. In 1970 a study suggested that encephalopathy and brain damage might be a rare complication of immunisation. By 1978, only 30 per cent of children under two years were immunised against whooping cough and large outbreaks followed in 1978 and 1982. New evidence suggested that the association between immunisation and encephalopathy was not causative and vaccine coverage rates increased. By 2000/01, 94 per cent of children in the United Kingdom had been immunised against whooping cough by their second birthday.

Measles immunisation was introduced in 1968 and, although immunisation was slow to gain general acceptance, notifications of measles outbreaks in the United Kingdom fell in the early 1980s. In 1988, the measles/mumps/ rubella (MMR) vaccine was introduced. Notifications of measles fell to their lowest recorded annual total of under 3,000 in 2001 (see Figure 7.4). The number of children who have received the MMR vaccine by their second birthday has fallen from 91 per cent in 1997/98 to 88 per cent in 2000/01. It is likely that reports in the media claiming a link between MMR, Crohn's disease and autism has contributed to this decline.

NHS screening programmes aim to prevent deaths from breast cancer and lower the incidence of cervical cancer. Currently there is no screening programme available for prostate cancer, however a risk management programme was introduced in 2001. Also, a pilot study into the feasibility of screening for colorectal cancer was completed in 2002, with a decision as to whether colorectal screening will be introduced on a national basis due to be made during 2003. Trials into ovarian cancer screening are also underway.

The national policy for cervical screening is that women aged 20 to 64 (20 to 60 in Scotland) should be screened every three to five years (three and a half to five and a half years in Scotland). The test identifies a pre-cancerous stage which after a long developmental period may sometimes proceed to invasive cancer. Although cervical screening was introduced in England in 1964 it was not until 1988, when a three-year national call and recall system was established, that coverage (the proportion of women screened out of those invited) began to grow, from 45 per cent in 1988/89 to 84 per cent in 1999/2000. The affect of the increased coverage can be seen in the reduction in the incidence of cervical cancer in England and Wales, which fell sharply from a rate of over 16 to around 10 per 100,000 between 1988 and 1997.

In 2000/01, 82 per cent of the target population in Great Britain had been screened compared with 84 per cent in each of the previous two years (Table 7.23). Coverage was

Table 7.23

Cervical screening coverage:[1] by age

Great Britain			Percentages
	1999	2000	2001[2]
25–34[3]	82	81	79
35–44	87	87	85
45–54	87	87	84
55–64[4]	80	81	80
All aged 25–64[5]	84	84	82

1 See Appendix, Part 7: Breast cancer and cervical screening programmes.
2 March 2002 for England.
3 20–34 for Wales and Scotland.
4 55–60 for Scotland.
5 20–64 for Wales and 20–60 for Scotland.
Source: Department of Health; National Assembly for Wales; National Health Service in Scotland

Table 7.24

Breast cancer screening coverage:[1,2] by region, 2000/01

	Percentages
United Kingdom	75
England	75
Northern and Yorkshire	79
North West	75
Trent	81
West Midlands	77
Eastern	76
London	62
South East	77
South West	78
Wales	78
Scotland	72
Northern Ireland	73

1 As a percentage of women aged 50 to 64 invited for screening.
2 See Appendix, Part 7: Breast cancer and cervical screening programmes.
Source: Department of Health; National Assembly for Wales; National Health Service in Scotland; Department of Health, Social Services and Public Safety, Northern Ireland

lowest among the 25 to 34 year age group (79 per cent), although this group could be most at risk, as research has shown that the risk of developing cervical cancer is closely related to increased sexual activity. Smoking is another significant risk factor associated with the development of cervical cancer. The higher incidence of the cancer among the most deprived women can be closely linked to the prevalence of cigarette smoking by socio-economic group (see Table 7.16).

Breast cancer survival rates are among the highest for the most common forms of cancer. Around three quarters of women in England now survive for at least five years following the diagnosis of breast cancer (see Table 7.13). At present, breast screening is offered every three years to all women aged between 50 and 64, and to women aged 65 and over on request. By 2004, this will be extended to women in England aged 65 to 70, and to women over 70 on request. In Scotland the extension to women aged 65 to 70 will begin in 2003/04 and be implemented over a three-year round of screening.

In 2001, three quarters of the women invited from the target population in the United Kingdom underwent screening for breast cancer (Table 7.24). However, some regional variation does exist. While the proportion screened in most regions and countries of the United Kingdom was between 72 and 79 per cent, in the Trent region it reached 81 per cent, whereas in London it was only 62 per cent. In England in 2000/01, 1.3 million women were screened and 8,345 cases of breast cancer were diagnosed. In Scotland 120,000 women were screened with 822 cases of cancer diagnosed.

More cancer deaths in the United Kingdom can be attributed to smoking tobacco than to any other single risk factor. Smokers who quit can therefore have a direct influence on improving their health and extending their life expectancy. To encourage more smokers to quit, NHS smoking cessation services are now available across England. The services offer information, counselling and motivational help to smokers who want to stop. The services also offer pharmacological products, nicotine replacement therapy (NRT) and bupropion (Zyban), to aid smokers who want to quit. The Government target for 2001/02 was for 50,000 smokers to have quit by the four-week follow-up stage. Results for 2001/02 show that of the 227,300 smokers who set a quit date, 119,800 reported that they had successfully quit at the four-week follow-up stage (Table 7.25). Among both men and women the highest proportions of those using the services were in the 45 to 59 year age group (32 per cent and 30 per cent, respectively, of those setting a quit date). The Government's target for 2002/03 is for 100,000 to quit at the four-week follow up stage (based on self-report).

Table **7.25**

Smoking cessation:[1] by age[2] and sex, 2001/02

England		Numbers
	Males	Females
Under 18	786	1,220
18–34	22,077	35,089
35–44	24,100	32,056
45–59	31,461	38,970
60 and over	19,810	21,766
All ages	98,234	129,101
Successfully quit after 4 weeks[3]	52,977	66,857

1 Smokers setting a quit date through smoking cessation services. See Appendix, Part 7: Smoking cessation services.
2 Age group is based on age at quit date.
3 Based on self-report.
Source: Department of Health

Chapter 8

Social protection

Expenditure

- In 2000/01 expenditure on social protection in the United Kingdom was £245 billion. Expenditure on benefits for old age and survivors increased by 70 per cent from 1990/91 to account for nearly half of the total in 2000/01 (Figure 8.1)

Carers and caring

- There were 341,000 places in residential care homes in the independent and public sectors in England in 2001. The majority of these were for older people. (Table 8.8)

- In Great Britain, around 6.8 million adults aged 16 or over, representing 16 per cent of adults, were caring for a sick, disabled or elderly person in 2000/01. This was a very similar proportion to 1990/91. (Page 151)

Sick and disabled people

- At the end of March 2002 there were just over a million people waiting for treatment as an in-patient or day case at NHS hospitals in England. This is 26,500 more than in March 2001. (Table 8.13)

- In 2000/01 there were 14.3 million attendances at hospital accident and emergency departments in England, an increase of 167,000 (1 per cent) since 1996/97. Over the same period emergency ambulance responses increased by 560,000 (19 per cent). (Page 153)

Older people

- In 2000/01, 61 per cent of male employees and 51 per cent of female employees in Great Britain contributed to either an occupational or personal pension or both. (Table 8.19)

Families and children

- In England, Wales and Northern Ireland the number of day care places in playgroups in 2001 was around a fifth less than in 1992, but this has been more than compensated for by the larger increase in the number of day nursery places. (Table 8.21)

- There were 58,900 children being looked after by local authorities in England in 2001, a rise of 16 per cent compared with 1996. The majority of these children (38,400) were cared for in foster placements. (Table 8.22)

Social protection describes the help given to those who are in need or are at risk of hardship, for example, through illness, low income, family circumstances or age. Central government, local authorities, private bodies (such as voluntary organisations) and individuals can provide help and support. Help may be provided through direct cash payments such as social security benefits or pensions; payments in kind such as free prescriptions or free school meals; or the provision of services such as through the National Health Service. Unpaid care, such as that provided by informal carers, also plays a major role in helping people in need.

Expenditure

In order for spending on social protection to be compared across the member countries of the European Union (EU), Eurostat has designed a framework for the presentation of information on such expenditure which has been adopted by member states as the European System of Integrated Social Protection Statistics (ESSPROS). For this purpose, programmes which are specifically designed to protect people against common sources of hardship are collectively described as expenditure on social protection benefits. Examples include government expenditure on social security (generally excluding tax credits) and personal social services, sick pay paid by employers, and payments made from occupational and personal pension schemes. Protected persons receive a direct benefit from these programmes, whether in terms of cash payments, goods or services.

In 2000/01 expenditure on social protection in the United Kingdom, using the ESSPROS definitions, was £245 billion. Expenditure on benefits for old age and survivors accounted for nearly half of this total while expenditure on benefits for sickness, healthcare and disability accounted for just over a third (Figure 8.1). Between 1990/91 and 2000/01 there was a 70 per cent increase in social protection expenditure on old age and survivors in real terms (after allowing for inflation). This reflects the increase in the number of older people (see Figure 1.3 on page 31).

Expenditure can be expressed in terms of purchasing power parities, to enable direct

Figure **8.1**

Expenditure on social protection benefits in real terms:[1] by function, 1990/91 and 2000/01

United Kingdom

£ billion at 2000/01 prices

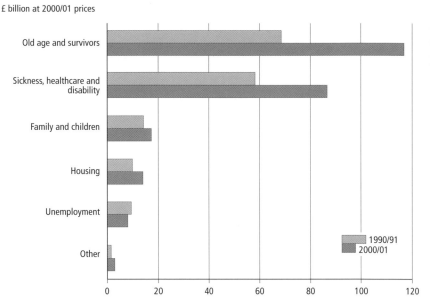

1 Adjusted to 2000/01 prices using the GDP market prices deflator.
Source: Office for National Statistics

Figure **8.2**

Expenditure[1] on social protection benefits per head: EU comparison, 1999

£ thousand per head

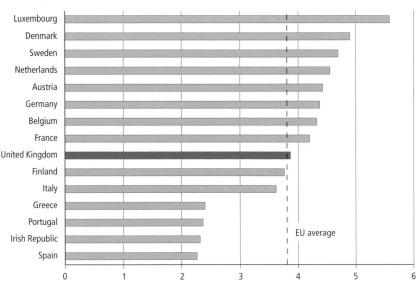

1 Before deduction of tax, where applicable. Tax credits are generally excluded. Figures are Purchasing Power Parities per inhabitant.
Source: Eurostat

Figure **8.3**

Real growth[1] in social security benefits and gross NHS expenditure
United Kingdom

£ billion at 2001/02 prices[1]

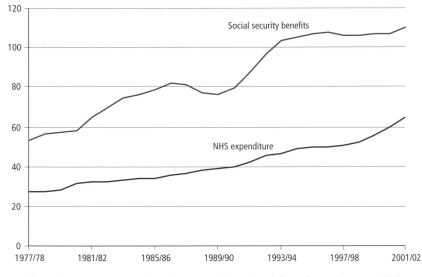

1 Adjusted to 2001/02 prices using the GDP market prices deflator (second quarter 2002).
Source: Department of Health; Department for Work and Pensions; Department for Social Development, Northern Ireland

Figure **8.4**

Social security benefit expenditure: by recipient group,[1] 2001/02
Great Britain

£ billion

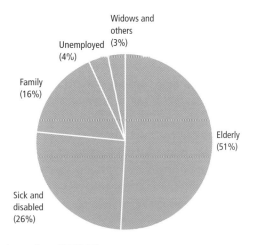

Total expenditure: £106.3 billion

1 See Appendix, Part 8: Benefits to groups of recipients.
Source: Department for Work and Pensions

comparisons in real terms between countries. These take account of differences in the general level of prices for goods and services within each country. The differences between countries therefore reflect the differences in the social protection systems, demographic structures, unemployment rates and other social, institutional and economic factors. Measured in this way, the United Kingdom's spending on social protection in 1999, at £3,870, was close to the EU average of £3,810 per person a year (Figure 8.2). Countries such as Luxembourg, Denmark, Sweden and the Netherlands spent more per head, while countries such as Greece, Portugal, the Irish Republic and Spain spent the least.

Spending on social security benefits and the National Health Service are large parts of social protection expenditure in the United Kingdom (Figure 8.3). In real terms, social security benefit expenditure rose from £53 billion in 1977/78 to £110 billion in 2001/02. Over the same period, spending on the National Health Service (NHS) grew from £27 billion to £64 billion. However, spending on social security benefits and NHS expenditure have followed differing patterns of growth, with increases in social security benefit expenditure following the general economic pattern. Spending on social security benefits fell sharply in the late 1980s before rising again in the early 1990s, reflecting changes in the number of unemployed people (see Figure 4.17 on page 82). However, recent falls in unemployment have not been so clearly reflected in the amount of social security benefit expenditure. Spending on the NHS rose more evenly between 1977/78 and 2001/02, although growth accelerated towards the end of this period, with spending rising by 17 per cent between 1999/2000 and 2001/02.

In 2001/02 social security expenditure in Great Britain was £106.3 billion. Figure 8.4 shows how this expenditure was distributed among the main groups of recipients. Benefit expenditure is classified where possible according to the main reason a benefit is paid. For example, a disability benefit paid to an elderly person is allocated to the sick and disabled rather than the elderly. Principally, benefits for the elderly are the state retirement pension and income-related benefits such as income support, housing

Table **8.5**

Receipt of selected social security benefits: by family type,[1] 2000/01

Great Britain

Percentages

	Working family tax credit or income support	Housing benefit	Council tax benefit	Jobseeker's allowance	State retirement pension	Incapacity or disablement benefits[2]	Child benefit	Any benefit/ tax credit
Pensioners[3]								
Couple	5	11	17	.	99	25	1	100
Single								
Male	13	25	32	.	98	20	–	99
Female	25	30	42	.	97	20	–	100
Couples								
Dependent children	14	7	9	2	–	9	98	98
No dependent children	4	4	7	1	9	15	–	27
Single person								
Dependent children	75	52	55	1	0	8	97	98
No dependent children								
Male	6	10	11	7	–	9	0	22
Female	8	10	12	4	0	8	–	23
All family types[4]	13	14	17	3	24	13	23	58

1 See Appendix 8: Benefit units.
2 Incapacity benefit, disability living allowance (care and mobility components), severe disablement allowance, industrial injuries disability benefit, war disablement pension, attendance allowance and disabled persons tax credit.
3 People aged 60 and over for females and 65 and over for males; for couples, where the head is over pension age.
4 Components do not add to the total as each benefit unit may receive more than one benefit.
Source: Family Resources Survey, Department for Work and Pensions

benefit and council tax benefit paid to people over 60. Over a half of all social security expenditure, £54 billion, was for the elderly, while over a quarter was for the sick and disabled.

Tax credits (which are excluded from Figures 8.1 to 8.4) are becoming an important part of the social protection system, particularly for families and those on low pay. Tax credits are additions to the net income of wage earners, credited to them if they meet certain criteria. For example, working families' tax credit (WFTC) gives working families with children additional financial help. At the end of February 2002 there were 1.3 million families receiving WFTC, adding, on average, an extra £83.14 a week to their income.

Benefits are available for a range of needs. In 2000/01, 58 per cent of families in Great Britain received some form of social security benefit or tax credit (Table 8.5). Nearly all people of pensionable age (women aged 60 and over

and men aged 65 and over) received a state retirement pension. In addition, many older people also receive other social security benefits such as council tax benefit or housing benefit, particularly if they are single. Many also receive occupational or personal pensions, which they have saved for throughout their working lives (see Table 8.19 on page 156).

Child benefit is paid for all children aged under 16 (or under 19 years and studying up to A level, NVQ level 3 or equivalent). It is a universal payment, not affected by income or savings or National Insurance contributions, which is received by nearly all families with dependent children. Single parent families with dependent children are more likely than couple families to be receiving some other benefits such as WFTC or income support, council tax benefit or housing benefit.

Local authorities offer a range of social protection such as the provision of home help (see Figure 8.9 on page 150), and the running

No. 33: 2003 edition

Figure **8.6**

Local authority personal social services expenditure,[1] 2000/01

England

Percentages

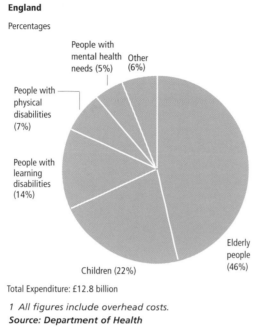

People with mental health needs (5%)

Other (6%)

People with physical disabilities (7%)

People with learning disabilities (14%)

Children (22%)

Elderly people (46%)

Total Expenditure: £12.8 billion

1 All figures include overhead costs.
Source: Department of Health

Figure **8.7**

Charitable expenditure on social protection of the top 500 charities:[1] by function, 1999/2000

United Kingdom

£ million

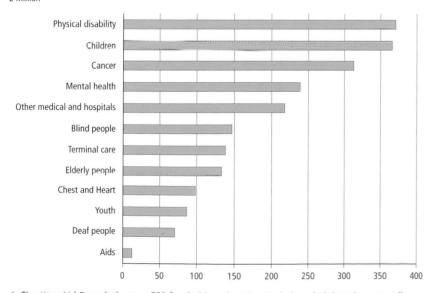

1 Charities Aid Foundation top 500 fundraising charities. Excludes administrative expenditure.
Source: Charities Aid Foundation

of children's homes (see Table 8.22 on page 158), day centres and residential homes (see Table 8.8). Spending on personal social services by local authorities in England was £12.8 billion in 2000/01 (Figure 8.6). Elderly people accounted for nearly a half of this expenditure (£5.9 billion) and children accounted for over a fifth (£2.9 billion). A seventh of this spending (£1.8 billion) went to people with learning disabilities, with smaller proportions accounted for by people with physical disabilities (£0.9 billion) and people with mental health problems (£0.7 billion).

Help for people in need is also provided by voluntary organisations. The Charities Aid Foundation combines data from the top 500 charities in the United Kingdom, to show their spending on social protection (Figure 8.7). In 1999/2000 the largest amounts of this type of expenditure went to helping people with a physical disability (£371 million), children (£367 million) and on cancer (£314 million). These three areas also received the most money from the top 500 charities in 1996/97. The charities helping children experienced the biggest increase in spending between 1996/97 and 1999/2000, at 44 per cent, while spending on helping those with a physical disability increased by 11 per cent and on cancer by 38 per cent. Overall during this period the largest increases in spending were in other medical areas and hospitals (75 per cent), mental health (61 per cent), terminal care (58 per cent) and chest and heart (57 per cent).

Carers and caring

The majority of residential care homes provide places for older people, people with physical or learning disabilities or for people with mental health problems. In 2001 there were 341,000 places in residential care homes in the independent and public sectors in England, the majority of which were for older people (Table 8.8 – see overleaf). The number of places for older people rose to a peak of 247,000 in 1998, and then decreased to 237,000 in 2001. This decrease can be attributed to a levelling off in the places available in the independent sector, coupled with a continued decline in places in the public sector. Between 1996 and 1998 a decrease of 7,000 places for older people in the public sector was more than offset by a increase of 11,000 in independent sector places. However between 1998 and 2001 public sector places decreased by 11,000 but places for older people available in the independent sector increased by only 600. To some extent these reductions reflect the Government's policy of promoting independence where it is safe to do so. Over the same period there has been an increase in intensive home care, which is seen as an alternative to residential care.

In 2001 almost six times as many residential care home places were available in the independent sector than in local authority run homes. While there had been a fall of 22,000 places in the public sector between 1996 and 2001, there was a rise of 40,000 places in the independent sector over the same period. The biggest increase was in the provision of independent sector places for people with mental health problems which increased by 15,000 places between 1996 and 2001.

Local authorities' home care services assist people to continue to live in their own home, and to function as independently as possible. During a survey week in September 2001, local authorities in England provided or purchased 2.9 million hours of home care services for around 381,000 households (or 396,000 clients). Between 1992 and 2001 the number of contact hours increased by 71 per cent and the average contact hours for each household visited rose from 3 to almost 8 hours (Figure 8.9).

The type of help provided is changing, with more hours of help being provided to fewer homes. Between September 2000 and September 2001 there was an increase of 3 per cent in the number of contact hours provided and a 4 per cent fall in the number of households receiving that care.

As with the provision of residential care homes, the independent sector (which includes the private and voluntary sectors) now provides much of the care, although the funding may well be provided by the public sector. The number of contact hours provided by the independent sector increased by 11 per cent between 2000 and 2001. Around 60 per cent of all contact hours were provided by the independent sector in 2001.

There were 264,000 personal social services staff in Great Britain in 2001, 23,000 more than there had been in 1981 – an increase of 10 per cent (see Table 8.15 on page 153). Over the last

Table 8.8

Places available in residential care homes: by sector[1]

England

Thousands

	1996	1998	2000	2001
Public sector[2]				
Older people	57.3	49.9	42.6	39.2
People with physical or sensory or learning disabilities	10.6	9.3	8.4	7.5
People with mental health problems[3]	4.7	4.5	4.1	3.9
Other people	0.1	0.2	0.3	0.2
All places in the public sector	72.7	64.0	55.5	50.9
Independent sector[4]				
Older people	185.3	196.9	197.8	197.6
People with physical or sensory or learning disabilities	41.0	48.7	53.7	52.9
People with mental health problems[3]	21.2	34.2	35.9	36.2
Other people	2.7	4.1	3.0	3.7
All places in the independent sector	250.3	283.9	290.4	290.3
All places in the public and independent sectors	323.0	347.9	345.9	341.2

1 At 31 March.
2 Places in staffed residential care homes.
3 Includes residential beds for older mentally infirm people.
4 Residential places in private, voluntary, small (less than 4 places) and dual registered places.
Source: Department of Health

Figure 8.9

Households visited by home help and home care

England

Average contact hours per household

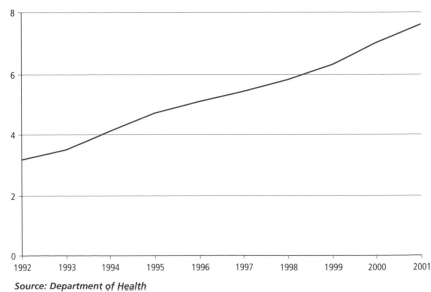

Source: Department of Health

Table **8.10**

Types of help given by informal carers, 2000/01

Great Britain Percentages

	Carers with main person cared for		
	In the same household	In another private household	All carers
Giving medicines	44	11	22
Personal care (eg washing)	51	15	26
Physical help (eg with walking)	57	25	35
Paperwork or financial matters	41	38	39
Taking out	49	53	52
Keeping company	49	58	55
Keeping an eye on person cared for	62	59	60
Other practical help	69	73	71

Source: General Household Survey, Office for National Statistics

Table **8.11**

Health symptoms felt by informal carers: by number of hours spent caring, 2000/01

Great Britain Percentages

	Number of hours spent caring per week			
	Under 20	20–49	50 or more	Total[1]
Feels tired	12	34	52	20
Feels depressed	7	27	34	14
Loss of appetite	1	5	8	3
Disturbed sleep	7	24	47	14
General feeling of strain	14	35	40	20
Physical strain	3	10	24	7
Short tempered	11	29	36	17
Had to see own GP	2	8	17	4
Other	2	4	2	2
Health not affected	72	39	28	61

1 Includes those who did not estimate the number of hours.
Source: General Household Survey, Office for National Statistics

ten years however there has been a decrease of 8 per cent in the number of personal social services staff, partially reflecting the increased use of the private sector in the provision of residential care and home care.

As well as care provided by central and local government, there are many informal carers who provide care for family members, friends or neighbours who are sick, disabled or elderly. The General Household Survey found that about 6.8 million adults aged 16 or over in Great Britain, representing 16 per cent of adults, were caring for a sick, disabled or elderly person in 2000/01. This was very similar to the figure in 1990/91.

Fifty eight per cent of these carers were women and 73 per cent were married or cohabiting. The majority, 65 per cent, were aged over 45. Nearly two fifths of carers were caring for a parent and nearly a fifth were caring for their spouse or partner. The majority of people cared for someone with a physical disability only (62 per cent), while 6 per cent cared for someone with a mental disability only, and a further 18 per cent cared for someone with both mental and physical disabilities. Fourteen per cent of carers looked after someone simply because they were old. The most common type of help given by informal carers was keeping an eye on the cared-for person, followed by keeping them company and taking them out (Table 8.10). A substantial proportion (71 per cent) of all carers provided other types of practical help.

Over a quarter of informal carers were caring for 20 or more hours a week. This group was more likely to be caring for a spouse or a child and less likely to be caring for a parent, parent-in-law, other relative or friend/neighbour. In 2000/01, 35 per cent of these carers said that they had a long-standing illness that had affected their activities and 20 per cent stated that their health over the last 12 months was not good, compared with 21 per cent and 13 per cent, respectively, of adults in the general population.

The perceived effects of caring on the health of the carer are shown in Table 8.11. Thirty nine per cent of all carers reported that their physical or mental health had been affected as a result of caring. The proportion of carers reporting health symptoms increased with the number of hours spent caring, with those caring for over 20 hours more likely to report each symptom than those who cared for less than 20 hours per week. Those caring for 50 hours or more were even more likely to report symptoms. Feeling tired and general feelings of strain were felt by 20 per cent of all carers, but among those who cared for 50 hours or more, 52 per cent reported feeling tired, 47 per cent reported disturbed sleep and 40 per cent reported general feelings of strain. Overall, only 4 per cent of carers had had to see their own GP about their symptoms, but this rose to 17 per cent of carers who spent 50 or more hours a week caring.

Sick and disabled people

The NHS offers care and help to sick and disabled people. The number of acute finished consultant episodes has risen by 42 per cent since 1981, to just over 8 million in 2000/01 in the United Kingdom (Table 8.12). Although episodes have declined for the mentally ill since 1994/95 and for people with learning disabilities since 1997/98, in 2000/01 they were 9 per cent and 26 per cent higher, respectively, than in 1981.

In 2000/01, acute patients stayed in hospital for an average of 5.1 days. In 1981 the mean duration of stay was 8.4 days, which had fallen to 6.0 days in 1991/92. Between 1996/97 and 2000/01 the average stay for acute patients was around 5.0 to 5.5 days. The mean duration of stay for the mentally ill was just over 58 days which is 49 per cent lower than in 1991. Despite the overall fall, the average stay increased between 1997/98 and 1998/99 to around 75 days before declining further.

For people with learning disabilities the average length of stay was just over 90 days, over 140 per cent lower than in 1991. As with the duration of stay for the mentally ill, this decline was not smooth, increasing by 3 per cent between 1998/99 and 1999/2000 before falling again.

The length of time people wait for treatment as an in-patient or day case at hospitals is one of the standards on which NHS performance is judged. At the end of March 2002 there were just over a million people waiting for treatment as an in-patient or day case at NHS hospitals in England (Table 8.13). This is 26,500 more than in March 2001. In 2002, 77 per cent

Table 8.12

NHS in-patient activity for sick and disabled people[1]
United Kingdom

	1981	1991/92	1998/99	1999/2000	2000/01
Acute[2]					
Finished consultant episodes[3] (thousands)	5,693	6,729	7,946	7,999	8,076
In-patient episodes per available bed (numbers)	31.1	45.9	58.5	63.5	63.7
Mean duration of stay (days)	8.4	6.0	4.9	5.6	5.1
Mentally ill					
Finished consultant episodes[3] (thousands)	244	281	276	271	265
In-patient episodes per available bed (numbers)	2.2	4.0	5.7	6.5	6.4
Mean duration of stay (days)	..	114.8	75.2	60.6	58.4
People with learning disabilities					
Finished consultant episodes[3] (thousands)	34	62	45	42	43
In-patient episodes per available bed (numbers)	0.6	2.2	4.0	4.8	5.3
Mean duration of stay (days)	..	544.1	101.9	104.8	90.4

1 Excludes NHS beds and activity in joint-user and contractual hospitals.
2 Wards for patients, excluding elderly, maternity and neonate cots in maternity units.
3 All data for Wales and Scotland, and for Northern Ireland except acute data after 1986, are for deaths, discharges and transfers between specialities. See Appendix, Part 8: In-patient activity.
Source: Department of Health; National Assembly for Wales; National Health Service in Scotland; Department of Health, Social Services and Public Safety, Northern Ireland

Table 8.13

NHS hospital waiting lists:[1,2] by patients' region of residence, 2002
Great Britain   Percentages

	Less than 6 months	6 to 12 months	12 months or longer	Total waiting (=100%) (thousands)
England	77	21	2	1,022
Northern & Yorkshire	78	22	–	122
North West	78	20	2	160
Trent	82	18	–	100
West Midlands	82	18	1	85
Eastern	75	22	3	124
London	75	22	3	139
South East	73	23	3	189
South West	75	21	3	103
Wales	63	23	14	71
Scotland	81	17	3	72

1 Waiting times refer to people waiting for admission as either an in-patient or a day case and the length of time they had waited to date. At 31 March.
2 There are differences between countries in the ways that waiting times are calculated. See Appendix, Part 8: Waiting times.
Source: Department of Health; National Assembly for Wales; Information and Statistics Division, NHS in Scotland.

Figure **8.14**

Total emergency calls[1] and those resulting in a response by an ambulance

England

Millions

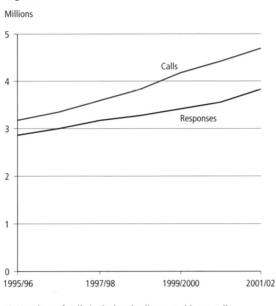

1 Number of calls includes duplicate and hoax calls.
Source: Department of Health

Table **8.15**

Health and personal social services staff[1]

Great Britain

Thousands

	1981	1991	2001
NHS hospital and community health service staff			
Direct care staff			
Medical and dental	48	56	76
Nursing, midwifery and health visitors	458	470	440
Other non-medical staff	95	113	171
All direct care staff	601	639	687
General medical practitioners	29	33	37
General dental practitioners	15	18	22
Personal social services	241	288	264

1 See Appendix, Part 8: Health and personal social services staff.
Source: Department of Health; National Assembly for Wales; National Health Service in Scotland

of the people had been waiting for less than six months, while 2 per cent had waited 12 months or longer. In Wales there were 71,000 people waiting for treatment at NHS hospitals, with the majority, 63 per cent, waiting for less than six months. A larger proportion of people on waiting lists in Wales had waited for 12 months or longer than in England – 14 per cent in Wales compared to 2 per cent in England.

About half of patients (not including live births) treated in hospitals are emergency cases and do not come from waiting lists. In 2000/01 there were 14.3 million attendances at hospital accident and emergency departments in England, an increase of 167,000 (1 per cent) since 1996/97. Over the same period emergency ambulance responses increased by 560,000 (19 per cent).

Emergency calls for ambulances are generally made via a 999 call but sometimes emergency requests can be made by GPs. In England, the number of emergency calls, including duplicate and hoax calls, rose from 3.2 million in 1995/96 to 4.7 million in 2001/02 (Figure 8.14). The number of emergency responses by ambulances increased less than this, from 2.9 million in 1995/96 to 3.8 million in 2001/02. However, emergency calls and responses both grew by 7 per cent between 2000/01 and 2001/02.

Between 1981 and 2001 the numbers of NHS hospital and community health direct care staff in Great Britain increased by 14 per cent, to 687,000 (Table 8.15). This rise is mainly due to an increase in the number of medical and dental staff and other non-medical employees. There were 18,000 fewer nurses, midwives and health visitors in 2001 than in 1981, representing a 4 per cent decrease. Between 1981 and 1991 there was an increase of 12,000 nurses, midwives and health visitors, but this was followed by a larger decrease of 30,000 between 1991 and 2001.

In 2001 there were 37,000 General Medical Practitioners (GPs) in Great Britain, an increase of 8,000 (28 per cent) between 1981 and 2001. Over this period the average number of NHS GP consultations per person per year increased slightly to five in the early and mid-1990s, but returned to its 1981 average of four in 2000/01. People can consult their GP for a number of services including vaccinations and general health advice, as well as the dispensing of prescriptions and the diagnosis of illness. Older people make more consultations with their GP than other age groups (Figure 8.16). In 2000/01 those aged 75 years or older visited their GP an average of seven times. Consultations with GPs for children aged under 5 took place on average five times in the year, while children aged between 5 and 15 visited their GP on average only twice. The average number of visits to a GP then increased from this age group onwards.

Older age groups are substantially more likely than younger age groups to be seen by an NHS GP at home. For the 75 and over age group, 23 per cent of consultations took place at home, compared with 9 per cent for those aged 65 to 74 and up to 2 per cent for those aged under 65. Of all age groups, telephone consultations were most likely to be made for the under 5s (17 per cent compared with between 7 and 11 per cent for other age groups).

People's satisfaction with their GP has fallen over recent years. In 2001 the British Social Attitudes survey found that 68 per cent of people in Great Britain regarded the quality of medical treatment provided by GPs as either satisfactory or very good (Table 8.17). This compares with 76 per cent in 1999. There was a more marked decline in the number of people who felt that the quality of medical treatment at hospitals in their area was satisfactory or very good – from 66 per cent in 1999 to 46 per cent in 2001. Most people felt that the staffing levels of doctors and of nurses in hospitals were inadequate. In 2001, around 80 per cent of people said that staffing levels were in need of either some improvement or a lot of improvement.

Waiting areas in accident and emergency departments were rated as in need of either some or a lot of improvement by 68 per cent of people. However, waiting areas in GP surgeries were more highly regarded with only 29 per cent of people saying that these areas were in need of some or a lot of improvement.

There are a number of benefits available to sick and disabled people. In 2001/02 it is estimated that 3.6 million long-term sick and/or disabled people in Great Britain

Figure **8.16**

NHS general medical practitioner consultations: by age, 2000/01
Great Britain

Average consultations per year

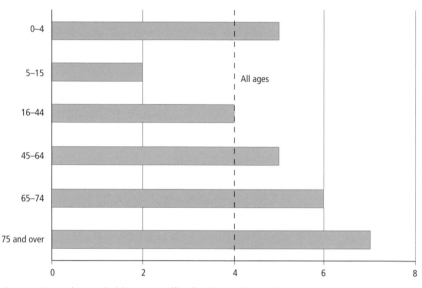

Source: General Household Survey, Office for National Statistics

Table **8.17**

Satisfaction with NHS hospitals and GPs in their area, 2001[1,2]
Great Britain   Percentages

	In need of a lot of improvement	In need of some improvement	Satisfactory	Very good
Hospital Services				
Quality of medical treatment	12	39	37	8
Quality of nursing care in hospitals	12	35	37	13
Staffing level of doctors in hospitals	34	45	17	2
Staffing level of nurses in hospitals	36	44	16	2
General condition of hospital buildings	18	39	34	7
Waiting areas in accident and				
emergency departments	30	37	27	2
Waiting areas for out-patients	21	38	35	3
GP services				
Quality of medical treatment by GPs	7	23	51	17
Being able to choose which GP to see	10	28	51	9
Waiting areas at GPs' surgeries	7	22	57	12

1 *Respondents' answer when asked 'From what you know or have heard, say whether you think the NHS in your area is, on the whole, satisfactory or in need of improvement'.*
2 *Percentages do not sum to 100 due to those who answered 'don't know' or 'not answered'.*
Source: British Social Attitude Survey, National Centre for Social Research

received either disability living allowance (DLA) or attendance allowance (AA), more than double the number who received these benefits or their equivalents in 1991/92 (Table 8.18). This increase is due to changes to conditions for benefit entitlement, demographic changes and increased take-up. DLA is a benefit for people who are disabled, have personal care needs, mobility needs or both and who claim before their 65th birthday. AA is paid to people who become disabled after age 65 and are so severely disabled (physically or mentally) that they need some one to help with their personal care needs.

In February 2002, 2.3 million people were receiving DLA and 1.3 million were receiving AA. The most common condition for which both DLA and AA were being received was arthritis (480,000 and 378,000 respectively). For DLA other common conditions included 'other mental health causes' such as psychosis and dementia (293,000), learning difficulties (230,000) and back ailments (204,000). Following arthritis, the most common

conditions for which AA was being received were frailty (176,00) and mental health causes (126,000).

Incapacity benefit (IB) and severe disablement allowance (SDA) are claimed by those who are unable to work because of illness and/or disability. The number of people receiving IB or SDA (or their earlier equivalents) increased by 46 per cent between 1981/82 and 2001/02 and is now at around 1.9 million. During this period there was an increase in the proportion of these people who receive IB and SDA on a long-term basis. This is partly due to the introduction in April 1983 of statutory sick pay which is paid to employees by their employer for the first 28 weeks of illness, reducing the need for people to claim benefits for short-term illness.

Older people

There has been a 51 per cent rise in the number of people aged 65 and over during the past 40 years in the United Kingdom (see Table 1.2). There are a number of care services available to older people. Older people occupy the majority of places in care homes (see Table 8.8 on page 150) and they make more consultations with GPs than any other group (see Figure 8.16 on page 154), a greater proportion of which are in the patients' home. Older people form the largest category of expenditure from both central government and local authorities (see Figure 8.4 on page 147 and Figure 8.6 on page 149). Much of government expenditure on social protection for older people is on the provision of the state retirement pension.

Most people in Great Britain feel that it should be the responsibility of the government to provide a decent standard of living for the old, according to data from the British Social Attitudes survey in 2001. Sixty three per cent thought that it definitely should be and a further 32 per cent thought that it probably should be. Despite this, there is an increasing emphasis on people making their own provision for retirement, through either an occupational or personal (private) pension. Occupational pensions are schemes set up and provided through people's employers. All employers who employ more than five employees are required by law to offer either an occupational pension, or access to a

Table **8.18**

Recipients of benefits for sick and disabled people[1]

Great Britain					Thousands
	1981/82	1991/92	1999/00	2000/01	2001/02
Long-term sick and people with disabilities					
Incapacity benefit/severe disablement allowance only	747	1,438	1,372	1,365	1,333
One of the above benefits plus income support	129	304	409	423	437
Income support only	..	..	586	620	655
Short-term sick					
Incapacity benefit only	369	107	69	70	64
Incapacity benefit and income support	24	28	22	23	20
Income support only	..	..	163	169	158
Disability living allowance/ attendance allowance	582	1,758	3,353	3,490	3,614

1 See Appendix Part 8: Recipients of benefits for sick and disabled people
Source: Department for Work and Pensions

Table **8.19**

Pension provision: by selected employment status,[1] sex and age, 2000/01

Great Britain
Percentages

	16–24	25–34	35–44	45–54	55–59	60–64	65 and over	All aged 16 and over
Male								
Employees								
Occupational pension only	14	46	58	58	55	38	2	46
Personal pension only	4	13	14	14	14	14	1	12
Either occupational or personal								
pension or both	18	61	75	76	71	54	2	61
No pension scheme	82	39	25	24	29	46	98	39
Self-employed								
Occupational pension only	..	1	1	2	1	1	0	2
Personal pension only	..	45	53	56	52	37	2	46
No pension scheme	..	53	45	40	47	61	98	52
Female								
Employees								
Occupational pension only	18	45	50	51	44	26	1	43
Personal pension only	2	8	7	8	7	2	2	7
Either occupational or personal								
pension or both	19	54	59	61	53	29	2	51
No pension scheme	81	46	41	39	47	71	98	49
Self-employed								
Personal pension only	..	29	30	30	..	..	..	27
No pension scheme	..	66	66	67	..	..	..	70

1 Includes employees and self-employed people, but not 'others'. See Appendix, Part 8: Pension provision.
Source: Family Resources Survey, Department for Work and Pensions

stakeholder pension (a form of personal pension), so long as the employee earns more than the 'lower earnings limit' (£72 per week in 2001/02). Personal pension schemes are offered by financial service companies into which people (and sometimes their employers) make contributions to provide a pension on retirement. Stakeholder pensions are a form of personal pension introduced in 2001 to provide a low cost option.

In 2000/01, 61 per cent of male employees and 51 per cent of female employees in Great Britain contributed to either an occupational or personal pension or both (Table 8.19). Self-employed people are less likely to save for their retirement in this way – only 48 per cent of men and 30 per cent of women made contributions to these schemes.

Those aged 16 to 24 were the least likely of those of working age to be contributing to a pension scheme. The proportion rose with age up to the 45 to 54 age group. People of state pension age were unlikely to be still contributing to a scheme but to be using the pension as a source of income, although it appears that a sizeable proportion of women carry on contributing after their state retirement age of 60. Twenty nine per cent of employed women aged 60 to 64 were still contributing to a pension scheme, although this percentage fell to 2 per cent for those aged 65 and over. For men the state retirement age is 65. Only 2 per cent of men aged 65 or over were still contributing to a pension.

Table **8.20**

Distribution of income[1] for pensioners by family type and pension scheme[2,3]

Great Britain

Percentages

	Income quintile group					All pensioners (millions)
	Bottom quintile	Second quintile	Third quintile	Fourth quintile	Top quintile	
Before housing costs[3]						
Couples	26	27	21	14	12	5.2
of which						
No pension scheme	52	28	13	5	3	1.1
Only one pension scheme	22	30	21	16	11	2.8
Both with pension scheme	10	20	29	20	22	1.3
Single	25	33	21	14	7	4.1
of which						
No pension scheme	34	34	17	11	4	1.9
With pension scheme	18	32	23	16	10	2.2
After housing costs[3]						
Couples	19	27	22	17	15	5.2
of which						
No pension scheme	45	34	12	6	3	1.1
Only one with pension scheme	15	30	23	18	14	2.8
Both with pension scheme	6	16	29	24	25	1.3
Single	21	31	21	15	11	4.1
of which						
No pension scheme	33	35	15	12	5	1.9
With pension scheme	12	29	25	18	16	2.2

1 Net equivalised disposable income.
2 Occupational or personal pension. Excludes self-employed.
3 Figures are presented on both a before and after housing costs basis to take into account variations in housing costs between groups. Both measures have imperfections, so it is not advisable to unduly favour one above another. See Appendix, Part 5: Housing costs.
Source: Households Below Average Income, Department for Work and Pensions

There were 5.2 million pensioners living as couples in 2001. In only a quarter of these couples did both partners have either a personal or occupational pension (Table 8.20). In one in five couples neither had one of these pensions. A higher proportion, almost half, of the 4.1 million single pensioners had neither an occupational or personal pension.

Occupational and personal pensions are a particularly important source of income for those over pensionable age (see Table 5.3 on page 94). Pensioners with no occupational or personal pension were more likely to be at the bottom end of the income distribution. Pensioner couples where neither partner had an occupational or personal pension were particularly likely to be in households in the bottom fifth of the income distribution.

Families and children

An important part of social protection provided to families is maternity care. In 2000/01 there were 550,000 NHS hospital deliveries in England, around 50,000 less than in 1980. The number of deliveries rose unevenly between 1980 and 1990/91 to 652,000, since when it has fallen for every year except 1996/97, when it rose slightly. Over 21 per cent of the deliveries in 2000/01 were by caesarean section, compared to 9 per cent in 1980. In 2000/01 more than half of caesareans were emergencies. Women with caesarean deliveries spent on average 3 to 4 days in hospital after delivery compared to 1 day for women who had spontaneous births . The average stay for all deliveries was just over 2 days.

Expectant mothers can be seen by midwives and health visitors in community clinics and by consultant obstetricians in outpatient clinics. While the total number of antenatal contacts in England grew by around 5 per cent between 1989/90 and 1999/2000, the balance between outpatient and community contacts shifted towards community programmes. In 1989/90, 52 per cent of contacts were in community programmes, while in 1999/2000 the proportion was 70 per cent.

In 1999/2000 the average number of contacts between a midwife or health visitor and an individual woman as part of a community maternity programme was just over 15, an increase of about one contact per maternity since 1989/90. In the ten years leading up to 1999/2000 there was a decline in the number of contacts made postnatally and a rise in antenatal contacts. Much of the rise in antenatal visits occurred in the mid-1990s and the figure remained at an average of around 8 between 1997/98 and 1999/2000. In 1999/2000 there were 8.8 million face to face contacts between a midwife or health visitor and an individual woman as part of a community maternity programme.

Changes in the labour market mean that there are more women in the workplace (see Chapter 4 on page 77), and the main component of the rise in the 1990s is the increased number of women with dependent children in the workplace. In spring 2002, 52 per cent of women whose youngest dependent child was under 5 years of age were working either part-time or full-time (36 per cent and 17 per cent, respectively). Seventy per cent of women whose youngest dependent child was aged 5-10 were working, 26 per cent full-time and 44 per cent part-time.

There are a number of day care and childminding options for parents with children aged under 8 and there has been an increased emphasis by the Government on the role of childcare and education in raising educational standards and enhancing children's social development. In England, Wales and Northern Ireland the number of day care places in playgroups in 2001 was around a fifth less than in 1992 but this has been more than compensated for by the larger increase in the number of day nursery places (Table 8.21). There were 455,000 playgroup places in 1992 and 369,000 in 2001, a decrease of 19 per cent. Over the same period the number of day nursery places more than doubled.

The majority of childminder, day nursery and playgroup places are provided by the private sector and the voluntary sector; and the number of nursery places they offer has been increasing in recent years. In 2001 there were nearly nine times as many registered day nursery places provided by these sectors as in 1987. Over the same period, the number of childminder places provided by these sectors doubled. The number of private and voluntary sector registered playgroup places decreased by a fifth between 1987 and 2001, the numbers falling between 2000 and 2001 after

Table **8.21**

Day care places for children[1]

England, Wales & Northern Ireland					Thousands
	1987	1992	1999	2000	2001
Day nurseries					
Local authority provided[2]	29	24	16	18	19
Registered	32	98	235	261	282
Non-registered[3]	1	1	12	2	2
All day nursery places[4]	62	123	262	281	304
Childminders					
Local authority provided[2]	2	2	9	3	3
Other registered person	159	275	360	349	331
All childminder places[4]	161	277	369	353	338
Playgroups					
Local authority provided	4	2	3	2	7
Registered	434	450	383	391	347
Non-registered[2]	7	3	3	1	1
All playgroup places[4]	444	455	389	394	369
Out of school clubs[5]	..	..	119	153	165

1 Under the age of 8 in England and Wales. Under the age of 12 in Northern Ireland.
2 England and Wales only.
3 England only before 2000; England and Wales only from 2000.
4 Figures do not add to totals. Total figures for England include an imputed figure for missing values.
5 For children aged five to seven in England and Wales. In Northern Ireland for children aged four to eight.
Source: Department for Education and Skills; National Assembly for Wales; Department of Health, Social Services and Public Safety, Northern Ireland

Table **8.22**

Children looked after by local authorities:[1] by type of accommodation[2]

England					Thousands
	1991	1996	1999	2000	2001
Foster placements	34.8	33.1	36.2	37.9	38.4
Placement with parents	..	4.7	6.3	6.5	6.9
Children's homes[3]	..	..	6.6	7.0	6.8
Placed for adoption	1.9	2.2	2.9	3.1	3.4
Living independently or in residential employment	1.7	1.4	1.2	1.2	1.2
Residential schools	..	..	1.0	1.1	1.1
Other accommodation	2.8	1.8	1.3	1.2	1.2
All looked after children	59.8	50.6	55.5	58.1	58.9

1 Excludes children looked after under an agreed series of short-term placements.
2 At 31 March.
3 Includes local authority, voluntary and private children's homes and secure units.
Source: Department of Health

Figure **8.23**

Adoptions by date of entry in Adopted Children Register: by age of child

Great Britain

Percentages

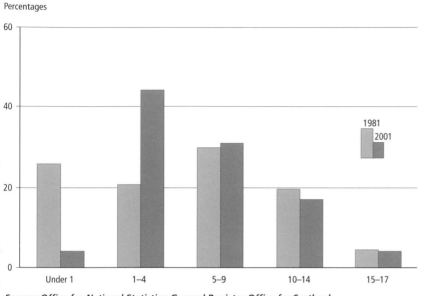

Source: Office for National Statistics; General Register Office for Scotland

a slight rise between 1999 and 2000. While the numbers remain relatively small, there was a sharp increase in local authority provided playgroup places between 2000 and 2001, from 2,000 to 7,000.

In cases where parents are unable to provide proper care for children, local authorities can take them into care. These children are usually described as being 'looked after'. In 2001 there were 58,900 children being looked after by local authorities in England (Table 8.22). The majority of these children (38,400) were cared for in foster placements. The number of children being looked after by local authorities decreased in the early 1990s but rose again

between 1996 and 2001 (by 16 per cent), when it almost returned to its 1991 level. This rise reflects not only an increase in the number of children being taken into care, but also an increase in the average duration of that care. There were 3,600 children in Wales and 2,400 children in Northern Ireland being looked after by local authorities in 2001. As in England, the majority of these children were being looked after by foster parents (although data are not collected in Northern Ireland on the number of these children who are placed for adoption).

A child is not necessarily being looked after by a local authority immediately prior to being adopted. Many are adopted by step-parents and relatives and will not be included in Table 8.22. In Great Britain there were 6,500 adoption orders in 2001, including those adopted by step-parents and other members of their family. An adoption order gives parental responsibility for a child to adoptive parent(s). Between 1981 and 2001 the number of adoptions fell from 10,400 to 6,500, although the number of adoptions has started to increase in recent years from a low of 4,800 in 1999.

In 2001, 4 per cent of adoptions were for children under 1, 44 per cent for children aged between 1 and 4, and 31 per cent for children aged 5 to 9 (Figure 8.23). The percentage of adoption orders declined as children approached adulthood with 17 per cent for 10-14 year olds and only 4 per cent of adoptions for children aged 15-17. Between 1981 and 2001 there was a decrease in the proportion of adopted children who were under 1 (from 26 to 4 per cent) and an increase in the proportion of adoptions of those aged 1-4 (from 20 to 44 per cent).

Chapter 9

Crime and justice

Crime rates

- In 2001/02, 5.5 million crimes were recorded by the police in England and Wales, 7 per cent more than in the previous year. (Table 9.1)

- Crime recorded by the police in England and Wales fell by 8 per cent between 1996 and 2000, compared with an average 1 per cent rise in EU countries. (Figure 9.4)

Offences

- In 2000, the number of drugs seizures in the United Kingdom fell by 7 per cent compared with the previous year to 124,000. (Table 9.6)

Victims

- Twenty eight per cent of those questioned in 2001/02 reported that they had been the victim of some sort of crime in the previous year. (Page 167)

Offenders

- In 2001, 467,000 people were cautioned for, or found guilty of, an indictable offence in England and Wales, 8,000 fewer than in 2000. (Table 9.13)

Police and courts action

- In 2001, 323,000 people were sentenced for indictable offences in England and Wales. Those sentenced for motoring offences were the most likely to be fined (46 per cent). (Table 9.16)

- In England and Wales the overall detection rate for crimes recorded by the police in 2001/02 was 23 per cent. (Table 9.18)

Prisons and probation

- The prison population in England and Wales increased to over 71,000 in mid-2002, a rise of over 25,000 since 1990, and the highest figure ever recorded. (Figure 9.19)

Civil justice

- Immigration, housing and welfare benefits make up two thirds of the new (non-family) matters handled by the Community Legal Service in England and Wales, where legal help is offered. (Figure 9.23)

Resources

- Police officer numbers in England and Wales reached record levels with 129,603 officers in March 2002. This was an increase of nearly 4,000 officers compared with a year earlier and the largest increase for 26 years. (Table 9.24)

Crime, in some form, affects many people during their lives. Dealing with crime and its impact is a continual problem for both society and government. The Government's current priorities include tackling street crime, introducing changes in the handling of drug offences and reforming the criminal justice system.

Crime rates

There are difficulties in determining the true level of crime in this country. Two main measures are used, each with its own strengths and weaknesses. One measure is the amount of crime recorded by the police, and the other comes from surveys of victims, including the British Crime Survey (BCS). The box opposite gives more details on these two measures of crime.

From recorded crime figures for England and Wales, it is estimated that in 2001/02 there was a 2 per cent increase in the underlying crime trend compared with the previous year. Although the 5.5 million crimes recorded by the police in 2001/02 (Table 9.1) was 7 per cent more than the previous financial year, a substantial part of this increase is likely to be due to the changes in the methods and rules for the recording of crime. These were estimated to have inflated the number of crimes recorded in 2001/02 by 5 per cent.

Crime in Scotland showed little overall change between 2000 and 2001, with a total of 421,000 crimes recorded by the police. In Scotland the term 'crimes' is used for the more serious criminal acts (roughly equivalent to 'indictable' and 'triable-either-way' offences in England and Wales). Less serious crimes are termed 'offences'. More details on these differences can be found in the Appendix, Part 9: Offences and crimes.

Recorded crime in Northern Ireland increased by around 17 per cent between 2000/01 and 2001/02. A major factor behind this increase was the implementation of a new recording system which resulted in more low level crime being recorded. In Northern Ireland the definitions used are broadly comparable with those in England and Wales.

After taking into account changes in the recording of crimes, there were rises in certain types of crime recorded by the police in

Table 9.1

Recorded crime: by type of offence,[1] 2001/02

Thousands

	England & Wales	Scotland[2]	Northern Ireland
Theft and handling stolen goods	2,267	171	42
of which			
theft of vehicles	328	23	12
theft from vehicles	655	40	7
Criminal damage	1,064	95	40
Burglary	879	45	17
Violence against the person	650	20	26
Fraud and forgery	317	21	9
Drugs offences	121	36	1
Robbery	121	4	2
Sexual offences	41	5	1
of which			
rape	10	1	0
Other offences[3]	65	25	1
All notifiable offences	5,527	421	140

1 See Appendix, Part 9: Types of offences in England, Wales and Northern Ireland, and Offences and crimes.
2 Figures for Scotland refer to 2001.
3 In Northern Ireland includes 'offences against the state'. In Scotland excludes 'offending while on bail'.
Source: Home Office; Scottish Executive; Police Service of Northern Ireland

Figure 9.2

Crime committed within last 12 months: by offence category, 2001/02

England & Wales

Percentages

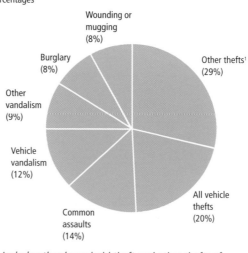

1 Include other household theft and other thefts of personal property.
Source: British Crime Survey, Home Office

Measures of crime

There are two main measures of crime: estimates from surveys of victims, such as the British Crime Survey (BCS), and from data collected by the police. Crime data collected by the police are a by-product of the administrative procedure of completing a record for crimes which they investigate. BCS data are collated by interviewing members of households. The survey measures all 'incidents' irrespective of whether they were reported to or recorded by the police.

Police recorded crime and BCS measured crime have a different coverage. Unlike crime data recorded by the police, the BCS is restricted to crimes against adults (aged 16 or over) living in private households and their property and does not include some types of crime (for example, fraud, murder and so-called victimless crimes).

England and Wales, most notably robbery, which increased by 27 per cent between 2000/01 and 2001/02. Non-vehicle thefts increased by 6 per cent over the same period. Household burglary rose, after the adjustments, by 3 per cent and other burglary rose by 5 per cent. Violent crimes against the person fell by 5 per cent, after adjusting for the recording changes, while sexual offences fell by 8 per cent. Theft and handling stolen goods accounted for around two fifths of all crimes recorded in 2001/02, around the same proportion as in the previous year.

The British Crime Survey estimated that just over 13 million crimes occurred in England and Wales, based on interviews taking place in the 2001/02 financial year (covering crimes occurring in the twelve months prior to interview) a decrease of 14 per cent compared with the estimate of crimes taking place in 1999. Within this, there were large falls in domestic burglary (23 per cent), vehicle thefts (14 per cent) and common assaults (24 per cent).

Theft (including vehicle and other household theft, but not including burglary) comprised almost half of all BCS crime in the 12 months prior to interview in 2001/02; with crimes against property (vandalism, vehicle vandalism and burglary) accounting for around 30 per cent of crimes, and the remaining percentage comprising offences against the person: wounding (5 per cent), mugging (3 per cent) and common assaults (14 per cent) (Figure 9.2).

Over three quarters of the incidents measured in the 2001/02 British Crime Survey, around 10 million crimes, are comparable with those recorded by police statistics. Over two fifths of comparable crimes in England and Wales in the twelve months prior to 2001/02 were reported to the police (Table 9.3). The proportion of crimes reported varies according to the type of offence. Reasons for not reporting crimes commonly include the perception on the part of the victim that the incident was too trivial, that the police could not do anything, or that the matter was dealt with privately. High proportions of vehicle thefts (52 per cent) are reported to the police as a formal record of the incident and is generally needed for insurance purposes. Lower proportions of incidents of vandalism (31 per cent) are reported to the police. Reporting rates have

Table **9.3**

Crimes committed within last 12 months: by outcome, 2001/02

England & Wales		Percentages
	Reported to the police	Recorded by the police
Vandalism	31	19
Comparable property crime[1]	51	34
Burglary	61	42
Vehicle thefts	52	36
Theft from the person[2]	34	15
Comparable violence[3]	35	17
All comparable crime[3]	42	25

1 Comprises all acquisitive crime: all burglary, vehicle thefts, bicycle theft and theft from the person.
2 Includes snatch theft, stealth theft and robbery.
3 See Appendix, Part 9: Comparable crime
Source: British Crime Survey, Home Office

fallen since 1991, when nearly half of crimes were reported to the police.

Not all crimes will be recorded by the police. Between 2000/01 and 2001/02, only one in four crimes in England and Wales were recorded by the police (60 per cent of those reported to the police). The police may choose not to record a reported crime for a number of reasons. They may consider that the report of a crime is mistaken, too trivial or that there is insufficient evidence. Alternatively, the victim may not wish the police to proceed. Recording rates also vary according to the type of offence, with 19 per cent of vandalism recorded by the police and 42 per cent of household burglaries.

Periodic surveys are carried out to compare crime in different countries. Making direct comparisons is complicated by a number of factors: laws are different across international boundaries, and methods of collecting crime data vary enormously from country to country, with some relying more on administrative data collected by the police and others relying more on surveys. For these reasons, international crime comparisons are invariably given in terms of percentage changes for each country rather than rates. When comparing 1996 with 2000, crime recorded by the police in England and Wales fell by 8 per cent compared with an average 1 per cent rise in EU countries (Figure 9.4). Recorded crime in Scotland fell by 6 per cent over the same period. Within the EU, crime in Belgium rose by the highest proportion (17 per cent); an increase which is far below the large increases in crime in a number of east European countries, including Slovenia (84 per cent), Estonia (63 per cent) and Poland (41 per cent).

The incidence of crime varies between different types of areas (Figure 9.5). Rural areas tend to have lower rates than non-rural areas, although the pattern of offences is similar. For three offence categories: burglary, vehicle-related thefts and violence, crime rates per 10,000 population in rural areas in England and Wales in 1999 were between a half and two thirds the crime rates in non-rural areas. Although rural crime did increase faster than non-rural crime in the mid-1980s and early 1990s, increases or decreases in crime in both types of areas have tended to follow national trends in more recent years.

Figure 9.4

Percentage change in serious crimes recorded by the police: EU comparison,[1] 1996 and 2000

Percentage change

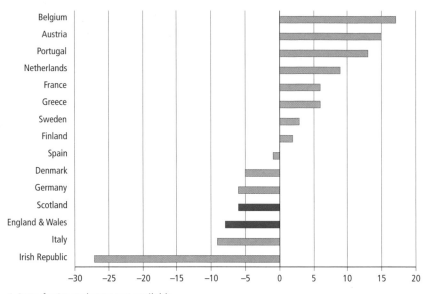

1 Data for Luxembourg not available.
Source: Home Office

Figure 9.5

Crime: by area type, 1999

England & Wales

Incidents per 10,000 population

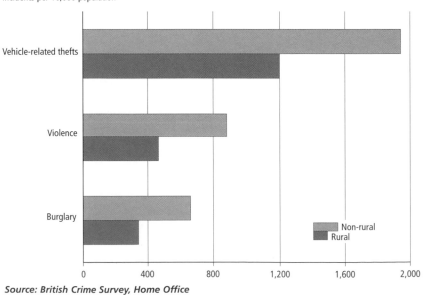

Source: British Crime Survey, Home Office

Table **9.6**

Seizures[1] of selected drugs

United Kingdom   Numbers

	1981	1991	1995	1998	1999	2000
Cannabis	17,227	59,420	90,935	114,691	98,450	91,306
Heroin	819	2,640	6,479	15,192	15,519	16,295
Ecstasy-type	..	1,735	5,521	4,850	6,637	9,664
Amphetamines	1,117	6,821	15,462	18,630	13,393	7,032
Cocaine	503	1,446	2,270	5,209	5,858	5,898
Crack	..	583	1,445	2,488	2,507	2,718
Methadone	402	427	942	1,584	1,215	1,150
LSD	384	1,636	1,158	623	480	292
All seizures	19,428	69,807	114,339	151,749	134,101	124,345

1 Seizures by the police and HM Customs. A seizure can include more than one type of drug. See Appendix, Part 9: Drug seizures.

Source: Home Office

Offences

Drugs and issues relating to the possible relaxation of drugs laws, have been the subject of much discussion in newspapers and public debate in recent years. Cannabis is the most commonly used drug in the United Kingdom. The Government intends to reclassify cannabis from Class B to Class C under the *Misuse of Drugs Act, 1971*. As a result, the maximum penalty for the possession of cannabis will fall from five years to two years imprisonment. Subject to approval by Parliament, the measures are likely to come into effect by July 2003.

Drugs offences can cover a range of activities including unlawful production, supply, and most commonly, possession of illegal substances. Half of all drug offences coming to the notice of the police do so as a result of stops and searches.

In 2000, the number of drug seizures in the United Kingdom fell by 7 per cent compared with the previous year to a total of 124,000 (Table 9.6). The continuing decline from a peak of nearly 152,000 in 1998 can be attributed to continuing falls in the number of seizures by the police and Customs involving cannabis and amphetamines. Cannabis seizures, at 91,000 in 2000, were broadly back down to the same level as they were in 1995. Seizures involving heroin rose by 7 per cent between 1998 and 2000 to 16,000.

In all EU countries as a whole cannabis seizures peaked at 327,000 in 1998. The number of seizures then fell by 40,000 in 1999, before rising to just under 300,000 in 2000. The United Kingdom had the highest number of seizures in 2000, followed by Spain (66,000), France (51,000) and Germany (32,000). These four countries accounted for four fifths of all EU cannabis seizures in 2000.

Mobile phone theft has also been the subject of recent media attention. Ownership of mobile phones has increased dramatically since they came onto the market in the mid-1980s. The small size of mobile phones, their visibility, accessibility and resale value make them attractive items to be stolen. Around 470,000 mobile phones were stolen in England and Wales in 2000, 16 per cent more than in 1999. But the number of mobile phone thefts still comprises a relatively small proportion (less than 6 per cent) of the total number of thefts (Table 9.7). Twenty nine per cent of mobile phone thefts over a two-year period, 1999-2000, were from vehicles, with 20 per cent in burglaries and 15 per cent from the person. A smaller proportion of phone thefts (4 per cent) involved robbery. Nearly one in three (32 per cent) occurred when the phone was left unattended. Overall, adults are more likely to fall victim to mobile phone theft when a phone is left in a car, or when they leave the phone unattended somewhere else, than they are to have a phone stolen in a robbery or directly from their person.

Theft from a vehicle remains the most commonly committed single offence in England and Wales with around 660,000 such incidents recorded by the police in 2001/02. Other types of theft-related offences include cheque and credit card fraud, which together accounted for 153,000 offences in 2001/02. The amount lost in credit card fraud was estimated at over £400 million in 2001, 30 per cent more than in 2000.

There were nearly 3 million violent (BCS) incidents in 2000/01 in England and Wales. There was no injury to the victim in half of violent incidents, and around two thirds of both robberies and common assaults. Fourteen per cent of these violent incidents resulted in medical attention from a doctor, with this percentage rising to 19 per cent for robbery victims and 39 per cent of victims of wounding. The type of weapons used in violent crimes in England and Wales include a mixture of 'obvious' weapons such as guns or knives and 'improvised' weapons such as sharp or heavy objects. A hitting implement was the most commonly used weapon in England and Wales, used in 8 per cent of BCS crimes in 1999, followed by a knife (5 per cent). In over 80 per cent of violent crimes in England and Wales in 2000/01, no weapon was used.

Crimes involving firearms still make up a low proportion (less than half a per cent) of all crimes recorded by the police. Air weapons are the most common items used. In 2000/01 air weapons were used in 10,200 crimes in England and Wales, compared with over 5,400 a decade earlier (Figure 9.8). Shotgun use has decreased in recent years. There were 1,600 crimes involving shotgun use in 1991 and 600 in 2000/01.

Figure **9.7**

Thefts of mobile phones:[1] by type of offence, 1999–2000
England & Wales

Percentages

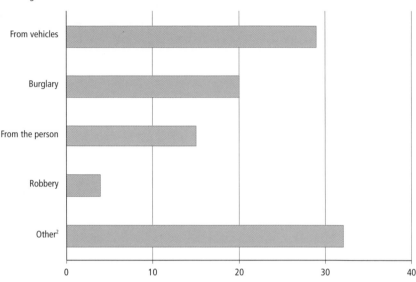

1 Theft or attempted theft.
2 Unattended phones left in offices, leisure facilities, and on public transport etc.
Source: British Crime Survey, Home Office

Figure **9.8**

Crimes[1] recorded by the police[2] in which firearms were reported to have been used: by principal weapon
England & Wales

Thousands

1 See Appendix, Part 9: Type of offences in England, Wales and Northern Ireland.
2 Data from 1998/99 onwards are for financial rather than calendar years.
3 Rifles (not air weapons), starting guns, imitation weapons, supposed type unknown, prohibited firearms (including CS gas) and other firearms.
Source: Home Office

Table **9.9**

Victims[1] of vehicle-related thefts and burglary within last 12 months: by age of head of household, 2001/02

England & Wales   Percentages

	Age of head of household				75 and over	All households
	16-24	25-44	45-64	65-74		
All vehicle theft[2]	18	14	12	5	3	11
of which						
theft of vehicle	4	2	2	1	–	2
theft from vehicle	12	9	7	3	1	7
attempted theft	5	4	4	1	1	3
All burglary	9	4	3	2	2	4
of which						
with entry	6	2	2	1	2	2
attempts	4	2	1	1	1	2

1 Victims once or more.
2 Vehicle-owning households.
Source: British Crime Survey, Home Office

Table **9.10**

Worry about crime,[1] by household income, 2001/02

England & Wales   Percentages

	Burglary	Mugging	Physical attack	Rape	Insulted or pestered	Theft of car[2]	Theft from car[2]
Less than £5,000	23	24	22	21	14	23	21
£5,000 but less than £10,000	20	21	19	19	11	21	16
£10,000 but less than £20,000	17	16	17	18	10	20	16
£20,000 but less than £30,000	14	12	14	16	7	17	14
£30,000 or more	9	8	9	11	5	13	12

1 Percentage of people who were 'very worried' about each type of crime.
2 Based on car owners only.
Source: British Crime Survey, Home Office

Victims

Some individuals and households are more at risk than others of being on the receiving end of crime. Twenty eight per cent of those questioned by the BCS in 2001/02 reported that they had been the victim of some sort of crime in the previous year. The risk of falling victim to either burglary or vehicle theft declines generally with the age of the head of household (Table 9.9). The most at risk group were those aged between 16 and 24, who were six times more likely to suffer some sort of vehicle theft, and four times more likely to fall victim to burglary, than those in the 75 and over age group. The type of housing in which people live can affect their likelihood of being a victim of burglary. In general, the risk of private renters being burgled is double the rate for owner occupiers.

Concern about crime depends on a number of factors. Levels of concern are higher among people in neighbourhoods where there is a low sense of community. Older people worry more about crime than younger people and women worry more than men about personal crime. One in twenty men, compared with one in five women, reported that they felt 'very unsafe' walking alone in their area after dark. Households in the lowest income groups tended to worry about all types of crime more than households in the higher income groups (Table 9.10). The proportion of households with incomes below £5,000 who were worried about falling victim to mugging was three times that for the highest income group (with incomes in excess of £30,000).

People's perceptions on whether crime is rising or falling has some part to play in determining how concerned they are about crime. In 2001/02, two thirds of people interviewed said that they believed that the national crime rate over the last two years rose a 'lot' or 'little more'; very few, just 6 per cent, said that they believed crime rates were falling (Figure 9.11 see overleaf). When asked about their local area, fewer (49 per cent) thought local crime had increased over the past two years, and more thought that it had remained the same. Estimates from the last three crime surveys reveal that in England and Wales since 1998 there have been little significant variations in peoples' perception about crime.

Violent crime can vary according to the nature of the relationship between the victim and the attacker. In incidents of domestic violence, there is a close relationship between victim and attacker. Women are far more likely to suffer domestic violence than men. Research estimates that in England and Wales, one woman in four reports experiencing domestic violence at some time in her life. There is widespread recognition of the difficulty in obtaining precise estimates of the real incidence of domestic violence, with many of the victims frightened or unwilling to admit that a violent incident has in fact taken place.

According to the British Crime Survey, one third of victims of any violence are victimised twice or more within a year (Figure 9.12). Nearly three fifths (57 per cent) of those who have been a victim of domestic violence, are then a victim of domestic violence again, not necessarily by the same perpetrator. In contrast to domestic violence, one in every five victims of stranger violence in England and Wales in 2000/01 was victimised on more than one occasion within a year.

Offenders

In 2001, 467,000 people were cautioned for or found guilty of an indictable offence in England and Wales (Table 9.13). Men commit more crimes than women. In 2001 in England and Wales, 167 per 10,000 men were found guilty of, or cautioned for, an indictable offence, compared with a rate of 37 per 10,000 women. The peak ages for offending were 18 for males and 15 for females. Theft was the most commonly committed offence by both male and female offenders. For indictable offences over half of all female offenders were found guilty or cautioned for theft-related offences compared with 36 per cent of all male offenders.

A relatively small number of offenders are responsible for a disproportionately high number of offences. Often, offending patterns of behaviour are established at an early age. Following the *Crime and Disorder Act 1998*, the treatment of young offenders within the criminal justice system changed, with many new orders being introduced, such as supervision orders and action plan orders. Recent research into juvenile offenders in England and Wales in 2000 found a reduction in reconviction rates across all offence

Figure **9.11**

Beliefs about the change in the national crime rate[1]
England & Wales

Percentages

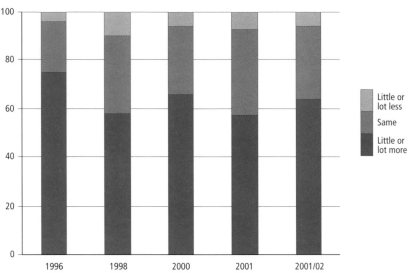

1 *Respondents were asked how they thought the recorded crime rate for the country as a whole had changed over the two previous years.*
Source: British Crime Survey, Home Office

Figure **9.12**

Violent crimes: repeat victimisation,[1] 2001/02
England & Wales

Percentages

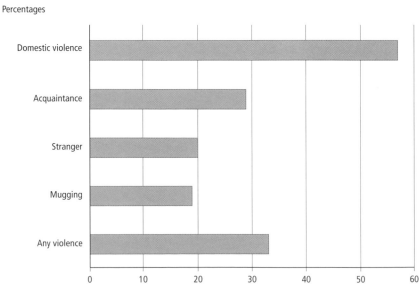

1 *Victimised twice or more within the 12 months prior to interview.*
Source: British Crime Survey, Home Office

Table **9.13**

Offenders found guilty of, or cautioned for, indictable offences:[1] by sex, type of offence and age, 2001

England & Wales

Rates per 10,000 population

	10–15	16–24	25–34	35 and over	All aged 10 and over (thousands)
Males					
Theft and handling stolen goods	104	196	91	16	137.8
Drug offences	17	140	52	8	76.1
Violence against the person	31	70	26	7	47.0
Burglary	31	48	16	2	29.4
Criminal damage	14	18	6	1	12.5
Robbery	7	13	3	0	6.7
Sexual offences	3	4	2	2	5.0
Other indictable offences	11	95	50	11	65.0
All indictable offences	218	584	246	46	379.3
Females					
Theft and handling stolen goods	64	72	30	6	52.7
Drug offences	2	15	7	1	8.9
Violence against the person	10	10	4	1	7.8
Burglary	3	3	1	0	1.8
Criminal damage	2	2	1	0	1.6
Robbery	1	1	0	0	0.7
Sexual offences	0	0	0	0	0.1
Other indictable offences	3	19	12	2	13.8
All indictable offences	86	121	55	10	87.5

1 See Appendix, Part 9: Types of offences in England and Wales.
Source: Home Office

Table **9.14**

Juvenile reconviction within one year: by offence category

England & Wales

Percentages

	1997[1]	2000[2]
Criminal damage	32	22
Burglary	39	21
Violence against the person	30	21
Drugs offences	31	20
Sexual offences	27	19
Theft	32	18
Fraud and forgery	24	17
Robbery	39	15
Other offences[3]	42	40

1 Original conviction in the first half of 1997.
2 Original conviction in July 2000.
3 Include breach, motoring offences and other offences not listed in other categories.
Source: Home Office

categories between 1997 and 2000. Robbery had the lowest reconviction rate of 15 per cent in 2000, and it also recorded the greatest fall, from 39 per cent in 1997 (Table 9.14). Burglary and theft were the offence categories with the second and third largest falls in reconviction rates, respectively. However, over 26 per cent of juvenile offenders, excluding those given custodial sentences, are still reconvicted within a year of their first conviction. Adult reconviction rates are calculated on a different basis to juveniles, with offenders followed for two years instead of one. For all community penalties the reconviction rate for adults for 1999 to 2001 was 45 per cent.

Police and courts action

In England and Wales a formal caution may be given by a senior police officer, when an offender has admitted their guilt, there is sufficient evidence for a conviction and it is not in the public interest to institute criminal proceedings. Cautions are more severe than a reprimand – in order for a caution to be given, there must be sufficient evidence gathered by the police of the likelihood of a successful prosecution. Details of cautions given remain on an individual's record. In 2001, 144,000 cautions for indictable offences in England and Wales were given – 59,000 fewer than the peak of 203,000 in 1995 (Table 9.15 - see overleaf). The two offence categories receiving the highest number of cautions were theft and handling stolen goods, and drugs offences.

Official research has shown that men and women have had different experiences in the way they are handled at this stage by the police and the courts. Women were less likely than men to request a lawyer and exercise their right of silence, and more likely than men to admit to offences, reflecting differences in the type of offences for which they were arrested. In 2001 the cautioning rate for women was 46 per cent compared with 28 per cent for men. Women were more likely than men to be cautioned because they were far more likely than men to admit their offences and more likely to be arrested for less serious offences (such as shoplifting).

When an offender has been charged, or received a summons, and then found guilty, the court will impose a sentence. Sentences in England, Wales and Northern Ireland can include immediate custody, a community sentence, a fine or, if the court considers that no punishment is necessary, a discharge. In 2001, 323,000 people were sentenced for indictable offences in England and Wales (Table 9.16). The form of sentence varied according to the type of offence committed. Those sentenced for motoring offences were the most likely to be fined, with 46 per cent receiving this form of sentence. Offenders sentenced for robbery were the most likely to be sentenced to immediate custody. In 2000, approximately 10 per cent of those sentenced by Scottish courts received either a probation or community service order, and 13 per cent received a custodial sentence.

The total number of motoring offences dealt with in England and Wales in 2000, was 10 million (Table 9.17). Motoring offences have fluctuated in recent years, rising from 6.9 million offences in 1993. In the early 1990s the majority of motoring offences were dealt with by fixed penalty notices. Penalty charge notices were introduced in 1994 and are issued by

Table **9.15**

Offenders cautioned for indictable offences:[1] by type of offence

England & Wales

Thousands

	1971[2]	1981	1991	1995	2000	2001
Theft and handling stolen goods	53.5	79.2	108.5	104.9	67.6	63.5
Drug offences[2]	..	0.3	21.2	48.2	41.1	39.4
Violence against the person	2.3	5.6	19.4	20.4	19.9	19.6
Burglary[3]	12.4	11.2	13.3	10.5	6.6	6.4
Fraud and forgery	1.0	1.4	5.6	7.9	6.2	5.8
Criminal damage	3.6	2.1	3.8	3.8	3.2	3.4
Sexual offences	3.9	2.8	3.3	2.3	1.3	1.2
Robbery	0.2	0.1	0.6	0.6	0.6	0.5
Other	0.3	1.3	4.1	4.0	4.4	4.2
All offenders cautioned	77.3	103.9	179.9	202.6	150.9	143.9

1 Excludes motoring offences.
2 Adjusted to take account of the Criminal Damage Act 1971. Drug offences data for 1971 are included in 'Other'.
3 See Appendix, Part 9: Offenders cautioned for burglary.
Source: Home Office

Table **9.16**

Offenders sentenced for indictable offences:[1] by type of offence and type of sentence,[2] 2001

England & Wales

Percentages

	Discharge	Fine	Community sentence	Fully suspended sentence	Immediate custody	Other	All sentenced (thousands)
Theft and handling stolen goods	21	20	35	0	21	2	126.4
Drug offences	18	44	18	1	19	1	45.7
Violence against the person	12	11	41	1	32	3	35.4
Burglary	4	2	40	0	51	2	24.7
Fraud and forgery	17	16	42	2	21	2	18.2
Criminal damage	22	17	41	0	11	8	10.5
Motoring	5	46	23	1	24	1	7.9
Robbery	1	0	27	0	70	2	6.8
Sexual offences	4	3	27	2	62	2	3.8
Other offences	10	43	18	1	17	10	43.8
All indictable offences	16	24	32	1	25	3	323.2

1 See Appendix, Part 9: Types of offences in England and Wales.
2 See Appendix, Part 9: Sentences and orders.
Source: Home Office

Figure **9.17**

Motoring offences: by action taken

England & Wales

Millions

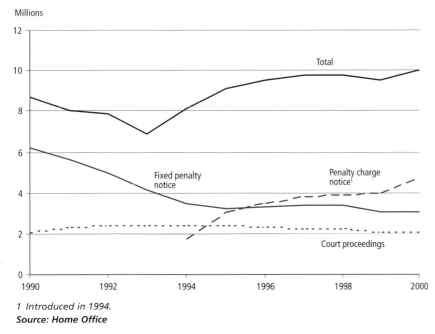

1 Introduced in 1994.
Source: Home Office

Table **9.18**

Detection rates for recorded crime:[1] by type of offence, 2001/02

Percentages

	England & Wales[2]	Scotland[3]	Northern Ireland
Drug offences	94	99	77
Violence against the person	58	82	47
Sexual offences	49	78	47
of which			
rape	42	82	52
Fraud and forgery	28	82	23
Robbery	17	37	14
Theft and handling stolen goods	17	34	13
of which			
theft of vehicles	14	32	9
theft from vehicles	6	17	2
Burglary	12	24	10
Criminal damage	13	22	11
Other crimes[4]	71	96	38
All recorded crime	23	45	20

1 See Appendix, Part 9: Types of offences in England and Wales, Types of offences in
  Northern Ireland, and Offences and crimes.
2 Detection rates may be influenced by the National Crime Recording Standard recording
  changes. See Appendix, Part 9: Changes in crime statistics.
3 Figures for Scotland refer to 2001.
4 The Northern Ireland figure includes offences against the State.
Source: Home Office; Scottish Executive; the Police Service of Northern Ireland

local authorities for offences of obstruction, waiting and parking. In 2000 they accounted for almost a half of motoring offences. Just over a fifth of offences resulted in court proceedings in 2000. Cameras provided evidence for 802,000 offences dealt with in 2000. Overall, these cameras provided evidence for 61 per cent of speeding offences.

Under recorded crime counting rules, a crime is 'detected' or 'cleared up' if a suspect has been identified and interviewed and there is sufficient evidence to bring a charge. There does not have to be a prosecution; for example, the offender may accept a caution or ask for the crime to be taken into consideration by the court, or the victim may not wish to give evidence.

Detection rates, still known as clear-up rates in Scotland, vary according to the type of offence. Drugs offences were the most likely type of crime to be detected and theft from vehicles was the least likely in 2001/02 in each of the constituent countries (Table 9.18). Less than a fifth of robberies were detected in England and Wales and Northern Ireland, compared with over a third of robberies cleared up in Scotland in 2001. In England and Wales, overall clear-up rates were 23 per cent in 2001/02, a 1 percentage point decrease on the previous year, although this change may have been due to recent changes in the recording of crime. It has been estimated that 60 per cent of all detections in England and Wales resulted in a charge or summons in 2001/02. Scotland had a clear-up rate of 45 per cent in 2001 and Northern Ireland had a comparable rate of 20 per cent in 2001/02. Often, there may be a time lapse between the committing of an offence and the police clearing it up.

Custodial sentences are normally given by courts to the most serious, dangerous and persistent offenders. A defendant may choose in court to either plead guilty or go on to contest the case by pleading not guilty. Appeals against decisions made at magistrates courts are heard in the Crown Court, while those against Crown Court decisions are made at the Court of Appeal. In 2001, just under 7,400 appeals were received in England and Wales by the Court of Appeal (Criminal Division): 1,943 against conviction and 5,497 against sentence.

Prisons and probation

Prisons are the usual and eventual destination for offenders receiving custodial sentences. Offenders initially given non-custodial sentences who break the terms of their sentence are then liable to receive custodial sentences. Sentenced prisoners are classified into different risk-level groups for security purposes. Women prisoners are held in separate prisons or in separate accommodation in mixed prisons. Young offenders receiving custodial sentences have traditionally been separated from adult offenders, enabling them to receive additional educational and rehabilitative treatment.

In England and Wales, after a period of fluctuation, there has been a recent increase in the prison population, to over 71,000 in mid-2002, an increase of over 25,000 since 1990, and the highest figure ever recorded (Figure 9.19). Remand prisoners comprise 18 per cent of the total prison population.

Measures taken to alleviate potential overcrowding in prisons include greater use of community (non-custodial) sentences for minor offenders, expanding the capacity of prisons, and the early release of prisoners under the Home Detention Curfew (HDC) scheme. The average annual prison population in Scotland is over 6,000 and the average prison population in Northern Ireland (based on monthly counts) is under 1,000.

While custodial sentences are given for some of the more serious offences, other crimes are more likely to result in the offender receiving a criminal supervision order. In 2001, some 122,000 people started a criminal supervision order in England and Wales, the same number as in the previous year (Table 9.20). Males starting orders outnumbered females by more than five to one. As the same people may receive more than one order, the number of orders exceeds the number of people receiving orders. Community punishment orders involve the offender carrying out unpaid work within the community, and community rehabilitation orders involve the offender being supervised within the community. Included in the 'other' category are drug treatment and testing orders, specifically designed for drug users who offend.

Figure 9.19

Prison population

England & Wales

Thousands

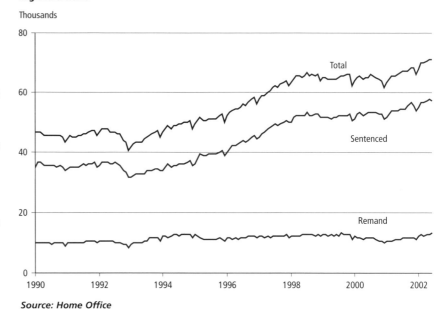

Source: Home Office

Table 9.20

People commencing criminal supervision orders[1]

England & Wales   Thousands

	1981	1986	1991	1996	2000	2001
Community rehabilitation order	36	40	45	49	54	54
Community punishment order	28	35	42	47	52	52
Community punishment and rehabilitation order	..	..	..	17	19	16
Under the *Children and Young Persons Act 1969*	12	6	2	3	–	–
Other	8	7	8	9	7	10
All[2]	79	83	91	115	122	122

1 *Supervised by the probation service. See Appendix, Part 9: Sentences and orders.*
2 *Individual figures do not sum to the total because each person may have more than one type of order.*
Source: Home Office

Figure **9.21**

Writs and summonses issued[1]

England & Wales

Millions

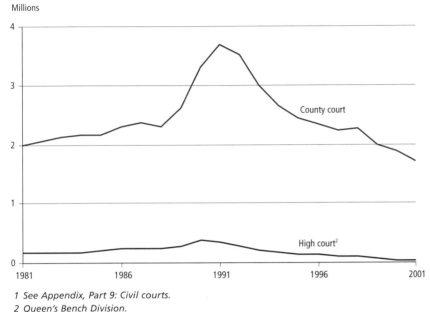

1 See Appendix, Part 9: Civil courts.
2 Queen's Bench Division.
Source: Court Service

Table **9.22**

Domestic violence applications and orders: by type of court and nature of proceedings, 2001

England & Wales   Numbers

	Magistrates court	County court	Total[1]
Non-molestation orders	179	20,725	20,968
Occupation orders	48	9,701	9,789
Number of cases where undertakings accepted[2]	27	4,212	4,245
Warrants of arrest	7	246	255

1 Includes High Court proceedings.
2 Cases where an application is made but a promise is given instead of an order granted.
Source: Judicial Statistics, Court Service

Civil justice

Cases may also be brought under civil law by, for example, an individual or a company. The majority of these cases are handled by the county courts and High Court in England, Wales and Northern Ireland and by the Sheriff Court and Court of Session in Scotland. The High Court and Court of Session deal with the more substantial and complex cases. Civil cases may include breach of contract, claims for debt, negligence and recovery of land. Smaller cases, such as claims for unfair dismissal and disputes over social security benefits, are held by tribunals.

The total number of claims issued in county courts in England and Wales rose sharply from just under 2.3 million in 1988 to peak at 3.7 million in 1991 (Figure 9.21). This rise may be explained, in part, by the increase in lending as a consequence of financial deregulation. Subsequent falls can be attributed to the effects of civil justice reforms. In 2001 claims connected with debt recovery still accounted for over half the total number of 1.7 million claims issued. After debt recovery, the second and third most common types of claims related to recovery of land and personal injury.

Many cases heard in family civil actions relate to a breakdown in relationships. Two types of order can be granted through the courts: a non-molestation order, which can either prohibit particular behaviour or general molestation; and an occupation order, which can define or regulate rights of occupation of the home. Most of these cases are heard in the county rather than magistrate's court and a few are heard on appeal to the High Court. Nearly 9,800 occupation orders were applied in 2001, and nearly 21,000 non-molestation orders (Table 9.22). Both orders must include the powers of arrest if threat of violence is used against the applicant. No power of arrest may be attached to any undertaking given and any undertaken given is enforceable as if it were an order of the court. Other civil actions included nearly 5,000 adoption applications and 161,600 petitions for divorce.

Resources

In England and Wales, the Legal Services Commission operates the Community Legal

Service (CLS), which funds civil legal and advice services and civil representation. The Commission was launched in April 2000, replacing the Legal Aid Board. The type of practical help offered by the CLS includes legal help, help at court, mediation and representation on tribunals. Legal help is available on any aspect of family law, including divorce or judicial separation, financial provision, domestic violence and residence and contact issues, as well as any matters arising under the *Child Support Act 1991* or the *Children Act 1989*. Immigration, housing and welfare benefits make up two thirds of the new (non-family) matters handled by the CLS where legal help is offered (Figure 9.23).

Police officer numbers in England and Wales reached record levels at 31 March 2002 with 129,603 officers. This was an increase of nearly 4,000 compared to a year earlier and was the largest increase for 26 years. In 1999, the Government set employment targets for the recruitment, retention and progression of officers from minority ethnic groups in England and Wales. The targets are intended to ensure that, by 2009, forces will reflect their minority ethnic population. On 31 March 2002, there were over 3,300 officers from minority ethnic backgrounds in England and Wales (up from around 3,000 a year previously), representing 2.6 per cent of the police service (Table 9.24). One in five police officers were female. Scotland had 15,149 police officers in 2001, and Northern Ireland had 10,387. Police resources across the United Kingdom are augmented by a range of other civilian staff, special constables and traffic wardens.

Figure 9.23

Community legal service: new matters[1] started in selected legal help categories, 2001/02

England & Wales

Thousands

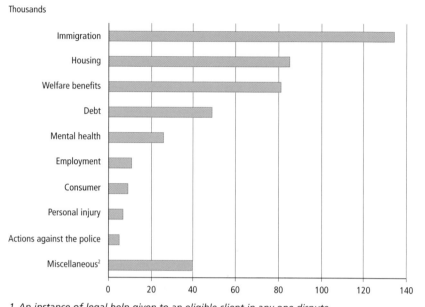

1 An instance of legal help given to an eligible client in any one dispute.

2 Includes help with clinical negligence, community care, education and public law matters, as well as any other legal question.

Source: Legal Services Commission

Table 9.24

Police officer strength: by sex,[1] minority ethnic group, and rank[2]

England & Wales

Numbers

	Males	Females	All minority ethnic groups
Chief Constable	47	6	1
Assistant Chief Constable	141	10	2
Superintendent	1,173	83	23
Chief Inspector	1,433	117	24
Inspector	5,717	479	99
Sergeant	16,621	1,953	369
Constable	79,351	20,137	2,844
All ranks	104,483	22,784	3,362

1 Full-time equivalents employed in the 43 police force areas in England and Wales. With officers on secondment, the total police force strength was 129,603. The figures may not add to the totals due to rounding.

2 At 31 March 2002.

Source: Home Office

Chapter 10

Housing

Housing stock and housebuilding

- There were 21.3 million dwellings in England in 2002, nearly three and a half times more than in 1901. (Figure 10.1)

- The number of owner-occupied dwellings in England increased by 38 per cent between 1981 and 2002 to reach almost 15 million. This was more than double the number of rented dwellings. (Figure 10.2)

Tenure and accommodation

- In 2000/01, 74 per cent of employers and managers in the United Kingdom were buying their home with a mortgage, almost double the proportion of unskilled manual workers. (Table 10.7)

- Lone parents with dependent children in the United Kingdom were far more likely to rent their property than to own it in 2000/01, with 52 per cent renting from the social sector and 14 per cent renting privately. (Page 183)

Homelessness

- By the end of 2001 there were almost 80,000 households in England living in temporary accommodation compared with 60,000 in 1991. Around 15 per cent were in bed and breakfast accommodation in 2001. (Figure 10.13)

Housing condition and satisfaction with area

- In 2001/02 in England, opportunities and facilities for children and young people was the aspect of their area that householders most commonly said they would like to see improved. (Table 10.18)

Housing mobility

- Of newly formed households in England in 2001/02, 43 per cent moved into the private rented sector, 35 per cent became owner-occupiers and 21 per cent social renters. (Page 188)

Housing costs and expenditure

- In 2001 the average dwelling price in the United Kingdom was £112,800, an increase of 11 per cent on 2000. (Table 10.22)

- There were regional variations in what buyers paid for their property in 2001. First time buyers in London, on average, paid £141,300 for their first home, compared with first time buyers in the North East who paid £53,100. (Page 190)

- In 1988, 83 per cent of new mortgages for house purchase in the United Kingdom were endowment mortgages but by 2001 this had fallen to 10 per cent. (Figure 10.24)

The last 10 years have seen a growth in the share of social sector housing provided by housing associations and other registered social landlords (RSLs) as well as a continued increase in home-ownership in the United Kingdom. House prices increased by around 11 per cent between 2000 and 2001. Of those houses financed with a mortgage in 2001, the majority were standard repayment mortgages. The popularity of endowment mortgages has continued to decline.

Housing stock and housebuilding

There were 6.3 million dwellings in England in 1901 and the number rose steadily throughout the century (Figure 10.1). By 2002 there were 21.3 million dwellings, nearly three and a half times more than in 1901. In contrast the population of England grew by around 60 per cent, from approximately 30 million in 1901 to just under 50 million in 2001. Demand for housing has increased at a higher rate than the population because of the trend to smaller households (see Table 2.1 on page 42 in the Households and Families chapter). It was estimated from the Labour Force Survey that there were 20.9 million households in England in 2002: 0.4 million fewer households than dwellings.

The number of owner-occupied dwellings increased by 38 per cent between 1981 and 2002 to reach almost 15 million. This was more than double the number of rented dwellings (Figure 10.2). During the same period the number of private rented dwellings increased by 7 per cent to 2.2 million and the number of dwellings rented from a registered social landlord increased by 250 per cent to 1.5 million. The only sector in which there was a decline in this period was the local authority rented sector – a reduction of 44 per cent to 2.7 million dwellings in 2002.

The increase in owner-occupied dwellings is partly due to the decrease in the number of local authority dwellings. There were fewer local authority dwellings in 2002 than in 1981 because of schemes such as the right to buy which have allowed local authority tenants to buy their homes (see also Figure 10.21). Also, the decision to concentrate public funding for new housing in the RSL sector rather than on local authorities has resulted in an increase in dwellings rented from RSLs. Similarly, the

Figure 10.1

Stock of dwellings[1]

England

Millions

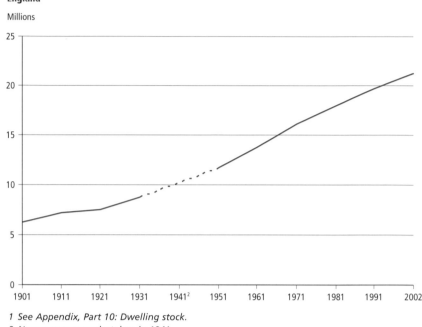

1 See Appendix, Part 10: Dwelling stock.
2 No census was undertaken in 1941.
Source: Census; Office of the Deputy Prime Minister

Figure 10.2

Stock of dwellings:[1] by tenure

England

Millions

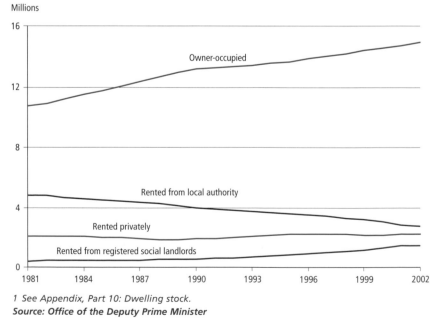

1 See Appendix, Part 10: Dwelling stock.
Source: Office of the Deputy Prime Minister

Table 10.3

Type of accommodation: by construction date, 2001/02

England   Percentages

	Before 1919	1919–1944	1945–1964	1965–1984	1985 or later	All
House or bungalow						
Detached	15	13	17	32	22	100
Semi-detached	10	30	32	21	7	100
Terraced	35	19	18	19	9	100
Flat or maisonette						
Purpose-built	4	9	26	42	19	100
Conversion	70	18	8	3	1	100
All dwellings[1]	20	20	23	25	12	100

1 Includes other types of accommodation, such as mobile homes.
Source: Survey of English Housing, Office of the Deputy Prime Minister

Figure 10.4

Housebuilding completion rates:[1] by sector,[2] 2001/02

Great Britain

Rate per 10,000 households

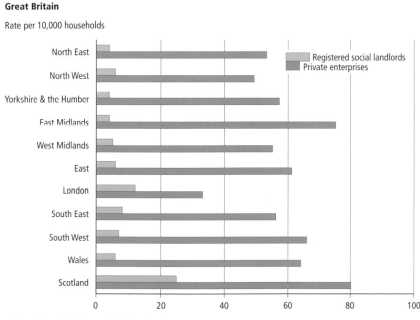

1 Based on 2001 household projections.
2 Completions by local authorities are negligible.
Source: Office of the Deputy Prime Minister

transfer of housing stock ownership from local authorities to RSLs has also contributed to the growth in the RSL sector.

In 2002 in England and Northern Ireland, and in 2001 in Wales, around 70 to 75 per cent of homes were owner-occupied and 20 per cent were rented from the social sector. Scotland has the lowest proportion of owners and the highest proportion of social renters – 63 per cent of stock was owner-occupied and 30 per cent rented from the social sector in 2000.

Between 1919 and 1944 there was a shift in the type of home that was being built in England – from terraced to semi-detached housing. It was in the second half of the 20th century that the majority of the current stock of purpose-built flats was built (Table 10.3). Sixty per cent of England's current housing stock was built after 1944, though this varies by region. Over 70 per cent of dwellings in the East of England were built after 1944 compared with under 40 per cent of dwellings in London. Around a third of all dwellings in England are in London and the South East.

The damage caused to the nation's housing stock during the Second World War made housing construction a post-war government priority. Local authorities undertook a massive housebuilding programme after 1945. The peak year for housebuilding in Great Britain was 1968 when total completions amounted to 414,000 dwellings, 54 per cent being completed by private enterprises, and 46 per cent by the social sector (mainly local authorities). In all, there were over 163,000 dwellings completed in 2001/02, 87 per cent being completed by private enterprises. RSLs are now the major developers of new social sector housing (accounting for 99 per cent of social sector completions in 2001/02).

In 2001/02, Scotland had the highest rate of completions by both private enterprises and RSLs in Great Britain (Figure 10.4). It is estimated there was a total of 104 completions per 10,000 households. London had the lowest overall rate with 45 completions per 10,000 households, although it had the highest rate of completions by RSLs outside of Scotland.

To minimise greenfield development (that is, building on land that has not previously been developed) and to encourage urban regeneration, the Government wishes to see unoccupied homes brought back into use. The number of empty homes in England fell from 869,000 in 1993 to 755,000 in 2001. Some dwellings are vacant for short periods pending sale or re-letting, but others may be vacant for longer while awaiting demolition or renovation. Four fifths of all vacant dwellings are private housing, with about half of these having been vacant for six months or more.

Over the last decade there has been a marked change in the number of bedrooms in newly built dwellings. Dwellings with one bedroom accounted for 20 per cent of total completions in England in 1990/91 but only 7 per cent ten years later (Figure 10.5). Dwellings with four or more bedrooms, on the other hand, increased from 20 per cent to 32 per cent over the same period. The number of bedrooms in a completed dwelling varies by tenure. Of the houses and flats completed by RSLs in 2000/01, around 5 per cent had four or more bedrooms compared with 36 per cent of those completed by private enterprises.

The rise in the number of bedrooms in dwellings may reflect an increased expectation that each child should have a separate bedroom. It may also reflect householders' aspirations to purchase homes with an extra room to use as a spare bedroom, a storage room or a home-office. The fall in the proportion of homes built with one bedroom contrasts with the increase in the proportion of one person households. They grew from 27 per cent of households in England in 1991 to 30 per cent in 2001; it is projected that one person households will account for 35 per cent of households by 2021.

Tenure and accommodation

In 2000/01, 80 per cent of households in the United Kingdom lived in a house or bungalow, whether it was detached, semi-detached or terraced (Table 10.6). Semi-detached houses and terraced houses were the most common type of dwelling, lived in by 31 per cent and 28 per cent respectively of all households. The type of accommodation varies according to tenure. In general, home-owners are more likely than social renters to live in houses, particularly in detached or semi-detached properties. Proportions living in a detached house or bungalow range from 1 per cent of

Figure **10.5**

Housebuilding completions:[1] by number of bedrooms
England

Percentages

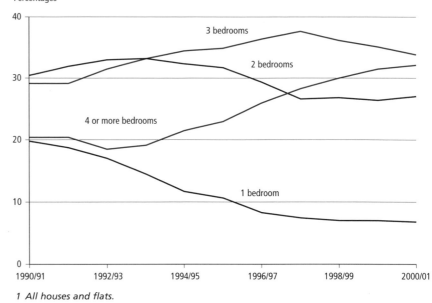

1 All houses and flats.
Source: Office of the Deputy Prime Minister

Table **10.6**

Tenure: by type of accommodation, 2000/01

United Kingdom   Percentages

	House or bungalow			Flat or maisonette		
	Detached	Semi-detached	Terraced	Purpose-built	Other[1]	All dwellings[2]
Owner-occupied						
Owned outright	34	35	22	7	2	100
Owned with mortgage	25	35	30	7	3	100
Rented from social sector						
Local authority	1	26	32	39	2	100
Housing association	1	23	30	39	7	100
Rented privately[3]						
Unfurnished[4]	12	21	30	20	16	100
Furnished	6	14	27	25	28	100
All tenures	21	31	28	15	4	100

1 Includes converted flats, part of a house and rooms.
2 Includes other types of accommodation, such as mobile homes.
3 Includes rent-free accommodation.
4 Includes partly furnished accommodation.
Source: General Household Survey, Office for National Statistics; Continuous Household Survey, Northern Ireland Statistics and Research Agency

Table **10.7**

Socio-economic group[1] of household reference person:[2] by tenure, 2000/01

United Kingdom   Percentages

	Owned outright	Owned with mortgage	Rented from social sector	Rented privately[3]	All tenures
Economically active					
Professional	12	68	3	17	100
Employers and managers	15	74	3	9	100
Intermediate non-manual	14	66	8	12	100
Junior non-manual	14	52	20	15	100
Skilled manual	18	58	14	9	100
Semi-skilled manual	12	47	29	13	100
Unskilled manual	14	38	35	13	100
All economically active	15	61	13	11	100
Economically inactive					
Retired	62	7	27	4	100
Other	18	13	54	15	100
All economically inactive	48	9	36	7	100
All socio-economic groups	27	41	21	10	100

1 Excludes members of the armed forces, economically active full-time students and those who were unemployed and had never worked.
2 See Appendix, Part 10: Household reference person.
3 Includes rent-free accommodation.
Source: General Household Survey, Office for National Statistics; Continuous Household Survey, Northern Ireland Statistics and Research Agency

Table **10.8**

Households living in the most deprived wards[1] and least deprived wards:[2] by tenure, 2001/02

England   Percentages

	Most deprived wards	Least deprived wards	Average
Owner-occupied			
Owned outright	17	34	29
Owned with mortgage	29	51	42
Rented from social sector			
Local authority	33	4	14
Registered social landlord	9	4	6
Rented privately			
Unfurnished	7	6	7
Furnished	4	1	3
All tenures	100	100	100

1 The 10 per cent most deprived wards ranked in the Index of Multiple Deprivation.
2 The 10 per cent least deprived wards ranked in the Index of Multiple Deprivation.
Source: Survey of English Housing, Office of the Deputy Prime Minister

social tenants to 34 per cent of those who own their home outright. On the other hand, proportions living in a purpose-built flat range from 7 per cent of owner-occupiers to 39 per cent of social renters. These patterns vary between regions. For example around 25 per cent of owner-occupiers in London lived in flats or maisonettes in 1999-2002 compared with only 6 per cent in the North East.

Tenure also varies with the socio-economic group of the household reference person. In 2000/01, 61 per cent of economically active households in the United Kingdom were buying their home with a mortgage and 15 per cent owned their home outright (Table 10.7). Those who had retired were by far the most likely group to have repaid their mortgage in full. The proportions of households among the economically active socio-economic groups who owned their home outright ranged from 12 to 18 per cent. Employers and managers were the most likely to be buying their home with a mortgage, while unskilled manual workers were the most likely to be renting their home from the social sector.

The type of accommodation in which people live also varies with socio-economic group. Among the economically active, a third of both professional, and employer and manager, households lived in a detached house in 2000/01, compared with fewer than one in ten unskilled manual households. Twenty per cent of economically inactive households lived in a purpose-built flat or maisonette compared with 12 per cent of economically active households.

Using the Index of Multiple Deprivation (see Appendix, Part 10: Index of Deprivation), comparisons can be made between households in England living in the 10 per cent most deprived wards and those living in the 10 per cent least deprived wards. In 2001/02, households in the most deprived wards were much more likely to be renting from the social sector (42 per cent) than households in the least deprived wards (8 per cent). Conversely, 47 per cent of those in the most deprived wards were owner-occupiers compared with 85 per cent of households in the least deprived wards (Table 10.8).

The type of accommodation also varied between the most deprived and the least deprived wards reflecting the greater proportion of social renters in the most deprived wards. Twenty seven per cent of those living in the most deprived wards lived in flats or maisonettes, compared with 11 per cent of those in the least deprived wards. Households in the most deprived wards were much less likely to live in detached houses than those in the least deprived wards (5 per cent compared with 42 per cent).

Tenure is also linked with economic status. In about one third of households in social housing, the reference person was in paid work compared with two thirds of those who rented privately in England in 2001/02 (Table 10.9). The proportion of paid workers was higher among those who were buying their home with a mortgage (92 per cent) while nearly two thirds of those who owned their home outright were retired. Unlike other tenures, social renters were almost equally divided between those where the reference person was in work, had retired or was unemployed or economically inactive.

Other members of a household may also be in work. Just under 50 per cent of those households buying with a mortgage had two people in paid work compared with only 11 per cent of social renters. Households renting furnished accommodation from a private landlord had the highest proportion with three or more people in paid work (14 per cent), reflecting the way that young adults, in particular, often share a flat or house.

Private renting is most common among the young (Table 10.10). Outright ownership is more common in the older age groups, although it is lower among those aged 75 and over than those aged 65-74. Of people aged between 35 and 74 there is a gradual shift out of mortgaging and into outright ownership. Only 1 per cent of households in the United Kingdom where the reference person was under 25 owned their home outright in 2000/01, compared with nearly two thirds of households aged 65-74. Renting from the social sector is highest in the under 25 and the 75 and over age groups.

The type of accommodation in which people live is also related to the age of the household reference person. Households where he/she

Table 10.9

Tenure: by economic status of household reference person,[1] 2001/02

England — Percentages

	Working						
	Full-time	Part-time	All	Unemployed	Retired	Other inactive[2]	All
Owner-occupied							
Owned outright	25	6	32	1	63	5	100
Owned with mortgage	86	5	92	1	4	4	100
Rented from social sector							
Local authority	22	9	31	5	36	28	100
Registered social landlord	24	10	34	5	34	27	100
Rented privately							
Unfurnished	59	8	67	3	15	16	100
Furnished	60	9	69	5	4	22	100
All tenures	53	7	60	2	28	10	100

1 See Appendix, Part 10: Household reference person.
2 Includes students, those looking after home or family and long term sick or disabled, who are not working or looking for work.
Source: Survey of English Housing, Office of the Deputy Prime Minister

Table 10.10

Age of household reference person:[1] by tenure, 2000/01

United Kingdom — Percentages

	Under 25	25–34	35–44	45–54	55–64	65–74	75 and over
Owner-occupied							
Owned outright	1	2	7	19	46	64	57
Owned with mortgage	17	57	67	58	31	8	3
Rented from social sector							
Local authority	26	15	12	12	14	18	25
Housing association	10	6	5	5	4	6	9
Rented privately[2]							
Unfurnished[3]	20	13	6	6	4	3	5
Furnished	25	7	3	1	1	1	1
All tenures	100	100	100	100	100	100	100

1 See Appendix, Part 10: Household reference person.
2 Includes rent-free accommodation.
3 Includes partly furnished accommodation.
Source: General Household Survey, Office for National Statistics; Continuous Household Survey, Northern Ireland

Table **10.11**

Ethnic group of head of household:[1] by tenure, 1999–2002

England   Percentages

	Owned outright	Owned with mortgage	Rented from social sector	Rented privately[2]	All tenures (=100%) (millions)
White	28	43	20	9	19.0
Black Caribbean	13	37	44	6	0.3
Black African	4	22	50	23	0.1
Indian	26	55	8	11	0.3
Pakistani	22	47	17	14	0.2
Bangladeshi	4	29	57	10	0.1
Other or mixed	14	33	32	21	0.5
All heads of household[1]	28	42	20	10	20.5

1 Household reference persons for 2001/02.
2 Includes rent-free accommodation.
Source: Survey of English Housing, Office of the Deputy Prime Minister

Table **10.12**

Household type: by type of accommodation, 2000/01

United Kingdom   Percentages

	House or bungalow			Flat or maisonette		
	Detached	Semi-detached	Terraced	Purpose-built	Other[1]	All dwellings[2]
One person	13	23	27	28	8	100
Two or more unrelated adults	9	21	36	27	7	100
Single family households[3]						
Couple						
No children	29	34	24	9	3	100
Dependent children[4]	28	37	28	6	1	100
Non-dependent children only	29	40	28	3	–	100
Lone parent						
Dependent children[4]	7	29	41	20	3	100
Non-dependent children only	16	34	34	14	1	100
Multi-family households	19	38	41	2	–	100
All households	21	31	28	15	4	100

1 Includes converted flats, part of a house and rooms.
2 Includes other type of accommodation, such as mobile homes.
3 May also include other individuals who were not family members.
4 May also include non-dependent children.
Source: General Household Survey, Office for National Statistics; Continuous Household Survey, Northern Ireland Statistics and Research Agency

was aged under 25 were most likely to live in purpose-built flats or terraced houses (38 per cent and 31 per cent respectively) in 2000/01. From the age of 35 the majority of people live in houses although from the age of 55 there is a slight shift into living in purpose-built flats – nearly a quarter of people aged 75 and over lived in this type of accommodation.

Tenure patterns also vary markedly with the ethnic group of the household head. A high proportion of households headed by someone of Bangladeshi or Black African ethnic origin lived in the social rented sector (57 per cent and 50 per cent respectively) (Table 10.11). This is six to seven times the proportion of households headed by someone of Indian descent. In contrast, 55 per cent of Indian and 47 per cent of Pakistani heads of household were buying their home with a mortgage. Households with a White or Indian head were the most likely to own their home outright. To some extent these patterns reflect the availability of housing in the areas where previous generations from minority groups originally settled and also difficulties experienced in gaining access to council housing. However, choice of tenure is also driven by people's economic circumstances and by their own aspirations.

The type of home in which people live is often a reflection of the size and type of their household, as well as what they can afford. In 2000/01, the majority of family households in the United Kingdom lived in detached, semi-detached or terraced houses (Table 10.12). Although the majority of lone parents with dependent children lived in a house, it was far less likely to be detached and more likely to be terraced than for households overall. Over a third of one person households lived in a flat or maisonette and these were three times more common for lone parents with dependent children than for couples with dependent children.

Around 40 per cent of couples without children, including those who have retired, owned their home outright, compared with only 7 per cent of couples with dependent children. Lone parents with dependent children were far more likely to rent their property than to own it with 52 per cent renting from the social sector and 14 per cent renting privately.

Homelessness

When a household makes a homelessness application the local housing authority must decide whether the applicant is eligible for assistance, unintentionally homeless and in a priority need group. Where all these criteria are met, the authority has a legal obligation to provide settled housing, or where not available, suitable temporary accommodation until settlement can be arranged. In England the number of households accepted as homeless by their local authority increased by 6 per cent over 12 months to 118,700 by 2001. In Wales the number of households accepted as homeless increased by 19 per cent over 12 months to 4,400 by 2000/01. Over the same period the number of homeless households in Northern Ireland increased by 25 per cent to 6,500. In Scotland the number of homeless households increased by 6 per cent over 12 months to reach approximately 18,000 by 1999/2000.

Most households who are accepted as homeless are provided with temporary accommodation. After a peak in the early 1990s when the number of households in temporary accommodation in England was almost 60,000, the number fell to 42,000 households in 1996. Since then there has been another steady rise, particularly in the number of households temporarily housed in local authority or housing association owned property (Figure 10.13). By 2001 the number in temporary accommodation had reached almost 80,000; around 15 per cent of these were in bed and breakfast accommodation.

Homelessness often results from changes in personal circumstances. In 1991 the main reason for homelessness in England (given by 42 per cent of households) was that parents, relatives or friends were no longer able or willing to accommodate them. By 2001 this proportion had reduced to 33 per cent but was still highest (Figure 10.14). The breakdown of a relationship is another significant reason for homelessness and has increased from 16 per cent of cases in 1991 to 22 per cent in 2001. In 1991 the ending of an assured shorthold tenancy agreement accounted for about 6 per cent of all acceptances, but by 2001 this had risen to 15 per cent. This reflects the increasing attraction of, and reliance on, shorthold lettings by private sector landlords.

Figure 10.13

Homeless households[1] in temporary accommodation[2]

England

Thousands

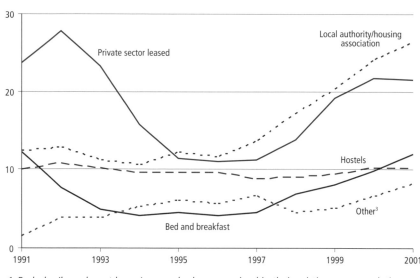

1 Excludes 'homeless at home' cases who have remained in their existing accommodation after acceptance but have the same rights to suitable alternative accommodation as those in accommodation arranged directly by authorities.
2 Data are at end year and include households awaiting the outcome of homeless enquiries.
3 Includes mobile homes such as caravans and portacabins or being accommodated directly with a private sector landlord.
Source: Office of the Deputy Prime Minister

Figure 10.14

Households accepted as homeless by local authorities: by main reason for loss of last settled home

England

Percentages

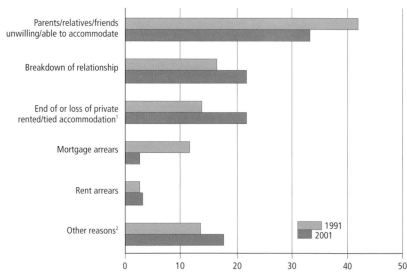

1 Mainly the ending of an assured tenancy.
2 Includes households leaving an institution (such as hospital, prison or a residential home), and those returning from abroad, sleeping rough or in hostels, or made homeless by an emergency such as fire or flooding.
Source: Office of the Deputy Prime Minister

Figure **10.15**

Accommodation without central heating: by tenure, 2001/02

England

Percentages

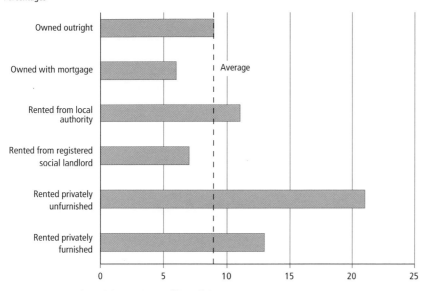

Source: Survey of English Housing, Office of the Deputy Prime Minister

Table **10.16**

Overcrowding and under-occupation:[1] by tenure of household, 2001/02

England   Percentages

	Overcrowded[2]	Under-occupied[3]
Owner-occupied		
Owned outright	1	56
Owned with mortgage	2	36
Rented from social sector		
Local authority	6	13
Registered social landlord	4	8
Rented privately[4]		
Unfurnished	4	21
Furnished	4	15
All tenures	2	35

1 See Appendix, Part 10: Bedroom standard.
2 One or more below bedroom standard.
3 Two or more above bedroom standard.
4 Includes rent-free accommodation.
Source: Survey of English Housing, Office of the Deputy Prime Minister

Housing condition and satisfaction with area

There are a number of means-tested grants available from local authorities to adapt, repair or convert existing housing. One of these grants is the disabled facilities grant (DFG). These are available for a wide range of works needed on a disabled person's home to allow them to live independently. For example, funding is provided to enable a housebound person to work from home, as well as to improve access and improve amenities, such as heating and lighting. Between 1997/98 and 2000/01 the number of these grants in England increased from 22,000 to 24,800, with a total value of £130.7 million in 2000/01. Other grants which provide for private sector housing renewal in England are those covering assistance for improvements and repairs to housing generally. In 2000/01 there were almost 99,000 of these grants with a total value of £293.7 million.

One of the Government's main criteria to assess housing fitness is room temperature and a key influence on this is the presence of central heating. In 2001/02 only 9 per cent of dwellings in England lacked central heating, though prevalence varied with tenure. Private renters were the most likely to be without central heating in their home (Figure 10.15).

Households living in the 10 per cent most deprived wards were over three times more likely to be living without central heating (13 per cent) than those in the 10 per cent least deprived wards (4 per cent). There were four times as many households without central heating who rented from the social sector in the most deprived wards compared with the least deprived wards (11 per cent and 3 per cent, respectively) and three times as many households who rented privately (26 per cent and 9 per cent, respectively).

The bedroom standard measures the number of bedrooms actually available to a household against the number of bedrooms required, given the household's size and composition (see Appendix, Part 10: Bedroom standard). In 2001/02, 2 per cent of households in England were below the bedroom standard and hence defined as overcrowded (Table 10.16). In contrast, 35 per cent of households had two or more bedrooms above the standard and could therefore be said to be under-occupying. Under-occupation was most common in the owner-occupied sector, where 56 per cent of households that owned their property outright and 36 per cent of those buying with a mortgage were two or more bedrooms above the bedroom standard. Overcrowding was most common among those renting in the social sector, where 6 per cent of local authority households were living below the bedroom standard. Higher proportions of households from the Bangladeshi (30 per cent), Pakistani (22 per cent) and Black African (15 per cent) ethnic groups lived in overcrowded accommodation on this bedroom standard measure than White households (2 per cent).

In 2001/02 owner-occupiers in England were generally satisfied with their locality with only 7 per cent expressing dissatisfaction. Households in the rented sector were more likely than those in other tenures to be dissatisfied, with around 15 per cent of social sector tenants, and around 10 per cent of private sector tenants, expressing dissatisfaction with the area in which they lived (Table 10.17).

Households living in 'affluent family', 'mature home-owning' and 'affluent suburban and rural areas' were more likely to be satisfied with both their area and accommodation than people who lived elsewhere (see Appendix, Part 10: Acorn classification). The lowest levels of satisfaction were in 'council estates and low-income areas', although here too 74 per cent were satisfied with their area and 85 per cent with their accommodation.

The 2001/02 Survey of English Housing asked householders in England what they would like to see improved in their area. The most desired improvement was a growth in the number of opportunities and facilities specifically for children and young people (Table 10.18). Other improvements wanted were a reduction in crime and vandalism, as well as more parks and leisure facilities (designed for all ages). More households were concerned with these issues than with the quality of housing in their area as only 12 per cent expressed a desire for an increase in the amount and quality of housing.

Table 10.17

Satisfaction with area: by tenure, 2001/02

England
Percentages

	Satisfied[1]	Neither satisfied nor dissatisfied	Dissatisfied[2]	Total
Owner-occupied				
Owned outright	89	3	8	100
Owned with mortgage	88	5	7	100
Rented from social sector				
Local authority	78	7	16	100
Registered social landlord	80	6	15	100
Rented privately				
Unfurnished	82	7	11	100
Furnished	80	12	8	100
All tenures	86	5	9	100

1 Those who replied that they were 'very satisfied' or 'fairly satisfied'.
2 Those who replied that they were 'slightly dissatisfied' or 'very dissatisfied'.
Source: Survey of English Housing, Office of the Deputy Prime Minister

Table 10.18

Aspects of their area that householders would like to see improved[1]

England
Percentages

	1995/96	1999/00	2000/01	2001/02
Opportunities and facilities for children and young people	39	40	45	38
Crime and vandalism	39	26	47	32
Local amenities, parks and leisure facilities	27	32	38	31
Public transport service	22	29	30	28
Shopping and commercial facilities	14	23	26	21
Local health services	11	15	20	18
Quality of environment	17	18	25	18
Availability of jobs	30	21	23	16
Amount and quality of housing	12	12	14	12
Schools and colleges	8	9	10	9
None of these	18	16	8	16

1 Respondents were asked to select only from those aspects listed in the table. Percentages do not add up to 100 per cent as respondents could give more than one answer.
Source: Survey of English Housing, Office of the Deputy Prime Minister

Table **10.19**

Households resident under one year: previous tenure by current tenure, 2001/02

England   Percentages

	Previous tenure						
	New household	Owned outright	Owned with mortgage	Rented from local authority	Rented from registered social landlord	Rented privately[1]	All tenures
Current tenure							
Owner-occupied							
Owned outright	3	62	25	1	1	9	100
Owned with mortgage	17	3	53	2	2	24	100
Rented from social sector							
Local authority	18	2	6	50	5	18	100
Registered social landlord	19	2	4	24	27	24	100
Rented privately							
Unfurnished	18	6	13	3	4	57	100
Furnished	23	1	15	4	3	55	100
All tenures	17	8	27	10	5	34	100

1 The split between privately rented unfurnished and privately rented furnished is not available for previous tenure.
Source: Survey of English Housing, Office of the Deputy Prime Minister

Social renters were more likely than owners to want a reduction in crime and vandalism, but less likely to feel that public transport facilities needed improving. About a fifth of renters wanted an improvement in the amount and quality of housing, double the proportion of owners. Households living in London, more than any region, wanted a reduction in crime and vandalism and an improvement in the amount and quality of housing.

Housing mobility

The 2000/01 General Household Survey showed that one in ten of all households in Great Britain had been resident for less than 12 months. Of the households in England who had been resident for under a year in 2001/02, the most common types of move had been from one owned property to another or from one privately rented property to another (Table 10.19). Overall movement within each of the three sectors was more common than movement between them. About half of all

Table **10.20**

Main reasons for moving: by post-move tenure,[1] 2001/02

England
Percentages

	Owned outright	Owned with mortgage	Rented from local authority	Rented from registered social landlord	Rented privately	All tenures
Different size accommodation						
Wanted larger or better house or flat	9	22	15	15	10	15
Wanted smaller or cheaper house or flat	20	2	3	4	3	4
Personal reasons						
Divorce or separation	7	8	8	7	10	9
Marriage or cohabitation	2	7	2	4	6	6
Other personal reasons	21	5	18	13	8	10
To move to a better area	15	10	9	12	6	9
Job related reasons	2	11	2	5	20	12
Accommodation no longer available	1	1	8	8	9	5
Wanted to buy	4	21	1	0	0	8
Could not afford mortgage or rent	0	0	1	2	1	1
To live independently	2	9	13	7	9	9
Other reasons	18	4	21	23	16	13
All households (=100%) (millions)	0.2	0.8	0.3	0.2	0.8	2.2

1 Current tenure of all household heads who moved in the year before interview.
Source: Survey of English Housing, Office of the Deputy Prime Minister

moves were either within, to, or from the private rented sector, showing how important this sector is in facilitating mobility within the housing market. Among newly formed households (where the household reference person was not the household reference person at their previous address), 43 per cent moved into the private rented sector, 35 per cent became owner-occupiers and 21 per cent social renters.

People have different motivations for moving home. The most common reasons given for moving in England in 2001/02 was the desire for a larger or better home or for work, though reasons varied by tenure (Table 10.20). Around a fifth of those who owned outright moved because they wanted a smaller or cheaper house or flat. A fifth of private renters cited job related reasons as their main motivation for moving, which was far higher than those living in any other tenure.

The distances people move home also varies by tenure. In 2001/02, of those who were owner-occupiers in England who had moved in the

previous year, over two thirds had moved less than 10 miles to their new home. Of those who rented privately, over a third had moved more than 20 miles away from their previous home. This compared with just over a tenth of those who rented from the social sector. One reason for this is that opportunities for social rented tenants to move to another local authority area can be fairly limited, whereas private tenants are free to move long distances, provided they can afford the rent in the new area.

One way of changing your tenure is to buy your current home from your landlord. The right to buy (RTB) scheme provides for public sector tenants to buy their home from the local authority and become home-owners. This scheme was introduced in Scotland in 1979 and across the rest of Great Britain in 1980. The Northern Ireland Housing Executive operates a voluntary house sales scheme which is comparable to the RTB scheme in Great Britain. Another type of scheme which aims to increase low-cost home-ownership across the United Kingdom is shared ownership, in which

Figure **10.21**

Sales and transfers of local authority dwellings[1]

Great Britain

Thousands

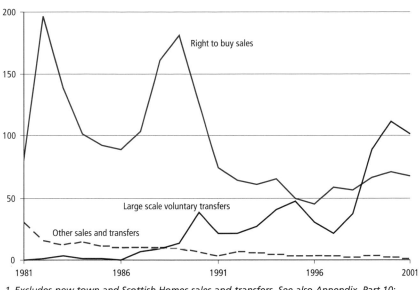

1 Excludes new town and Scottish Homes sales and transfers. See also Appendix, Part 10:
Sales and transfers of local authority dwellings.

Source: Office of the Deputy Prime Minister; National Assembly for Wales; Scottish Executive

home-owners buy a share of their property from a registered social landlord and pay rent for the remainder. The RTB scheme was particularly popular in the 1980s, though since the late 1990s large scale voluntary transfers (LSVT) have been the main contributor to the transfer of ownership of stock from local authorities to other owners: in this case mainly housing associations (Figure 10.21). In 1991, 22,000 dwellings were transferred from local authority ownership under this scheme in Great Britain. There continued to be a general increase in the annual number of LSVTs throughout the 1990s, and by 2001, 101,000 dwellings had been transferred from local authority ownership in this way.

Housing costs and expenditure

In 2001 the average dwelling price in the United Kingdom was £112,800, although there were marked variations by region and type of accommodation (Table 10.22). House prices in London and the South East are well above the rest of England – the amount buyers in London

Table **10.22**

Average dwelling prices: by region and type of accommodation, 2001

	House or bungalow				Flat or maisonette		All dwellings
	Bungalow	Detached	Semi-detached	Terraced	Purpose-built	Other[1]	
United Kingdom	113,419	173,295	99,412	87,470	90,356	121,456	112,835
England	121,577	182,487	104,220	92,193	101,867	130,306	119,563
North East	79,281	116,619	60,170	45,945	52,544	68,483	69,813
North West	95,386	139,939	75,486	54,486	69,710	76,864	82,403
Yorkshire & the Humber	87,588	127,888	65,334	52,775	58,499	71,512	76,368
East Midlands	91,274	134,679	68,850	58,028	52,973	74,093	87,280
West Midlands	111,508	162,802	78,857	65,879	69,063	77,526	97,650
East	118,186	202,021	118,771	96,546	78,346	78,349	127,858
London	196,184	331,324	213,228	187,493	138,939	176,471	182,325
South East	169,281	254,138	146,033	117,133	93,559	94,913	156,964
South West	130,157	185,670	107,483	87,641	81,472	88,955	118,639
Wales	87,675	126,644	66,922	53,079	61,009	55,525	79,628
Scotland	89,983	121,705	66,255	58,190	53,585	69,609	73,570
Northern Ireland	82,441	124,012	76,529	57,302	38,838	50,145	79,885

1 Includes converted flats.
Source: Survey of Mortgage Lenders; Office of the Deputy Prime Minister

paid for a terraced house was more than three times the amount paid by buyers in the North West. Between 2000 and 2001 house prices increased by 11 per cent across the United Kingdom with the largest increase in the East of England (14 per cent). Prices increased by 12 per cent on average in England, while prices in Wales and Northern Ireland increased by 10 per cent each and in Scotland by 5 per cent.

The cost of rented accommodation also varies across Great Britain. The average weekly private sector rent in 2000/01 was £91. The cheapest region was the North East at £61 per week, while the most expensive was London at £154 per week. The average weekly private sector rent was £72 in Scotland and £65 in Wales.

Affordability is a particular concern for first-time buyers. In 2001 first time buyers in the United Kingdom paid an average of around £85,000 for their home compared to previous owners who paid £131,800 (Figure 10.23). However there were regional variations and first time buyers in London, on average, had to pay £141,300 for their first home, while first time buyers in the North East paid £53,100.

The average age of first time buyers has increased. In 1974 the average age of a first time buyer in the United Kingdom was 30. By 2001 this had risen to 34 (ranging from 32 in the North West and Northern Ireland to 36 in the South East and East Anglia). The proportion of first time buyers, out of all buyers, has fallen from 54 per cent in 1994 to 40 per cent in 2001. In 2001 first time buyers put down a deposit in the region of £18,000, on average, whereas five years previously the average was around £5,000. In 2001 the average deposit put down on a property by previous owners in the United Kingdom was in the region of £47,600. This was almost a 50 per cent increase on the average deposit in 1996.

The purchase of a home with a mortgage represents the largest and most long-term financial commitment most people are likely to enter in to. Approximately three quarters of house purchases in the United Kingdom are financed with a mortgage. In 2001, 77 per cent of loans for home purchase were obtained through banks and 18 per cent through building societies, with 5 per cent through

Figure 10.23

Average dwelling prices: by type of buyer

United Kingdom

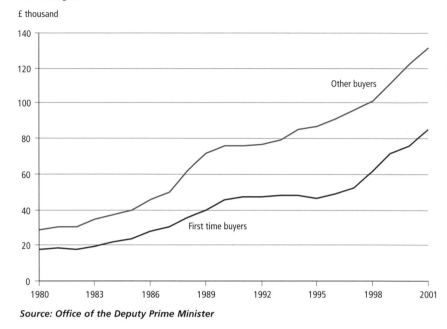

Source: Office of the Deputy Prime Minister

Figure 10.24

Type of mortgage for house purchase[1]

United Kingdom

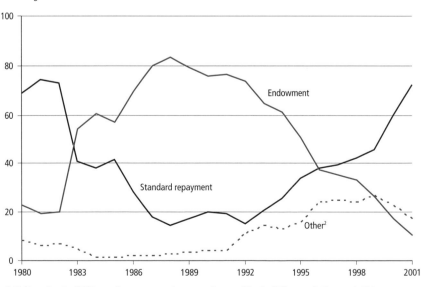

1 Data prior to 1992 are for new mortgages advanced by building societies and Abbey National plc; since 1992 new mortgages advanced by other major lenders have been included. Includes sitting tenants.
2 Includes interest only, PEP or ISA and pension.
Source: Office of the Deputy Prime Minister

Figure **10.25**

Mortgage loans in arrears and repossessions[1]

United Kingdom

Thousands

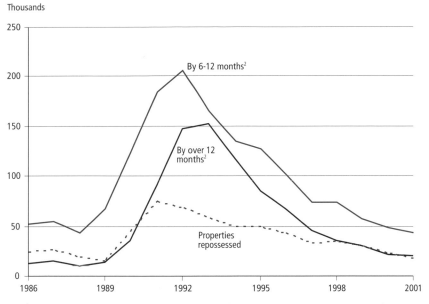

1 *Estimates cover only members of the Council of Mortgage Lenders; these account for 98 per cent of all mortgages outstanding.*
2 *Length of time mortgage loans have been in arrears at end of period.*
Source: Council of Mortgage Lenders

other lenders. Those who are buying a house can choose from a variety of different types of mortgage – the most common being repayment, and interest-only. With repayment mortgages, the debt and the interest are both repaid during the life of the mortgage (usually 25 years). Around 72 per cent of all new mortgages were standard repayment mortgages in 2001 (Figure 10.24). Interest-only mortgages, which include endowment policies, ISAs (individual savings accounts) and personal pensions, accounted for the bulk of other mortgages. Since the late 1980s there has been a decrease in the popularity of endowment mortgages because of the possibility that investments may not grow fast enough to repay the capital borrowed. In 1988, 83 per cent of new mortgages for house purchase were of this type but by 2001 this had fallen to 10 per cent.

Research published in July 2002 by the Council of Mortgage Lenders suggested that flexible mortgages are accounting for a rapidly growing share of the mortgage market.

Flexible mortgages allow people to pay off some of the loan early through overpayments and lump sum investments; and to borrow funds back by withdrawing lump sums, underpaying or taking breaks from payment. Flexible mortgage holders are more likely than other new borrowers to be slightly older, have slightly higher incomes, be professionals, managers or those with a high degree of responsibility in their job. They also tend to be experienced borrowers who have had previous mortgages.

The warning given with every mortgage is that 'your home is at risk if you do not keep up repayments on a mortgage or other loan secured on it' (the same is true of rented property). When people fall behind with rent or mortgage payments and are unable to reach an alternative payment arrangement with their landlord or mortgage lender, a county court possession summons may be issued, with the view to obtaining a court order. Not all orders will result in repossession; it is not uncommon for courts to make suspended orders which provide for arrears to be paid off within a reasonable period. If the court decides not to adjourn the proceedings or suspend a possession order, the warrant will be executed and the home repossessed by the landlord or mortgage lender.

The base interest rate began to increase from the middle of 1988, and mortgage rates followed, increasing from 9.8 per cent in the second quarter of 1988 to 13.4 per cent a year later (for mortgages from building societies). In 1990 mortgage rates had reached 15.3 per cent. The resulting increased payments led to a rise in financial difficulties as new home-buyers who had borrowed a high proportion of the value of their properties were particularly exposed to the increased rates. Arrears and repossessions increased in the late 1980s and even though base rates and mortgage rates began to decrease from 1990, many households still suffered from the effects of the earlier increases. Repossessions continued and peaked in 1991 (Figure 10.25). By 2001 however, base rates had fallen to their lowest level since the 1960s. The lower base rates eased financial difficulties for many households and as a result the number of loans in arrears by 6 to 12 months declined from 205,000 in 1992 to 43,000 in 2001.

Chapter 11

Environment

Environmental concerns and behaviour

- More than 9 out of 10 adults aged 18 and over in England said they were 'very' or 'fairly' concerned about the environment in 2001. (Table 11.1)

- In 2001, over half of those aged 18 and over in England said they regularly took paper to a recycling centre or separated it for recycling, and over two fifths did the same with glass. (Page 194)

Global warming and climate change

- The United Kingdom reduced its emissions of carbon dioxide, the most significant greenhouse gas, by 11 per cent between 1990 and 2000. (Table 11.8)

Countryside, farming and wildlife

- The amount of land used for agriculture in the United Kingdom fell between 1991 and 2001, by 1.6 per cent or just under 300,000 hectares. (Table 11.11)

- The area of forested land in the United Kingdom fell to a low of around 1.1 million hectares at the beginning of the 20th century, but has been increasing since then and reached 2.8 million hectares in 2002. (Page 201)

The local environment and waste

- In November 2001 most adults in Great Britain thought the condition of elements of their local environment, such as air quality, street lighting and the level of traffic noise, were good. (Table 11.16)

- In 2000/01, 12 per cent of municipal waste was recycled or composted, while 78 per cent was disposed in landfill. The proportion recycled has grown since 1996/97, as the proportion disposed to landfill has fallen. (Table 11.17)

Use of resources

- Most energy in the United Kingdom is produced from fossil fuels – petroleum, natural gas and coal – which accounted for 91 per cent of primary fuel production in 2001. (Page 204)

The World Summit on Sustainable Development, held in Johannesburg in August/September 2002, focused the attention of many on environmental concerns, both global and local. It followed on from the Rio 'Earth' summit ten years previously, after which both governments and individuals became more aware of environmental issues. The issue of sustainable development has become a key part of the UK Government's environment policy, with the aim of ensuring a better quality of life, now and for future generations. It has developed a set of core sustainable development indicators to monitor progress towards this goal, which cover economic, social and environmental issues.

Environmental concerns and behaviour

Most people say they are concerned to some extent about the environment. The 2001 Survey of Public Attitudes to Quality of Life and to the Environment found that more than 9 out of 10 adults aged 18 and over in England said they were 'very' or 'fairly' concerned about the environment (Table 11.1). The level of concern has changed little since 1993, although the proportion of people saying they are 'very' concerned has increased – from 30 per cent in 1993 to 35 per cent in 2001.

Concern about the environment is spread relatively evenly across different groups in society. In 2001, 94 per cent of those aged 45-64 said that they were 'very' or 'fairly' concerned about the environment, compared with 81 per cent of those aged 18-24, the age group least likely to express concern about the environment.

The environmental issue causing most concern to individuals in 2001 was the disposal of hazardous waste – 66 per cent of respondents said they were 'very worried' about the issue. Next came the effects of livestock methods (including BSE) (58 per cent), and pollution in rivers (55 per cent). These largely domestic issues were seen as more worrying than global issues, of which ozone layer depletion caused the most concern (49 per cent).

Many adults say they carry out some sort of action which may be beneficial for the environment. In 2001, over half of adults in England said they regularly took paper to a recycling centre or separated it for recycling,

Table 11.1

Concern about the environment:[1] by age, 2001

England
Percentages

	18–24	25–44	45–64	65 and over	All ages
Very concerned	21	29	42	42	35
Fairly concerned	60	62	52	48	56
Not very concerned	16	6	5	8	7
Not at all concerned	1	2	1	2	1
Do not know/refusal	2	-	-	1	1
All	100	100	100	100	100

1 Respondents were asked, "How concerned are you about the environment in general?"
Source: Department for Environment, Food & Rural Affairs

Table 11.2

Personal actions[1] taken on a regular basis which may have a positive environmental impact: by settlement size, 2001

England
Percentages

	Settlement size			
	Less than 3,000	3,000 to 9,999	10,000 to 100,000	Greater than 100,000
Recycling				
Collected for recycling[2]				
Paper	62	62	55	43
Glass	58	50	43	34
Cans	37	45	29	24
Plastic	27	38	22	17
Made compost out of kitchen waste	34	23	21	13
Resource use				
Cut down the amount of electricity/gas your household uses	41	42	39	40
Cut down on use of water	33	37	29	25
Car use				
Deliberately used public transport, walked or cycled instead of a car	28	38	44	49
Cut down the use of a car for short journeys	26	39	41	42
Other				
Made sure that your noise did not disturb others	73	87	80	77
Done things to encourage wildlife in garden	70	60	57	46

1 Based on respondents to whom action was applicable. Does not include 'don't know' and refused to answer.
2 Taken to recycling bank or separated from rubbish so that it could be collected for recycling.
Source: Department for Environment, Food & Rural Affairs

Table **11.3**

Air pollutants: by source, 2000

United Kingdom   Percentages

	Carbon monoxide	Sulphur dioxide	Nitrogen oxides	Volatile organic compounds[1]	PM$_{10}$[1]
Road transport	69	1	42	24	18
Power stations	1	71	24	–	13
Production processes	3	3	–	12	7
Power generation within industry[2]	9	11	11	–	12
Solvent use	0	–	–	27	–
Domestic	5	4	5	2	16
Extraction and distribution of fossil fuels	–	–	–	18	–
Refineries	–	6	2	–	2
Other	11	5	17	16	33
All sources (=100%) (thousand tonnes)	4,171	1,165	1,512	1,676	172

1 See Appendix, Part 11: Air pollutants.
2 Includes iron and steel and other industrial combustion.
Source: National Environmental Technology Centre

Figure **11.4**

Emissions of selected air pollutants

United Kingdom

Million tonnes

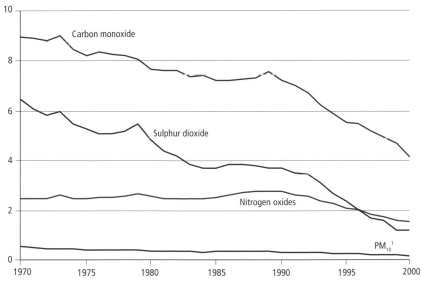

1 Particulate matter that is less than 10 microns.
Source: Department for Environment, Food & Rural Affairs

and over two fifths did the same with glass. People living in smaller settlements are in general more likely to recycle or compost their waste, and cut down their use of resources such as electricity and water, than people living in larger towns or cities (Table 11.2). However people living in urban areas appear to be more likely than their rural counterparts to use public transport, cycle or walk instead of using the car.

The Survey of Public Attitudes to the Environment also found that there is widespread support for actions which central or local government, or other appropriate bodies, could take which may have a positive environmental impact. Particularly popular measures include recycling and renewable energy. Over four fifths of adults supported the provision of more recycling facilities, and nine in ten supported the increased use of renewable energy sources such as solar power, wind and water. Protection of the countryside is another key issue, with three quarters of adults saying they would support only paying agricultural subsidies to farmers if they protect the environment.

Pollution

Many of the activities we undertake each day produce pollutants which can harm the environment as well as impact on human health. The main source of most atmospheric pollutants is fossil fuel combustion of one kind or another (Table 11.3). In 2000 road transport was the main source of carbon monoxide (CO) in the United Kingdom, while electricity supply generated the most sulphur dioxide. Emissions of other pollutants are more evenly spread among different sources, although road transport and electricity supply are, again, important contributors.

Emissions of the major air pollutants in the United Kingdom have been falling, and generally the rate of decline accelerated in the 1990s (Figure 11.4). Emissions of CO fell by 42 per cent between 1990 and 2000, largely as a result of the introduction of catalytic converters to petrol-engined cars. CO reduces the capacity of the blood to carry oxygen and deliver it to the body tissues, and even at low concentrations can cause fatigue in healthy people and chest pain in people with heart disease.

Particulate matter that is less than 10 microns in diameter, known as PM_{10}, is generated primarily by combustion processes and also from processes such as stone abrasion during construction, mining or quarrying. Emissions fell by 45 per cent between 1990 and 2000. Particulate air pollution is responsible for causing premature deaths among those with pre-existing lung and heart conditions.

Nitrogen oxides (NOx) are acid gases which can harm both vegetation and human health. Nitrogen dioxide, for example, is thought to have both acute and chronic effects on airways and lung function, particularly in people with asthma. NOx emissions fell by 45 per cent between 1990 and 2000, again largely due to the fitting of catalytic converters to cars. Sulphur dioxide (SO_2), another acid gas, affects the lining of the nose, throat and airways of the lungs, again especially among asthma sufferers, and those with chronic lung disease. Between 1990 and 2000, emissions fell by 69 per cent, mainly as a result of a reduction in coal use by power stations and the introduction of flue gas desulphurisation, a process by which sulphur dioxide is removed from the gases produced by burning fossil fuels.

The quality and quantity of water supplies is also important to the health and wellbeing of both people and the natural environment. A number of different factors impact on the quality of rivers and other bodies of water, including fertiliser run-off, climate, and industrial and sewage discharge.

The Environment Agency monitors water pollution in England and Wales – in 2001 there were 33,722 substantiated incidents. There were 978 category 1 and 2 incidents, the two most common identified sources of which were agriculture and the sewage and water industry (Figure 11.5). Category 1 incidents are defined as those which have a persistent and/or extensive effect on water quality. They may cause major damage to aquatic ecosystems; cause the closure of a drinking water abstraction plant; cause major damage to agriculture and/or commerce; or have a

Figure **11.5**

Water pollution incidents:[1] by source, 2001

England & Wales

Numbers

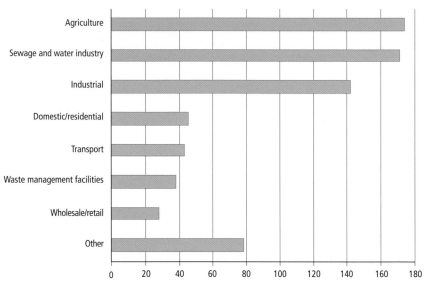

1 Incidents where the source was identified. Category 1 (most severe) and 2 (severe) incidents.

Source: Environment Agency

Table **11.6**

Chemical quality[1] of rivers and canals: by country

	England	Wales	Scotland[2]	Northern Ireland
				Percentage of total river length
1990[3]				
Good	43.5	86.3	..	44.2
Fair	40.1	11.3	..	50.8
1995				
Good	55.4	93.2	..	44.7
Fair	34.6	5.3	..	43.2
2000				
Good	64.4	93.4	86.7	58.8
Fair	29.3	5.2	9.6	36.9
2001				
Good	66.1	92.5	86.9	58.4
Fair	28.1	6.0	9.2	37.1

1 See Appendix, Part 11: Rivers and canals.
2 Data from Scotland are collected on a different basis to the rest of the UK.
3 Northern Ireland figures are for 1991.

Source: Environment Agency; Environment and Heritage Service, Northern Ireland; Scottish Environment Protection Agency

serious impact on the human population. Category 2 incidents have similar but less serious effects.

Rivers and canals in the United Kingdom are generally of a good quality, and both chemical and biological quality has improved in recent years. In particular, the chemical quality of rivers in England improved markedly between 1990 and 2001, although by the latter date England still had the lowest percentage of river length in a good or fair condition of any of the constituent countries of the United Kingdom (Table 11.6).

River water quality is a headline indicator of sustainable development, and improvements in water quality since 1990 are thought to be largely attributable to the impact of the investment programme of the water industry and pollution control measures. However, the chemical quality of rivers and canals is not only affected by human activity. Lower than average rainfall and low river flows can also have an adverse effect on river quality through a reduced dilution of pollutants.

Global warming and climate change

Both global and local (central England) average temperatures rose during the 20th century (Figure 11.7). Global temperatures rose consistently during the first half of the 20th century and, after a period of levelling off, rose again steeply from 1975. Nine of the ten hottest years on record have been during the period 1990 to 2001, with 1998 being the warmest year since global records began in 1860. Temperatures in central England also rose in the first half of the century and, after a period with little change, mirrored the global pattern and rose steeply from the 1970s. Four of the five warmest years in central England since 1772 occurred after 1990.

The Intergovernmental Panel on Climate Change (IPCC) reported in 2001 that there is new and stronger evidence that most of the warming over the last 50 years is attributable to human activities – chief among these is the emission of 'greenhouse gases', such as carbon dioxide, methane and nitrous oxide.

Temperature changes are not the only indication that climate change is occurring. Phenology – the study of the timing of natural seasonal events – suggests that events such as the flowering of plants are being thrown out of their traditional sequences. The Woodland Trust and the Centre for Ecology and Hydrology found that higher than average temperatures from January to April 2002 led to almost every characteristic of spring happening earlier than in 2001, with insect species such as bumble bees and butterflies occurring up to three weeks early.

The IPCC 2001 report also predicted that, unless action to control emissions is taken, global temperatures will rise by between 1.4 and 5.8°C by the end of the century. This increase would be a much larger change than any experienced over at least the last 10,000 years, and is likely to have a major impact on the global environment. Mean sea levels are expected to rise by 9 to 88 centimetres, causing flooding of low lying areas, and other effects could include increases in rainfall and the frequency of extreme weather events.

Figure **11.7**

Difference in average surface temperature: comparison with 1961–90 average

Global and Central England

Degrees C

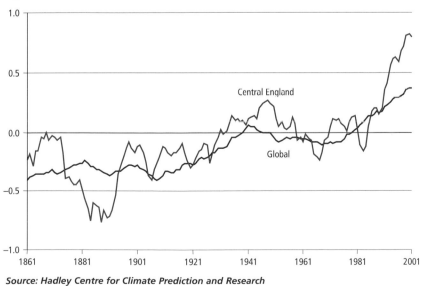

Source: Hadley Centre for Climate Prediction and Research

Under the Kyoto Protocol, ratified by the United Kingdom and its European Union (EU) partners in May 2002, the EU as a unit is committed to reducing emissions of six greenhouse gases by 8 per cent below the 1990 level over the 'commitment period' of 2008 to 2012. The United Kingdom has a legally binding target to reduce emissions by 12.5 per cent relative to 1990 over the same period, and the Government intends to move beyond that target towards a goal of reducing its carbon dioxide emissions to 20 per cent below 1990 levels by 2010. Emissions of greenhouse gases are one of the Government's headline indicators of sustainable development, and fell by 13 per cent between 1990 and 2000.

In 2000, the United Kingdom emitted 9.1 tonnes of carbon dioxide (CO_2) per person (Table 11.8). CO_2 is the most significant greenhouse gas, and contributed 84 per cent of the potential warming effect of man-made emissions in the United Kingdom in 2000. Other greenhouse gases, such as hydrochlorofluorocarbons (HFCs), have much higher warming potentials but are produced in much lower quantities. The United Kingdom is one of the EU countries that has succeeded in reducing its emissions of CO_2, with a reduction of 11 per cent between 1990 and 2000.

Between 1970 and 2000, CO_2 emissions from transport grew by 87 per cent, more than doubling the sector's share of overall emissions (Figure 11.9). In contrast, emissions from industrial, domestic and services end-users have all fallen over the same period. The largest reduction came from industry, where emissions fell rapidly but erratically up to the early 1980s and then continued declining steadily to just over half their 1970 level by 2000. In contrast, emissions from domestic users fell more steadily and then levelled off to around four fifths of their 1970 level, while emissions from services fell the least, and were less than a fifth lower by 2000.

The use of renewable sources in electricity generation will be vital in reducing CO_2 emissions. The United Kingdom produces far less of its electricity from renewable sources than do most other countries in the EU, only 3 per cent in 2000, compared with an EU average of 16 per cent (Figure 11.10).

Table **11.8**

Emissions of carbon dioxide: EU comparison

Tonnes per capita

	1990	2000	Percentage change 1990–2000
Belgium	11.8	12.4	4.7
Luxembourg	..	12.3	..
Finland	12.5	12.0	–3.9
Irish Republic	9.0	11.6	28.4
Netherlands	10.7	10.9	2.1
Germany	12.8	10.4	–18.2
Greece	8.4	10.2	20.7
Denmark	10.2	9.9	–3.3
United Kingdom	10.3	9.1	–11.2
Austria	8.1	8.2	1.1
Italy	7.7	8.0	3.7
Spain	5.9	7.8	32.8
France	6.9	6.8	–1.7
Portugal	4.5	6.3	41.6
Sweden	6.6	6.3	–3.9

Source: European Environment Agency

Figure **11.9**

Emissions of carbon dioxide: by end user

United Kingdom

Million tonnes

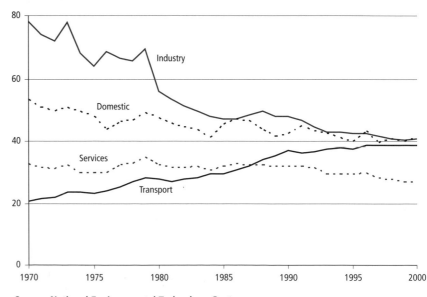

Source: National Environmental Technology Centre

Figure **11.10**

Proportion of electricity produced by renewable sources:[1] EU comparison, 2000

Percentages

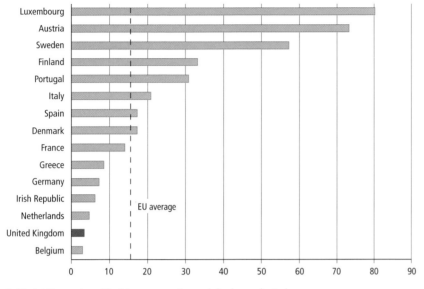

1 Electricity produced by biomass, geothermal, hydro and wind power.
Source: Eurostat

Table **11.11**

Agricultural land use[1]

United Kingdom   Thousand hectares

	1971	1981	1991	2001
Crop areas				
Wheat	1,097	1,491	1,981	1,635
Barley	2,288	2,327	1,395	1,245
Other cereals (excluding maize)	424	161	127	134
Rape grown for oil seed	5	125	440	404
Sugar beet not for stock feeding	190	210	196	177
Potatoes (early and main crop)	256	191	177	165
Other crops	577	490	643	694
All crop areas	4,838	4,995	4,957	4,454
Grasses	7,240	7,013	6,935	6,789
Sole right rough grazing	5,550	5,021	4,950	4,435
Common rough grazing	1,128	1,214	1,233	1,232
Set-aside land	..	..	..	800
Woodland	154	277	372	514
All other land on agricultural holdings	131	211	242	287
Bare fallow	74	76	67	43
All agricultural land	19,115	18,808	18,853	18,555

1 Includes estimates for minor holdings for all countries. Northern Ireland data are based on all active farm businesses.
Source: Department for Environment, Food & Rural Affairs; National Assembly for Wales; Scottish Executive; Department of Agriculture, Northern Ireland

In contrast to increases in recent years, the amount of electricity produced from renewable sources in the United Kingdom fell between 2000 and 2001, due to a reduction in hydro generation. Large scale hydro generation was 21 per cent lower than in 2000, because of a low level of precipitation in the catchment areas, especially in the winter of 2000-01. However, generation from renewables other than hydro was 12 per cent higher in 2001 than in 2000. Generation from landfill gas grew the most, by 14.5 per cent.

Under the Renewables Obligation, the Government is committed to increase the contribution of electricity from renewables in the United Kingdom so that by 2010, 10 per cent of licensed electricity sales should be from eligible renewable sources. The EU-wide target is 22 per cent of electricity from renewables by 2010.

Countryside, farming and wildlife

The 'natural' landscape of much of the United Kingdom is a product of many centuries of human intervention. The majority of the land is used for agriculture, 70 per cent of the total in 2000. However, the amount of land used for agricultural purposes fell between 1991 and 2001, by 1.6 per cent or just under 300,000 hectares (Table 11.11). A fall in the area given to crops more than accounted for this reduction, which is the continuation of a long term trend – between 1961 and 2001, the area of land used for agriculture fell by 900,000 hectares (5 per cent). One reason for this decrease is an improvement in agricultural techniques which means that more food can be produced from the same amount of land.

There have also been large scale changes in the area of land given to different crops in recent years. Between 1971 and 1991, the area used to grow wheat increased by 81 per cent, to almost 2 million hectares. It exceeded 2 million hectares several times during the 1990s, and again in 2000, although it then fell to 1.6 million hectares in 2001, due to wet weather the previous autumn. Oil seed rape was rarely grown in 1971, but in 2001 more than 0.4 million hectares was given over to it. However, the area used to grow barley fell by 46 per cent over the same 30 years, to 1.2 million hectares.

Over 1 million hectares of farmland in England is in a government-sponsored environment scheme of some sort (Table 11.12). Agri-environment measures are a publicly funded means of maintaining and enhancing the natural beauty and diversity of the countryside. Payments are made to farmers who adopt land management practises that protect biodiversity, landscape and historical features. Environmentally sensitive areas (ESAs) are designated throughout the United Kingdom, covering nearly 3.4 million hectares, nearly 14 per cent of the land area. Payments are made to farmers in respect of nearly half this area.

The scheme which had the largest growth in area between 1996 and 2001 was the organic conversion scheme, which aims to encourage the expansion of organic production. This provides benefits to soil health and fertility, biodiversity and the wider landscape, resulting from the use of crop rotations, as well as from the absence of synthetic pesticides, herbicides and fertilisers. Demand for organic food has increased in recent years, in response to growing concern about the use of pesticides and about the development of genetically modified crops. As at June 2002, almost 700,000 hectares of land in the United Kingdom was under organic production, a sixth more than in the previous year and 22 times more than in 1993.

In an attempt to minimise the effect of house building on the countryside, the Government has set targets for the amount of new housing which is to be built on 'brownfield', or previously developed sites in England. In 2001, 33 per cent of land changing to residential use in England was previously used for agriculture, compared with 51 per cent which was previously developed urban land (Table 11.13). In 1985 these figures were 44 per cent and 38 per cent respectively. The area of land changing to residential use each year fell between 1985 and 1999, which could in part be a reflection of the fact that fewer houses were being built (see Chapter 10: Housing). However, the area changing increased in both 2000 and 2001.

Over 11 per cent of the United Kingdom is covered by woodland of some kind. Cover varies throughout the United Kingdom: in 2002, it was 17 per cent in Scotland, 14 per

Table **11.12**

Land in environment schemes

England				Thousand hectares
	1996	1999	2000	2001
Environmentally sensitive areas[1]	434	524	532	577
Countryside stewardship	91	140	192	263
Organic conversion	5	16	96	135
Woodland schemes	23	33	36	38
Moorland	11	16	16	16
Nitrate sensitive areas	20	28	16	10
Other[2]	7	9	9	9
Total	589	765	897	1,047

1 Land under management agreement only.
2 Arable stewardship, countryside access and habitat schemes.
Source: Department for Environment, Food & Rural Affairs

Table **11.13**

Land changing to residential use: by previous use[1,2]

England						Percentages
	1985	1990	1995	1999	2000	2001
Rural uses						
Agriculture	44	41	38	38	35	33
Minerals, landfill and defence	1	1	1	1	1	2
Other rural uses	7	5	5	5	5	4
All rural uses	52	47	43	43	41	39
Urban uses						
Residential	21	22	17	15	14	15
Previously developed vacant and derelict land	11	13	21	20	24	24
Other urban uses	7	7	8	12	12	13
All land previously developed for urban uses	38	42	46	47	49	51
Vacant – not previously developed	10	10	11	9	10	10
All urban uses	48	53	57	57	59	61
All uses	100	100	100	100	100	100
All previously developed land	39	43	47	48	51	48
All land changing to residential use (hectares)	8,755	8,160	6,685	4,730	4,890	5,470

1 The information relates only to map changes recorded by the Ordnance Survey between 1985 and 2000 for which the year of change is judged to have been the year shown for each column as appropriate. (See also Appendix, Part 11: Land use change).
2 Excludes conversion of existing buildings.
Source: Department for Environment, Food & Rural Affairs

Figure **11.14**

New woodland creation[1]

Great Britain

Thousand hectares

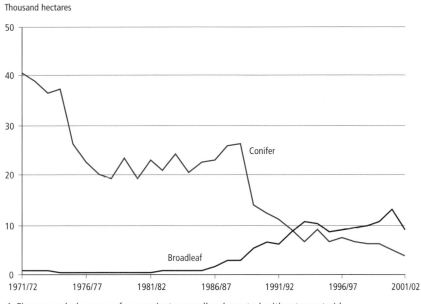

1 Figures exclude areas of new private woodland created without grant aid.
Source: Forestry Commission

Table **11.15**

Breeding populations of selected birds

Great Britain   Indices[1] (1971=100)

	1971	1981	1991	2000
Woodland[2] birds				
Great tit	100	107	122	127
Pheasant	100	97	112	127
Chaffinch	100	108	123	125
Robin	100	102	96	121
Wren	100	110	102	116
Blue tit	100	106	113	115
Blackbird	100	93	79	74
Dunnock	100	92	61	57
Song thrush	100	79	49	43
Farmland[2] birds				
Woodpigeon	100	105	143	174
Yellowhammer	100	97	83	53
Skylark	100	99	60	50
Starling	100	93	69	40

1 Figures are ten year rolling averages ending in the year shown.
2 Principal breeding season habitat.
Source: British Trust for Ornithology

cent in Wales, 8 per cent in England and 6 per cent in Northern Ireland. In international terms, however, the United Kingdom has relatively low forest cover. In 2000, the EU average figure was 37 per cent, with the Irish Republic having the lowest cover, at 10 per cent, and Finland the highest, at 72 per cent.

The area of forested land in the United Kingdom fell to a low of around 1.1 million hectares at the beginning of the 20th century and has been increasing since then, reaching 2.8 million hectares in 2002. Ancient woodland, which has existed since the earliest reliable records began (over 400 years in England and Wales) and which may contain complex and fragile ecosystems, and preserve historical features, only covers around 2 per cent of the United Kingdom.

Although there are more conifers in Great Britain than broadleaved trees, since the early 1990s broadleaved planting has exceeded that of conifer (Figure 11.14). Prior to the 1990s timber production remained the key priority, resulting in the planting of conifer trees, which were suitable for timber but mainly not native to Britain. Since then, additional incentives for planting broadleaves and native pinewood, and for planting on former agricultural land, have led to a growth in the number of broadleaved trees planted.

Bird populations are thought to be good indicators of the condition of Britain's wildlife and the countryside, as birds have a wide-range of habitats and tend to be at or near the top of the food chain. The British Trust for Ornithology found that between 1971 and 2000, breeding populations of common birds such as the song thrush, skylark and starling fell by a half or more, while those of other species, such as woodpigeon, great tit and pheasant increased by more than a quarter (Table 11.15). The Government's indicator of wild bird populations showed a fall of 15 per cent for woodland species, and 43 per cent for farmland species, between the baseline year of 1970 and 2000.

Changes in farming practices have contributed to the decline in certain species, particularly those whose principal breeding habitat is farmland. Increased use of chemicals and loss of hedgerows have lead to a decline and deterioration in suitable breeding and feeding areas. Bird populations are a headline indicator of sustainable development, and the Government has set a target to reverse the long term decline in the number of farmland birds by 2020.

The local environment and waste

The condition of the local environment is often central to people's perception of their quality of life. In November 2001, the ONS Omnibus Survey found that most adults in Great Britain thought the condition of elements of their local environment, such as air quality, street lighting, and the level of traffic noise, were good (Table 11.16). Women were in general less likely than men to perceive elements of their environment as good. The biggest differences came in the areas of personal safety, air quality and traffic noise. A fifth of women felt that personal safety at rail stations was poor, double the proportion of men.

According to the Omnibus Survey, one of the most common concerns people had was over the condition of pavements. This perception is supported by the Local Environmental Quality Survey of England (LEQSE), commissioned by the Department for Environment, Food & Rural Affairs and conducted in 2001/02. It showed that on 35 per cent of the sites surveyed, paved areas suffered from a significant degree of physical deterioration. The survey also found that 18 per cent of sites monitored were significantly or heavily littered.

The collection and disposal of household waste, and litter and rubbish from public areas, is the responsibility of local authorities throughout the United Kingdom. Around 90 per cent of such 'municipal' waste is generated by households, and much of this has traditionally been disposed of to landfill, a method which makes little use of the waste and produces greenhouse gases (mainly CO_2 and methane).

In 2000/01, 12 per cent of municipal waste was recycled or composted, while 78 per cent was disposed in landfill (Table 11.17). The proportion recycled has grown since 1996/97, as the proportion disposed to landfill has fallen. However, the absolute volume of waste disposed in landfill sites has increased over the same period, as the overall amount of

Table **11.16**

Perception of local conditions: by sex, November 2001

Great Britain

Percentages[1]

	Males			Females		
	Good	Poor	Neither	Good	Poor	Neither
Condition of pavements	44	37	18	39	40	18
Level of crime	46	32	19	40	31	25
Ease of crossing roads on foot	62	26	12	60	28	12
Traffic noise	64	22	13	57	25	17
Street lighting	64	19	16	63	22	13
Personal safety at rail stations	48	11	17	32	21	18
Air quality	73	12	15	66	16	16
Personal safety at bus stops	54	9	16	47	16	15

1 Percentages do not sum to 100 as "don't knows" are not shown. Adults aged 16 and over.
Source: Omnibus Survey, Office for National Statistics

Table **11.17**

Management of municipal waste: by method

England

Percentages

	1996/97	1998/99	2000/01
Landfill	84	82	78
Incineration with energy from waste	6	8	9
Incineration without energy from waste	2	–	–
Refuse derived fuel manufacture	1	1	–
Recycled/composted[1]	7	10	12
Other[2]	0	–	–
Total (=100%) (million tonnes)	24.6	26.3	28.2

1 Includes household and non-household sources collected for recycling or for centralised composting; home composting estimates are not included in this total.
2 Excludes any processing prior to landfilling and materials sent to materials reclamation facilities (MRFs).
Source: Department for Environment, Food & Rural Affairs

Map **11.18**

Household waste recycling: by area, 2000/01

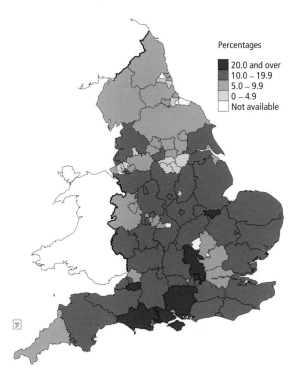

Percentages

- 20.0 and over
- 10.0 – 19.9
- 5.0 – 9.9
- 0 – 4.9
- Not available

Source: Department for Environment, Food & Rural Affairs

Figure **11.19**

Environmental impacts of households

Great Britain

Indices (1971=100)

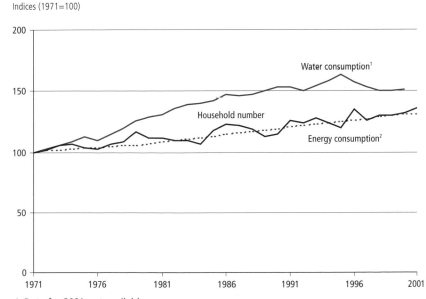

1 Data for 2001 not available.
2 Data are for United Kingdom.
Source: Department of Trade and Industry; Office of the Deputy Prime Minister; Office of Water Services

municipal waste continues to grow year on year. Much of this waste is packaging, and factors such as the increasing number of smaller households and changes in lifestyles (such as eating more convenience foods) have contributed to the growth in volume of waste produced.

The Government has set an overall target to recycle 25 per cent of household waste in England by 2005, and local authorities have been set individual statutory standards. Recycling rates vary widely across the country (Map 11.18). In 2000/01, over two thirds of authorities recycled at least 10 per cent of household waste. One in ten recycled over 20 per cent, while less than one in twenty authorities had household recycling rates of less than 5 per cent. In general, authorities in the north of England had lower rates than those achieved in other parts of the country.

The Survey of Public Attitudes to the Environment 2001 (see Tables 11.1 and 11.2) found that the most common reasons given by people for not regularly recycling paper were that recycling facilities were too far away (26 per cent) and that there was no kerbside collection (25 per cent).

Use of resources

Transport accounted for 32 per cent of final energy consumption in the United Kingdom in 2001, while the domestic sector consumed 28 per cent of the total. The number of households in the United Kingdom increased by 34 per cent between 1970 and 2001 (Figure 11.19). Household energy consumption increased roughly in line with household numbers, at 32 per cent over the same period, while water consumption grew faster, at 51 per cent. However, after peaking in the mid-1990s, when there were droughts (households tend to use more water during droughts, for example to water gardens), water consumption fell somewhat in the second half of the 1990s as rainfall increased.

In terms of energy use, changes such as an increased efficiency of appliances and improved thermal insulation of houses have been counterbalanced by an increased use of those appliances and a tendency for people to heat their homes to higher temperatures than previously. The Building Research Establishment estimate that average temperatures inside domestic dwellings increased from 16.5°C in 1991 to 18°C in 2000. The increase in water consumption can be linked to greater ownership of appliances such as washing machines and washer-dryers (64 per cent of households had at least one of these in 1970 compared with 92 per cent in 2001), the increased use of those appliances within the home, and also the greater number of smaller households (see Chapter 10, Housing).

If predicted changes in precipitation patterns due to climate change occur, water resources could become a major issue in many parts of the world over the next century. According to the United Nations, 1.7 billion people already live in 'water-stressed countries'. In a global context, Britain does not in general suffer from a lack of rain. However, precipitation amounts vary greatly both through time and from region to region (Table 11.20). On average, rainfall is lowest in eastern and southern England, where population densities and water demand are high.

Climate change may increase the vulnerability of parts of the country to the threat of drought or flooding. Notable climatic variability has been a feature of the last decade with very wide departures from seasonal average river flows, groundwater levels and reservoir stocks. Protracted drought conditions in the early and mid-1990s were followed by a sequence of wet years in southern Britain, which triggered a sustained recovery in water resources. They culminated, however, in the remarkably widespread and protracted flooding in the autumn and winter of 2000-01 – the most severe in England and Wales since the snowmelt-generated flooding of March 1947. Rainfall for the September 2000 to April 2001 period was well below average in much of Scotland, but for England and Wales a new maximum rainfall total was established for any eight-month period since the series started in 1766. As a consequence, overall water resources were exceptionally healthy in almost all regions throughout 2001.

Most energy used in the United Kingdom is produced from fossil fuels – petroleum, natural gas and coal – which accounted for 91 per cent

Table 11.20

Average annual rainfall: by region[1,2]

United Kingdom   Index (1961–90 average rainfall = 100)

	1981	1991	2001	1961–90 average rainfall (millimetres)
United Kingdom	109	94	95	1,080
England	111	87	103	823
North West	115	93	90	1,201
Northumbria	104	94	95	853
Severn Trent	111	86	102	754
Yorkshire	114	82	96	821
Anglian	109	79	123	596
Thames	111	88	113	688
Southern	108	90	111	778
Wessex	110	91	98	839
South West	115	93	86	1,173
Wales[2]	113	94	97	1,355
Scotland	106	102	88	1,436
Northern Ireland	115	96	83	1,059

1 The regions of England shown in this table correspond to the original nine English regions of the National Rivers Authority (NRA); the NRA became part of the Environment Agency upon its creation in April 1996. See Appendix, Part 11: Environment Agency.
2 The figures in this table relate to the country of Wales; not the Environment Agency Welsh Region.
Source: Meteorological Office; Centre for Ecology and Hydrology

of primary fuel production in 2001. Overall, primary fuel production was 4 per cent lower than in the previous year (Figure 11.21). Production of petroleum fell by 8 per cent as production from older, established fields continued to decline. Production of natural gas fell by 2 per cent from the record level seen in 2000, while production of coal rose by 2 per cent. There was a 5 per cent increase in production of primary electricity, largely due to an increase in the generation of nuclear energy.

Production of petroleum was negligible at the beginning of the 1970s, but rose sharply between 1976 and 1985, before falling and then rising again in the 1990s. Coal consumption has been in decline since the

Figure **11.21**

Production of primary fuels

United Kingdom

Millions tonnes of oil equivalent

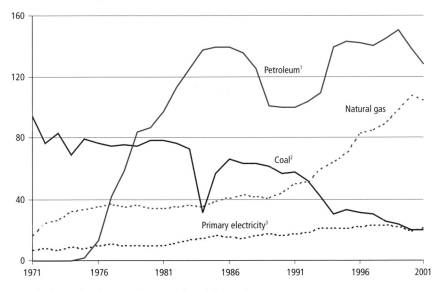

1 Includes crude oil, natural gas liquids and feedstocks.
2 Includes colliery methane.
3 Nuclear, natural flow hydro-electricity and, from 1988, generation at wind stations.
Source: Department of Trade and Industry

Table **11.22**

Oil and gas reserves, 1991 and 2001

United Kingdom Extra-Regio

	1991		2001	
	Oil (million tonnes)	Gas (billion cubic metres)	Oil (million tonnes)	Gas (billion cubic metres)
Fields already discovered				
Proven reserves[1]	555	540	605	695
Probable reserves	675	695	350	445
Possible reserves	730	570	475	395
Total remaining reserves in present discoveries	1,960	1,805	1,430	1,535
Already recovered	1,465	804	2,687	1,625
Maximum estimates of potential future discoveries	3,395	1,252	1,930	1,680
Maximum recoverable reserves	6,820	3,860	6,050	4,815
Maximum potential additional reserves	360	305	420	245

1 Excludes volumes of oil and gas already recovered.
Source: Department of Trade and Industry

1980s, while consumption of natural gas rose sharply from the end of that decade, primarily due to electricity generators switching to gas as a cheaper source of fuel. Coal production in 1984 was less than half that in 1983 because of the miners strike at the time and, although it recovered when the strike ended, it never returned to previous levels. The small increase in coal production in 2001 was triggered by an increase in gas prices which allowed coal powered generators to produce electricity more cheaply than some gas powered stations.

Although the amounts extracted each year have grown over the last decade, new discoveries mean that the United Kingdom's proven and probable reserves of oil and gas are not much lower than the levels of 10 years ago (Table 11.22). In 1991, 1.2 billion tonnes of oil remained in proven and probable reserves. By 2001, this figure was 1.0 billion tonnes, even though 1.2 billion tonnes had been recovered over the same period. For gas, proven plus probable reserves were 1,235 billion cubic metres in 1991 and 1,140 billion cubic metres in 2001. A total of 821 billion cubic metres of gas were recovered over the decade.

It is difficult to make accurate predictions, but if all discovered oil reserves were to be developed they would last 12 years at 2001 rates of extraction. If estimates of as yet undiscovered reserves are also considered, it is thought that UK oil reserves will last between 14 and 29 years, although the upper estimate is unlikely. Similarly, discovered natural gas reserves will last 14 years at current rates of extraction, with estimates of undiscovered reserves increasing this estimate to between 17 and 30 years.

Chapter 12

Transport

Overview

- In 1999-2001, British residents of all ages travelled an average of 11,000 kilometres a year within Great Britain. (Page 208)

- Although people in Great Britain are travelling further each year than ever before, in recent years the number of trips made has fallen. In 1989-91 each person made 1,091 trips per year on average, but by 1999-2001 this had decreased to 1,019. (Page 208)

Prices and expenditure

- After taking into account the effect of inflation, UK household expenditure on transport and travel increased by 20 per cent between 1990 and 2001-02. (Table 12.6)

Access to transport

- In 1999-2001, 85 per cent of households in rural areas had access to at least one car. In large urban areas the proportion was 68 per cent, and in London boroughs, 63 per cent. (Figure 12.10)

Travel to work and school

- The average length of commuting trips in Great Britain in 1989-91 was 11.6 kilometres with an average journey time of 23 minutes. By 1999-2001 these had increased to 13.6 kilometres and 25 minutes respectively. (Page 215)

The roads

- In 2001, 73 per cent of people aged 18 and over agreed that it was 'very' or 'fairly' important to cut down the number of cars on Britain's roads. (Page 216)

The railways

- The number of passenger journeys taken on Britain's rail systems fell by 7 million between 2000/01 and 2001/02, to 2,054 million. (Table 12.17)

International travel

- In 2001 there were 23 million overseas visits to the United Kingdom by overseas residents, compared with 58 million visits overseas by UK residents. (Table 12.19)

Transport safety

- There were 3,450 deaths from road accidents in Great Britain in 2001, 41 per cent less than the 5,846 in 1981. (Page 220)

- In 2000, the United Kingdom had the lowest road death rate in the EU, at 6 deaths per 100,000 population. (Figure 12.24)

The last ten years have seen the continuation of long-term trends in many areas of transport and travel, for example the increase in the distance each person travels in a year, the rising number of cars on the roads, and the ever-increasing reliance on those cars. Travel overseas, and particularly air travel, has increased substantially over the same period. Pronounced variations in the amount and way people travel depend, for example, on their age, sex, where they live, and their income. Such variations include the longer distances travelled by people on high incomes compared with those on low incomes and the much greater reliance on the car by people in rural areas than those living in London.

Overview

The total distance that people in Great Britain travelled was almost two and a half times higher in 2001 than in 1961 (Table 12.1). Travel in cars, vans and taxis more than accounted for this increase, while travel by other forms of road transport - bus and coach, bicycle and motorcycle - fell over the period. The increasing dominance of the car as a form of transport is demonstrated by the substantial rise in the proportion of passenger kilometres covered in cars. In 1961 cars, vans and taxis accounted for 53 per cent of all passenger kilometres travelled, but by 2001 this figure had risen to 85 per cent.

There are considerable variations in the distances travelled by individuals. The National Travel Survey (NTS) found that, in 1999-2001, British residents of all ages travelled on average 11,000 kilometres a year within Great Britain. Males travelled 13,000 kilometres on average, compared with 9,200 kilometres for females. Men aged 40-49 travelled the furthest, 19,000 kilometres a year, whereas women aged 70 and over travelled the shortest overall distance, 4,600 kilometres.

The type of area a person lives in can also affect the distance they travel each year. People living in metropolitan areas travelled the shortest distance on average, at 8,600 kilometres, and those in the London boroughs 8,800 kilometres. Those living in rural areas travelled the furthest, at 14,300 kilometres.

The increase in distance travelled is due to longer trips being undertaken. The average length of trip increased from 9.6 kilometres in 1989-91 to 10.8 kilometres in 1999-2001.

Table 12.1

Passenger transport: by mode

Great Britain						Billion passenger kilometres
	1961	1971	1981	1991	1996	2001
Road						
Car and van[1]	157	313	394	582	606	624
Bus and coach	76	60	48	44	44	46
Motorcycle	11	4	10	6	4	5
Bicycle	11	4	5	5	4	4
All road	255	381	458	638	658	679
Rail[2]	39	35	34	39	39	47
Air[3]	1	2	3	5	6	8
All modes	295	419	495	681	703	734

1 Includes taxis.
2 Data relate to financial years.
3 Includes Northern Ireland and Channel Islands.
Source: Department for Transport

Although people in Great Britain are travelling further each year than ever before, in recent years the numbers of trips made has fallen. In 1989-91, the average number made each year was 1,091 per person, but by 1999-2001 this had fallen to 1,019. The fall has been greatest among males, who took 9 per cent fewer trips in 1999-2001 than in 1989-91, whereas females took only 4 per cent fewer.

Males make, on average, slightly more trips each year than females (Table 12.2). In 1999-2001, females made proportionately more trips for shopping and taking children to school, but fewer commuting and business trips. Overall, males were more likely to travel by car, using it for 65 per cent of trips, while females made 61 per cent of their trips by car. Females were more likely than males to walk, making 28 per cent of their trips on foot, compared with 24 per cent of trips made by males.

There are also marked differences in the numbers of trips made each year by people living in households on different incomes. In 1999-2001, people living in households in the highest equivalised income quintile made 43 per cent more trips within Great Britain than those in the lowest (see Appendix, Part 12:

Table **12.2**

Trips per person per year: by sex, main mode and trip purpose,[1] 1999–2001

Great Britain   Percentages

	Males					Females				
	Car	Walk	Bus, coach and rail[2]	Other	All modes	Car	Walk	Bus, coach and rail[2]	Other	All modes
Social/entertainment	25	21	19	25	23	27	18	18	32	24
Shopping	18	22	18	10	19	23	23	29	15	23
Commuting	20	7	29	31	18	13	7	24	19	13
Other escort and personal business	21	13	10	8	18	22	14	11	13	19
Education	3	13	16	13	7	4	10	13	11	6
Escort education	2	4	1	–	3	6	10	1	1	6
Business	7	2	4	5	5	2	1	2	3	2
Holiday/day trip	3	1	3	8	3	3	1	2	7	3
Other, including just walk	–	18	–	–	4	–	15	–	–	4
All purposes (=100%) (numbers)	667	246	70	48	1,031	613	278	85	33	1,008

1 See Appendix, Part 12: National Travel Survey.
2 Includes London Underground.
Source: National Travel Survey, Department for Transport

Table **12.3**

Trips per person per year: by real household income quintile group[1] and trip purpose, 1999–2001

Great Britain   Trips per person per year

	Bottom quintile	Second quintile	Third quintile	Fourth quintile	Top quintile
Social/entertainment	208	225	246	259	264
Commuting	45	103	170	221	229
Shopping	213	225	210	214	209
Other escort and personal business	138	169	197	206	217
Business	7	15	29	45	76
Education	88	62	79	52	52
Escort education	54	45	56	40	37
Holiday/day trip	21	26	31	31	33
Other, including just walk	40	44	44	46	47
All purposes	811	913	1,063	1,115	1,164

1 See Appendix, Part 12: National Travel Survey.
Source: National Travel Survey, Department for Transport

Real household income equivalent) (Table 12.3). The biggest differences across the income range were in commuting and travel for business: those in the highest income quintile of households made eleven times as many business trips, and five times as many commuting trips, as those in the lowest quintile. However, people living in households in the lowest income quintile made more education and escort education trips than those in the highest. The number of trips made on average each year varies more among females, with those in the highest income quintile making 1,173 trips a year in 1999-2001 compared with 802 made by those in the lowest quintile. Males in the same groups made on average 1,155 and 824 trips respectively.

Within the general pattern of a fall in the number of trips made each year over the last decade, the largest reduction occurred among those in the highest income quintile, who made on average 9 per cent fewer trips a year in 1999-2001 than in 1989-91. The average number of trips made by people in the lowest income quintile remained almost unchanged over the same period.

There is considerable variation by equivalised household income in the average lengths of the trips people make. In 1999-2001, this was 15.3 kilometres for those living in households in the highest income quintile. For those in the next highest quintile, it was 11.9, while for those in the lowest, it was 6.7 kilometres.

The movement of goods around Great Britain has also increased markedly in the last 30 years (Figure 12.4). Almost all this increase can be attributed to the movement of goods by road, which grew from 88 billion tonne kilometres in 1972 to 157 billion tonne kilometres in 2001. The volume of goods moved by rail in 2001, 20 billion tonne kilometres, was 5 per cent less than it was in 1972; it fell to a low of 13 billion tonne kilometres in 1994 and 1995, but has increased steadily since then.

The increase in road freight reflects an increase in distance travelled rather than in the overall quantity of goods lifted. In recent years there has been a decrease in total weight lifted by heavy goods vehicles (those over 3.5 tonnes) at the same time as an increase in tonne kilometres travelled. The total weight of goods lifted by such vehicles in Great Britain peaked in 1989 at 1.70 billion tonnes. It fell during the recession in the early 1990s, and then recovered to 1.64 billion tonnes in 1997, after which it fell again, to 1.58 billion tonnes in 2001. The average length of haul for goods lifted by road, however, steadily increased during the 1990s. In 1991 it was 83 kilometres, and by 2001 had grown to 94 kilometres. For food, drink and tobacco, which accounted for a fifth of goods lifted in 2001, the average length of haul was 129 kilometres in 2001, compared with 112 in 1991.

Prices and expenditure

Transport prices increased substantially during the 1980s and 1990s (Table 12.5). There were rises between 1981 and 1991 of 63 per cent in the 'All motoring' index of the retail prices index (RPI) and 86 per cent in the 'All fares and other travel' index. These were greater than the increases between 1991 and 2002 in motoring prices (45 per cent) and in fares and other travel costs (47 per cent). However, the increases in transport prices in the later period

Figure **12.4**

Goods moved by domestic freight transport: by mode
Great Britain

Billion tonne kilometres

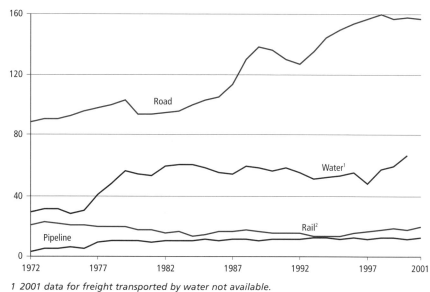

1 2001 data for freight transported by water not available.
2 From 1991 data for rail are financial years.
Source: Department for Transport

Table **12.5**

Passenger transport prices[1]
United Kingdom   Indices (1991=100)

	1981	1986	1991	1996	2001	2002
Motoring costs						
Vehicle tax and insurance	45	66	100	136	195	198
Maintenance[2]	51	71	100	129	160	169
Petrol and oil	64	93	100	137	188	172
Purchase of vehicles	70	81	100	114	106	106
All motoring expenditure	61	81	100	125	146	145
Fares and other travel costs						
Bus and coach fares	51	70	100	132	158	163
Rail fares	50	68	100	130	151	155
Other	74	79	100	115	133	135
All fares and other travel	54	72	100	123	144	147
Retail prices index	54	74	100	115	131	133

1 At January each year based on the retail prices index. See Appendix, Part 6: Retail prices index.
2 Includes spares and accessories, repairs and motoring organisation membership fees.
Source: Office for National Statistics

Table **12.6**

Household expenditure on transport in real terms[1]

United Kingdom   £ per week[1]

	1980	1990	1991	2000/01	2001/02
Motoring					
Cars, vans and motorcycle purchase	..	22.37	20.54	22.99	25.29
Repairs, servicing, spares and accessories	..	6.17	5.56	6.07	6.70
Motor vehicle insurance and taxation	..	6.24	6.16	8.25	9.08
Petrol, diesels and other oils	..	10.78	11.02	15.82	14.79
Other motoring costs	..	1.12	1.15	1.78	1.83
All motoring expenditure	34.20	46.66	44.43	54.91	57.70
Fares and other travel costs					
Rail and tube fares	..	1.50	1.25	1.78	1.62
Bus and coach fares	..	1.70	1.62	1.27	1.34
Taxi, air and other travel costs[2]	..	4.38	3.42	4.94	4.69
All fares and other travel costs[3]	7.00	8.54	7.26	8.87	8.71
All transport and travel	41.22	55.20	51.69	63.78	66.41
All expenditure groups	282.10	340.91	337.29	383.77	394.92

1 At 2001/02 prices deflated by the 'All items' RPI.
2 Includes combined fares.
3 Includes expenditure on bicycles and boats – purchases and repairs.

Source: Family Expenditure Survey and Expenditure and Food Survey, Office for National Statistics

outpaced general inflation, which was not the case between 1981 and 1991. The 'All items' RPI increased by 33 per cent between 1991 and 2002. Over the same period, public transport prices increased by considerably more than motoring prices. For example, from January 1991 to January 2002, bus and coach fares rose by almost two thirds, while motoring prices rose by under a half.

Different components of motoring expenditure have experienced different price increases over the last decade. Vehicle tax and insurance prices rose by 98 per cent between January 1991 and January 2002, whereas the cost of purchasing a vehicle was only 6 per cent more in 2002 than it was in 1991. Petrol and oil prices rose by 72 per cent over the same period. The cost of purchasing vehicles has actually been falling in recent years, and remained virtually unchanged in January 2002 compared with the previous year.

After taking into account the effect of inflation, household expenditure on transport and travel increased by 20 per cent between 1990 and 2001/02 (Table 12.6). If expenditure in 2001/02 is compared with 1991, the increase is even larger – 28 per cent – because expenditure on transport and travel fell in real terms between 1990 and 1991 due to the recession at that time. The increase in expenditure over the 1990s was smaller than over the previous decade – for example, household expenditure on motoring rose by 36 per cent between 1980 and 1990, and by 18 per cent between 1990 and 2000/01.

There are marked variations in the amount spent on transport and travel by households of different incomes. The Expenditure and Food Survey found that in 2001/02, the difference in expenditure on transport and travel between households in the highest gross income quintile and those in the lowest was considerably greater than the difference in overall expenditure.

In June 2002, the United Kingdom and the Netherlands were the most expensive countries in the EU in which to buy premium unleaded petrol (Figure 12.7 - see overleaf). The cheapest country was Greece, where a litre cost on average 35 per cent less than it did in the United Kingdom. The average price of unleaded petrol in the United Kingdom, 74 pence a litre in June 2002, has fallen in recent years – it was 79 pence in June 2001 and 84 pence in June 2000 (at current prices).

Taxes and duties form a major component of petrol prices across the EU – 67 per cent on average in mid-June 2002. If taxes and duties are excluded from prices, the United Kingdom had the cheapest premium unleaded petrol in the EU, at 17 pence compared with an EU average of 20 pence. The tax component of prices in the United Kingdom is the largest of any EU country, 77 per cent in June 2002. In the same month, France and Germany had the next highest tax components, 73 per cent each, whereas Greece had the lowest, at 55 per cent.

Access to transport

The number of licensed cars on Britain's roads continued to increase during the 1990s, from just under 22 million in 1991 to over 26 million in 2001 (Table 12.8). This latter figure is four times greater than it was in 1961, when there were only 6.2 million licensed cars. The number of licensed motorcycles has declined since the early 1980s, reaching a low of 594,000 in 1995, although there has been something of a recovery in recent years. In 1995, 69,000 motorcycles were registered for the first time – by 2000 this number had grown to 183,000, although it fell back slightly in 2001.

In 1999-2001, an estimated 18 million men and 14 million women in Great Britain held full car driving licences. Historically, men have been much more likely than women to hold licences; in 1975-76, 69 per cent of men held a full driving licence compared with only 29 per cent of women. However, women are catching up – in 1999-2001, the proportions were 82 per cent and 60 per cent respectively. The gap between the sexes is smallest in the youngest age groups and largest in the oldest. Forty one per cent of men and 31 per cent of women aged 17-20 held licences in 1999-2001, whereas among those aged 70 and over 69 per cent of men held a licence compared with only 25 per cent of women.

The proportion of people holding full driving licences is highest among those aged 40-49: 91 per cent of men and 77 per cent of women did so in 1999-2001. Older people are less likely to

Figure **12.7**

Premium unleaded petrol[1] prices: EU comparison, mid-June 2002
Pence per litre[2]

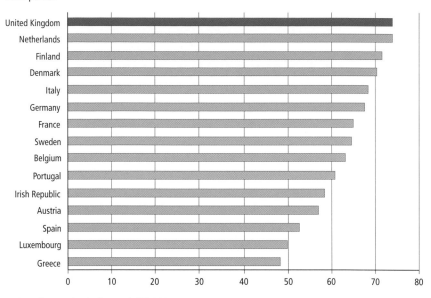

1 Premium unleaded petrol, 95RON.
2 Prices converted to pounds sterling using mid month exchange rates.
Source: Department of Trade and Industry

Table **12.8**

Cars[1] and motorycles[2] currently licensed[3] and new registrations[4]
Great Britain   Thousands

	Currently licensed		New registrations	
	Cars	Motorcycles	Cars	Motorcycles
1961	6,240	1,577	743	212
1971	11,895	899	1,462	128
1981	16,490	1,371	1,643	272
1991	21,955	750	1,709	77
1996	23,439	609	2,093	90
2001	26,443	882	2,710	177

1 Includes light goods vehicles.
2 Includes scooters and mopeds.
3 At 31 December each year.
4 New methods of estimating vehicle stock were introduced in 1992, and changes to the vehicle taxation system were introduced from 1 July 1995.
Source: Department for Transport

Figure **12.9**

Households with regular use of a car[1]

Great Britain

Percentages

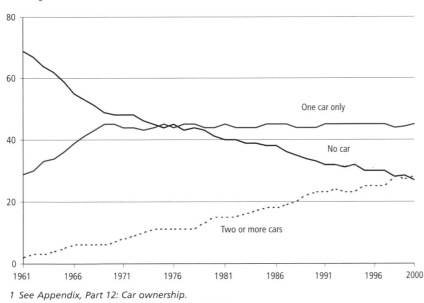

1 See Appendix, Part 12: Car ownership.
Source: National Travel Survey, Department for Transport

Figure **12.10**

Households with access to one or more cars: by type of area, 1989–91 and 1999–2001

Great Britain

Percentages

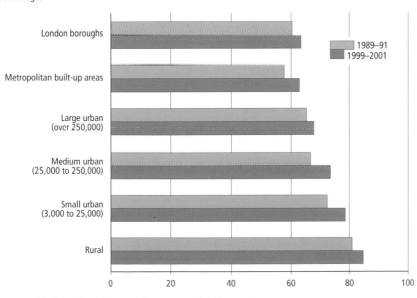

Source: National Travel Survey, Department for Transport

hold a licence, largely because fewer learned to drive when they were younger. Very few people gain licences after the age of 60.

The increase in licensed cars during the 1990s is reflected in the growth in the number of households with two or more cars. Throughout the 1990s around 45 per cent of households owned one car only, while the percentage with no car fell from 32 per cent in 1991 to 27 per cent in 2000 (Figure 12.9). The percentage owning two or more cars increased from 23 per cent to 28 per cent over the same period.

The higher a household's income, the more likely it is to have access to a car. Only 38 per cent of households in the lowest equivalised income quintile had access to a car in 1999-2001. For those in the next quintile, this figure was 57 per cent; for those in the middle quintile it was 82 per cent; while for those in the highest, it reached 93 per cent. However, over the last ten years, car access has grown most among households in the lowest quintile, only 26 per cent of which had access to a car in 1989-91. Conversely, the same proportion of households in the highest quintile had access to at least one car in the earlier period as in the latter.

Whether a person lives in a household with access to a car or not can have a major impact on both the distance they travel each year and the time they spend doing so. Adults (aged 17 and over) who live in a household with no car access travelled on average around 4,740 kilometres a year in 1999-2001. Those living in households with two or more cars travelled over three and a half times further, more than 17,860 kilometres. The former group spent on average 295 hours a year travelling, the latter, 447 hours.

Car ownership is higher in rural areas and lower in large urban areas, reflecting a greater reliance on the car outside urban areas. In 1999-2001, 85 per cent of households in rural areas had access to at least one car (Figure 12.10). In large urban areas, this figure was 68 per cent, and in London boroughs, 63 per cent. Over the last ten years the growth in car access has been greatest in small and medium urban areas at around 6 percentage points. This compares with an increase of around 3 percentage points in London boroughs and large urban areas.

People in rural areas drive further in their cars than those who live in more urban areas. In 1999-2001, cars owned by households in rural areas travelled 16,700 kilometres on average, compared with 12,300 kilometres travelled by cars owned by London households and 13,800 kilometres covered by those owned by households in large urban areas. Household cars covered less distance each year on average in 1999-2001 than in 1989-91, reflecting the greater level of second car ownership in the later period.

Overall, 46 per cent of the distance covered by household cars is for commuting and business reasons. This proportion does not vary greatly by the type of area in which the household is located, although cars owned by London households covered proportionately the least distance for commuting and business reasons.

For households with no, or only limited access to a car, public transport can be vital. The availability of bus services is fairly good overall, with almost nine in ten households in Great Britain living within 13 minutes' walk of a bus stop with a service at least once an hour, although there is variation between different regions (Table 12.11). There is also variation by area type – 99 per cent of households in London boroughs live within 13 minutes' walk of a bus stop with a service at least once an hour, compared with 73 per cent in small urban areas and 50 per cent in rural areas.

Travel to work and school

For men aged 17 to 59, over a quarter of all trips made are for commuting, compared with just under a fifth for women in the same age range. In general, men's journeys to work take more time than women's (Figure 12.12). Overall, men took 28 minutes on average to travel to work and women 22 minutes in 1999-2001. There was little variation between different types of area, except for residents of London boroughs where men took 40 minutes on average compared with 35 minutes for women. One reason for these differences is the distance of the commuting trip, which on average was 9.7 kilometres for women and 16.6 kilometres for men. Women are also more likely to walk or use public transport than men – for example, one in five women in large urban areas walk to work, compared with one in ten men.

Table **12.11**

Time taken to walk to nearest bus stop: by region, 1999–2001

Great Britain   Percentages

	6 minutes or less	7–13 minutes	14 minutes or more	Bus availability indicator[1]
Great Britain	87	10	3	89
England	87	10	3	89
North East	92	7	2	98
North West	90	9	1	96
Yorkshire and the Humber	89	9	3	92
East Midlands	86	9	4	77
West Midlands	87	10	3	94
East	84	12	4	79
London	88	11	1	99
South East	84	13	4	89
South West	83	12	5	78
Wales	88	6	6	79
Scotland	89	8	3	92

1 Households within 13 minutes walk of a bus stop with a service at least once an hour.
Source: National Travel Survey, Department for Transport

Figure **12.12**

Mean time taken to travel to work: by sex and area type of residence, 1999-2001

Great Britain

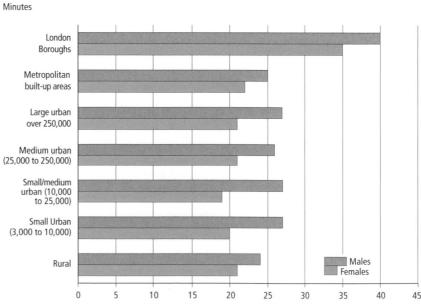

Source: National Travel Survey, Department for Transport

No. 33: 2003 edition

Table **12.13**

Average time taken to travel to school: by age of child and area type of residence

Great Britain   Minutes

	Aged 5–10			Aged 11–16		
	1989–91	1995–97	1999–01	1989–91	1995–97	1999–01
London boroughs	25	22	26	35	35	43
Metropolitan built-up areas	27	21	23	31	30	29
Large urban over 250,000	24	21	19	29	27	29
Medium urban 25,000 to 250,000	23	19	20	26	29	29
Small urban 3,000 to 25,000	22	18	20	27	26	27
Small/medium urban 10,000 to 25,000	..	..	19	..	..	29
Small urban 3,000 to 10,000	..	..	20	..	..	25
Rural	18	17	18	30	27	28

Source: National Travel Survey, Department for Transport

Table **12.14**

Average daily flow[1] of motor vehicles: by class of road

Great Britain   Thousands

	1981	1991	1996	1999[2]	2000[2]	2001[1]
Motorways[3]	30.4	53.8	62.4	74.2	74.4	75.3
Major roads						
Built-up	12.4	15.5	15.5	15.0	15.0	15.3
Non built-up	5.9	9.5	10.1	10.8	10.8	10.9
All major roads	9.1	13.8	14.9	16.3	16.4	16.6
Minor roads	1.0	1.4	1.4	1.4	1.4	1.4
All roads	2.2	3.1	3.3	3.3	3.3	3.3

1 Flow at an average point on each class of road.
2 Estimates from 1999 onwards on new basis (see Appendix, Part 12: Road traffic).
3 Includes motorways owned by local authorities.
Source: Department for Transport

The commute to work has increased in both distance and duration over the last decade. The average length of commuting trips in 1989-91 was 11.6 kilometres and average journey time was 23 minutes. By 1999-2001 these figures had increased to 13.6 kilometres and 25 minutes. The biggest increase in distance was for those living in smaller urban areas, 3.3 kilometres, while those living in London had the smallest increase, just 0.3 kilometres.

Trips to school account for over a quarter of all trips taken by under 16s. In 1999-2001, children of secondary school age took considerably longer on average to get to school than younger children, and those living in London took the most time of all (Table 12.13). One factor in these variations is the distance children live from their schools. Children aged 5-10 travel, on average, 2.6 kilometres to their school, while for those aged 11-16 this figure is 4.8 kilometres.

The ways in which children travel to school have changed over the last ten years. In general, fewer are walking and more are travelling in cars. For example, in 1989-91, 27 per cent of trips to school taken by 5-10 year olds were in a car or van; by 1999-2001 this figure had risen to 39 per cent. Since trips to school usually take place at the same time each morning and evening, they can have a major impact on levels of congestion in residential areas. At the morning peak at 8.50am, an estimated 17 per cent of all cars on the road in urban areas are taking children to school.

The roads

In total, 474 billion vehicle kilometres were travelled on Great Britain's roads in 2001; over 80 per cent of this was accounted for by cars, vans and taxis. As both car ownership and usage have increased, so have traffic volumes. In terms of traffic flow, motorways had by far the biggest increase in traffic volume between 1981 and 2001, with daily flows almost two and a half times greater in the latter year (Table 12.14). Vehicle flows on major built–up roads grew by much less over the same period, and actually fell slightly during the 1990s. In 2001, the busiest roads were motorways in the Greater London area, which had average daily flows of over 107,000 vehicles. The quietest were non-built-up minor roads in Scotland, which had average daily flows of only 500 vehicles.

Average vehicle speeds suggest that on motorways and dual carriageways where traffic is free-flowing, most drivers drive at or over the speed limit that applies. In 2001, the average speed of cars on motorways was 70 miles per hour, which is the speed limit for cars on that type of road, with 54 per cent of cars exceeding the speed limit. Similar results were noted on dual carriageways.

While buses and coaches accounted overall for only 1 per cent of motor vehicle traffic in 2001, they remain an important form of public transport. Local buses are the most widely used form of public transport, with over 4.3 billion journeys made by local bus in Great Britain in 2001/02, more than twice the number of journeys made by rail (see Table 12.17). Travel in London accounted for about a third of all passenger journeys on local buses.

After a long period of post-war decline, which continued into the early 1990s, local bus use in terms of passenger journeys stabilised towards the end of the decade (Figure 12.15). The distance travelled by buses increased from a low point in the mid-1980s up to the mid-1990s, before it too stabilised.

In 1999-2001, people in Great Britain used local buses for 61 journey stages a year on average. (See Appendix, Part 12: National Travel Survey for the definition of journey stages). The biggest users of buses are those aged 16-24, who used local buses for 126 journey stages each year, and those aged 70 and over, who used them for 76 stages. Education, and commuting and business are the main trip purposes for users aged 16-24, while shopping is the main reason for travel by bus among those 70 and over.

The British Social Attitudes survey in 2001 found that 73 per cent of people aged 18 and over thought it was 'very' or 'fairly' important to 'cut down the number of cars on Britain's roads', while 94 per cent thought it was 'very' or 'fairly' important to 'improve public transport in Britain'. These opinions held across different socio-economic groups, although there was a wider range of opinion on cutting the number of cars. In the intermediate and junior non-manual group 77 per cent thought

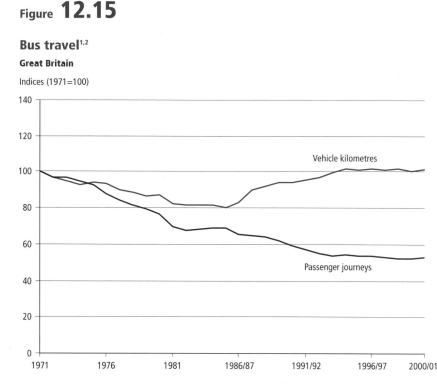

Figure 12.15

Bus travel[1,2]

Great Britain

Indices (1971=100)

1 Local services only. Includes street running trams and trolley buses but excludes modern 'supertram' systems.
2 Financial years from 1985/86.
Source: Department for Transport

this was important, compared with 66 per cent of people in the unskilled manual group, and 68 per cent in the professional group.

Underlying these general positions are some contradictory views. Forty seven per cent agreed to some extent with the proposition that 'building more roads just encourages more traffic', with 29 per cent disagreeing (Table 12.16). However, 38 per cent of respondents agreed with the proposition, that 'the Government should build more motorways to reduce traffic congestion', with 34 per cent disagreeing. While attitudes to the first proposition have remained relatively stable in recent years, attitudes to the second have altered somewhat – in 1997, 30 per cent of respondents agreed and 42 per cent disagreed.

The railways

The number of journeys taken on Britain's railways fell by 7 million between 2000/01 and 2001/02 to 2,054 million (Table 12.17). The number of passenger journeys made on the

Table **12.16**

Attitudes to road transport and the environment,[1] 2001

Great Britain   Percentages

	Agree strongly	Agree	Neither agree nor disagree	Disagree	Disagree strongly	Can't choose
For the sake of the environment, car users should pay higher taxes	3	12	15	47	19	2
The Government should build more motorways to reduce traffic congestion	8	30	22	29	5	4
Driving one's car is too convenient to give up for the sake of the environment	8	37	24	21	4	4
Building more roads just encourages more traffic	9	38	18	25	4	3

1 Figures do not sum to 100 per cent as respondents who didn't answer are not included.
Source: British Social Attitudes Survey, National Centre for Social Research

Table **12.17**

Rail journeys:[1] by operator

Great Britain   Millions

	1981	1991–92	1995–96	1999–00	2000–01	2001–02
Main line/underground						
National Rail	719	792	761	931	957	960
London Underground	541	751	784	927	970	953
Glasgow Underground	11	14	14	15	14	14
All national rail and underground	1,271	1,557	1,559	1,873	1,941	1,927
Light railways and trams						
Nexus, Tyne and Wear Metro	14	41	36	33	33	33
Docklands Light Railway	.	8	14	31	38	41
Manchester Metrolink	.	.	13	14	17	18
Stagecoach Supertram	.	.	5	11	11	11
West Midlands Metro	.	.	.	5	5	5
Croydon Tramlink	.	.	.	.	15	18
All light railways and modern trams	14	49	68	94	120	127
All journeys by rail	1,285	1,605	1,627	1,967	2,061	2,054

1 Excludes railways and tramways operated principally as tourist attractions.
Source: Department for Transport

railways fell to a low of less than 1,200 million in 1982 but, apart from a period in the early 1990s, have generally increased since then, and grew by over a quarter between 1995/96 and 2001/02.

Just under half of all rail travel is on national rail, although travel on London Underground has twice recently exceeded that on national rail, in 1995/96 and 2000/01. Despite the difficulties of recent years, for example the accidents at Ladbroke Grove (1999), Hatfield (2000) and Potters Bar (2002), the number of journeys made on national rail in 2001/02 was the highest since 1962. However, passenger kilometres travelled are much higher now than in the 1960s, suggesting that people are using the national railways for longer journeys than before. Light rail and tram systems are also increasingly popular, and were used for more than double the number of journeys in 2001/02 than in 1991/92. Such systems are often key components in integrated transport systems, and several more will come into operation over the next few years.

The Strategic Rail Authority (SRA) has recently started compiling a rail fare price index, which covers all rail services previously operated by franchise holders (Table 12.18). While overall fares increased by 8 per cent from 1999 to 2002 (compared with an increase of 6 per cent in the 'All items' RPI, so the increase in real terms was 2 per cent), prices charged by long distance operators rose by 16 per cent (a 9 per cent increase in real terms). The SRA's National Passenger Survey (NPS) found that in spring 2002, 34 per cent of passengers were dissatisfied with the value for money of their rail journey, compared with 42 per cent who were satisfied.

The NPS also found that 23 per cent of passengers were dissatisfied with the punctuality of their service. However, 65 per cent were satisfied, up from 59 per cent in spring 2001. As measured by the SRA's Public Performance Measure, 81 per cent of trains arrived on time in the fourth quarter of 2001/02, compared with 71 per cent in the previous quarter and 76 per cent in the fourth quarter of 2000/01. Regional operators recorded most services on time in the fourth quarter of 2001/02, 81 per cent, while long distance operators recorded the least, at 76 per cent.

International travel

United Kingdom residents now take almost twice as many trips abroad each year as they did ten years ago, and these trips abroad outnumber visits to the UK by overseas residents by well over two to one. In 2001 there were 23 million overseas visits to the United Kingdom by overseas residents, compared with 58 million visits overseas by United Kingdom residents (Table 12.19). The majority of trips in both directions were made by air.

Although the numbers are still increasing year on year, the rate of growth in trips abroad by UK residents has slowed somewhat in recent years. The number taken grew by 3 per cent between 2000 and 2001, compared with increases of 5 per cent between 1999 and 2000, 6 per cent between 1998 and 1999, and 11 per cent between 1997 and 1998. In contrast, there was a 10 per cent fall in the number of visits by foreign nationals to the United Kingdom between 2000 and 2001, against a background of relatively stable numbers during the second half of the 1990s.

Table **12.18**

National rail fare price index[1]

Great Britain				Indices (1999=100)
	1999	2000	2001	2002
All operators	100	103	106	108
London and South East	100	101	103	103
Long distance	100	107	110	116
Regional	100	102	105	107
Retail prices index (all items)	100	102	105	106

1 As at January each year.
Source: Strategic Rail Authority

Table **12.19**

International travel: by mode[1]

United Kingdom						Millions
	1981	1991	1996	1999	2000	2001
Visits abroad by UK residents						
Air	11.4	20.4	27.9	37.5	41.4	43.0
Sea	7.7	10.4	10.7	10.4	9.6	9.7
Channel Tunnel	.	.	3.5	5.9	5.8	5.6
All visits abroad	19.0	30.8	42.1	53.9	56.8	58.3
Visits to the United Kingdom						
by overseas residents						
Air	6.9	11.6	16.3	17.3	17.8	16.1
Sea	4.6	5.5	6.2	5.0	4.3	4.0
Channel Tunnel	.	.	2.7	3.1	3.1	2.8
All visits to the United Kingdom	11.5	17.1	25.2	25.4	25.2	22.8

1 Mode of travel from, and into, the United Kingdom.
Source: International Passenger Survey, Office for National Statistics

Figure **12.20**

UK residents visiting abroad: by month, 1991 and 2001

United Kingdom

Millions

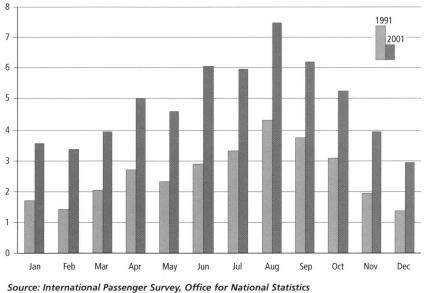

Source: International Passenger Survey, Office for National Statistics

Figure **12.21**

International passenger movements by air:[1] 1991 and 2001

United Kingdom

Millions

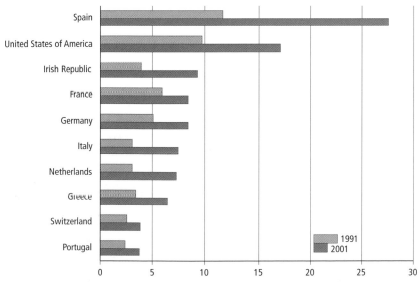

1 Arrivals plus departures.
Source: Civil Aviation Authority Economic Regulation Group

In 2001 two thirds of visits abroad by United Kingdom residents were for holidays (a similar proportion to 2000), compared with a third of visits by overseas residents to the United Kingdom (33 per cent, compared with 37 per cent in 2000). Trips by overseas residents are more likely than those by UK residents to be for business or to visit friends and family.

Although the peak period for UK residents to travel abroad remains the summer, the distribution of trips through the year has altered slightly over the last decade. There has been a rise in the proportion of trips taken in the winter and spring, and a fall in the proportion taken in the summer and early autumn (Figure 12.20). August is still the most popular month in absolute terms, although trips in February rose by 135 per cent between 1991 and 2001, the largest such rise for any month. One reason for the change in the distribution of trips through the year could be that more people are taking second and third holidays abroad.

As Table 12.19 demonstrates, air travel is by far the most important form of international travel as far as the United Kingdom is concerned. In 2001, the country with which the UK had the most air passenger movements, by a considerable margin, was Spain, with 27.6 million arrivals plus departures (Figure 12.21). The second greatest volume of traffic was with the US, with over 17 million air passenger movements. Figure 12.21 shows the ten countries with which the United Kingdom had the highest volume of passenger traffic in 2001. The country ranked fourteenth, Turkey, was the European country with which the United Kingdom increased its traffic the most between 1991 and 2001. There were 525,000 air passenger movements between the two countries in 1991, but by 2001, this figure had grown to 2.1 million.

The ONS February 2002 Omnibus Survey found that 49 per cent of adults had travelled by plane in 2001. Of these, 50 per cent had made one return trip, compared with 26 per cent who had made two, and 6 per cent who had made more than six trips. Those aged 45-54 were the most likely to have flown, and those aged 75 and over the least likely. Although men and women were equally likely to have flown, men who did so flew more often than women. Fifty five per cent of men who flew in 2001 made more than one trip, compared with 46 per cent of women.

Transport safety

Most major forms of transport were safer in 2001 than they were in 1981, and there have been continued improvements in the last 10 years. However, despite improvements in road safety in recent years, other forms of transport, such as rail, air and sea continue to have much lower death rates from accidents (Table 12.22). In general it is much safer to use public rather than private transport, and safer to be in an enclosed vehicle than exposed. Motorcycling, cycling and walking are by some margin the most dangerous forms of transport, death rates for motorcycling being over 42 times greater than those for the car.

In total there were 3,450 deaths from road accidents in Great Britain in 2001, compared with 5,846 in 1981. In 2001, 24 per cent of those who died were pedestrians, 4 per cent pedal cyclists, 17 per cent riders or passengers of two wheeled motor vehicles, and 51 per cent occupants of cars, while occupants of buses, coaches and heavy goods vehicles accounted for the remaining 4 per cent of deaths.

Casualty rates from transport accidents are not distributed evenly across the population. In 2001, children aged 12 to 15 had the highest killed or seriously injured casualty rate among pedestrians, at 41 per 100,000 population. The lowest was for those aged 40 to 59, at 8 per 100,000. For all road users, those aged 16 to 19 are most likely to be killed or seriously injured in an accident. This age group had a rate of 173 per 100,000 population in 2001, compared with 70 per 100,000 for the population as a whole.

Two major contributors to road accidents are excessive speed and alcohol. The Department for Transport has estimated that in 2000, 6 per cent of all road casualties, and 16 per cent of road deaths, occurred when someone was driving while over the legal alcohol limit. There was an overall rise of 23 per cent in the

Table **12.22**

Passenger death rates:[1] by mode of transport

Great Britain					Rate per billion passenger kilometres	
	1981	1986	1991	1996	2000	2001
Motorcycle	115.8	100.3	94.7	97.0	124.5	122.7
Walk	76.9	75.3	69.3	55.3	48.3	46.9
Bicycle	56.9	49.6	46.5	47.2	31.8	34.5
Car	6.1	5.1	3.7	3.1	2.8	2.9
Van	3.8	3.8	2.1	1.0	1.0	0.9
Water[2]	0.4	0.5	0.0	0.8	0.4	0.5
Bus or coach	0.3	0.5	0.6	0.2	0.3	0.2
Rail[3]	1.0	0.9	0.8	0.4	0.4	0.1
Air[2]	0.2	0.5	0.0	0.0	0.0	0.0

1 See Appendix, Part 12: Passenger death rates.
2 Data are for United Kingdom.
3 Financial years. Includes train accidents and accidents occurring through movement of railway vehicles.

Source: Department for Transport

Figure **12.23**

Casualties from road accidents involving illegal alcohol levels
United Kingdom

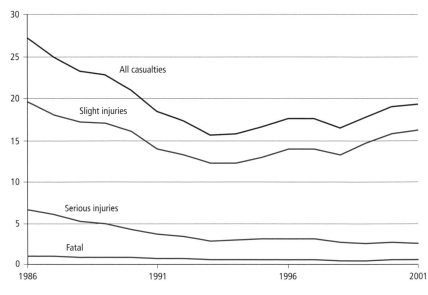

Source: Department for Transport; The Police Service for Northern Ireland

Figure **12.24**

Road deaths: EU comparison, 2000

Rate per 100,000 population

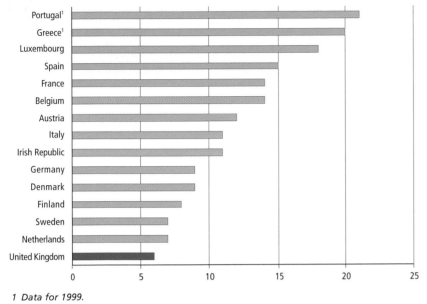

1 Data for 1999.
Source: Department for Transport

number of casualties from road accidents involving alcohol between the low point of 1993 and 2001 (Figure 12.23). However, although over 500 people died in road accidents involving illegal alcohol levels in 2001, this compares with nearly 700 in 1991.

Driving too fast for the road conditions causes, or contributes to, around one third of road accidents. The Department for Transport has estimated that there are about 72,000 speed–related accidents each year on Britain's roads, killing 1,100 people and seriously injuring a further 12,600.

The United Kingdom has a relatively good record for road safety compared with most other EU countries. In 2000, it had the lowest road death rate in the EU, at 6.0 deaths per 100,000 population (Figure 12.24). This was also substantially lower than the rates in other industrialised countries such as Japan (8.2 per 100,000 population), Australia (9.5), Canada (9.7), and the USA (15.2).

The United Kingdom also has the lowest rate in the EU in terms of overall road accidents involving children. The UK death rate for children aged 0-14 of 1.5 per 100,000 population in 2000, compared with 1.9 in Germany and the Netherlands, and 3.2 in France. However, in terms of child pedestrian deaths, the United Kingdom rate of 0.9 per 100,000 children in 2000 is above that of many EU countries, including France (0.7), Germany (0.5), and the Netherlands (0.4).

Chapter 13

Lifestyles and social participation

Time use

- Women spent nearly 3 hours a day on average on housework (excluding shopping and childcare) in the United Kingdom in 2000-01. This was 1 hour and 40 minutes longer than men. (Figure 13.2)

- Half of the men in the United Kingdom in 2000-01 liked DIY repair work, compared with about one fifth of women. Conversely, three quarters of women surveyed said they liked non-food shopping, compared with just under half of men. (Table 13.3)

Social activities

- Almost three fifths of those aged 70 and over in Great Britain knew most or many people in their neighbourhood, compared with just over a third of those aged between 16 and 29 in 2000/01. (Table 13.5)

Leisure time

- Walking/hiking and swimming were the two sporting activities with the highest participation rates in the United Kingdom, of around 20 per cent and 15 per cent, respectively in 2000-01. (Table 13.6)

Holidays and tourism

- In 2001, the most popular holiday destinations visited by United Kingdom residents continued to be Spain and France, accounting for 28 per cent and 18 per cent of holidays. (Table 13.12)

Media and communications

- The proportion of households in the United Kingdom with a mobile phone nearly quadrupled from 17 per cent in 1996/97 to 65 per cent in 2001/02. (Figure 13.13)

- In 2001/02, London and the South East had the highest proportions of households with access to the Internet, at 49 and 48 per cent respectively. Wales, the North East of England (32 per cent each) and Northern Ireland (31 per cent) had the lowest proportions of households with Internet access. (Figure 13.14)

- Adults in the United Kingdom aged 16 and over spent an average of nearly 20 hours a week, or just under 3 hours a day, watching television in 2000-01. (Table 13.16)

- About 406 million books, an average of nearly seven per person, were borrowed from public libraries in the United Kingdom in 2000/01. (Figure 13.18)

The ways in which people spend their time outside work have altered significantly over the past few decades. Changes in working patterns as well as technological advances have influenced the amount of time people spend on different activities.

Time use

The UK 2000 Time Use Survey asked adults aged 16 and over to keep a detailed diary of how they spent their time. It found that at 8am on a weekday 23 per cent of adults were sleeping, 23 per cent were eating or performing tasks associated with personal care, while 19 per cent were at work (Table 13.1). At 12 noon, work or study became the main activities, carried out by 42 per cent of all adults; a further 22 per cent of people were engaged in housework or childcare and 14 per cent were involved in leisure pursuits. By 8pm the proportion engaged in leisure activities of some sort rose to 57 per cent, while 7 per cent were working or studying. Peak weekday travel times were 8am in the morning and 5pm in the evening, with 12 and 18 per cent, respectively, of those surveyed undertaking some sort of journey at these times.

From Monday to Thursday 81 per cent of adults were asleep at midnight, and 11 per cent were engaged in leisure activities. The proportion of adults engaged in leisure activities at midnight on Friday increased to 17 per cent with 72 per cent asleep. While for many, weekends were a time for rest and recuperation, adults were engaged in a range of other activities too: at noon on a weekend, 33 per cent of adults were engaged in housework or childcare, 12 per cent were travelling, 12 per cent were eating or involved with tasks associated with personal care, and 10 per cent were working or studying. Weekend evenings were a favoured leisure slot; at 9pm, two thirds of adults were engaged in leisure activities such as reading or socialising.

Women still do the majority of the household chores, despite their increased participation in the labour market. Women spent nearly 3 hours a day on average on housework (excluding shopping and childcare) compared with the 1 hour and 40 minutes spent by men (Figure 13.2). Women also spent more time than men looking after children. Men, on the

Table **13.1**

Activities[1] on weekdays at selected times, 2000–01

United Kingdom   Percentages

	4am	8am	12 noon	4pm	8pm	12 midnight
Sleep	97	23	2	2	1	79
Eating/personal care	1	23	11	6	13	3
Work and study	1	19	42	36	7	2
Housework and childcare	0	16	22	21	15	1
Leisure	1	7	14	23	57	13
Travel	0	12	9	12	7	2

1 Adults aged 16 years and over.
Source: UK 2000 Time Use Survey, Office for National Statistics

Figure **13.2**

Time spent on various activities: by sex, 2000–01[1]
United Kingdom

Hours per day

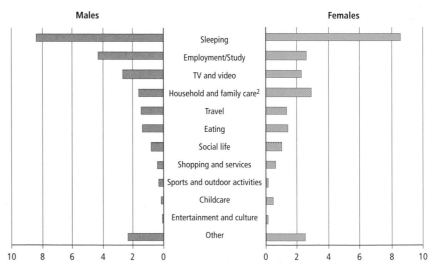

1 Adults aged 16 and over.
2 Excludes shopping and childcare.
Source: UK 2000 Time Use Survey, Office for National Statistics

other hand, worked or studied on average for nearly 2 hours a day more than women (4 hours 20 minutes a day for men compared with 2 hours 30 minutes for women). Both sexes spent roughly the same amount of time sleeping and eating.

Young people aged between 8 and 15 were also asked to complete a diary as part of the UK 2000 Time Use Survey. Findings from this aspect of the survey revealed some differences between how children and adults choose to spend their time. Young people spend more time sleeping – over 10 hours each day, compared with around 8 hours 30 minutes a day for both men and women. The amount of

time young people spent working or studying (at nearly four hours) was, on average, 20 minutes a day less than for men and an hour and 30 minutes more than for women. For young people it is not all work and no play – half an hour a day was spent on sport.

Women taking part in the survey were more likely than men to say that they 'like' most household tasks. The main exception is DIY repair work – half of the men said they liked this compared with about one fifth of women, and over two fifths of women did not do DIY at all (Table 13.3). Conversely, three quarters of women said they liked non-food shopping compared with just under half of men. Ironing clothes was one of the least popular activities, disliked by almost half of the women surveyed. Fewer men said they disliked ironing (less than a third), but that figure is low because a large proportion of men (42 per cent) did not iron.

Table 13.3

Attitudes to various activities[1] for the home: by sex, 2000–01

United Kingdom   Percentages

	Like	Neither like nor dislike	Dislike	Do not do activity
Males				
Cooking a meal	58	15	12	15
DIY repair work	50	14	20	16
Gardening	47	10	23	20
Shopping non-food	48	18	27	7
Cooking a meal for a special occasion	44	10	13	33
Decorating	39	15	28	18
Going to the shops to buy food	38	22	28	12
Tidying the house	33	24	30	13
Helping children with homework[2]	25	5	4	66
Washing clothes	15	22	24	39
Ironing clothes	14	14	30	42
Females				
Cooking a meal	69	16	12	3
DIY repair work	21	11	22	46
Gardening	50	8	20	22
Shopping non-food	75	10	12	3
Cooking a meal for a special occasion	68	8	14	10
Decorating	43	10	20	27
Going to the shops to buy food	51	19	25	5
Tidying the house	49	21	26	4
Helping children with homework[2]	31	5	4	60
Washing clothes	44	34	17	5
Ironing clothes	31	15	46	8

1 Adults aged 16 and over.
2 All adults not just parents.
Source: UK 2000 Time Use Survey, Office for National Statistics

Social activities

Over a long period, participation by individuals in formal, political and other community-based institutions has declined in some areas. These trends have been examined in more detail in the lead article on social capital (on page 19). Increased academic and official interest in the area of social capital (and its policy implications) have resulted in more surveys commissioned and a greater range of data becoming available.

The majority of people in the United Kingdom use their right to vote at general elections even though the proportions doing so have fluctuated over the last half a century. Over the past ten years, political involvement, expressed as the proportion of the registered electorate turning out to vote, has been declining. Official turnout at the 2001 general election, at 59 per cent, was at its lowest level since 1918. Academic research and opinion polls have suggested that recent low turnouts have been due in part to voter apathy and a distrust of politicians (see page 20).

Many people choose to become more involved in the community through activities such as fundraising, serving on committees, organising or helping to run clubs or groups (such as brownies or guides) or by giving advice. In 2001, the Omnibus Survey asked adults aged 16 and over in Great Britain about the sorts of volunteering activities they had undertaken during the previous twelve months. Personally raising or collecting money was found to be the most common activity for both men and women (Table 13.4). Organising or helping to run clubs or groups was more common among people aged between 16 and 24, and this declined with age. In contrast, the proportion of adults who personally raised or collected money generally increased with age (except for those aged 75 and over).

The number of times people speak to their neighbours, and the number of people they know within their area, give some indication of 'neighbourliness'. The proportion of people who say that they know many people in their neighbourhood increases with age. Almost three fifths of those aged 70 and over in Great Britain in 2000/01 said that they knew many people in their neighbourhood, compared with just over a third of those aged between 16 and 29 (Table 13.5). Over two fifths of those in the 70 and over age group said they spoke to their neighbours daily, compared with less than a fifth of those aged 16 to 29. In general a greater proportion of women (48 per cent) knew many people in their neighbourhood, compared with men (43 per cent).

For some people, religion is an important part of their lives, providing spiritual inspiration, contact with others and a means to participate in the life of the local community. The British Social Attitudes survey estimated that in Great Britain in 2001 just over half of the population (54 per cent) regarded themselves as Christian: 29 per cent were Church of England/Anglican; 11 per cent Catholic, and 14 per cent were of other Christian denominations. A further 4 per cent regarded themselves as belonging to another religion, such as the Islamic, Hindu, Jewish, or Sikh faiths. In contrast, 41 per cent said that they belonged to no religion. In 2001 a question on religion was included in the census in all the countries of the United Kingdom; this was the first time since 1851. These data will provide extensive information on religious identity in the United Kingdom.

Table 13.4

Volunteering:[1] by type of activity carried out and sex, 2001

Great Britain		Percentages
	Males	Females
Personally raising or collecting money	12	19
Organising or helping a club or group	10	11
Serving on committees	8	9
Giving non-professional advice	5	4
Giving professional advice	5	3
Giving other kinds of practical help	4	7
Providing administrative/clerical help	4	3
Any other type of voluntary activity	3	4

1 By adults aged 16 and over. In 12 months prior to interview.
Source: Omnibus Survey, Office for National Statistics

Table 13.5

Indicators of neighbourliness: by age, 2000/01

Great Britain						Percentages
	16–29	30–39	40–49	50–59	60–69	70 and over
Frequency of speaking to neighbours						
Daily	17	25	21	28	39	43
3–6 days per week	20	23	25	24	23	22
1–2 days per week	32	31	37	32	27	23
Less than once a week	30	21	17	16	11	12
Number of people known in the neighbourhood						
Most/many	35	39	48	50	54	57
A few	51	54	48	47	44	41
None	14	8	4	3	2	3

Source: General Household Survey, Office for National Statistics

Table **13.6**

Participation in selected sports:[1] by sex, 2000–01

United Kingdom		Percentages
	Men	Women
Walking/hiking	19	23
Snooker	15	4
Swimming	13	17
Cycling	12	7
Football	10	1
Golf	9	1
Weights	8	4
Keep fit	8	18
Running/athletics	7	3
Racket sports	6	4
Darts	4	2
Bowls	2	2

1 Percentage of adults aged 16 and over reporting participation in four weeks before survey.
Source: UK 2000 Time Use Survey, Office for National Statistics

Table **13.7**

Attendance[1] at cultural events[2]

Great Britain						Percentages
	1986/87	1991/92	1996/97	1999/00	2000/01	2001/02
Cinema	31	44	54	56	55	57
Plays	23	23	24	23	23	24
Art galleries/exhibitions	21	21	22	22	21	22
Classical music	12	12	12	12	12	12
Ballet	6	6	7	6	6	6
Opera	5	6	7	6	6	6
Contemporary dance	4	3	4	4	4	5

1 Percentage of resident population aged 15 and over attending 'these days'.
2 See Appendix, Part 13: Cultural events.
Source: Target Group Index, BMRB International; Cinema Advertising Association

Leisure time

Participating in sporting activities, either alone or as a member of a team or a club, is a popular way of spending leisure time. The UK 2000 Time Use Survey found that adults aged 16 and over were most likely to have participated in walking/hiking (Table 13.6). Around a quarter of women and a fifth of men had walked/hiked during the month before interview. Keep fit and swimming were the next most common activities for women, while snooker, swimming and cycling were the other most common activities for men.

Around ten times the proportion of men had participated in football or golf, during the month prior to interview, compared with women. Conversely more than twice the proportion of women as men participated in keep fit exercises. However nearly half of those surveyed mentioned they did not participate in any form of sport.

Attending a cultural event, such as a play, or visiting an art gallery or museum, is another way that people spend their leisure time. Over half those surveyed in Great Britain in 2001/02 said they went to the cinema; a quarter said they had attended plays and over a fifth said they had gone to art galleries or exhibitions recently (Table 13.7). Over the last 15 years, the proportion of adults going to the cinema almost doubled, while attendance at other cultural events remained relatively stable. Attendance varies across the socio-economic groups. For example, around four in ten managers and professional people attended plays once a year or more in 2001/02, compared with around one in twenty unskilled manual workers.

The Arts Council of England asked people the reasons why they attended arts events. Although more than one reason could be given, 'like going to that type of event' was the most commonly given reason for attending by those in the 75 and over age group. One in five of the 25 to 44 age group, described attending the arts event as a 'social event' as a reason for going (Table 13.8). Most frequently cited reasons for not attending more arts and cultural events were difficulty in finding time (mentioned by 48 per cent of respondents) and cost (by 38 per cent).

The proportion of adults attending the cinema has increased over recent years. Frequent cinema attendance in Great Britain has consistently been highest among those aged between 15 and 24. In 2001, 50 per cent of this age group reported attending the cinema once a month or more compared with 15 per cent of those aged 35 and over (Figure 13.9). The success of 'family' films such as *Shrek* and *Cats and Dogs*, with the third and fifth highest takings in the UK box office in 2001, may have contributed to recent increases in attendance among those aged between 7 and 14. The type of films released through mainstream cinemas tend to be large budget blockbusters and the increase in cinema attendance may be related to the expansion and investment in multiplex cinemas across the country. In addition to the multiplexes, smaller independent cinemas cater for more specialist 'art house' audiences.

Holidays and tourism

From 1995 to 1999, domestic tourism trips increased by 20 per cent. There were an estimated 102 million domestic holidays taken in the United Kingdom in 2001, compared with 106 million holidays taken in 2000. A range of different accommodation is used on holidays in the United Kingdom. In 2001 staying with friends or relatives was the most popular choice, accounting for four in ten domestic holidays (Table 13.10). A quarter of domestic holidays were spent at a hotel/motel or guesthouse. Static caravans and rented houses were the third and fourth most popular types of holiday accommodation used. The South West, the Heart of England, Scotland and London were the four most popular destinations for domestic holidays taken by UK residents within the United Kingdom.

The UK's historic towns and cities, and its scenic rural and coastal areas, continue to have great appeal for domestic and overseas tourists alike. Their popularity reflects an interest in British heritage, arts and culture. There are an estimated 6,400 visitor attractions in the United Kingdom. In 2001 free and paying attractions combined received 452 million

Table **13.8**

Reasons for attending the arts:[1] by age, 2001[2]

England   Percentages

	16–24	25–44	45–54	55–64	65–74	75 and over	All
Like going to that type of event	25	29	36	44	46	51	35
See specific performer or event	23	17	19	23	21	18	19
Social event	17	20	18	13	18	18	18
Invited to go	13	9	10	11	8	12	10
Accompanying children	4	17	8	7	6	2	10
Special occasion/celebration	10	10	8	8	7	5	9
Recommended by a friend or relative	11	7	4	4	6	6	6
Happened to be passing by	4	5	5	5	6	4	5
Other	14	12	14	14	10	13	13

1 Percentages do not total 100 as respondents could give more than one reason.
2 Fieldwork was carried out in July, September, October and November.
Source: Arts Council of England; Office for National Statistics

Figure **13.9**

Cinema attendance:[1] by age

Great Britain

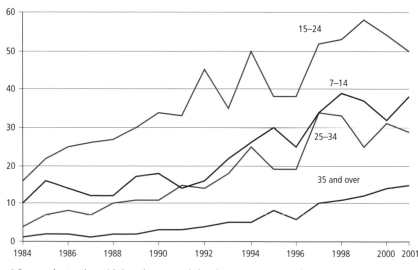

1 Respondents who said that they attend the cinema once a month or more.
Source: Cinema Advertising Association/Cinema and Video Industry Audience Research

Table **13.10**

Type of accommodation used on holidays[1] in the United Kingdom

Percentages[2]

	2000	2001
Friends/relatives' home	40	41
Hotel/motel/guesthouse	23	24
Static caravan	10	8
Rented house/flat/chalet	7	8
B&B	8	7
Towed caravan	4	4
Camping	4	3
Second home/Timeshare	1	2
Hostel/university/school	1	1
Holiday camp/village	1	1
Boats	1	1
Other	4	4

1 Holiday trips taken by United Kingdom residents aged 16 and over within the UK.

2 Percentages add to more than 100 due to more than one accommodation type being used per trip.

Source: United Kingdom Tourism Survey, National Tourist Boards

visits. These attractions include museums, art galleries, historic houses and castles, churches and cathedrals, gardens, wildlife sites, visitor centres and workplaces, as well as leisure parks and other recreational facilities. Tourist attractions not charging admission have proved just as popular in terms of the estimated admissions they receive (Table 13.11). The 'free' tourist attraction with the highest number of visits in 2001 was Blackpool Pleasure Beach in Lancashire. Many churches and museums do not 'charge' admission but receive voluntary donations from their visitors. Tate Modern, the London Eye and the Eden Gardens in Cornwall all opened within the last three years and have established themselves among the country's leading tourist attractions.

Table **13.11**

Visits to the most popular tourist attractions

United Kingdom
Millions

	2000	2001		2000	2001
Museums and galleries			**Theme parks**		
National Gallery, London[1]	4.9	4.9	Blackpool Pleasure Beach[1]	6.8	6.5
British Museum, London[1]	5.5	4.8	Pleasureland Theme Park, Southport[1]	2.1	2.1
Tate Modern, London[1]	3.9	3.6	Legoland, Windsor	1.5	1.6
Victoria and Albert Museum, London	1.3	1.5	Pleasure Beach, Great Yarmouth[1]	1.5	1.5
Science Museum, London	1.3	1.4	Flamingo Land Theme Park	1.3	1.3
Historical houses and monuments			**Churches and cathedrals**		
Tower of London	2.3	2.0	York Minster[1]	1.8	1.6
Edinburgh Castle	1.2	1.1	Canterbury Cathedral	1.3	1.2
Windsor Castle	1.1	0.9	Westminster Abbey, London	1.2	1.0
Roman Baths, Bath	0.9	0.9	Chester Cathedral	1.0	0.9
Somerset House, London	0.6	0.7	St Paul's Cathedral, London	0.9	0.8

1 Free tourist attractions.

Source: National Tourist Boards

UK residents took almost 39 million holidays abroad in 2001. Since 1994 Spain has been the most popular destination, accounting for 28 per cent of holidays taken in 2001, while France was the second most popular destination at 18 per cent of holidays (Table 13.12).

The United States of America was the most popular non-European destination. Overall, the average length of stay on holiday was 10 nights. Holiday makers travelling to Australia and New Zealand spent the longest time away from home, an average of 47 nights; holiday trips within the European Union averaged 9 nights. The number of visits to the United States of America fell by 341,000 between 2000 and 2001 to 4.0 million. Other countries which had large falls in the number of visits between 2000 and 2001 were Germany, Canada and Israel.

The countries with the highest growth in the number of visits in 2001 were predominantly Mediterranean destinations, such as Spain, Greece, Cyprus and Italy.

Media and communications

Advances in technology and greater general levels of prosperity over the past ten years have led to more and more people having access to new and sophisticated media products. These new products have been introduced alongside well-established communications media such as television and the printed word.

The past few years have been notable for a large increase in two areas: ownership of mobile phones and home access to the Internet. Mobile phone ownership nearly quadrupled from 17 per cent of households in the United Kingdom in 1996/97 to 65 per cent in 2001/02, while access to the Internet at home rose at a similar rate between 1998/99 and 2001/02, to reach 40 per cent (Figure 13.13).

According to the ONS Omnibus Survey, 57 per cent of adults in Great Britain had accessed the Internet at least once by June 2002, equivalent to 26 million adults. Over three quarters of adults who have accessed it for private use have used it to find information about goods

Table **13.12**

Holidays[1] abroad: by destination

United Kingdom | | | | Percentages
	1971	1981	1991	2001
Spain[2]	34	22	21	28
France	16	27	26	18
Greece	5	7	8	8
United States	1	6	7	6
Italy	9	6	4	4
Irish Republic	..	4	3	4
Portugal	3	3	5	4
Cyprus	1	1	2	4
Netherlands	4	2	4	3
Belgium	..	2	2	2
Turkey	..	-	1	2
Germany	3	3	3	1
Austria	6	3	2	1
Malta	..	3	2	1
Other countries	19	14	12	14
All destinations (=100%) (millions)	4.2	13.1	20.8	38.7

1 A visit made for holiday purposes. Business trips and visits to friends or relatives are excluded.
2 Excludes the Canary Islands prior to 1981.
Source: International Passenger Survey, Office for National Statistics

Figure **13.13**

Households with selected durable goods[1]
United Kingdom

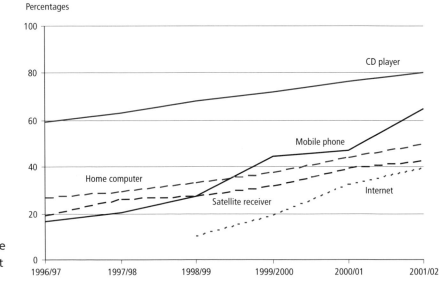

1 Data for 1998/99 onwards are based on weighted data and include children's expenditure.
Source: Family Expenditure Survey and Expenditure and Food Survey, Office for National Statistics

Figure **13.14**

Households with access to the Internet: by region, 2001/02

Percentages

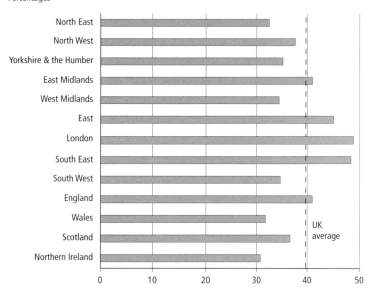

Source: Expenditure and Food Survey, Office for National Statistics

Table **13.15**

VHS/DVD video rentals and purchases

United Kingdom				£ million
	Purchases		Rentals	
	VHS	DVD	VHS	DVD
1999	814	68	408	0
2000	840	264	422	22
2001	844	646	399	65

Source: British Video Association

or services, or for e-mail. Men still use the Internet more than women; 68 per cent of men who accessed the Internet for private use did so more than once a week, compared with 50 per cent of women. A further 17 per cent of women did so less than once a month; the equivalent figure for men was 9 per cent.

Household access to the Internet varies across the United Kingdom. In 2001/02, London and the South East had the highest proportions of households with access to the Internet, at 49 and 48 per cent respectively (Figure 13.14); Wales, the North East of England (32 per cent each) and Northern Ireland (31 per cent) had the lowest proportions of households with Internet access.

Another media product that has increased in popularity over recent times is the Digital Versatile Disc (DVD). DVDs, which can play music, video and games, were launched in the United Kingdom in April 1998. Since then, both hardware and software sales have increased rapidly. According to the British Video Association, the DVD is the fastest growing consumer electronics format of all time, selling faster than the video and audio compact disc (CD) players did at the same stage after their launch.

Around 41 million DVDs of all genres were purchased in 2000/01, ten times the number purchased in 1999 (Figure 13.15). Households with a videocassette recorder (VCR) have traditionally had the choice of buying or renting new video titles. Those with DVD players are more likely than households with only VCRs to purchase rather than rent new titles. In 2001 DVDs accounted for 43 per cent of the total value of DVD and VHS videos purchased in the United Kingdom but only 14 per cent of the value of all rentals.

Television has traditionally played an important part in people's leisure time. Adults aged 16 and over completing the UK 2000 Time Use Survey spent nearly 20 hours a week, or just under 3 hours a day, watching television. This activity was almost exclusively carried out in the respondent's own home. Nearly 2 hours a day were spent watching television while not engaged in any other activity. While watching television, respondents spent an average of 25 minutes per day eating and drinking, and only 3 minutes per day entertaining friends (Table 13.16). Around half of television viewing (one and three quarter hours a day) was carried out in the company of other household members. The single programme with the highest audience in 2001 was the *Only Fools and Horses Christmas Special*, attracting over 20 million viewers.

Playing music on home music systems is another popular activity. While CD sales in the UK continued to increase, sales of music cassettes continued to fall, from 11.4 million in 2000 to 4.6 million in 2001 (Figure 13.17). Sales of singles (all formats) decreased by 10 per cent between 2000 and 2001, while CD sales increased by 8 per cent.

Technology for downloading music from the Internet is still being developed, with a growing number of websites offering this facility. Pop and rock remain the most popular music categories in terms of albums purchased, accounting between them for over half of all albums sold; with dance, Rhythm and Blues and 'middle of the road' accounting for around a quarter of all albums sold.

The printed word is still enjoyed by many, despite competition from other media. Books can be purchased, or borrowed from public libraries. In 2001 there were almost 5,000 public libraries in the United Kingdom. In Great Britain more than 34 million people (58 per cent of the population) were registered members of their local library, and 20 per cent borrow at least once a week. About 406 million books, an average of nearly seven per person, were borrowed from public libraries in the United Kingdom in 2000/01 (Figure 13.18). 'Adult fiction' comprised the most popular category of book borrowed, followed by 'adult non–fiction' and 'junior'. The total number of books borrowed has declined since 1981, when an average over 11 books per person were borrowed.

Many libraries have collections of CDs, records, audio- and video-cassettes, and DVDs for loan to the public. Thirty nine million audio-visual items were also borrowed in 2000/01. The

Table **13.16**

Television viewing patterns, 2000

United Kingdom	Minutes per day per person
	Average viewing
Exclusively watching television	114
Watching television along with other activities	
Eating/drinking	25
Housework	9
Other activities	26
Location of viewing	
Own home	163
Friends' home	6
Other	2
Watching with others	
Alone or with people you don't know	42
Children up to 9 living in your household	18
Other household members	86
Other persons that you know	13
Total TV viewing	171

Source: UK 2000 Time Use Survey, Office for National Statistics

Figure **13.17**

Sales[1] of CDs, LPs, cassettes, and singles[2]
United Kingdom

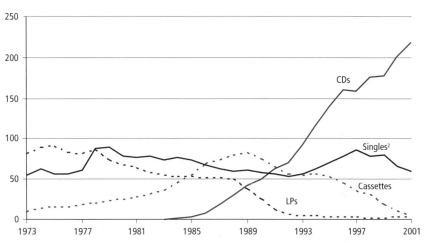

1 *Trade deliveries – sales of records, cassettes and CDs invoiced to all retailers, distributors, wholesalers and mail order houses.*
2 *All formats combined (7", 12", cassette and CD).*
Source: British Phonographic Industry

Figure **13.18**

Library books issued per person: by type of book
United Kingdom

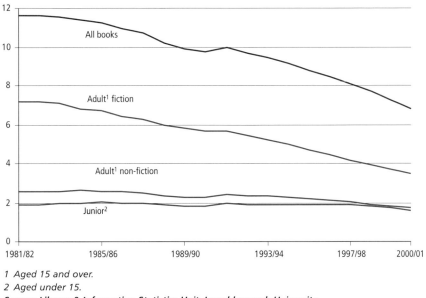

1 Aged 15 and over.
2 Aged under 15.
Source: Library & Information Statistics Unit, Loughborough University

information role is becoming increasingly important for all libraries: nearly all have personal computers for public use and, in May 2002, 70 per cent had Internet connections.

Reading newspapers is an important part of many people's daily routine. On an average weekday it was estimated that around 55 per cent of people aged 15 and over in the United Kingdom read a national morning newspaper in 2001 (59 per cent of men and 50 per cent of women). Over 80 per cent of adults read a regional or local newspaper every week.

There are marked variations in the spending patterns of income groups on different types of reading material. Households in the highest income group spent more than three times as much on books and magazines as on newspapers; the lowest income group spent more on newspapers than books or magazines (Table 13.19). In 2001/02 UK households in the highest income group spent five times more on books than the lowest income group (an average of £6.29 per household per week compared with £1.17 for the lowest income group) but less than twice as much on newspapers (£2.17 and £1.45, respectively).

Figure **13.19**

Spending on selected reading materials: by gross income quintile group, 2001/02
United Kingdom

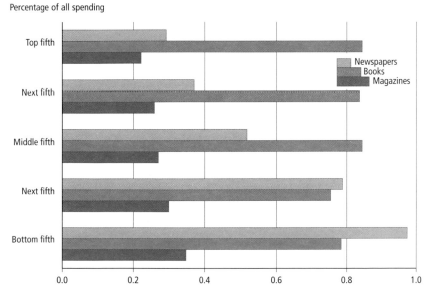

Source: Expenditure and Food Survey, Office for National Statistics

Websites and Contacts

Chapter 1 – Population

Websites

National Statistics	www.statistics.gov.uk
Eurostat	www.europa.eu.int/comm/eurostat
General Register Office for Scotland	www.gro-scotland.gov.uk
Government Actuary's Department	www.gad.gov.uk

Home Office

Immigration and Asylum Statistics	www.homeoffice.gov.uk/rds
National Assembly for Wales	www.wales.gov.uk
Northern Ireland Statistics Research Agency	www.nisra.gov.uk
Scottish Executive	www.scotland.gov.uk
The Commonwealth	www.thecommonwealth.org

United Nations

Population Information Network	www.un.org/popin/
United Nations Statistics Division	unstats.un.org/unsd

Contacts

Office for National Statistics

Chapter author	020 7533 5773
Internal Migration	01329 813872
International Migration	01329 813255
Labour Market Statistics Helpline	020 7533 6094
Population Estimates General Enquiries	01329 813318
Eurostat	00 352 4301 35487
General Register Office for Scotland	0131 314 4254
Government Actuary's Department	020 7211 2622
Home Office	020 8760 8280
National Assembly for Wales	029 2082 6399
Northern Ireland Statistics and Research Agency	028 9034 8100
General Register Office	028 9025 2000
United Nations Information Centre	020 7630 1981

Chapter 2 – Households and Families

Websites

National Statistics	www.statistics.gov.uk
ESRC Research Centre for Analysis of Social Exclusion	
	sticerd.lse.ac.uk/case
Eurostat	www.europa.eu.int/comm/eurostat
General Register Office for Scotland	www.gro-scotland.gov.uk
Institute for Social and Economic Research	www.iser.essex.ac.uk
National Assembly for Wales	www.wales.gov.uk/keypub
National Centre for Social Research	www.natcen.ac.uk
Northern Ireland Statistics Research Agency	www.nisra.gov.uk
Office of the Deputy Prime Minister	www.odpm.gov.uk
Scottish Executive	www.scotland.gov.uk
Teenage Pregnancy Unit	www.teenagepregnancyunit.gov.uk

Contacts

Office for National Statistics

Chapter author	020 7533 5773
Fertility and Birth Statistics	01329 813758
General Household Survey	020 7533 5444
Labour Market Statistics Helpline	020 7533 6094
Marriages and Divorces	01329 813758
ESRC Research Centre for Analysis of Social Exclusion	020 7955 6679
Eurostat	00 352 4301 33527
General Register Office for Scotland	0131 314 4243
Home Office Family Policy Unit	020 7217 8393
Institute for Social and Economic Research	01206 872957
London School of Hygiene and Tropical Medicine	020 7299 4636
National Assembly for Wales	029 2082 5055
National Centre for Social Research	020 7250 1866
Northern Ireland Statistics and Research Agency	028 9034 8100
General Register Office	028 9025 2000
Office of the Deputy Prime Minister	020 7944 3303

Chapter 3 – Education and Training

Websites

National Statistics	www.statistics.gov.uk
Department for Education and Skills	www.dfes.gov.uk
Scottish Executive	www.scotland.gov.uk
Northern Ireland Department of Education	www.deni.gov.uk
Northern Ireland Department for Employment and Learning	www.delni.gov.uk
National Assembly for Wales	www.wales.gov.uk
Higher Education Statistics Agency	www.hesa.ac.uk
Office for Standards in Education	www.ofsted.gov.uk
Organisation for Economic Co-operation and Development	www.oecd.org

Contacts

Office for National Statistics

Chapter author	020 7533 5283
Department for Education and Skills	01325 392754
National Assembly for Wales	029 2082 3507
Scottish Executive	0131 244 0442
Northern Ireland Department of Education	028 9127 9279
Northern Ireland Department for Employment and Learning	028 9025 7400

Chapter 4 – Labour Market

Websites

National Statistics	www.statistics.gov.uk
Department for Work and Pensions	www.dwp.gov.uk
Department of Trade and Industry	www.dti.gov.uk
Eurostat	www.europa.eu.int/comm/eurostat/
Jobcentre Plus	www.jobcentreplus.gov.uk
National Centre for Social Research	www.natcen.ac.uk

Contacts

Office for National Statistics

Chapter Author	020 7533 6174
Labour market enquiry helpline	020 7533 6094
New Deal	0114 259 5741

Jobcentre Plus (Job seekers direct)   0845 6060 234

Eurostat   00 352 4301 33209

Chapter 5 – Income and Wealth

Websites

National Statistics	www.statistics.gov.uk
Department for Work and Pensions	www.dwp.gov.uk
Inland Revenue	www.inlandrevenue.gov.uk
Institute for Fiscal Studies	www.ifs.org.uk
Institute for Social and Economic Research	www.iser.essex.ac.uk
National Centre for Social Research	www.natcen.ac.uk
EUROSTAT	www.europa.eu.int/comm/eurostat
Women and Equality Unit	www.womens-unit.gov.uk
NOMIS	www.nomisweb.co.uk

Contacts

Office for National Statistics

Chapter author	020 7533 6108
Effects of taxes and benefits	020 7533 5770
National accounts	020 7533 5938
New Earnings Survey	01633 819024
Regional accounts	020 7533 5809
Retail prices index	020 7533 5874

Department for Work and Pension

Survey of Low Income Families	020 7962 8000
Households Below Average Income	020 7962 8232
Individual Income	020 7712 2258
Pensioners' Incomes	020 7962 8975

Eurostat

Data Shop Luxembourg	00 352 4335 2251
Data Shop London	020 7533 5676
Inland Revenue	020 7438 7370
Institute for Fiscal Studies	020 7291 4800
Institute for Social and Economic Research	01206 872957
National Centre for Social Research	020 7549 9571

Chapter 6 – Expenditure

Websites

National Statistics	www.statistics.gov.uk
National Centre for Social Research	www.natcen.ac.uk
Department of Trade and Industry	www.dti.gov.uk
Department for Work and Pensions	www.dwp.gov.uk
Jobcentre Plus	www.jobcentreplus.gov.uk
Eurostat	www.europa.eu.int/comm/eurostat/

Contacts

Office for National Statistics

Chapter author	020 7533 5130
Household expenditure	020 7533 5999
Expenditure and food survey	020 7533 5752
Volume of retail sales	01633 812713
Retail prices index	020 7533 5853
Harmonised index of consumer prices	020 7533 5818
Comparative price levels	020 7533 5818
Association for Payment Clearing Services	020 7711 6265
Bank of England	020 7601 4878
Department for Trade and Industry	020 7215 3305

Chapter 7 – Health

Websites

National Statistics	www.statistics.gov.uk
Department of Health	www.doh.gov.uk
Department of Health, Social Services and Public Safety, Northern Ireland	www.dhsspsni.gov.uk/iau
General Register Office for Northern Ireland	www.groni.gov.uk
General Register Office for Scotland	www.gro-scotland.gov.uk
Government Actuary's Department	www.gad.gov.uk
Information and Statistics Division (Scotland)	www.show.scot.nhs.uk/isd
Department for Environment, Food and Rural Affairs	www.defra.gov.uk
National Assembly for Wales	www.wales.gov.uk
Northern Ireland Cancer Registry	www.qub.ac.uk/nicr
Northern Ireland Statistics and Research Agency	www.nisra.gov.uk

Public Health Laboratory Service   www.phls.org.uk

Scottish Executive   www.scotland.gov.uk

Welsh Cancer Intelligence and Surveillance Unit

www.velindre-tr.wales.nhs.uk/wcisu

Eurostat   www.europa.eu.int/comm/eurostat

European Monitoring Centre for Drugs and Drug Addiction

www.emcdda.eu.int

Contacts

Office for National Statistics

Chapter author	020 7533 5081
Cancer statistics	020 7533 5641
Drug related poisoning deaths	020 7533 5242
General Household Survey	020 7533 5444
General Practice Research Database	020 7273 0206
Infant mortality statistics	020 7533 5205
Life expectancy by social class	020 7533 5186
Mortality statistics	01329 813379
Psychiatric morbidity survey	020 7533 5305

Department of Health

Contraceptive services	020 7972 5533
Health Survey for England	020 7972 5718
Immunisation and cancer screening	020 7972 5533
Infant Feeding Survey	020 8433 4405
Prescription analysis	020 7972 5513
Smoking, misuse of alcohol and drugs	020 7972 5551

Department for Environment, Food & Rural Affairs	020 7270 8547
Department of Health, Social Services and Public Safety, Northern Ireland	028 9052 2800
General Register Office for Northern Ireland	028 9025 2031
General Register Office for Scotland	0131 314 4227
Government Actuary's Department	020 7211 2635
Home Office	020 7273 2084
National Assembly for Wales	029 2082 5080
NHS Scotland Information and Statistics Division	0131 551 8899
Northern Ireland Statistics and Research Agency	**028 9034 8132**
Continuous Household Survey	028 9034 8243
Northern Ireland Cancer Registry	028 9026 3136

Public Health Laboratory Service	020 8200 6868
Royal College of General Practitioners	0121 426 1125
Welsh Cancer Intelligence and Surveillance Unit	029 2037 3500
Eurostat	00 352 4301 32 056
European Monitoring Centre for Drugs and Drug Addiction	00 351 21 811 3000

Chapter 8 – Social Protection

Websites

National Statistics	www.statistics.gov.uk
Department of Health	www.doh.gov.uk
Department for Work and Pensions	www.dwp.gov.uk
Department for Education and Skills	www.dfes.gov.uk
Northern Ireland Statistics and Research Agency	www.nisra.gov.uk
Department of Health, Social Services and Public Safety, Northern Ireland	www.dhsspsni.gov.uk/iau/index.html
Department for Social Development, Northern Ireland	www.dsdni.gov.uk
Scottish Executive	www.scotland.gov.uk
NHS in Scotland	www.show.scot.nhs.uk/isd
National Assembly for Wales	www.wales.gov.uk
Eurostat	www.europa.eu.int/comm/eurostat
Charities Aid Foundation	www.cafonline.org
The National Centre for Social Research	www.natcen.ac.uk/

Contacts

Office for National Statistics

Chapter author	020 7533 5781
General Household Survey	020 7533 5444

Department of Health

Acute services activity	0113 254 5522
Adults' services	020 7972 5591
Children 's services	020 7972 5581
Community and cross-sector services	020 7972 5524
General dental and community dental service	020 7972 5392
General medical services statistics	0113 254 5911
Mental illness/handicap	020 7972 5546
NHS expenditure	0113 254 6012
NHS medical staff	0113 254 5892

NHS non-medical manpower	0113 254 5744
Non-psychiatric hospital activity	020 7972 5529
Personal social services expenditure	020 7210 5699
Residential care and home help	020 7972 5591
Social services staffing and finance data	020 7972 5595
Waiting lists	0113 254 5200
Department for Work and Pensions	**020 7962 8000**
Family Resources Survey	020 7962 8092
Number of benefit recipients	0191 225 7373
Households Below Average Income	020 7962 8232
Department for Education and Skills	
Day care for children	01325 392827
Department of Health, Social Services and Public Safety, Northern Ireland	
Health and personal social services activity	028 9052 2800
Health and personal social services manpower	028 9052 2468
Department for Social Development, Northern Ireland	028 9052 2280
National Assembly for Wales	029 2082 5080
National Health Service in Scotland	0131 551 8899
Northern Ireland Statistics and Research Agency	028 9034 8243
Scottish Executive	
Children's social services	0131 244 3551
Adult community care	0131 244 3777
Social work staffing	0131 244 3740
Eurostat	00 352 4301 34122
Charities Aid Foundation	01732 520 125

Chapter 9 – Crime and Justice

Websites

National Statistics	www.statistics.gov.uk
Lord Chancellor's Department	www.lcd.gov.uk
Court Service	www.courtservice.gov.uk
Home Office	www.homeoffice.gov.uk
Home Office (Criminal Justice System)	www.criminal-justice-system.gov.uk
National Assembly for Wales	www.wales.gov.uk
Scottish Executive	www.scotland.gov.uk
Northern Ireland Office	www.nio.gov.uk
Police Service of Northern Ireland	www.psni.police.uk
Legal Services Commission	www.legalservices.gov.uk

Contacts

Office for National Statistics

Chapter Author	020 7533 5776
Home Office	020 7273 2084
Lord Chancellor's Department	020 7210 8500
National Assembly for Wales	029 2080 1388
Northern Ireland Office	028 9052 7538
Police Service for Northern Ireland	028 9065 0222 Ext. 24865
Scottish Executive Justice Department	0131 244 2227

Chapter 10 – Housing

Websites

National Statistics	www.statistics.gov.uk
Office of the Deputy Prime Minister	www.odpm.gov.uk
Court Service	www.courtservice.gov.uk
Department for Social Development, Northern Ireland	www.dsdni.gov.uk
Department for Work and Pensions	www.dwp.gov.uk
National Assembly for Wales	www.wales.gov.uk
Northern Ireland Statistics Research Agency	www.nisra.gov.uk
Scottish Executive	www.scotland.gov.uk
Social Exclusion Unit	www.cabinet-office.gov.uk/seu
Council of Mortgage Lenders	www.cml.org.uk
Land Registry	www.landreg.gov.uk

Contacts

Office for National Statistics

Chapter Author	020 7533 5807
Expenditure and Food Survey	020 7533 5754
General Household Survey	020 7533 5444
Office of the Deputy Prime Minister	**020 7944 3303**
Planning and Land Use Statistics	020 7944 5533
Court Service	020 7210 1773
Department for Social Development, Northern Ireland	028 9052 2762
Department for Work and Pensions	
Family Resources Survey	020 7962 8092
National Assembly of Wales	029 2082 5063
Northern Ireland Statistics and Research Agency	028 9034 8243
Scottish Executive	0131 244 7236
Council of Mortgage Lenders	020 7440 2251
Land Registry	0151 473 6008

Chapter 11 – Environment

Websites

National Statistics	www.statistics.gov.uk
Department for Environment, Food & Rural Affairs	www.defra.gov.uk/environment/index.htm
Department of Trade and Industry	www.dti.gov.uk/energy/index.htm
Scottish Executive	www.scotland.gov.uk
National Assembly for Wales	www.wales.org.uk
Northern Ireland Department of Environment	www.nics.gov.uk
Centre for Ecology and Hydrology, Wallingford	www.ceh-nerc.ac.uk
Countryside Agency	www.countryside.gov.uk
Countryside Council for Wales	www.ccw.gov.uk
Environment Agency	www.environment-agency.gov.uk
Environment and Heritage Service (NI)	www.ehsni.gov.uk
European Environment Agency	www.eea.eu.int
Eurostat	www.europa.eu.int/comm/eurostat
Forestry Commission	www.forestry.gov.uk/statistics
Joint Nature Conservation Committee	www.jncc.gov.uk
Northern Ireland Statistics and Research Agency	www.nisra.gov.uk
OFWAT	www.ofwat.gov.uk
Scottish Environment Protection Agency	www.sepa.gov.uk
Scottish Natural Heritage	www.snh.org.uk

Contacts

Office for National Statistics

Chapter author	020 7533 5701
Department for Environment Food & Rural Affairs	020 7944 6497
Department of Trade and Industry	020 7215 2697
Scottish Executive	0131 244 0445
National Assembly for Wales	029 2082 5111
Northern Ireland Department of Environment	028 9054 0540
Centre for Ecology and Hydrology	01491 838 800
Countryside Agency	020 7340 2900
Countryside Council for Wales	01248 385 500
CADW	029 2082 5111
Environment Agency	0845 9333 111
Environment and Heritage Services (Northern Ireland)	028 9023 5000
European Environment Agency	0045 3336 7100
Eurostat	00352 4301 33023
Forestry Commission	0131 314 6337
Joint Nature Conservation Committee	01733 562 626

OFWAT	0121 625 1300
Scottish Environment Protection Agency	01786 457 700
Scottish Natural Heritage	0131 447 4784
Northern Ireland Statistics Research Agency	028 9034 8200

Chapter 12 – Transport

Websites

National Statistics	www.statistics.gov.uk
Department of Trade and Industry	www.dti.gov.uk
Department for Transport	www.transtat.dft.gov.uk
Department of the Environment for Northern Ireland	www.doeni.gov.uk
Civil Aviation Authority Economic Regulation Group	www.caaerg.co.uk
Police Service of Northern Ireland	www.psni.police.uk
Scottish Executive	www.scotland.gov.uk
Strategic Rail Authority	www.sra.gov.uk
National Centre for Social Research	www.natcen.ac.uk

Contacts

Office for National Statistics

Chapter author	020 7533 5701
Expenditure and Food Survey	020 7533 5754
Household expenditure	020 7533 6001
International Passenger Survey	020 7533 5765
Retail Prices Index	020 7533 5874
Department of Trade and Industry	020 7215 5000

Department for Transport

General Queries	020 7944 8300
National Travel Survey	020 7944 3097
Civil Aviation Authority Economic Regulation Group	020 7453 6213
Department of the Environment for Northern Ireland	01232 540807
Driving Standards Agency	0115 901 2852
Police Service of Northern Ireland	028 9065 0222 Ext 24135
National Centre for Social Research	020 7250 1866
Scottish Executive	0131 244 7255/7256
Strategic Rail Authority	020 7654 6072

Chapter 13 – Lifestyles and Social Participation

Websites

National Statistics	www.statistics.gov.uk
Department for Culture, Media and Sport	www.culture.gov.uk
Northern Ireland Statistics and Research Agency	www.nisra.gov.uk
British Video Association	www.bva.org.uk
British Broadcasting Corporation	www.bbc.co.uk
British Film Industry	www.bfi.org.uk
British Phonographic Industry	www.bpi.co.uk
Library & Information Statistics Unit	
	www.lboro.ac.uk/departments/dils/lisu/lisuhp.html
Cinema Advertising Association	www.carltonscreen.com www.pearlanddean.com
English Tourism Council	www.englishtourism.org.uk
Arts Council of England	www.artscouncil.org.uk
British Market Research Bureau	www.bmrb.co.uk
National Centre for Social Research	www.natcen.ac.uk
Centre for Research into Elections and Social Trends	www.crest.ox.ac.uk
The Electoral Commission	www.electoralcommission.gov.uk
The National Tourism Statistics	www.staruk.org.uk

Contacts

Office for National Statistics

Chapter Author	020 7533 5776
Expenditure and Food Survey	020 7533 5756
General Household Survey	020 7533 5444
International Passenger Survey	020 7533 5765
Omnibus Survey	020 7533 5321
UK 2000 Time Use Survey	020 7533 5933
Department for Culture, Media and Sport	020 7211 2179
Northern Ireland Statistics and Research Agency	028 9034 8246
British Broadcasting Corporation	020 7765 1064
British Phonographic Industry	020 7851 4000
British Video Association	020 7436 0041
Cinema Advertising Association	020 7534 6363
English Tourism Council	020 5863 3011
Library & Information Statistics Unit	01509 223 071
National Centre for Social Research	020 7250 1866

References and further reading

Those published by The Stationery Office are available from the addresses shown on the back cover of *Social Trends*. Many can also be found on the National Statistics website: www.statistics.gov.uk

General

Regional Trends, The Stationery Office

Social Focus on Ethnic Minorities, The Stationery Office

Social Focus on Families, The Stationery Office

Social Focus on Men, The Stationery Office

Social Focus on Older People, The Stationery Office

Social Focus on Women and Men, The Stationery Office

Social Focus on Young People, The Stationery Office

UK 2003: The Official Yearbook of the United Kingdom of Great Britain and Northern Ireland, The Stationery Office

1: Population

Annual Abstract of Statistics, The Stationery Office

Annual Report of the Registrar General for Northern Ireland, The Stationery Office

Annual Report of the Registrar General for Scotland, General Register Office for Scotland

Asylum Statistics – United Kingdom, Home Office

Birth Statistics (Series FM1), The Stationery Office

Census 2001: First results on population for England and Wales, The Stationery Office

Control of Immigration: Statistics, United Kingdom, The Stationery Office

European Social Statistics – Demography, Eurostat

Health Statistics Quarterly, The Stationery Office

International Migration Statistics (Series MN), The Stationery Office

Key Population and Vital Statistics (Series VS/PP1), The Stationery Office

Mid-year Population Estimates for England and Wales, The Stationery Office

Mid-year Population Estimates, Northern Ireland, Northern Ireland Statistics and Research Agency

Mid-year Population Estimates, Scotland, General Register Office for Scotland

Migration Statistics, Eurostat

Mortality Statistics for England and Wales (Series DH1, 2,3,4), The Stationery Office

National Population Projections, UK (Series PP2), The Stationery Office

Patterns and Trends in International Migration in Western Europe, Eurostat

Persons Granted British Citizenship – United Kingdom, Home Office

Population and Projections for areas within Northern Ireland, Northern Ireland Statistics and Research Agency

Population Projections for Wales (sub-national), National Assembly for Wales/Welsh Office

Population Projections, Scotland (for Administrative Areas), General Register Office for Scotland

Population Trends, The Stationery Office

The State of World Population, United Nations

United Nations Demographic Yearbook, United Nations

World Population Prospects: The 2000 Revision, United Nations

World Statistics Pocketbook, United Nations

2: Households and Families

Abortion Statistics (Series AB), The Stationery Office

Annual Report of the Registrar General for Northern Ireland, The Stationery Office

Annual Report of the Registrar General for Scotland, General Register Office for Scotland

Attitudes towards ideal family size of different ethnic/nationality groups in Great Britain, France and Germany, Population Trends 108, Penn R and Lambert P, Office for National Statistics, The Stationery Office

Birth Statistics (Series FM1), The Stationery Office

Birth Statistics: historical series, 1837 –1983 (Series FM1), The Stationery Office

British Social Attitudes, National Centre for Social Research

Choosing Childlessness, Family Policy Studies Centre

European Social Statistics – Demography, Eurostat

Grandparents and the care of children: The research evidence, Clarke L and Cairns H, in Broad B (ed.) Kinship Care: The placement choice for children and young people, Russell House Publishing

Health Statistics Quarterly, The Stationery Office

Human Fertilisation and Embryology Authority Annual Report, Human Fertilisation and Embryology Authority

Key Population and Vital Statistics (Series VS/PP1), The Stationery Office

Living in Britain: results from the 2001 General Household Survey, The Stationery Office

Marriage, Divorce and Adoption Statistics (Series FM2), The Stationery Office

Marriage and Divorce Statistics 1837 –1983 (Series FM2), The Stationery Office

Population Trends, The Stationery Office

Personal Relationships and Marriage Expectations: Evidence from the 1998 British Household Panel Study, Institute for Social and Economic Research, University of Essex

Policy and rhetoric: The growing interest in fathers and grandparents in Britain, Clarke L and Roberts C, in Carling A, Duncan S and Edwards R (eds.) Analysing families: Morality and rationality in policy and practice, Routledge

Projections of Households in England to 2021, Office of the Deputy Prime Minister

Recent Demographic Developments in Europe, Council of Europe

Housing in England: Survey of English Housing, The Stationery Office

Teenage Pregnancy, Report by the Social Exclusion Unit, The Stationery Office

The British Population, Oxford University Press

3: Education

Education at a Glance, OECD Indicators 2002, Organisation for Economic Co-operation and Development, 2002

Fifth Survey of Parents of Three and Four Year Old Children and Their Use of Early Years Service, National Centre for Social Research, for the Department for Education and Skills, Research Report 351, 2002, The Stationery Office

Knowledge and Skills for Life, Organisation for Economic Co-operation and Development, 2001

Learning and Training at Work 2001, IFF Research Ltd, for the Department for Education and Skills, Research Report 334, 2002, The Stationery Office

National Adult Learning Survey 2001, National Centre for Social Research, for the Department for Education and Skills, Research Report 321, 2002, The Stationery Office

Statistical Volume: Education and Training Statistics for the United Kingdom, Department for Education and Skills, 2002, The Stationery Office

4: Labour Market

European Social Statistics – Labour Force Survey results, Eurostat

How Exactly is Unemployment Measured? Office for National Statistics

Labour Force Survey Historical Supplement, Office for National Statistics

Labour Force Survey Quarterly Supplement, Office for National Statistics

Labour Market Trends, The Stationery Office

*Northern Ireland Labour Force Survey,
Department of Enterprise,* Trade and
Investment, Northern Ireland

The State of the Labour Market, Office for
National Statistics

The State of Working Britain, Cregg P and
Wadsworth J, Manchester University Press,
1999

What exactly is the Labour Force Survey?
Office for National Statistics

5: Income and Wealth

*Changing Households: The British Household
Panel Survey,* Institute for Social and Economic
Research

Economic Trends, The Stationery Office

*European Community Finances: Statement on
the 2002 EC Budget and Measures to Counter
Fraud and Financial Mismanagement,* The
Stationery Office

Eurostat National Accounts ESA, Eurostat

Family Resources Survey, Department for Work
and Pensions

Fiscal Studies, Institute for Fiscal Studies

For Richer, For Poorer, Institute for Fiscal
Studies

*Households Below Average Income, 1994/5 –
2000/01,* Department for Work and Pensions

Income and Wealth. The Latest Evidence,
Joseph Rowntree Foundation

Individual Incomes 1996/97 2000/01, Women
and Equality Unit

*Labour Market Trends (incorporating
Employment Gazette),* The Stationery Office

*Low/moderate-income Families in Britain:
Changes in 1999 and 2000,* Marsh A and
Rowlingson K, Research Report, Department
for Work and Pensions

Monitoring Poverty and Social Exclusion,
Joseph Rowntree Foundation

New Earnings Survey, The Stationery Office

Poverty and Social Exclusion in Britain, 2000,
Joseph Rowntree Foundation,

Social Security, Departmental Report, The
Stationery Office

Social Security Statistics, The Stationery Office

The Distribution of Wealth in the UK, Institute
for Fiscal Studies

The Pensioners' Incomes Series, Department for
Work and Pensions

*United Kingdom National Accounts (The ONS
Blue Book),* The Stationery Office

6: Expenditure

*Business Monitor MM23 (Consumer Price
Indices),* The Stationery Office

Consumer Trends, Internet only publication,
Office for National Statistics
www.statistics.gov.uk/consumertrends

Economic Trends, The Stationery Office

Family Spending, The Stationery Office

In Brief 2002, Payment Markets Briefing,
Association for Payment Clearing Services

Financial Statistics, The Stationery Office

*United Kingdom National Accounts (The ONS
Blue Book),* The Stationery Office

7: Health

*The Annual Report of the Registrar General for
Northern Ireland,* Northern Ireland Statistics
and Research Agency

*Annual Report on the State of the Drugs
Problem in the European Union, 2001,*
European Monitoring Centre for Drugs and
Drug Addiction

*Annual Report of the Registrar General for
Scotland,* General Register Office for Scotland

*Cancer Trends in England and Wales 1950
–1999,* The Stationery Office

Community Statistics, Department of Health,
Social Services and Public Safety, Northern
Ireland

Geographic Variations in Health, The
Stationery Office

*Health in Scotland. The Annual Report of the
Chief Medical Officer on the State of Scotland's
Health,* Scottish Executive

Health Statistics Quarterly, The Stationery Office

Health Statistics Wales, National Assembly for Wales

Health Survey for England, The Stationery Office

Infant Feeding Survey 2000, The Stationery Office

Key Health Statistics from General Practice 1998, Office for National Statistics

Living in Britain: results from the 2001 General Household Survey, The Stationery Office

Mortality trends by cause of death in England and Wales 1980-94: the impact of introducing automated cause coding and related changes in 1993, Population Trends 86, Rooney C and Devis T, Office for National Statistics, The Stationery Office

National Food Survey 2000, The Stationery Office

On the State of the Public Health – The Annual Report of the Chief Medical Officer of the Department of Health, The Stationery Office

Population Trends, The Stationery Office

Psychiatric Morbidity Survey Among Adults Living in Private Households 2000, The Stationery Office

Report of the Chief Medical Officer, Department of Health, Social Services and Public Safety, Northern Ireland

Results of the ICD-10 bridge coding study, England and Wales, 1999, Health Statistics Quarterly 14, Office for National Statistics, The Stationery Office

Scottish Health Statistics, Information and Statistics Division, NHS Scotland

Smoking, Drinking and Drug Use among Young People in 2001, Press release, Department of Health (internet only publication) www.doh.gov/public/press15march02.htm

Statistical Publications on Aspects of Health and Personal Social Services Activity in England (various), Department of Health

Trends in life expectancy by social class – an update, Hattersley L, Health Statistics Quarterly 2, Office for National Statistics, The Stationery Office

Welsh Health: Annual Report of the Chief Medical Officer, National Assembly for Wales

World Health Statistics, World Health Organisation

8: Social Protection

Annual News Releases (various), Scottish Executive

Carers 2000, The Stationery Office

Community Statistics for Northern Ireland, Department of Health, Social Services and Public Safety, Northern Ireland

Department of Health Departmental Report, The Stationery Office

Dimensions of the Voluntary Sector, Charities Aid Foundation

ESSPROS manual 1996, Eurostat

Family Resources Survey, Department for Work and Pensions

Health and Personal Social Services Statistics for England, The Stationery Office

Hospital Episode Statistics for England, Department of Health

Hospital Statistics for Northern Ireland, Department of Health, Social Services and Public Safety, Northern Ireland

Health Statistics Wales, National Assembly for Wales

Scottish Community Care Statistics, Scottish Executive

Scottish Health Statistics, National Health Service in Scotland, Common Services Agency

Social Protection Expenditure and Receipts, Eurostat

Social Security Departmental Report, The Stationery Office

Social Services Statistics Wales, National Assembly for Wales

Statistical Publications on Aspects of Community Care in Scotland (various), Scottish Executive Health Department

Statistical Publications on Aspects of Health and Personal Social Services Activity in England (various), Department of Health

Work and Pension Statistics, The Department for Work and Pensions

9: Crime and Justice

A Commentary on Northern Ireland Crime Statistics, The Stationery Office

Chief Constable's Annual Report, Police Service of Northern Ireland

Civil Judicial Statistics, Scotland, The Stationery Office

Costs, Sentencing Profiles and the Scottish Criminal Justice System, Scottish Executive

Crime and the Quality of Life: Public Perceptions and Experiences of Crime in Scotland, Scottish Executive

Crime in England and Wales 2001–02, Home Office

Criminal Statistics, England and Wales, The Stationery Office

Crown Prosecution Service, Annual Report, The Stationery Office

Digest 4: Information on the Criminal Justice System in England and Wales, Home Office

Digest of Information on the Northern Ireland Criminal Justice System 3, The Stationery Office

Home Office Annual Report and Accounts, The Stationery Office

Home Office Research Findings, Home Office

Home Office Statistical Bulletins, Home Office

Judicial Statistics, England and Wales, The Stationery Office

Legal Services Commission Annual Report 2001/02, The Stationery Office

Local Authority Performance Indicators, Volume 3, Audit Commission

Northern Ireland Judicial Statistics, Northern Ireland Court Service

One Year Juvenile Reconviction Rates July 2000 Cohort, Home Office

Police Statistics, England and Wales, CIPFA

Prison Service Annual Report and Accounts, The Stationery Office

Prison Statistics, England and Wales, The Stationery Office

Prison Statistics Scotland, Scottish Executive

Prisons in Scotland Report, The Stationery Office

Race and the Criminal Justice System, Home Office

Report of the Parole Board for England and Wales, The Stationery Office

Report on the work of the Northern Ireland Prison Service, The Stationery Office

Scottish Crime Survey, Scottish Executive

Statistics on Women and the Criminal Justice System, Home Office

The Criminal Justice System in England and Wales, Home Office

Scottish Executive Statistical Bulletins: Criminal Justice Series, Scottish Executive

The Work of the Prison Service, The Stationery Office

Review of Police Forces' Crime Recording Practices, Home Office

Review of Crime Statistics: a Discussion Document, Home Office

10: Housing

A Review of Flexible Mortgages, The Council of Mortgage Lenders

Becoming a Home-owner in Britain in the 1990s The British Household Panel Survey, ESRC Institute for Social and Economic Research

Bringing Britain Together: A National Strategy for Neighbourhood Renewal, Social Exclusion Unit, Cabinet Office

Changing Households: The British Household Panel Survey, Institute for Social and Economic Research

Department for Transport, Local Government and the Regions Annual Report, The Stationery Office

Divorce, Remarriage and Housing: The Effects of Divorce, Remarriage, Separation and the Formation of New Couple Households on the Number of Separate Households and Housing Demand Conditions, Department of the Environment, Transport and the Regions

English House Condition Survey, The Stationery Office

Housing Finance, Council of Mortgage Lenders

Housing in England: Survey of English Housing, The Stationery Office

Housing Statistics, The Stationery Office

Living conditions in Europe – Statistical Pocketbook, Eurostat

Local Housing Statistics, The Stationery Office

My Home Was My Castle: Evictions and Repossessions in Britain, ESRC Institute of Social and Economic Research and Institute of Local Research

Northern Ireland House Condition Survey, Northern Ireland Housing Executive

Northern Ireland Housing Statistics, 2001–02, Department for Social Development, Northern Ireland

On the Move: The Housing Consequences of Migration, YPS

Private Renting in England, The Stationery Office

Private Renting in Five Localities, The Stationery Office

Projections of Households in England to 2021, The Stationery Office

Scotland's People: Results from the 1999 Scottish Household Survey, The Stationery Office

Scottish House Condition Survey 1996, Scottish Homes

Statistical Bulletins on Housing, Scottish Executive

Statistics on Housing in the European Community, Commission of the European Communities

The Social Situation in the European Union, European Commission

Welsh House Condition Survey, National Assembly for Wales

Welsh Housing Statistics, National Assembly for Wales

11: Environment

A Better Quality of Life, The Stationery Office

Accounting for Nature: Assessing Habitats in the UK Countryside, Department for Environment, Food & Rural Affairs

Air Quality Strategy for England, Scotland, Wales and Northern Ireland, The Stationery Office

Bathing Water Quality in England and Wales, The Stationery Office

Biodiversity: The UK Action Plan, The Stationery Office

British Social Attitudes, National Centre for Social Research

Development of the Oil and Gas Resources of the United Kingdom, The Stationery Office

Digest of Environmental Statistics, Internet only publication, Department for Environment, Food & Rural Affairs www.defra.gov.uk/environmental/statistics/des/index.htm

Digest of United Kingdom Energy Statistics, The Stationery Office

Farming and Food: A Sustainable Future, Policy Commission on the Future of Farming and Food

Forestry Commission Facts and Figures 2002, Forestry Commission

Forestry Statistics 2002, Forestry Commission

General Quality Assessment, The Environment Agency

Hydrological Summaries for the United Kingdom, Centre for Hydrology and British Geological Survey

Municipal Waste Management Survey, Department for Environment, Food & Rural Affairs

OECD Environmental Data Compendium, OECD

Organic Farming, Department for Environment, Food & Rural Affairs

Planning Public Water Supplies, The Environment Agency

Pollution Incidents in England and Wales, 2000, Environment Agency

Progress in Water Supply Planning, The Environment Agency

Quality of Life Counts, The Stationery Office

Scottish Environmental Statistics, Scottish Executive

Survey of Public Attitudes to Quality of Life and to the Environment 2001, Department for Environment, Food & Rural Affairs

Sustainable Scotland: Priorities and Progress, Scottish Executive

The Environment in your Pocket, Department for Environment, Food & Rural Affairs

The State of the Countryside 2002, The Countryside Agency

The State of the Environment of England and Wales: The Atmosphere, The Stationery Office

The State of the Environment of England and Wales: The Land, The Stationery Office

The State of the Environment of England and Wales: Fresh Waters, The Stationery Office

The State of the Environment of England and Wales: Coasts, The Stationery Office

Waste Strategy 2000, England and Wales, Department of the Environment, Transport and the Regions

Waterfacts, Water Services Association

12: Transport

A New Deal for Transport: Better for Everyone, The Stationery Office

A Strategy for Sustainable Development for the United Kingdom, The Stationery Office

Annual Report, Central Rail Users Consultative Committee

British Social Attitudes, National Centre for Social Research

Driving Standards Agency Annual Report and Accounts, The Stationery Office

Focus on Personal Travel, The Stationery Office

Focus on Public Transport, The Stationery Office

Focus on Roads, The Stationery Office

International Passenger Transport, The Stationery Office

National Rail Trends, Strategic Rail Authority

Rail Complaints, Office of the Rail Regulator

Road Accidents Great Britain – The Casualty Report, The Stationery Office

Road Accidents, Scotland, Scottish Executive

Road Accidents Statistics English Regions, The Stationery Office

Road Accidents: Wales, National Assembly for Wales

Road Traffic Accident Statistics Annual Report, Police Service of Northern Ireland

Road Traffic Statistics Great Britain, The Stationery Office

Scottish Transport Statistics, Scottish Executive

Transport Statistics Bulletins and Reports, Department for Transport

Transport Statistical Bulletins, Scottish Executive

Transport Statistics Great Britain, The Stationery Office

Transport Trends, The Stationery Office

Travel Trends, The Stationery Office

Vehicle Licensing Statistics, Department for Transport

Vehicle Speeds in Great Britain, Department for Transport

Welsh Transport Statistics, National Assembly for Wales

13: Lifestyles and Social Participation

Annual Report of Department for Culture, Media and Sport, The Stationery Office

Arts in England and Wales: Attendance, Participation and Attitudes in 2001, Arts Council of England

BBC Annual Reports and Accounts, BBC

BPI Statistical Handbook, British Phonographic Industry

British Social Attitudes, National Centre for Social Research

BVA Yearbook, British Video Association

Cinema and Video Industry Audience Research, CAA

Cultural Trends in Scotland, Policy Studies Institute

Cultural Trends, Policy Studies Institute

Family Spending, The Stationery Office

Film and Television Handbook, British Film Institute

LISU Annual Library Statistics, LISU, Loughborough University

Living in Britain: results from the 2001 General Household Survey, The Stationery Office

The UK Tourist: Statistics, English Tourism Council, VisitScotland, Wales Tourist Board and Northern Ireland Tourist Board

Travel Trends, The Stationery Office

UK 2000 Time Use Survey, Office for National Statistics

UK Day Visits Survey, Countryside Recreation Network, University of Wales Cardiff

Visits to Visitor Attractions, English Tourism Council, VisitScotland, Wales Tourist Board and Northern Ireland Tourist Board

Young People and Sport in England, Sport England

Geographical areas of the United Kingdom

Government Office Regions

ENGLAND

— GOR boundary

SCOTLAND

NORTHERN IRELAND

NORTH EAST

YORKSHIRE AND THE HUMBER

NORTH WEST

EAST MIDLANDS

WEST MIDLANDS

WALES

EAST OF ENGLAND

LONDON

SOUTH WEST

SOUTH EAST

Environment Agency regions

ENGLAND and WALES

— Environment Agency region boundary

SCOTLAND

NORTHERN IRELAND

NORTH WEST

NORTH EAST

MIDLANDS

ANGLIAN

WELSH

THAMES

SOUTH-WESTERN

SOUTHERN

NHS Regional Office areas (from April 2001)

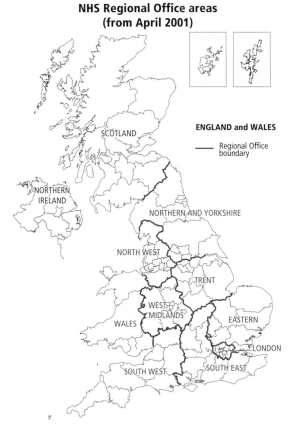

ENGLAND and WALES

— Regional Office boundary

SCOTLAND

NORTHERN IRELAND

NORTHERN AND YORKSHIRE

NORTH WEST

TRENT

WEST MIDLANDS

WALES

EASTERN

LONDON

SOUTH WEST

SOUTH EAST

Police Force areas

Northern

Northern

GREAT BRITAIN

— Police Force area boundary

Northern

Grampian

Tayside

Fife

Central

Strathclyde

Lothian & Borders

Dumfries & Galloway

Northumbria

Cumbria

Durham

Cleveland

North Yorkshire

Lancashire

Humberside

Merseyside

G.M.P.

W. Yorks

S. Yorks

Cheshire

Derbys

Lincolnshire

North Wales

Notts

Staffs

Leicester

Norfolk

West Mercia

W. Mids

Warks

Northants

Cambs

Suffolk

Dyfed-Powys

Beds

Gwent

Gloucs

Thames Valley

Herts

Essex

City

South Wales

Avon and Somerset

Wiltshire

Met

Surrey

Kent

Devon and Cornwall

Dorset

Hampshire

Sussex

Major Surveys

	Frequency	Sampling frame	Type of respondent	Coverage	Effective sample size[1] (most recent survey included in Social Trends)	Response rate (percentages)
Adult Dental Health Survey	Decennial	Postcode Address File in GB, Rating and Valuation lists in NI	All adults in household	UK	4,984 households	74
Agricultural and Horticultural Census	Annual	Farms	Farmers	UK	238,000 farms	80
British Crime Survey	Annual	Postcode Address File	Adult in household	EW	33,000 addresses	74
British Household Panel Survey	Annual	Postal Addresses in 1991, members of initial wave households followed in subsequent waves	All adults in households	GB	5,160 households	97[2]
British Election Survey	With each election	Postcode Address File	One adult per household	UK	4,659 households	65
British Social Attitudes Survey	Annual	Postcode Address File	One adult per household	GB	5,523 addresses	62[3]
Census of Population	Decennial	Detailed local	Adult in household	UK	Full count	98
Continuous Household Survey	Continuous	Valuation and Lands Agency Property	All adults in household	NI	4,147 addresses	70
Employers Skill Survey	Annual	BT Database	Employers	E	27,031 interviews achieved	53
English House Condition Survey	Quinquennial	Postcode Address File	Any one householder	E	27,200 addresses	49[4]
European Community	Annual	Various	All household members aged 16 and over	EU	60,000 households	90[5]
Expenditure and Food Survey	Continuous	Postcode Address File	Household in GB, Rating and Valuation lists in NI	UK	12,096 addresses[6]	62[7]
Family Resources Survey	Continuous	Postcode Address File	All adults in household	GB	34,636 households	66
General Household Survey	Continuous	Postcode Address File	All adults in household	GB	11,845 households	76
Health Education Monitoring Survey	Ad hoc	Postcode Address File	One adult aged 16 and over in household	E	8,168 households	71
Health Survey for England	Continuous	Postcode Address File	Adults, children over 2	E	12,250 addresses	74[8]
International Passenger Survey	Continuous	International passengers	Individual traveller	UK	254,000 individuals	81
Labour Force Survey	Continuous	Postcode Address File	All adults in household	UK	61,000 households	78[9]
Learning and training at work	Annual	BT Business database	Employers	E	4,006 interviews achieved	63
National Readership Survey	Continuous	Postcode Address File	Adults aged 15 and over	GB	54,074 individuals	60
National Travel Survey	Continuous	Postcode Address File	All household members	GB	5,075 households per year	65[10]
New Earnings Survey	Annual	Inland Revenue PAYE records	Employee	GB	[11]	[11]
National Statistics Omnibus Survey	Continuous	Postcode Address File	Adults aged 16 or over living in private households	GB	Approximately 1,800[12]	66
Survey of English Housing	Continuous	Postcode Address File	Household	E	26,277 households	71
Survey of Personal Incomes	Annual	Inland Revenue	Individuals administrative data	UK	125,000	95
Survey of public attitudes to quality of life and to the environment	Ad hoc	Postcode Address File	One adult per household	E	3,700 interviews	68
UK Time Use Survey	Ad hoc	Postcode Address File	Adults and children 8 years and over	UK	10,503	61[13]
Youth Cohort Study	Biennial	School records	Young people (Aged 16 to 19)	EW	22,500 individuals	65

1   Effective sample size includes non-respondents but excludes ineligible households.
2   Wave on wave response rate at wave eight. Around 76 per cent of eligible wave one sample members were respondent in wave eight.
3   Response rate refers to 2000 survey.
4   The 1996 EHCS response combines successful outcomes from two linked surveys where information is separately gathered about the household and the dwelling for each address.
5   Response rates vary between EU countries.
6   Basic sample only.
7   Response rate refers to Great Britain.
8   Response rate for fully and partially responding households.
9   Response rate to first wave interviews quoted. Response rate to second and fifth wave interviews 91 per cent off those previously accepting.
10 Response rate for the period January 1999 to January 2001.
11 In the New Earnings Survey employers supply data on a 1 per cent sample of employees who are members of PAYE schemes. For the 2002 sample approximately 241 thousand were selected and there was an 87.1 per cent response, but some 47 thousand returned questionnaires were not taken onto the results file for various reasons.
12 Achieved sample size per Omnibus cycle. The Omnibus interviews at one household per sampled address and one adult per household. Data are weighted to account for the fact that respondents living in smaller households would have a greater chance of selection.
13 Responses rate for the household questionnaire.

Symbols and conventions

Reference years. Where, because of space constraints, a choice of years has to be made, the most recent year or a run of recent years is shown together with the past population census years (1991, 1981, 1971, etc) and sometimes the mid-points between census years (1986, etc). Other years may be added if they represent a peak or trough in the series.

Rounding of figures. In tables where figures have been rounded to the nearest final digit, there may be an apparent discrepancy between the sum of the constituent items and the total as shown.

Billion. This term is used to represent a thousand million.

Provisional and estimated data. Some data for the latest year (and occasionally for earlier years) are provisional or estimated. To keep footnotes to a minimum, these have not been indicated; source departments will be able to advise if revised data are available.

Seasonal adjustment. Unless otherwise stated unadjusted data have been used.

Non-calendar years

Financial year - eg 1 April 2001 to 31 March 2002 would be shown as 2001/02

Academic year - eg September 2000/July 2001 would be shown as 2000/01

Combined years - eg 2000-02 shows data for more than one year that have been combined

Data covering more than one year - eg 1998, 1999 and 2000 would be shown as 1998 to 2000

Units on tables. Where one unit predominates it is shown at the top of the table. All other units are shown against the relevant row or column. Figures are shown in italics when they represent percentages.

Dependent children. Those aged under 16, or single people aged 16 to 18 and in full-time education.

Germany. Unless otherwise stated data relate to Germany as constituted since 3 October 1990.

Symbols. The following symbols have been used throughout Social Trends:

..	not available
.	not applicable
-	negligible (less than half the final digit shown)
0	nil

Appendix

Part 1: Population

Population estimates and projections

The estimated and projected populations are of the resident population of an area, i.e. all those usually resident there, whatever their nationality. Members of HM forces stationed outside the United Kingdom are excluded; members of foreign forces stationed in the United Kingdom are included. Students are taken to be resident at their term-time addresses. Figures for the United Kingdom do not include the population of the Channel Islands or the Isle of Man.

The population estimates for mid-2001 are based on results from the 2001 Census and incorporate an allowance for census under-enumeration. The figures for 1982 to 2000 are not consistent with the 2001 estimates, apart from national estimates for the UK, or those for England and Wales combined, where interim revised population estimates are available. All population estimates for 1982 to 2000 are subject to revision in 2003, including the United Kingdom and England and Wales interim estimates. The following items will be updated on the National Statistics website in late Spring 2003 using the final revised population estimates: 1.1, 1.2, 1.3, 1.7, 1.9, 1.12, 7.11 and 7.12.

The most recent set of national population projections published for the United Kingdom are based on the populations of England, Wales, Scotland and Northern Ireland at mid-2001. Further details of these can be found on the Government Actuary's Department's website (www.gad.gov.uk).

Boundaries

Map boundaries show government office regions, counties/unitary authorities and, where available, local authority districts in England; unitary authorities in Wales; the council areas in Scotland; health and social service boards/education and library boards/districts as available in Northern Ireland. See page 256 for reference maps showing these borders.

Classification of ethnic groups

The recommended classification of ethnic groups for National Statistics data sources was changed in 2001 to bring it broadly in line with the 2001 Census.

There are two levels to this classification. Level 1 is a coarse classification into five main ethnic groups. Level 2 sub-divides Level 1, and provides a finer classification. The preference is for the Level 2 (detailed) categories to be adopted wherever possible. The two levels and the categories are:

Level 1	Level 2
White	White
	British
	Irish
	Other White background
	All White groups
Mixed	White and Black Caribbean
	White and Black African
	White and Asian
	Other Mixed background
	All Mixed groups
Asian or Asian British	Indian
	Pakistani
	Bangladeshi
	Other Asian background
	All Asian groups
Black or Black British	Caribbean
	African
	Other Black Background
	All Black Groups
Chinese or other ethnic group	
	Chinese
	Other ethnic group
	All Chinese or Other groups
All ethnic groups	All ethnic groups
Not stated	Not stated

Direct comparisons should not be made between the figures produced using this new classification and those based on the previous classification.

Further details can be found on the National Statistics website:

www.statistics.gov.uk/about/classifications/downloads/ns_ethnicity_statement.doc

National Statistics Socio-economic Classification

From 2001 the National Statistics Socio-economic Classification (NS-SEC) has been used for all official statistics and surveys. It replaces Social Class based on Occupation (SC) and Socio-economic Groups (SEG).

The NS-SEC is an occupationally-based classification designed to provide coverage of the whole adult population. The version of the classification, which will be used for most analyses, has eight classes, the first of which can be subdivided. These are:

1. Higher managerial and professional occupations

1.1 Large employers and higher managerial occupations

1.2 Higher professional occupations

2. Lower managerial and professional occupations

3. Intermediate occupations

4. Small employers and own account workers

5. Lower supervisory and technical occupations

6. Semi-routine occupations

7. Routine occupations

8. Never worked and long-term unemployed

For complete coverage, the three categories: Students; Occupations not stated or inadequately described; and Not classifiable for other reasons are added as 'Not classified'.

Further details can be found on the National Statistics website:

www.statistics.gov.uk/methods_quality/ns_sec/default.asp

International migration estimates

A migrant is defined as a person who changes his or her country of usual residence for a period of at least a year, so that the country of destination effectively becomes the country of usual residence.

Data from 1991 onwards are derived from three data sources and represent total international migration:

1. The International Passenger Survey (IPS) is a sample survey of all passengers travelling through major air and seaports of the United Kingdom. Routes to and from the Irish Republic are excluded from the survey as well as diplomats and military personnel. The IPS data also exclude persons seeking asylum after entering the country and short-term visitors granted extensions of stay. Migration between the Channel Islands or the Isle of Man and the rest of the world was previously included in the total migration to the United Kingdom. From 1988 this has been excluded.

2. The Home Office provides data on people who entered the United Kingdom as asylum seekers, or as short-term visitors who were subsequently granted an extension of stay for a year or more, for example as asylum seekers, students or on the basis of marriage. Also included is an estimate of those asylum seekers that failed in their application and were subsequently removed.

3. Information on migration between the United Kingdom and the Irish Republic from the Irish Labour Force Survey and the National Health Service Central Register agreed between the Irish Central Statistics Office and the Office for National Statistics.

For years prior to 1991 data are based only on data from the IPS. After taking account of persons leaving the United Kingdom for a short-term period, but who stayed overseas for longer than originally intended, the adjustment needed to net migration ranges from about 10,000 in 1981 to just over 20,000 in 1986.

Results from the 2001 Census have shown that, by combining data from these three sources, net inward migration to the UK has been overestimated. Therefore, an adjustment has been made to these data to take account of this known overestimation. After allowing for the removal of failed asylum seekers, this is approximately 76,000 each year. This adjustment is consistent with the interim population estimates and the interim 2001-based population projections.

These estimates will be further revised following additional information from the 2001 Census and subsequent research in 2003. These revisions will affect both the internal and international migration estimates shown in the volume.

Citizenship

Citizenship of the country groups in Table 1.12 refers to the countries as they were constituted on 1 January 2000.

European Union (EU) is defined as Austria, Belgium, Denmark, Finland, France, Germany, Greece, Italy, Luxembourg, the Netherlands, Portugal, Spain, Sweden, the Irish Republic and the United Kingdom.

Old Commonwealth is defined as Australia, Canada, New Zealand and South Africa.

New Commonwealth is defined as all other Commonwealth countries, British Dependent Territories and British Overseas citizens in tables by citizenship. This excludes Hong Kong.

Other includes the Middle East (defined as Bahrain, Iran, Iraq, Israel, Jordan, Kuwait, Lebanon, Oman, Qatar, Saudi Arabia, Syria, the United Arab Emirates and Yemen), the rest of Europe, rest of America, rest of Asia, rest of Africa and rest of Oceania.

Part 2: Households and Families

Although definitions differ slightly across surveys and the census, they are broadly similar.

Households

A household: is a person living alone or a group of people who have the address as their only or main residence and who either share one meal a day or share the living accommodation.

Students: living in halls of residence are recorded under their parents' household and included in the parents' family type in the Labour Force Survey (LFS), although some surveys/projections include such students in the institutional population.

Families

Children: are never-married people of any age who live with one or both parents. They also include stepchildren, adopted children (but not foster children) and also grandchildren (where the parents are absent).

Dependent children: in the 1971 Census, dependent children were defined as never-married children in families who were either under 15 years of age, or aged 15 to 24 and in full-time education. In the 1991 Census, the LFS and the General Household Survey (GHS), dependent children are childless never-married children in families who are aged under 16, or aged 16 to 18 and in full-time education.

A family: is a married or cohabiting couple, either with or without their never-married child or children (of any age), including couples with no children or a lone parent together with his or her never-married child(ren). A family could also consist of grandparent(s) with grandchild or grandchildren if the parents of the grandchild or grandchildren are not usually resident in the household. In the LFS, a family unit can also comprise a single person. LFS family units include non-dependent children (who can in fact be adult) – those aged 16 or over and not in full-time education provided they are never married and have no children of their own in the household.

A lone-parent family: (in the census) is a father or mother together with his or her never-married child or children.

A lone-parent family (in the LFS) consists of a lone parent, living with his or her never-married children, provided these children have no children of their own living with them.

A lone-parent family (in the GHS) consists of a lone parent, living with his or her never-married dependent children, provided these children have no children of their own. Married lone mothers whose husbands are not defined as resident in the household are not classified as lone parents. Evidence suggests the majority are separated from their husband either because he usually works away from home or for some other reason that does not imply the breakdown of the marriage.

Conceptions

Conception statistics used in Tables 2.14 and 2.15 include pregnancies that result in one or more live or still births, or a legal abortion under the *Abortion Act 1967*. Conception statistics do not include miscarriages or illegal abortions. Dates of conception are estimated using recorded gestation for abortions and still births, and assuming 38 weeks gestation for live births.

Average teenage fertility rate

Teenage fertility rates for Figure 2.18 are calculated for each age, summed and then divided by five to obtain the average rate for women aged 15 to 19. This methodology is consistent with the Council of Europe publication.

Part 3: Education and Training

Main categories of educational establishments

Educational establishments in the United Kingdom are administered and financed in several ways. Most schools are controlled by local education authorities (LEAs), which are part of the structure of local government, but some are 'assisted', receiving grants direct from central government sources and being controlled by governing bodies which have a substantial degree of autonomy. Outside the public sector and run by individuals, companies or charitable institutions are non-maintained schools.

Up to March 2001, further education (FE) courses in FE sector colleges in England and in Wales were largely funded through grants from the respective Further Education Funding Councils (FEFC). In April 2001, however, the Learning and Skills Council (LSC) took over the responsibility for funding the FE sector in England, and the National Council for Education and Training for Wales (part of Education and Learning Wales – ELWa) did so for Wales. The LSC in England is also responsible for funding provision for FE and some non-prescribed higher education in FE sector colleges; it also funds some FE provided by LEA maintained and other institutions referred to as 'external institutions'. In Wales, the National Council – ELWa, funds FE provision made by FE institutions via a third party or sponsored arrangements. The Scottish FEFC funds FE colleges in Scotland, while the Department for Employment and Learning funds FE colleges in Northern Ireland.

Higher education courses in higher education establishments are largely publicly funded through block grants from the HE funding councils in England and Scotland, the Higher Education Council – ELWa in Wales, and the Department of Employment and Learning in Northern Ireland. In addition, some designated HE (mainly HND/HNC Diplomas and Certificates of HE) is also funded by these sources. The FE sources mentioned above fund the remainder.

Numbers of school pupils are shown in Table 3.3. Nursery school figures for Scotland prior to 1998/99 only include data for local authority pre-schools. Data thereafter include partnership pre-schools. Secondary 'Other' schools largely consist of middle schools in England, and Secondary Intermediate schools in Northern Ireland. Special schools include maintained and non-maintained sectors, whilst public sector and non-maintained schools totals exclude special schools.

Stages of education

Education takes place in several stages: nursery (now part of the foundation stage in England), primary, secondary, further and higher education, and is compulsory for all children between the ages of 5 (4 in Northern Ireland) and 16. The non-compulsory fourth stage, further education, covers non-advanced education, which can be taken at both further (including tertiary) education colleges, higher education institutions and increasingly in secondary schools. The fifth stage, higher education, is study beyond GCE A levels and their equivalent, which, for most full-time students, takes place in higher education institutions.

Foundation stage

In recent years there has been a major expansion of pre-school education. Many children under 5 attend state nursery schools or nursery classes within primary schools. Others may attend playgroups in the voluntary sector or in privately run nurseries. In England and Wales many primary schools also operate an early admissions policy where they admit children under 5 into what are called 'reception classes'. The *Education Act 2002* extended the National Curriculum for England to include the foundation stage. The foundation stage was introduced in September 2000 and covers children's education from the age of three to the end of the reception year, when most are just five and some almost six years old. The 'Curriculum guidance for the foundation stage' supports practitioners in their delivery of the foundation stage.

In Table 3.2 the nursery education providers covered are nursery schools, nursery classes, reception classes, special day schools and nurseries (which usually provide care, education and play for children up to the age of five), playgroups and pre-schools (which provide childcare, play and early years education usually for children aged between two and five), and combined/family centres.

Primary education

The primary stage covers three age ranges: nursery (under 5), infant (5 to 7 or 8) and junior (up to 11 or 12) but in Scotland and Northern Ireland there is generally no distinction between infant and junior schools. Most public sector primary schools take both boys and girls in mixed classes. It is usual to transfer straight to secondary school at age 11 (in England, Wales and Northern Ireland) or 12 (in Scotland), but in England some children make the transition via middle schools catering for various age ranges between 8 and 14. Depending on their individual age ranges middle schools are classified as either primary or secondary.

Secondary education

Public provision of secondary education in an area may consist of a combination of different types of school, the pattern reflecting historical circumstances and the policy adopted by the LEA. Comprehensive schools largely admit pupils without reference to ability or aptitude and cater for all the children in a neighbourhood, but in some areas they co-exist with grammar, secondary modern or technical schools. In Northern Ireland, post-primary education is provided by secondary intermediate and grammar schools.

Special schools

Special schools (day or boarding) provide education for children who require specialist support to complete their education, for example because they have physical or other difficulties. Many pupils with special educational needs are educated in mainstream schools. All children attending special schools are offered a curriculum designed to overcome their learning difficulties and to enable them to become self-reliant.

Pupil referral units

Pupil referral units (PRUs) are legally a type of school established and maintained by a LEA to provide education for children of compulsory school age who may otherwise not receive suitable education. The aim of such units is to provide suitable alternative education on a temporary basis for pupils who may not be able to attend a mainstream school. The focus of the units should be to get pupils back into a mainstream school. Pupils in the units may include: teenage mothers, pupils excluded from school, school phobics and pupils in the assessment phase of a special educational needs statement.

Further education

The term further education may be used in a general sense to cover all non-advanced courses taken after the period of compulsory education, but more commonly it excludes those staying on at secondary school and those in higher education, i.e. courses in universities and colleges leading to qualifications above GCE A Level, Higher Grade (in Scotland), GNVQ/NVQ level 3, and their equivalents. Since 1 April 1993 sixth form colleges have been included in the further education sector.

In Table 3.12, snapshots were taken at around November to estimate the number of further education students each year up to 1997/98. Since 1998/99, whole year further education figures have been collected (except in Northern Ireland). Figures exclude adult education centres.

Higher education

Higher education is defined as courses that are of a standard that is higher than GCE A level, the Higher Grade of the Scottish Certificate of Education/National Qualification, GNVQ/NVQ level 3 or the Edexcel (formerly BTEC) or SQA National Certificate/Diploma. There are three main levels of HE course:

1. postgraduate courses are those leading to higher degrees, diplomas and certificates (including postgraduate certificates of education and professional qualifications) which usually require a first degree as entry qualification;

2. undergraduate courses which include first degrees, first degrees with qualified teacher

status, enhanced first degrees, first degrees obtained concurrently with a diploma, and intercalated first degrees;

3. other undergraduate courses which includes all other higher education courses, for example HNDs and Diplomas in HE. As a result of the *Further and Higher Education Act 1992*, former polytechnics and some other higher education institutions were designated as universities in 1992/93. Students normally attend HE courses at higher education institutions, but some attend at further education colleges. Some also attend institutions which do not receive public grants (such as the University of Buckingham) and these numbers are excluded from the tables.

Figures for higher education students in Table 3.12 are annual snapshots taken around November or December each year, depending on the type of institution, except for Scotland further education colleges from 1998/99, for which counts are based on the whole year. The Open University is included in these estimates.

For the destinations of first degree graduates in Table 3.16, 'Others' includes those students whose main activity was given as 'Seeking employment or training' and who had employment, study or training as a secondary activity. Up to 1990/91, this category also included Overseas graduates reported as returning overseas (no other information available) and those not available for employment, study or training. For 'All destinations known' from 1994/95, the number is based on known destinations excluding Overseas graduates reported as returning overseas (no other information available).

The National Curriculum

The *Education Act 2002* extended the National Curriculum for England to include the foundation stage. It has six areas of learning namely, personal, social and emotional development; communication, language and literacy; mathematical development; knowledge and understanding of the world; physical development; and creative development.

Under the *Education Reform Act 1988* a National Curriculum has been progressively introduced into primary and secondary schools in England and Wales. This consists of English (or the option of Welsh as a first language in

Wales), mathematics and science. The second level of curriculum additionally comprises the so-called 'foundation' subjects, such as history, geography, art, music, information technology, design and technology and physical education (and Welsh as a second language in Wales).

Measurable targets have been defined for four key stages, corresponding to ages 7, 11, 14 and 16. Pupils are assessed formally at the ages of 7, 11 and 14 by their teachers and by national tests in the core subjects of English, mathematics and science (and in Welsh speaking schools in Wales, Welsh). Sixteen year olds are assessed by means of the GCSE examination. Statutory authorities have been set up for England and for Wales to advise government on the National Curriculum and promote curriculum development generally. Statutory assessment at the end of key stage 1 in Wales in 2002 was by means of teacher assessment only.

In Wales the National Curriculum Tests/Tasks were discontinued in 2002 following the outcome of the public consultation on proposed changes to the assessment arrangements contained in *The Learning Country – A Comprehensive Education and Lifelong Learning Programme to 2010 in Wales*.

Northern Ireland has its own common curriculum that is similar but not identical to the National Curriculum in England and Wales. Assessment arrangements in Northern Ireland became statutory from September 1996 and key stage 1 pupils are assessed at the age of 8. Pupils in Northern Ireland are not assessed in science at key stages 1 and 2.

In Scotland there is no statutory national curriculum. Pupils aged 5 to 14 study a broad curriculum based on national guidelines, which set out the aims of study, the ground to be covered and the way the pupils' learning should be assessed and reported.

Progress is measured by attainment of six levels based on the expectation of the performance of the majority of pupils on completion of certain stages between the ages of 5 and 14: primary 3 (age 7/8), primary 4 (age 8/9), primary 7 (age 11/12) and secondary 2 (age 13/14). It is recognised that pupils learn at different rates and some will reach the various levels before others.

The curriculum areas are: language; mathematics; environmental studies; expressive arts; and religious and moral education with personal and social development and health education. Though school curricula are the responsibility of education authorities and individual head teachers, in practice almost all 14 to 16 year olds study mathematics, English, science, a modern foreign language, a social subject, physical education, religious and moral education, technology and a creative and aesthetic subject.

England	Attainment expected
Key stage 1	Level 2 or above
Key stage 2	Level 4 or above
Key stage 3	Level 5/6 or above
Key stage 4	GCSE

Qualifications

In England, Wales and Northern Ireland the main examination for school pupils at the minimum school leaving age is the General Certificate of Secondary Education (GCSE) which can be taken in a wide range of subjects. This replaced the GCE O Level and CSE examinations in 1987 (1988 in Northern Ireland). In England, Wales and Northern Ireland the GCSE is awarded in eight grades, A* to G, the highest four (A* to C) being regarded as equivalent to O level grades A to C or CSE grade 1.

GCE A Level is usually taken after a further two years of study in a sixth form or equivalent, passes being graded from A (the highest) to E (the lowest).

Following the 'Qualifying for Success' consultation in 1997, a number of reforms were introduced to the 16 to 19 qualifications structure in September 2000. Under these reforms, students were encouraged to follow a wide range of subjects in their first year of post-16 study, with students expected to study four Advanced Subsidiaries before progressing three of them on to full A levels in their second year. In addition, students are encouraged to study a combination of both general and vocational advanced level examinations. A new vocational A level is replacing the Advanced GNVQ.

The Advanced Subsidiary (AS) qualification covers the first half of the full A level. New specifications introduced in 2001 are now in place and A levels now comprise of units, normally six for a full A level (now A2) and three for the AS level. The full A level is normally taken either over two years (modular) or a set of exams at the end of the two years (linear). The AS is a qualification in its own right, whereas A2 modules do not make up a qualification in their own right.

From 1999/2000 National Qualifications (NQ) were introduced in Scotland. NQs include Standard Grades, Intermediate 1 and 2 and Higher Grades. Pupils study for the Scottish Certificate of Education (SCE)/NQ Standard Grade, approximately equivalent to GCSE, in their third and fourth years of secondary schooling (roughly ages 14 and 15). Each subject has several elements, some of which are internally assessed in school, and an award is only made (on a scale of 1 to 7) if the whole course has been completed and examined. The Higher Grade requires one further year of study and for the more able candidates the range of subjects taken may be as wide as at Standard Grade with as many as five or six subjects spanning both arts and science. Three or more Highers are regarded as being approximately the equivalent of two or more GCE A levels.

After leaving school, people can study towards higher academic qualifications such as degrees. However, a large number of people choose to study towards qualifications aimed at a particular occupation or group of occupations – these qualifications are called vocational qualifications.

Vocational qualifications can be split into three groups, namely National Vocational Qualifications (NVQs), General National Vocational Qualifications (GNVQs) and other vocational qualifications.

NVQs are based on an explicit statement of competence derived from an analysis of employment requirements. They are awarded at five levels. Scottish Vocational Qualifications (SVQs) are the Scottish equivalent.

GNVQs are a vocational alternative to GCSEs and GCE A levels. They are awarded at three levels: Foundation, Intermediate and Advanced. The Advanced level is being replaced by vocational A levels. General Scottish Vocational Qualifications (GSVQs) are the Scottish equivalent.

There are also a large number of other vocational qualifications, which are not NVQs, SVQs, GNVQs or GSVQs, for example, a BTEC Higher National Diploma or a City and Guilds Craft award.

Other qualifications (including academic qualifications) are often expressed as being equivalent to a particular NVQ level so that comparisons can be made more easily.

An NVQ level 5 is equivalent to a Higher Degree.

An NVQ level 4 is equivalent to a First Degree, a HND or HNC, a BTEC Higher Diploma, an RSA Higher Diploma, a nursing qualification or other Higher Education.

An NVQ level 3 is equivalent to two A levels, an advanced GNVQ, an RSA advanced diploma, a City & Guilds advanced craft, an OND or ONC or a BTEC National Diploma.

An NVQ level 2 is equivalent to five GCSEs at grades A* to C, an Intermediate GNVQ, an RSA diploma, a City and Guilds craft or a BTEC first or general diploma.

For achievement at GCE A level shown in Table 3.9, data up to 1999/00, for England, Wales and Northern Ireland, are for pupils in schools and students in further education institutions aged 17 to 19 at the start of the academic year as a percentage of the 18 year old population. For 2000/01, data are for pupils in schools and students in further education institutions aged 18 to 19 at the end of the academic year in England, for those aged 18 in Wales, and those aged 17 to 19 in Northern Ireland, as a percentage of the 18 year old population. In Scotland pupils generally sit Highers one year earlier than the rest of the UK sit A levels. The figures for Scotland relate to the results of pupils in year 5 (secondary) as a percentage of the 17 year old population.

In Table 3.17 'Other qualifications' includes the academic qualifications GCSE grades D to G, NVQ Level 1 and Foundation GNVQ, and vocational qualifications such as BTEC general certificates, YT certificates, RSA qualifications (below diploma) and City and Guilds (below craft award).

Student Support

Up to and including academic year 1997/98 students were funded under the student support system. The system was introduced in 1990/91 when non income-assessed student loans were introduced to provide extra resources towards living expenses and to partially replace grants. The main grant rates were frozen at their 1990/91 values until 1994/95 when the shift from grant to loan was accelerated by reducing the level of grant rates and increasing loan rates. Broad parity between the main rates of grant and loans was achieved in the academic year 1996/97.

New student support arrangements in higher education came into effect on 12 August 1998. In 1998/99, new entrants to full-time higher education courses were, with certain specified exceptions, expected to contribute up to around £1,000 a year (£1,075 in 2001/02) towards the cost of their tuition. The amount depends on their own and, if appropriate, their parents' or spouse's income. The exceptions were entitled to pre-1998/99 support arrangements. For the first year of the new scheme (1998/99), eligible new entrants received support for living costs through both grants and loans. Grants, which were assessed against family income formed about a quarter of the support available, on average. All students were entitled to a non income-assessed loan, which comprised the remaining three quarters of support available.

Apart from the transitional year of 1998/99, most new students entering higher education from this date received support mostly through loans. The 'standard grant' figures from 1998/99 in Figure 3.26 refer to rates of grant applicable to students who are eligible to receive grants under the mandatory awards scheme funding arrangements.

New students from 1999/2000, together with those who started in 1998/99, received support for living costs mainly through loans which are partly income-assessed. Grants for living costs are no longer available except for some limited allowances, eg for students with dependants; students who require assistance with travel, books and equipment, lone parent students, students leaving care, students with dependent children who are eligible for school meals grants, and disabled students. The amount available to students through loans has increased to compensate for the reduction in grants. Repayment of these loans will be linked to income after leaving university or college so that leavers only repay as and when they can afford to (while the loans of those who started their course before 1998/99 are repayable on a mortgage style basis).

The financial support arrangements for existing mandatory award holders and other students on courses which began before 1 August 1998, and those new students who are exceptionally treated as existing award holders for the purposes of the Mandatory Awards Regulations, remain largely unchanged. Tuition fees for these students continue to be paid in full by LEAs where the student is eligible for a mandatory award. These students will also receive a grant towards their maintenance for the duration of their course. All existing students remain eligible for loans repayable on a mortgage-style (fixed term) basis.

Mandatory awards are made to students who fulfil certain residence conditions and who satisfy the other conditions laid down by the Education (Mandatory Awards) Regulations, attending 'designated' higher education courses in the United Kingdom. 'Designated' courses are principally those leading to a first degree or equivalent qualification, all approved initial teacher training qualifications (including the Postgraduate Certificate in Education), a University Certificate or Diploma, Higher National Diploma and the Diploma of Higher Education. Students not eligible for mandatory awards may qualify for other forms of support including discretionary awards and Career Development Loans.

Adult education

Academic and vocational courses (Schedule 2 courses which generally lead to some form of qualification) are those courses of further education for which the *Further and Higher Education Act 1992* required the then FEFC, and from April 2001, the LSC to secure adequate national provision. Other courses are those not included in Schedule 2 to the *Further and Higher Education Act 1992*.

In Table 3.13 'Independent living' courses are for adults with learning difficulties which are not aiming to prepare them for entry to a

schedule course. 'Role education' includes courses on pre-retirement, stress management, assertiveness training, managing investments, committee skills, parenting, counselling, the 'gender agenda' and self-advocacy.

Learning and Training at Work

Learning and Training at Work 2001 (LTW 2001) is the third in what is now an annual series of employer surveys that investigate the provision of learning and training at work.

Learning and training information had previously been collected, along with information on recruitment difficulties, and skill shortages and gaps, in the annual Skill Needs in Britain (SNIB) surveys, which were carried out between 1990 and 1998.

The objectives of the LTW 2001 survey were to collect information about:

1. the volume, type and pattern of off-the-job training;

2. key indicators of employers' commitment to training, such as Investors in People;

3. learning opportunities offered; and

4. awareness of, and involvement with, a number of initiatives relevant to training.

The LTW 2001 survey consisted of 4,006 telephone interviews with employers having 1 or more employees at the specific location sampled. All business sectors, public and private, with the exception of schools and LEAs were covered. The main stage of interviewing was carried out between 20 October and 4 December 2001. The overall response rate from employers was 63 per cent, acceptable for a study of this nature. Sample design involved setting separate sample targets for each cell on a government office region by industry sector by establishment size matrix. In contrast the former SNIB survey covered employers with 25 or more employees in all business sectors, except agriculture, hunting, forestry and fishing, in Great Britain.

Programme for International Student Assessment

The Programme for International Student Assessment (PISA) is a collaborative study among 28 member countries of the Organisation for Economic Co-operation and Development (OECD), plus Hungary, Latvia,

Liechtenstein and the Russian Federation. Its main purpose is to assess the knowledge and skills of 15 year olds in three broad areas of literacy: reading, mathematics and science. PISA was carried out in 32 countries in 2000 when the main focus was on reading literacy, and will be repeated in 2003 and 2006, when the main focuses will be literacy in mathematics and science, respectively. ONS carried out the Survey in England and Northern Ireland. The Scottish Executive carried out a separate study in Scotland.

In each domain of literacy, a student's score is expressed as a number of points on a scale, and shows the highest difficulty of task that the student is likely to be able to complete. The scales are constructed so that the average score for students from all countries participating in PISA 2000 is 500 and its standard deviation is 100 – that is, about two thirds of students internationally score between 400 and 600. Each country contributes equally to this average irrespective of its size.

Differences in PISA scores between countries should not be taken to result solely from differences in schooling, but rather from differences in the cumulative effect of learning experiences, because learning starts before school and occurs in different institutional and out-of-school settings. It should be noted that some of these differences are due to the standard errors around the estimates.

Part 4: Labour Market

Labour Force Survey (LFS) reweighting

The results from the 2001 Census, published in September 2002, showed that previous estimates of the total UK population were around one million too high. As a result, ONS published interim revised estimates of the population for the years 1982 to 2001 which are consistent with the 2001 Census findings. In addition the Government Actuary's Department has published interim national population projections for 2002 onwards. Interim national LFS estimates consistent with the latest population data have now been produced.

The interim mid-year population estimates and projections are available by age and sex and these have been used to produce interim revised LFS estimates of employment, unemployment and inactivity by age and sex. Other LFS analyses, eg full/part-time, have been produced by scaling to this age/sex adjusted data. A full reweighting of the LFS dataset is not available until further population estimates and projections are published. In the meantime, national LFS estimates will be adjusted using a time series of factors based on age bands and sex. These factors have been applied to the existing LFS data and summed to obtain new aggregate LFS totals.

The working age employment rate – the percentage of the working-age population who are in employment – was little affected. Almost all of the population revisions were among men aged 25 to 49. As a result it is the estimates of employment for men in this age group which are most affected. The employment revisions for women are small. Estimates of unemployment and unemployment rates are relatively little affected by the population revisions.

Initial analysis work conducted by the ONS has shown that revisions to the LFS census-adjusted data have a greater impact on levels than on rates. Generally, revisions to rates are within sampling variability whilst those for levels are not.

ONS will complete a full re–weighting of all series and databases by summer 2003. This will allow the interim revised series to be replaced by final estimates. The following items will be updated on the National Statisitics website: 4.1, 4.2, 4.5, 4.7, 4.10, 4.17 and 4.19

For more information see: www.statistics.gov.uk/cci/nugget.asp?id=207

Annual Local Area Labour Force Survey

Estimates coming from the Annual Local Area Labour Force Survey (ALALFS) use data compiled annually from the main LFS together with additional interviews in England and Wales.

The ALALFS data presented here have been weighted to be consistent with the best population estimates available before the results of the 2001 Census were published. New regional and local mid-year population estimates for 1992 to 2000, which are consistent with the 2001 Census figures, will be published by ONS in early spring 2003. When these data are available, a reweighting of all the LFS series will be carried out. The data presented here will then be replaced by final estimates, which are consistent with the new population estimates derived from the 2001 Census.

Unemployment

The ILO definition of unemployment refers to people without a job who were available to start work within two weeks and had either looked for work in the previous four weeks or were waiting to start a job they had already obtained. Estimates on this basis are not available before 1984, as the LFS did not then collect information on job search over a four week period. The former GB/UK Labour Force definition of unemployment, the only one available for estimates up to 1984, counted people not in employment and seeking work in a reference week (or prevented from seeking work by a temporary sickness or holiday, or waiting for the results of a job application, or waiting to start a job they had already obtained), whether or not they were available to start (except students not able to start because they had to complete their education).

Following a quality review of its labour market statistics, the ONS have re-labelled 'ILO unemployment' as 'unemployment'. This emphasises that the LFS figures provide the official, and only internationally comparable, measure of unemployment in the UK. Claimant count data will continue to be published monthly to provide further information about the labour market, but these will not be presented as an alternative measure of UK unemployment.

Standard Occupation Classification

The new Standard Occupation Classification (SOC) 2000 replaces SOC90 in analyses of the LFS from spring 2001. The main features of the revision include a tighter definition of managerial occupations and an overhaul of new occupations introduced as a result of new technology (for example areas such as computing, the environment and conservation, and customer service occupations). There is no exact correspondence between SOC90 and SOC2000 at any level. Most of the major

groups have been renamed and all have a different composition in SOC2000 compared with SOC90. More details may be found in an article in *Labour Market Trends*, July 2001 (pp357-364).

Disabled People

The focus and number of questions in the heath and disability module of the LFS questionnaire changed in spring 1997 to reflect the *Disability Discrimination Act 1995 (DDA)*. From spring 2001 the LFS asks all its working age respondents: 'Do you have any health problems or disabilities that you expect will last more that a year?'

If they answer yes to this question, they are also asked to say what kind(s) of health problem or disability(ies) they have, based on a list read to them by the interviewer.

If they then answer yes to the following question:

'Does this (do these) health problem(s) or disability(ies) (when taken singly or together) substantially limit your ability to carry out normal day-to-day activities?'

or they said they had the following health problems:

Progressive illness not included elsewhere (eg cancer, multiple sclerosis, symptomatic HIV, Parkinson's disease, muscular dystrophy) then they are defined as having a current disability covered by the DDA.

People whose health problem(s) or disability(ies) are expected to last more than a year are also asked the following questions: 'Does this health problem affect the kind of paid work that you might do? Or the amount of paid work that you might do?'

If the respondent fulfils either of these criteria, they are defined as having a work-limiting disability.

Those who meet the criteria for either (or both) DDA or work-limiting definitions of disability are described as having a current long-term disability.

For more information, see 'Labour Market experiences of people with disabilities', pp415-427, *Labour Market Trends*, August 2002.

Part 5: Income and Wealth

Household sector

The data for the household sector as derived from the national accounts have been compiled according to the definitions and conventions set out in the European System of Accounts 1995 (ESA95). At present, estimates for the household sector cannot be separated from the sector for non-profit institutions serving households and so the data in *Social Trends* cover both sectors. The most obvious example of a non-profit institution is a charity: this sector also includes many other organisations of which universities, trade unions and clubs and societies are the most important. The household sector differs from the personal sector, as defined in the national accounts prior to the introduction of ESA95, in that it excludes unincorporated private businesses apart from sole traders. More information is given in *United Kingdom National Accounts Concepts, Sources and Methods* published by The Stationery Office.

In ESA95, household income includes the value of National Insurance contributions made by employers on behalf of their employees. It also shows property income (that is, income from investments) net of payments of interest on loans. In both these respects, national accounts conventions diverge from those normally used when collecting data on household income from household surveys. Employees are usually unaware of value of the National Insurance contributions made on their behalf by their employer, and so such data are rarely collected. Payments of interest are usually regarded as items of expenditure rather than reductions of income. Thus for the first time in *Social Trends*, the national accounts data for household sector income have been adjusted to omit employers' National Insurance contributions and to express property income gross of any payments of interest on loans, in order to increase comparability with the data on income derived from household surveys used elsewhere in the chapter.

Individual income

Gross individual income refers to the weekly personal income of women and men before deduction of income tax and National Insurance contributions as reported in the Family Resources Survey. Net individual income is weekly gross income plus tax credits, less deductions for National Insurance contributions and income tax payments. Gross income includes: earnings, income from self-employment, investments and occupational pensions/annuities, benefit income, and income from miscellaneous other sources. It excludes income which accrues at household level, such as council tax benefit. Income from couples' joint investment accounts is assumed to be received equally. Benefit income paid in respect of dependants such as Child Benefit is included in the individual income of the person nominated for the receipt of payments, except for married pensioner couples, where state retirement pension payments are separated and assigned to the man and woman according to their entitlements. Full details of the concepts and definitions used may be found in *Individual Income 1996/97 to 2000/01* available on the Women and Equality Unit website www.womenandequalityunit.gov.uk or from the Information and Analysis Division, Department for Work and Pensions.

Equivalisation scales

The Department for Work and Pensions (DWP), the Office for National Statistics (ONS), the Institute for Fiscal Studies (IFS) and the Institute for Social and Economic Research (ISER) all use McClements equivalence scales in their analysis of the income distribution, to take into account variations in the size and composition of households. This reflects the common sense notion that a household of five adults will need a higher income than will a single person living alone to enjoy a comparable standard of living. An overall equivalence value is calculated for each household by summing the appropriate scale values for each household member. Equivalised household income is then calculated by dividing household income by the household's equivalence value. The scales conventionally take a married couple as the reference point with an equivalence value of 1; equivalisation therefore tends to increase relatively the incomes of single person households (since their incomes are divided by a value of less than 1) and to reduce incomes of households with three or more persons. For further information see *Households Below Average Income*, Corporate Document Services, Department for Work and Pensions.

The DWP and IFS both use different scales for adjustment of income before and after the deduction of housing costs.

McClements equivalence scales:

Household member	Before housing costs	After housing costs
First adult (head)	0.61	0.55
Spouse of head	0.39	0.45
Other second adult	0.46	0.45
Third adult	0.42	0.45
Subsequent adults	0.36	0.40
Each dependant aged:		
0-1	0.09	0.07
2-4	0.18	0.18
5-7	0.21	0.21
8-10	0.23	0.23
11-12	0.25	0.26
13-15	0.27	0.28
16 or over	0.36	0.38

Redistribution of income (ROI)

Estimates of the incidence of taxes and benefits on household income, based on the Expenditure and Food Survey (EFS), formally the Family Expenditure Survey (FES), are published by the ONS in *Economic Trends*. The article covering 2000/01 was published on the NS website in April 2002 and appeared in the May 2002 edition of *Economic Trends*, and contains details of the definitions and methods used.

Households Below Average Income (HBAI)

Information on the distribution of income based on the Family Resources Survey is provided in the DWP publication *Households Below Average Income: 1994/95 – 2000/01*, available both in hard copy and on the DWP website. This publication provides estimates of patterns of personal disposable income in Great Britain, and of changes in income over time in the United Kingdom. It attempts to measure people's potential living standards as determined by disposable income. Although as the title would suggest, HBAI concentrates on the lower part of the income distribution, it also provides estimates covering the whole of the income distribution.

Disposable household income includes all flows of income into the household, principally earnings, benefits, occupational and private pensions, and investments. It is net of tax, employees' National Insurance contributions, Council Tax, contributions to occupational pension schemes (including additional voluntary contributions), maintenance and child support payments, and parental contributions to students living away from home.

Two different measures of disposable income are used in HBAI: before and after housing costs are deducted. Housing costs consist of rent, water rates, community water charges and council water charges, mortgage interest payments, structural insurance, ground rent and service charges.

Difference between Households Below Average Income and Redistribution of Income series

These are two separate and distinct income series produced by two different government departments. Each series has been developed to serve the specific needs of that department. The DWP series, HBAI, provides estimates of patterns of disposable income and of changes over time and shows disposable income before and after housing costs (where disposable income is as defined in the section on HBAI above). The ONS series, ROI, shows how Government intervention through the tax and benefit system affects the income of households. It covers the whole income distribution and includes the effects of indirect taxes, like VAT and duty on beer, as well as estimating the cash value of benefits in kind (eg from state spending on education and healthcare). The ROI results are designed to show the position in a particular year rather than trends in income levels over time, although trends in the distribution of income are given. An important difference between the two series is that HBAI counts individuals and ROI counts households. Also, whereas ROI provides estimates for the United Kingdom, from 1994/95 onwards HBAI provides estimates for Great Britain only.

Net wealth of the household sector

Revised balance sheet estimates of the net wealth of the household (and non-profit institutions) sector were published in an article in *Economic Trends* (November 1999). These figures are based on the new international system of national accounting and incorporate data from new sources. Quarterly estimates of net financial wealth (excluding tangible and intangible assets) are published in *Financial Statistics.*

Distribution of personal wealth

The estimates of the distribution of the marketable wealth of individuals relate to all adults in the United Kingdom. They are produced by combining Inland Revenue (IR) estimates of the distribution of wealth identified by the estate multiplier method with independent estimates of total personal wealth derived from the ONS national accounts balance sheets. Estimates for 1995 onwards have been compiled on the basis of the new System of National Accounts, but estimates for earlier years are on the old basis. The methods used were described in an article in *Economic Trends* (October 1990) entitled 'Estimates of the Distribution of Personal Wealth'. Net wealth of the personal sector differs from marketable wealth for the following reasons:

Difference in coverage: the ONS balance sheet of the personal sector includes the wealth of non-profit making bodies and unincorporated businesses, while the IR estimates exclude non-profit making bodies and treat the bank deposits and debts of unincorporated businesses differently from ONS;

Differences in timing: the ONS balance sheet gives values at the end of the year, whereas IR figures are adjusted to mid-year;

IR figures: exclude the wealth of those under 18.

Funded pensions: are included in the ONS figures (including personal pensions) but not in the IR marketable wealth. Also the ONS balance sheet excludes consumer durables and includes non-marketable tenancy rights, whereas the IR figures include consumer

durables and exclude non-marketable tenancy rights.

Household Satellite Account

The ONS is developing a Household Satellite Account (HHSA) which for the first time measures and values the outputs produced by households in the UK. This unpaid work is not included in the UK National Accounts.

The HHSA brings together estimates of the output of housing, transport, nutrition, clothing and laundry, childcare, adult care and voluntary activity, and shows the related inputs of intermediate consumption and household capital, and the calculation of gross and net value added.

A variety of sources have been used to estimate the volume of output (number of journeys provided, number of meals produced etc) and value them using the price of an equivalent good or service provided by the market. The value of inputs of purchased goods and services is then subtracted.

Adjustments have to be made to avoid double-counting. For example the price of a meal in a restaurant includes the cost of the premises and any transport required for food shopping. The household production of these is valued in the housing and transport elements respectively. Thus a proportion of total housing and transport output must therefore be deducted from the nutrition output to avoid double-counting.

Removing the inputs of purchased goods and services and making the adjustment for inputs of household production gives the gross value added by households.

More information on the concepts and methodology may be found on the ONS website: www.statistics.gov.uk/hhsa.

Contributions to and receipts from the EC budget

The figures in Table 5.32 come from the European Commission's Report on the Allocation of 2000 EU Operating Expenditure and the European Court of Auditors' (ECA) Annual Report on the 2000 EC Budget.

Contribution figures are after account is taken of the UK's abatement and the bringing to account of surpluses and deficits in respect of

Member States' contributions in earlier years. The information in the ECA report does not attribute all Community expenditure to the Member States. For example, not all administrative expenditure is attributed. The figures shown for the net position should not, therefore, be regarded as definitive.

Part 6: Expenditure

Household expenditure

The national accounts definition of household expenditure, within household final consumption expenditure, consists of: personal expenditure on goods (durable, semi-durable and non-durable) and services, including the value of income in kind; imputed rent for owner-occupied dwellings; and the purchase of second-hand goods less the proceeds of sales of used goods. Excluded are interest and other transfer payments; all business expenditure; and the purchase of land and buildings (and associated costs). This national accounts definition is also used for regional analysis of household income.

In principle, expenditure is measured at the time of acquisition rather than actual disbursement of cash. The categories of expenditure include that of non-resident as well as resident households and individuals in the United Kingdom.

The methods used for estimating expenditure at constant prices often depend on the methods used for the current price estimates. Where the current price estimate is in value terms only, it is deflated by an appropriate price index. The indices most widely used for this purpose are components of the retail prices index (RPI). The index does not, however, cover the whole range of household final consumption expenditure, and other indices have to be used or estimated where necessary. If no other appropriate price index is available the general consumer price index implied by the estimates of household expenditure at current and constant prices on all other goods and services is used. Where the estimate at current prices is one of quantity multiplied by current average value, the estimate at constant prices is in most cases the same quantity multiplied by the average value in the base year. All these revaluations are

carried out in as great detail as practicable.

For further details see the article entitled 'Consumers expenditure' in *Economic Trends,* September 1983.

From April 2001, the Family Expenditure Survey (FES) was replaced by the Expenditure and Food Survey (EFS). This was formed by merging the FES with the National Food Survey (NFS). It continues to produce the information previously provided by the FES.

The EFS definition of household expenditure represents current expenditure on goods and services. This excludes those recorded payments that are savings or investments (eg life assurance premiums). Similarly, income tax payments, National Insurance contributions, mortgage capital repayments and other payments for major additions to dwellings are excluded. For further details see *Family Spending.*

Household reference person

The concept of head of household has been replaced on all government-sponsored household surveys after 2000/01 with 'household reference person'. The household reference person is identified during the interview and is defined as the member of the household who:

1. owns the household accommodation;

2. is legally responsible for the rent of the accommodation;

3. has the household accommodation as an emolument or perquisite, or

4. has the household accommodation by virtue of some relationship to the owner who is not a member of the household.

The household reference person must always be a householder, whereas the head of household was always the husband, who might not be a householder. If there are joint householders, the household reference person will be the householder with the highest income.

Classification of individual consumption by purpose

From 2001/02, the Classification of Individual Consumption by Purpose (COICOP) was introduced as a new coding frame for expenditure items in the Expenditure and Food Survey. COICOP has been adapted to the needs of Household Budget Surveys (HBS) across the EU and, as a consequence, is compatible with similar classifications used in national accounts and consumer price indices. This allows the production of indicators which are comparable Europe-wide, such as the Harmonised Indices of Consumer Prices.

Twelve categories are used and in this edition of Social Trends they are labelled as food and non-alcoholic drink; alcohol and tobacco; clothing and footwear; housing, water and fuel; household goods and services; health; transport; communication; recreation and culture; education; restaurants and hotels; and miscellaneous goods and services. Categories using the new COICOP and the old FES coding frame are not comparable and consequently time series data have not been published in this year's expenditure chapter of Social Trends.

A major difference also exists in the treatment of rent and mortgages which were included as part of 'housing' expenditure in the previous editions of Social Trends in the FES coding frame. Rent and mortgages are now excluded from the COICOP 'housing, water and fuel' category and are recorded under 'other expenditure items.'

Retired households

Retired households are those where the head of the household is retired. All male heads of household are 65 years of age or more; all female heads of household are 60 years of age or more. For analysis purposes two categories are used in this report:

a. 'A retired household mainly dependent upon state pensions,' also known as a pensioner household, is one in which at least three quarters of the total income of the household is derived from National Insurance retirement and similar pensions, including housing and other benefits paid in supplement to or instead of such pensions. The term 'National Insurance retirement and similar pensions' includes National Insurance disablement and war disability pensions, and income support in conjunction with these disability payments.

b. 'Other retired households'" are households that do not fulfil the income conditions of 'pensioner' households because more than a quarter of the household income derives from occupational retirement pensions and/or income from investments, annuities etc.

Retail Prices Index

The general index of retail prices (RPI) is the main domestic measure of inflation in the UK. It measures the average change from month to month in the prices of goods and services purchased by most households in the United Kingdom. The spending pattern on which the index is based is revised each year, mainly using information from the Family Expenditure Survey and its successor, the Expenditure and Food Survey, which was introduced in April 2001. The expenditure of certain higher income households, and of pensioner households mainly dependent on state pensions, is excluded.

These households are:

a. the 4 per cent (approximately) where the total household recorded gross income exceeds a certain amount (£1,363 a week in 2000/01).

b. 'pensioner' households consisting of retired people who derive at least three quarters of their income from state benefits.

Expenditure patterns of one-person and two-person pensioner households differ from those of the households upon which the general index is based. Separate indices have been compiled for such pensioner households since 1969, and quarterly averages are published on the National Statistics website, Focus on Consumer Price Indices (formerly known as the Consumer Price Indices (CPI) Business Monitor MM23). They are chain indices constructed in the same way as the general index of retail prices. It should, however, be noted that the pensioner indices exclude housing costs.

A guide to the RPI can be found on the National Statistics website: www.statistics.gov.uk/rpi. Additional information on data, articles and publication can be found under 'Related links' on this page.

Harmonised index of consumer prices

The harmonised indices of consumer prices (HICPs) are calculated in each member state of the European Union for the purposes of European comparisons, as required by the Maastricht Treaty. From January 1999 the HICP has been used by the European Central Bank (ECB) as the measure for its definition of price stability across the Euro area. Further details are contained in an ECB Press Notice released on 13 October 1998: 'A stability oriented monetary policy strategy for the ESCB'.

The methodology of the HICP is similar to that of the RPI but differs in the following ways:

1. in the HICP, the geometric mean is used to aggregate the prices at the most basic level whereas the RPI uses arithmetic means;

2. a number of RPI series are excluded from the HICP, most particularly, those mainly relating to owner occupiers' housing costs (eg mortgage interest payments, house depreciation, council tax and buildings insurance);

3. the coverage of the HICP indices is based on the international classification system, COICOP (classification of individual consumption by purpose). Whereas the RPI uses its own bespoke classification;

4. the HICP includes series for air fares, university accommodation fees, foreign students' university tuition fees, unit trust and stockbrokers charges, none of which are included in the RPI;

5. the index for new car prices in the RPI is imputed from movements in second hand car prices, whereas the HICP uses a quality adjusted index based on published prices of new cars;

6. the HICP weights are based on expenditure by all private households, foreign visitors to the UK and residents of institutional households. In the RPI, weights are based on expenditure by private households only, excluding the highest income households, and pensioner households mainly dependent on state benefits, and

7. in the construction of the RPI weights, expenditure on insurance is assigned to the relevant insurance heading. For the HICP weights, the amount paid out in insurance claims is distributed amongst the COICOP headings according to the nature of the claims expenditure with the residual (i.e. the service charge) being allocated to the relevant insurance heading.

Comparative price levels

Comparative price levels (CPL) are defined as the ratio of Purchasing power parities (PPP) to exchange rates and provide a measure of the differences in price levels between countries. PPPs are the rates of currency conversion that eliminate the differences in price levels between countries.

Part 7: Health

Expectation of life

The expectation of life is the average total number of years which a person of that age could be expected to live, if the rates of mortality at each age were those experienced in that year. The mortality rates that underlie the expectation of life figures are based, up to 2001, on total deaths occurring in each year for England and Wales and the total deaths registered in each year in Scotland and Northern Ireland.

Social class

Social class is based on occupation and is a classification system that has grown out of the original Registrar-General 's social class classification. These are defined in the Classification of Occupations 1990) prepared by the Office for National Statistics. The five categories are:

I. Professional, etc. occupations

II Managerial and technical occupations

III. Skilled occupations

(N) non-manual

(M) manual

IV. Partly skilled occupations

V. Unskilled occupations

For Table 7.2, social class is based on the occupation of the father (or where not available, the mother) at the first census or at the registration of the birth. For Table 7.3, social class is based on the occupation of the father at the registration of the infant death.

General Practice Research Database (GPRD)

The GPRD is a large data collection system of continuous data on patients registered with participating general practices in the United Kingdom. The practices follow an agreed protocol for the recording of clinical data and submit anonymised, patient based clinical records on a regular basis to the database. Practices are recruited to GPRD on a volunteer basis rather than as a statistically representative sample. Data from 210 practices in England and Wales are included in the analysis presented here. These practices cover on average 2.6 per cent of the population of England and Wales in 1998. Patients are allocated to regions according to the location of the practice at which they are registered. The Medicines Control Agency (MCA) has been responsible for the overall management and financial control of the GPRD since April 1999,and its operation since October 1999.

Prescription Cost Analysis system

Data from the Prescription Cost Analysis system and cover all prescriptions dispensed by community pharmacists and dispensing doctors in England. The system covers prescriptions originating from general practices and also those written by nurses, dentists and hospital doctors which are dispensed in the community. Also included are prescriptions written in Wales, Scotland, Northern Ireland and the Isle of Man but dispensed in England. Information on items dispensed in hospitals is not available.

Accidental deaths

The data in Table 7.10 exclude deaths where it was not known whether the cause was accidentally or purposely inflicted, misadventure during medical care, abnormal reactions and late complications.

International Classification of Diseases

The International Classification of Diseases (ICD) is a coding scheme for diseases and causes of death. The Tenth Revision of the ICD (ICD10) was introduced for coding the underlying cause of death in Scotland from 2000 and in the rest of the United Kingdom from 2001. The causes of death included in Figure 7.11 correspond to the following ICD10 codes: circulatory diseases I00–I09: cancer C00–D48: respiratory diseases J00–J99 and infectious diseases A00–B99. Rates for 2000 are for England and Wales only.

The data presented in Figure 7.11 cover five different revisions of the International Classification of Diseases, and although they have been selected according to codes that are comparable, there may still be differences between years that are due to changes in the rules used to select the underlying cause of death.

Standardised rates

Directly age-standardised incidence rates enable comparisons to be made over time and between the sexes, which are independent of changes in the age structure of the population. In each year, the crude rates in each five-year age group are multiplied by the European standard population for that age group. These are then summed and divided by the total standard population for these age groups to give an overall standardised rate.

Alcohol consumption

A unit of alcohol is 8 grams by weight or 1 cl (10 ml) by volume of pure alcohol. This is the amount contained in half a pint of ordinary strength beer or lager, a single pub measure of spirits (25 ml), a small glass of ordinary strength wine (9 per cent alcohol by volume), or a small pub measure of sherry or fortified wine. Sensible Drinking, the 1995 report of an inter-departmental review of the scientific and medical evidence of the effects of drinking alcohol, concluded that the daily benchmarks were more appropriate than previously recommended weekly levels since they could help individuals decide how much to drink on single occasions and to avoid episodes of intoxication with their attendant health and social risks. The report concluded that regular consumption of between three and four units a day for men and two to three units for women does not carry a significant health risk. However, consistently drinking more than four units a day for men, or more than three for women, is not advised as a sensible drinking level because of the progressive health risk it carries. The government's advice on sensible drinking is now based on these daily benchmarks.

Weekly income of head of household

Breakdown of gross weekly income of head of household by income group and year as shown in Figure 7.19. OAPs have no specified pay band.

1975

Households with one or more earners

A1 - £110 and over

A2 - £82 and under £110

All A - £82 and over

B - £49 and under £82

C - £28 and under £49

D - Under £28

Households without an earner

E1- £28 or more

E2 - Under £28

1980

Households with one or more earners

A1 - £250 and over

A2 - £180 and under £250

All A - £180 and over

B - £110 and under £180

C - £67 and under £110

D - Under £67

Households without an earner

E1- £67 or more

E2 - Under £67

1985

Households with one or more earners

A1 - £395 and over

A2 - £300 and under £395

All A   £300 and over

B - £165 and under £300

C - £85 and under £165

D - Under £85

Households without an earner

E1- £85 or more

E2 - Under £85

1990

Households with one or more earners

A1 - £645 and over

A2 - £475 and under £645

All A - £475 and over

B - £250 and under £475

C - £125 and under £250

D - Under £125

Households without an earner

E1- £125 or more

E2 - Under £125

1995

Households with one or more earners

A1 - £790 and over

A2 - £570 and under £790

All A - £570 and over

B - £300 and under £570

C - £140 and under £300

D - Under £140

Households without an earner

E1- £140 or more

E2 - Under £140

2000

Households with one or more earners

A1 - £1070 and over

A2 - £725 and under £1070

All A - £725 and over

B - £375 and under £725

C - £180 and under £375

D - Under £180

Households without an earner

E1- £180 and over

E2 - Under £180

Body mass index

The body mass index (BMI) shown in Figure 7.20, is the most widely used index of obesity which standardises weight for height and is calculated as weight (kg)/height (m)^2. Underweight is defined as a BMI of 20 or less, desirable over 20 to 25, overweight over 25 to 30 and obese over 30.

Immunisation

Data shown in Table 7.22 for 1991/92 onwards for England, Wales and Northern Ireland relate to children reaching their second birthday and immunised by their second birthday. Data for 1981 in England, Wales and Northern Ireland relate to children born two years earlier and immunised by the end of the second year. For Scotland, rates prior to 1995/96 have been calculated by dividing the cumulative number of immunisations for children born in year X and vaccinated by year X+2, by the number of live births (less neonatal deaths) during year X.

Breast cancer and cervical screening programmes

Screening programmes are in operation in the United Kingdom for breast and cervical cancer. Under the breast screening programme, every women aged between 50 and 64 is invited for mammography (breast X-ray) every three years by computerised call-up and recall systems. In addition, all women over the age of 64 can refer themselves for screening. In England, the call-up and recall system is to be extended to women aged 65 to 70 by 2004. In Scotland, the extension to women aged 65 to 70 will begin in 2003/04. National policy for cervical screening is that women should be screened every three to five years (three-and-a-half to five-and-a-half years in Scotland). The programme invites women aged 20 to 64 (20 to 60 in Scotland) for screening. However, since many women are not invited immediately when they reach their 20th birthday, the age group 25 to 64 is used to give a more accurate estimate of coverage of the target population in England.

Smoking cessation services

The establishment and development of smoking cessation services in the NHS is an important element of the Government's strategy, in recognition that many smokers want to stop but find it hard to do so. Smoking cessation services provide a new approach to helping people to quit smoking through advice from health care professionals and the use of pharmacological products. Nicotine Replacement Therapy and bupropion (Zyban). General Practitioners (GPs) are also encouraged to provide brief advice to smokers to stop, in the course of their normal duties.

Part 8: Social Protection

Benefits to groups of recipients

Elderly people

Retirement pension (including non-contributory retirement pension)
Christmas bonus paid with retirement pension and other non-disability benefits
Winter fuel payments
Over 75 TV licence
Minimum income guarantee (income support)
Housing benefit/council tax benefit
Social fund

Sick and disabled people

Incapacity benefit
Attendance allowance
Disability living allowance
Industrial disablement benefit
Other industrial injuries benefits
Severe disablement allowance
Invalid care allowance
Independent living fund
Motability
Christmas bonus paid with disability benefits
Statutory sick pay
Income support
Housing benefit/council tax benefit
Social fund

Family

Maternity allowance
Statutory maternity pay
Child benefit
Vaccine damage payments
Income support
Housing benefit/council tax benefit
Social fund

Unemployed people

Jobseekers allowance (contribution based and income based)
Job grant
Housing benefit/council tax benefit
Social fund

Widows and others

Widows/bereavement benefits
War pensions (including war widows'/widower's' pension and war disablement pension)

Christmas bonus - contributory paid with widow/bereavement benefits

Industrial death benefit

Guardian's allowance & child's special allowance

Pensions compensation board

New deal 50 plus employment credits

Income support paid to people who do not fall within the other client groups

Housing benefit/council tax benefit

Social fund

Benefit units

A benefit unit is a single adult or couple living as married and any dependent children. A pensioner benefit unit is where the head is over state pension age.

Informal Carers

The definition of carers in Tables 8.10 and 8.11 is a self-defined measure of caring based on respondents' own view of whether there is anyone (either living with them or not) who is sick, disabled or elderly whom they look after or give special help to, other than in a professional capacity (for example, a sick, disabled or elderly relative/friend, etc.).

The definition of care used includes all types of caring task and does not impose limits on the number of hours given to caring.

Recipients of benefits for sick and disabled people

Incapacity benefit and severe disablement figures are given as at the end of February from 1996/97 onwards. Prior to this they are as at the end of March. Incapacity benefit was introduced in April 1995 to replace sickness and invalidity benefits. Statutory sick pay was introduced in April 1993. Prior to this date employees sick for less than 28 weeks claimed sickness benefit and are included in the 'incapacity benefit only' row.

Income-based jobseekers allowance (JSA) replaced income support for the unemployed from October 1996. Since then, the income support rows include a small number of income-based JSA claimants.

Disability living allowance (DLA) and attendance allowance are given as at the end of February. DLA was introduced in August 1992. Before April 1992 the figures include mobility allowance.

In-patient activity

In-patient data for England and later years for Northern Ireland are based on finished consultant episodes (FCEs). Data for Wales and Scotland, and for Northern Ireland except acute data after 1986, are based on deaths and discharges and transfers between specialities (between hospitals in Northern Ireland). An FCE is a completed period of care of a patient using a bed, under one consultant, in a particular NHS Trust or directly managed unit. If a patient is transferred from one consultant to another within the same hospital, this counts as an FCE but not a hospital discharge. Conversely if a patient is transferred from one hospital to another provider, this counts as a hospital discharge and as a finished consultant episode.

Waiting times

Patients undergoing a series of repeat admissions and those who were temporarily suspended from the waiting list for medical or social reasons are excluded.

Comparisons between the constituent countries should be made with caution because there are differences between countries in the ways that waiting times are calculated. Figures for Scotland exclude all patients awaiting deferred or planned repeat admission. In Scotland, once a person is classed as deferred they remain as deferred and these patients are excluded from the waiting list figures. In England and Wales patients who have been classed as deferred but who are now available for treatment are included. This means that figures for Scotland are not directly comparable with those for other areas of Great Britain.

For the regions of England the data are for the 'responsible population'. This is all those patients resident within the Health Authority (HA) boundary; plus all patients registered with GPs who are members of a Primary Care Group for which the HA is responsible, but are resident within another HA; minus any patients resident in the HA but registered with a GP who is a member of a PCG responsible to a different HA.

In Scotland, waiting lists are based on NHS lists for each trust irrespective of the patient's residence.

Emergency transport request

An emergency transport request is defined as a request for transport generally made via a 999 call but may also include some calls from GPs. emergency calls include:

a. all accident and sudden illness patients;

b. maternity admissions, unless there is a clear indication to the contrary eg that an ambulance is not required until a later specified time; and

c. any other type of patient for whom an emergency procedure is necessary.

A maternity admission is an admission of a pregnant woman to a maternity ward except where the intention is to terminate the pregnancy.

Health and personal social services staff

Nursing, midwifery and health visitors comprise qualified and unqualified staff, and exclude nurse teachers, nurses in training and students on '1992' courses.

Other non-medical staff comprises scientific and professional, and technical staff. A new classification of the non-medical workforce was introduced in 1995. Information based on this classification is not directly compatible with earlier years.

General medical practitioners includes unrestricted principals, PMS contracted GPs, PMS salaried GPs, restricted principals, assistants, GP registrars and PMS others. It excludes GP retainers.

The number of general dental practitioners is a headcount of General Dental Service (GDS) at 30 September. It includes principals on a Health Authority/Family Health list, assistants and vocational dental practitioners.

Personal social services staff includes staff employed only at local authority social work departments (whole time equivalent). The figures for Scotland relate to the first Monday in October.

Pension provision

In Table 8.19 the 'other' category is all those who are not employed or self-employed based on the International Labour Organisation definition. The table excludes the unemployed, retired people, students, those who are

looking after their family/home, those who are temporarily or permanently sick/disabled and those not classified elsewhere.

Part 9: Crime and Justice

Types of offences in England and Wales

The figures are compiled from police returns to the Home Office or directly from court computer systems.

Recorded crime statistics broadly cover the more serious offences. Up to March 1998 most indictable and triable either way offences were included, as well as some summary ones; from April 1998, all indictable and triable either way offences were included, plus a few closely related summary ones. Recorded offences are the most readily available measures of the incidence of crime, but do not necessarily indicate the true level of crime. Many less serious offences are not reported to the police and cannot, therefore, be recorded, while some offences are not recorded due to lack of evidence. Moreover, the propensity of the public to report offences to the police is influenced by a number of factors and may change over time.

In England and Wales, indictable offences cover those offences which must or may be tried by jury in the Crown Court and include the more serious offences. Summary offences are those for which a defendant would normally be tried at a magistrates ' court and are generally less serious – the majority of motoring offences fall into this category. Triable either way offences are triable either on indictment or summarily.

Changes in crime statistics

Changed to counting rules for recorded crime in England and Wales has been revised in recent years, in order to promote greater consistency between police forces. In 1998 there was an increase in the offences covered, and also a greater emphasis on counting crimes in terms of numbers of victims. In April 2002, a new National Crime Recording Standard (NCRS) was introduced across England and Wales, which aims to take a more victim-oriented approach to crime recording. Under the Standard, police forces record a crime if the circumstances as reported amount to a crime defined by law, and there is no credible evidence to the contrary. Some police forces adopted the principles of the standard in advance of April 2002. Changes in crime statistics in Durham, Cumbria, Greater Manchester, Lancashire, Lincolnshire, North Yorkshire, Staffordshire, West Mercia, West Midlands, Suffolk, Kent, Avon and Somerset, Dyfed Powys, North Wales and South Wales will be strongly influenced by the changes in recording practice.

Significant changes have also taken place within the British Crime Survey (BCS) which used to be carried out every two years. The most recent survey (2001/02) has incorporated substantial methodological changes and has now moved to cover financial rather than calendar years, to cover the same time frame as crime figures collected by the police. Because of the significant changes taking place in both measures of crime, direct comparisons with figures for previous years cannot be made.

BCS comparable crime

Over three quarters of British Crime Survey (BCS) offences reported via interviews in the 2001/02 interview sample fall into categories which can be compared with crimes recorded under the new police coverage of offences adopted from 1 April 1998. The new comparable subset includes common assaults (and assaults on a constable) and vehicle interference and tampering. The comparable subset is used to observe differences between police and BCS figures.

Comparable violence comprises wounding, robbery and common assault – the violent crimes measured by the BCS which can now be compared with violent crimes recorded by the police. It excludes the small category of snatch theft that is not separately identified in police recorded crime figures but is part of the police recorded crime category of theft from the person.

Notifiable offences: are broadly the more serious offences. They include most indictable offences and triable either way offences and certain summary offences (for example, unauthorised taking of a motor vehicle).

Indictable only offences: are those for which an adult must be tried at the Crown Court, for example robbery, arson and rape. Figures for

indictable offences given in this chapter include those for offences which are triable either way (see below).

Triable either way offences: are offences triable either on indictment or summarily. They may be tried in a magistrates' court unless either the defendant or the magistrate requests a Crown Court hearing. Most thefts, drug offences and less serious violence against the person offences fall into this category.

Summary offences: are those offences which are normally tried at a magistrates ' court.

Crime across the UK

There are a number of reasons why recorded crime statistics in England and Wales, Northern Ireland and Scotland cannot be directly compared:

Different legal systems: the legal system operating in Scotland differs from that in England and Wales, and in Northern Ireland. For example, in Scotland children aged under 16 are normally dealt with for offending by the Children's Hearings system rather than the courts.

Differences in classification: there are significant differences in the offences included within the recorded crime categories used in Scotland and the categories of notifiable offences used in England, Wales and Northern Ireland. Scottish figures of 'crime' have therefore been grouped in an attempt to approximate to the classification of notifiable offences in England, Wales and Northern Ireland.

Counting rules: in Scotland each individual offence occurring within an incident is recorded whereas in England, Wales and Northern Ireland only the main offence is counted.

Types of offences in Northern Ireland

In recording crime, the Police Service of Northern Ireland broadly follow the Home Office rules for counting crime. As from 1st April 1998 notifiable offences are recorded on the same basis as those in England and Wales (i.e. under the revised Home Office rules – see above). Prior to the revision of the rules, criminal damage offences in Northern Ireland excluded those where the value of the property damaged was less than £200.

Offences and crimes

Burglary: this term is not applicable to Scotland where the term used is 'housebreaking'.

Theft from vehicles: in Scotland data have only been separately identified from January 1992. The figures include theft by opening lock-fast places from a motor vehicle and other theft from a motor vehicle.

Offenders cautioned for burglary

In England and Wales offenders cautioned for going equipped for stealing, etc were counted against Burglary offences until 1986 and against Other offences from 1987. Historical data provided in Table 9.16 have been amended to take account of this change. Drug offences were included under Other offences for 1971.

Sentences and orders

The following are the main sentences and orders that can be imposed upon those persons found guilty. Some types of sentence or order can only be given to offenders in England and Wales in certain age groups. Under the framework for sentencing contained in the *Criminal Justice Acts 1991* and *1993*, the sentence must reflect the seriousness of the offence. The following sentences are available for adults (a similar range of sentences is available to juveniles aged 10 to 17):

Absolute and conditional discharge: a court may make an order discharging a person absolutely or (except in Scotland) conditionally where it is inexpedient to inflict punishment and, before 1 October 1992, where a probation order was not appropriate. An order for conditional discharge runs for such period of not more than three years as the court specifies, the condition being that the offender does not commit another offence within the period so specified. In Scotland a court may also discharge a person with an admonition.

Community service: an offender who is convicted of an offence punishable with imprisonment may be sentenced to perform unpaid work for not more than 240 hours (300 hours in Scotland), and not less than 40 hours. Twenty hours minimum community service is given for persistent petty offending or fine default. In Scotland the *Law Reform (Miscellaneous Provisions) (Scotland) Act 1990*

requires that community service can only be ordered where the court would otherwise have imposed imprisonment or detention. Probation and community service may be combined in a single order in Scotland.

Community rehabilitation orders (probation orders prior to April 2001): an offender sentenced to a community rehabilitation order is under the supervision of a probation officer (social worker in Scotland), whose duty it is (in England and Wales and Northern Ireland) to advise, assist and befriend him or her but the court has the power to include any other requirement it considers appropriate. A cardinal feature of the order is that it relies on the co-operation of the offender. Community rehabilitation orders may be given for any period between six months and three years inclusive.

Community punishment orders (community service orders prior to 1 April 2001): an offender aged 16 or over who is convicted of an offence for which a court can send an adult to prison may be required to perform unpaid work on behalf of the community. Such orders involve a minimum of 40 hours and a maximum of 240 hours to be completed within 12 months. The work is under the direction of a community service organiser, working within the Probation Service. A wide variety of work is done including, for example, outdoor conservation projects, building adventure playgrounds, and painting and decorating for the elderly or disabled.

Community punishment and rehabilitation orders (combination orders prior to 1 April 2001): this order was introduced in October 1992 by the *Criminal Justice Act 1991* and amended by the *Criminal Justice and Courts Act 2000.* It combines elements of both probation supervision and community service and may be given to any offender aged 16 or over. The maximum duration of the probation element of the Community Punishment and Rehabilitation Order is three years and the minimum 12 months. When a Community Punishment and Rehabilitation Order is made, probation supervision continues for at least as long as community service is being performed. The minimum number of community service hours is 40 and the maximum 100.

Meanwhile, Article 15 of the *Criminal Justice (NI) Order 1996* introduced the combination order to Northern Ireland.

Attendance centre order: available in England, Wales and Northern Ireland for offenders under the age of 21 and involves deprivation of free time.

Imprisonment: is the custodial sentence for adult offenders. In the case of mentally disordered offenders, hospital orders, which may include a restriction order may be considered appropriate. Home Office or Scottish Executive consent is needed for release or transfer. A new disposal, the 'hospital direction', was introduced in 1997.

The court, when imposing a period of imprisonment, can direct that the offender be sent directly to hospital. On recovering from the mental disorder, the offender is returned to prison to serve the balance of their sentence. The *Criminal Justice Act 1991* abolished remission and substantially changed the parole scheme in England and Wales. Those serving sentences of under four years, imposed on or after 1 October 1992, are subject to Automatic Conditional Release and are released, subject to certain criteria, halfway through their sentence. Home Detention Curfews result in selected prisoners being released up to 2 months early with a tag that monitors their presence during curfew hours. Those serving sentences of four years or longer are considered for Discretionary Conditional Release after having served half their sentence, but are automatically released at the two-thirds point of sentence.

The *Crime (Sentences) Act 1997,* implemented on 1 October 1997 (as amended by the *Powers of Criminal Courts Sentencing Act 2000,* included, for persons aged 18 or over, an automatic life sentence for a second serious violent or sexual offence unless there are exceptional circumstances. All offenders serving a sentence of 12 months or more are supervised in the community until the three quarter point of sentence. A life sentence prisoner may be released on licence subject to supervision and is always liable to recall. In Scotland the *Prisoners and Criminal Proceedings (Scotland) Act 1993* changed the system of remission and parole for prisoners sentenced on or after 1 October 1993.

Those serving sentences of less than four years are released unconditionally after having served half of their sentence, unless the court specifically imposes a Supervised Release Order which subjects them to social work supervision after release.

Those serving sentences of four years or more are eligible for parole at half sentence. If parole is not granted then they will automatically be released on licence at two thirds of sentence subject to days added for breaches of prison rules. All such prisoners are liable to be 'recalled on conviction' or for breach of conditions of licence i.e. if between the date of release and the date on which the full sentence ends, a person commits another offence which is punishable by imprisonment or breaches his/her licence conditions, then the offender may be returned to prison for the remainder of that sentence whether or not a sentence of imprisonment is also imposed for the new offence.

Fully suspended sentences may only be passed in exceptional circumstances. In England, Wales and Northern Ireland, sentences of imprisonment of two years or less may be fully suspended. A court should not pass a suspended sentence unless a sentence of imprisonment would be appropriate in the absence of a power to suspend. The result of suspending a sentence is that it will not take effect unless during the period specified the offender is convicted of another offence punishable with imprisonment. Suspended sentences are not available in Scotland.

Fines: the *Criminal Justice Act 1993* introduced new arrangements on 20 September 1993 whereby courts are now required to fit an amount for the fine which reflects the seriousness of the offence, but which also takes account of an offender's means. This system replaced the more formal unit fines scheme included in the *Criminal Justice Act 1991.*The Act also introduced the power for courts to arrange deduction of fines from income benefit for those offenders receiving such benefits. The *Law Reform (Miscellaneous Provision) (Scotland) Act 1990* as amended by the *Criminal Procedure (Scotland) Act 1995* provides for the use of supervised attendance orders by selected courts in Scotland. The *Criminal Procedure (Scotland) Act 1995* also makes it easier for courts to impose a supervised attendance order in the event of a default and enables the court to impose a supervised attendance order in the first instance for 16 and 17 year olds.

Custody probation order: an order unique to Northern Ireland reflecting the different regime there which applies in respect of remission and the general absence of release on licence. The custodial sentence is followed by a period of supervision for a period of between 12 months and three years.

Young offender institutions

The *Criminal Justice Act 1991* made a number of changes to the custodial sentencing arrangements for young offenders in England and Wales. A common minimum age of 15 for boys and girls was set for the imposition of a sentence of detention in a young offender institution thus removing boys aged 14 from the scope of this sentence.

Civil courts

England and Wales: the main civil courts are the High Court and the county courts. Magistrates' courts also have some civil jurisdiction, mainly in family proceedings. Most appeals in civil cases go to the Court of Appeal (Civil Division) and may go from there to the House of Lords. Since July 1991, county courts have been able to deal with all contract and tort cases and actions for recovery of land, regardless of value. Cases are presided over by a judge who almost always sits without a jury. Jury trials are limited to specified cases, for example, actions for libel.

Scotland: the Court of Session is the supreme civil court. Any cause, apart from causes excluded by statute, may be initiated in, and any judgement of an inferior court may be appealed to, the Court of Session. The Sheriff Court is the principal local court of civil jurisdiction in Scotland. It also has jurisdiction in criminal proceedings. Apart from certain actions the civil jurisdiction of the Sheriff Court is generally similar to that of the Court of Session.

Publicly Funded Legal Services

In England and Wales, the Legal Services Commission operates two funding schemes: the Community Legal Service (CLS), which funds civil legal and advice services and civil representation; and the Criminal Defence Service (CDS) of which the Commission principally funds duty solicitor work and advice, and representation at the magistrates' court. The Commission was launched in April 2000, replacing the Legal Aid Board, and funds services through contracts agreed with quality assured service providers.

Community Legal Service

For clients whose capital and income are within certain financial limits, the Commission funds a range of legal and advice services in civil matters, either on a contributory or a free basis. The services include:

Legal help: this provides for initial advice and assistance with legal problems. This work was previously carried out under the advice and assistance, or 'green form', scheme.

Help at court: this allows for somebody (a solicitor or adviser) to speak on a client's behalf at certain court hearings.

Approved family help: this provides for help in relation to a family dispute, including assistance in resolving that dispute through negotiation or otherwise. It can be in the form of either:

1. *Help with mediation:* this is legal advice and assistance if the client is attending family mediation; or

2. *General family help:* this is legal advice and assistance on family matters where no family mediation is involved.

Family mediation: this covers mediation for a family dispute.

Controlled legal representation: for cases heard by the Mental Health Review Tribunal, the Immigration Appeal Tribunal and immigration adjudicators.

Legal representation: previously known as civil legal aid, this provides for representation if the client is taking or defending court proceedings. It is available in two forms: Investigative Help and Full Representation.

Support funding: this is partial funding of very expensive cases that are otherwise funded privately under conditional fee agreements. It is available in two forms: Investigative Support and Litigation Support.

Criminal Defence Service

During 2000/01, the Commission provided criminal legal aid within the meaning of the *Legal Aid Act 1988* and prepared for the launch of the Criminal Defence Service from April 2001. The services provided during the period covered legal advice and assistance (the 'green form' scheme) and representation in criminal cases. A similar range of services are now available through the CDS network of contracted suppliers.

The Commission also provides two duty solicitor schemes. One makes advice and representation available for certain criminal hearings in the magistrates' court. The second, known as the 24 hour duty solicitor scheme, provides for legal advice and assistance to people arrested or helping with enquiries at police stations.

The Commission is concerned only with funding proceedings in the magistrates' courts; funding of criminal legal aid in the higher courts is the responsibility of the Lord Chancellor's Department. In the criminal courts in England and Wales a representation order may be made if this appears desirable in the interest of justice. No limit of income or capital above which a person is ineligible for public funding is specified. However, since April 2001, the higher criminal courts have been able to order costs against defendants at the end of a case, usually following conviction.

Civil Legal Aid in Scotland operates on a similar basis to that operating prior to April 2000 in England and Wales. Advice and assistance has similar scope in Scotland but is available to those who are financially eligible either for free or on payment of a contribution. Assistance by way of representation (ABWOR) is granted mainly for summary criminal cases where a plea of guilty is made, though it also covers proceedings in mental health review cases, designated life prisoners before the parole board and disciplinary hearings before a prison governor, and other specified civil or criminal proceedings. Criminal Legal Aid, which is granted by the Scottish Legal Aid Board for summary cases and for all appeals, and by the courts for solemn cases, is not subject to a contribution.

Drugs seizures

The figures in this table, which are compiled from returns to the Home Office, relate to seizures made by the police and officials of HM Customs and Excise, and to drugs controlled under the *Misuse of Drugs Act 1971*. The Act divides drugs into three main categories according to their harmfulness. A full list of drugs in each category is given in Schedule 2 to the *Misuse of Drugs Act 1971,* as amended by Orders in Council.

Part 10: Housing

Dwelling stock

The definition of dwelling used follows the census' definition applicable at that time – currently the 1991 Census is used. This defined a dwelling as 'structurally separate accommodation'. This was determined primarily by considering the type of accommodation, as well as separate and shared access to multi-occupied properties.

In all stock figures, vacant dwellings are included but non-permanent dwellings are generally excluded. For housebuilding statistics, only data on permanent dwellings are collected.

Estimates of the total dwelling stock, stock changes and the tenure distribution for each country are made by the Office of the Deputy Prime Minister (ODPM), the Scottish Executive, the National Assembly for Wales, and NI Department for Social Development. These are primarily based on census output data for the number of dwellings (or households converted to dwellings) from the censuses of population for Great Britain. Adjustments were carried out if there were specific reasons to do so. Census years' figures are based on outputs from the censuses. For years between censuses, the total figures are obtained by projecting the base census year's figure forward yearly. The increment is based on the annual total number of completions plus the annual total net gain due to other housing flows statistics, i.e. conversions, demolitions and change of use.

Estimates of dwelling stock by tenure category are primarily based on the census except in the situation where it is considered that for some specific tenure information, there are other more accurate sources. In this situation, it is assumed that the other data sources contain vacant dwellings also but it is not certain and it is not expected that these data are very precise. Thus the allocation of vacant dwellings to tenure categories may not be completely accurate. This means that the margin of error for tenure categories are wider than for estimates of total stock.

For the 1991 Census, a comparison with other available sources indicated that for local authorities' stock, figures supplied by local authorities are more reliable. Similarly, it was found that Housing Corporation's own data are more accurate than those from the census for the Registered Social Landlord's (RSL's) stock. Hence only the rented privately or with a job or business tenure data directly from the census was used. The owner-occupied data was taken as the residual of the total from the census. For non-census years, the same approach was adopted except for the privately rented or with a job or business for which Labour Force Survey results were considered to be appropriate for use.

In the Survey of English Housing, data for privately rented unfurnished accommodation includes accommodation that is partly furnished.

For further information on the methodology used to calculate stock by tenure and tenure definitions see Appendix B: Notes and Definitions in the ODPM annual volume Housing Statistics or the housing statistics page of the ODPM website: www.odpm.gov.uk.

Dwellings completed

In principle, a dwelling is regarded as completed when it becomes ready for occupation whether it is in fact occupied or not. In practice, there are instances where the timing could be delayed and some completions are missed, for example, because no completion certificates were requested by the owner.

Tenure definition for housebuilding is only slightly different from that used for stock figures. For details see Housing Statistics.

Household reference person

As of April 2000 the General Household Survey adopted the term 'household reference person' in place of 'head of household'. As of

April 2001 the Survey of English Housing also adopted the term. For more information and the definition of the term see Appendix, Part 6: Household reference person.

Socio-economic group

The basic occupational classification used is the Registrar General's socio-economic grouping in Standard Occupational Classification 1990, Volume 3 OPCS (HMSO, London 1991), pp13-14. Table 10.7 uses a collapsed version of this classification, which is as follows:

Descriptive definition	SEG numbers
Professional	3, 4
Employers and managers	1, 2, 13
Intermediate non-manual	5
Junior non-manual	6
Skilled manual (including foremen and supervisors) and own account non-professional	8, 9, 12, 14
Semi-skilled manual and personal service	7, 10, 15
Unskilled manual	11

Index of Multiple Deprivation

As the result of a review of the 1998 Index of Local Deprivation (1998 ILD), the former Department for Transport, Local Government and the Regions constructed the Index of Multiple Deprivation (IMD 2000). This is a ward level index made up from six ward level indices: income; employment; health deprivation and disability; education, skills and training; housing; and geographical access to services. The index ranks the 8,414 wards in England with 1 being the most deprived and 8,414 being the least deprived.

Homeless households

England and Wales: households for whom local authorities accepted responsibility to secure accommodation under the Housing Act 1985, and subsequently the Housing Act 1996. Data for Wales include some households given advice and assistance only. Figures for the period 1986–1996 are not strictly comparable with information provided for 1997 due to a change in legislation.

Scotland: households assessed as being unintentionally homeless or potentially homeless (likely to become homeless within 28 days) in priority need by local authorities.

Northern Ireland: households for whom the Northern Ireland Housing Executive has accepted responsibility to secure permanent accommodation, not necessarily those for whom permanent accommodation has been found.

Bedroom standard

The concept is used to estimate occupation density by allocating a standard number of bedrooms to each household in accordance with its age/sex/marital status composition and the relationship of the members to one another. A separate bedroom is allocated to each married or cohabiting couple, any other person aged 21 or over, each pair of adolescents aged 10–20 of the same sex, and each pair of children under 10. Any unpaired person aged 10–20 is paired if possible with a child under 10 of the same sex, or, if that is not possible, is given a separate bedroom, as is any unpaired child under 10. This standard is then compared with the actual number of bedrooms (including bedsitters) available for the sole use of the household, and deficiencies or excesses are tabulated. Bedrooms converted to other uses are not counted as available unless they have been denoted as bedrooms by the informants; bedrooms not actually in use are counted unless uninhabitable.

The fitness standard

The fitness standard in England and Wales was set out in section 604 of the Local Government and Housing Act 1989 with guidance in DoE circulars 5/90 and 6/90. It came into operation from 1 April 1990. A property is fit for human habitation unless it fails to meet any of the following requirements in the opinion of the local authority:

a. it is structurally stable;

b. it is free from serious disrepair;

c. it is free from dampness prejudicial to the health of any occupants;

d. it has adequate provision for lighting, heating and ventilation;

e. it has adequate supply of wholesome, piped water;

f. it has satisfactory facilities for preparing and cooking food including a sink with supplies of hot and cold water;

g. it has a suitably located WC;

h. it has a bath or shower and basin, each with supplies of hot and cold water; or

i. it has an effective system for draining foul, waste and surface water.

There is also a separate fitness standard for houses in multiple occupation (HMOs), apart from the general standard described above, that compares the available facilities with the number of occupants, and that also ensures that there are adequate means of escape from fire and other fire precautions. When a property has been surveyed by the local authority and the condition assessed, the authority has then to decide on the most satisfactory course of action. If a property is identified as unfit, then the authority is obliged by statute to take action.

This action can include serving a notice, making a closing order or a demolition order, or including the property in a clearance area. The authority can also consider if the property could be dealt with by including it in a group repair scheme. Lastly there is a direct link between the standard of fitness and eligibility for mandatory renovation grants. Thus applications for renovation grants must be approved where the work is to bring a property up to the fitness standard, and the applicant meets the various conditions and undergoes the test of resources.

Acorn classification

The ACORN classification is a means of classifying areas according to various census characteristics devised by CACI limited. An ACORN code is assigned to each Census Enumeration District (ED) which is then copied to all postcodes within the ED.

The list below shows the 6 ACORN major categories and the 17 groups. Each ACORN group is further divided in a number of area types (not shown here).

The descriptions are CACI's:

Category A: Affluent suburban and rural areas

1. Wealthy Achiever, Suburban Areas

2. Affluent Greys, Rural Communities

3. Prosperous Pensioners, Retirement Areas

Category B: Affluent family areas

4. Affluent Executives, Family Areas

5. Well-Off Workers, Family Areas

Category C: Affluent urban areas

6. Affluent Urbanites, Town and City Areas

7. Prosperous Professionals, Metropolitan Areas

8. Better-Off Executives, Inner City Areas

Category D: Mature home owning areas

9. Comfortable Middle Agers, Mature Home Owning Areas

10. Skilled Workers, Home Owning Areas

Category E: New home owning areas

11. New Home Owners, Mature Communities

12. White Collar Workers, Better-Off Multi-Ethnic Areas

Category F: Council estates and low income areas

13. Older People, Less Prosperous Areas

14. Council Estate Residents, Better-Off Homes

15. Council Estate Residents, High Unemployment

16. Council Estate Residents, Greatest Hardship

17. People in Multi-Ethnic, Low-Income Areas

Sales and transfers of local authority dwellings

Right to buy was established by the Housing Act 1980 and was introduced across Great Britain in October 1980.

In England, large scale voluntary transfers (LSVTs) of stock have been principally to housing associations/registered social landlords; figures include transfers supported by estate renewal challenge funding (ERCF). The figures for 1993 includes 949 dwellings transferred under Tenants' Choice.

Scotland includes large scale voluntary transfers to registered social landlords and trickle transfers to Housing Associations.

Part 11: Environment

Air Pollutants

Volatile organic compounds (VOCs) are ozone precursors and comprise a wide range of chemical compounds including hydrocarbons,

oxygenates and halogen containing species. Methane (CH_4) is an important component of VOCs but its environmental impact derives principally from its contribution to global warming. The major environmental impact of non-methane VOCs lies in their involvement in the formation of ground level ozone. Most VOCs are non-toxic or are present at levels well below guideline values. Others, such as benzene and 1,3-butadiene, are of concern because of their potential impact on human health.

PM_{10} is airborne particulate matter. Specifically, it is that fraction of 'black smoke' which is thought most likely to be deposited in the lungs. It can be defined as the fraction resulting from a collection from black smoke by a size selective sampler which collects smaller particles preferentially, capturing 50 per cent of 10 micron aerodynamic diameter particles, more than 95 per cent of 5 micron particles, and less than 5 per cent of 20 micron particles.

Water pollution incidents

The Environment Agency defines four categories of pollution incidents. Only category one and two incidents are covered in Figure 11.5.

Category 1: The most severe, incidents which involve one or more of the following:

1. potential or actual persistent effect on water quality or aquatic life;

2. closure of potable water, industrial or agricultural abstraction necessary;

3. major damage to aquatic ecosystems;

4. major damage to agriculture and/or commerce;

5. serious impact on man;

6. major effect on amenity value.

Category 2: Severe incidents, which involve one or more of the following:

1. notification to abstractors necessary;

2. significant damage to aquatic ecosystems;

3. significant effect on water quality;

4. damage to agriculture and/or commerce;

5. impact on man;

6. impact on amenity value to public, owners or users.

Category 3: Minor incidents, involving one or more of the following:

1. a minimal effect on water quality;

2. minor damage to aquatic ecosystems;

3. amenity value only marginally affected;

4. minimal impact on agriculture and/or commerce.

Category 4: Incidents where no impact on the environment occurred.

Rivers and canals

The chemical quality of rivers and canal waters in the United Kingdom are monitored in a series of separate national surveys in England and Wales, Scotland and Northern Ireland. In England, Wales and Northern Ireland the General Quality Assessment (GQA) Scheme provides a rigorous and objective method for assessing the basic chemical quality of rivers and canals based on three determinands: dissolved oxygen, biochemical oxygen demand (BOD) and ammoniacal nitrogen). The GQA grades river stretches into six categories (A-F) of chemical quality Table 11.6 uses two broader groups – good (classes A and B) and fair (classes C and D). Classification of biological quality is based on the River Invertebrate and Classification System (RIVPACS).

The length of rivers chemically classified in Northern Ireland increased by more than 40 per cent between 1991 and 2001.

In Scotland, water quality is based upon the Scottish River Classification Scheme of 20 June 1997 which combines chemical, biological, nutrient and aesthetic quality using the following classes: excellent (A1), good (A2), fair (B), poor (C) and seriously polluted (D). In 2000 a new Digitised River Network was introduced.

Land use change

Between 1989 and 1992 only changes judged to have occurred in the previous five years were recorded to the nearest year. Changes occurring more than five years before the survey were recorded in bands to the nearest five years. Only changes in 1985 to 1987 are affected.

The uses of land given are as defined in *Land Use Change Statistics No.16,* published by the Office of the Deputy Prime Minister.

The Environment Agency

The Environment Agency for England and Wales was formally created on 8 August 1995 by the *Environment Act (1995)*. It brought together the functions previously carried out by the National Rivers Authority, Her Majesties Inspectorate of Pollution, the waste regulatory functions of 83 local authorities and a small number of units from the then Department of Environment dealing with waste regulation and contaminated land.

Part 12: Transport

The National Travel Survey

The NTS has been conducted on a small scale continuous basis since July 1988. The last of the previous ad hoc surveys was carried out in 1985–1986.

Information is collected from about 3,000 households in Great Britain each year. Each member of the household provides personal information (for example, age, sex, working status, driving licence, season ticket) and details of trips carried out in a sample week, including the purpose of the trip, method of travel, time of day, length, duration, and cost of any tickets bought.

Travel included in the NTS covers all trips by Great Britain residents within Great Britain for personal reasons, including travel in the course of work.

A trip is defined as a one-way course of travel having a single main purpose. It is the basic unit of personal travel defined in the survey. A round trip is split into two trips, with the first ending at a convenient point about half-way round as a notional stopping point for the outward destination and return origin.

A stage is that portion of a trip defined by the use of a specific method of transport or of a specific ticket (a new stage being defined if either the mode or ticket changes).

Cars are regarded as household cars if they are either owned by a member of the household, or available for the private use of household members. Company cars provided by an employer for the use of a particular employee (or director) are included, but cars borrowed temporarily from a company pool are not.

The main driver of a household car is the

household member that drives the furthest in that car in the course of a year.

The purpose of a trip is normally taken to be the activity at the destination, unless that destination is 'home' in which case the purpose is defined by the origin of the trip. The classification of trips to 'work' is also dependent on the origin of the trip. The following purposes are distinguished:

Commuting: trips to a usual place of work from home, or from work to home.

Business: personal trips in the course of work, including a trip in the course of work back to work. This includes all work trips by people with no usual place of work (eg site workers) and those who work at or from home.

Education: trips to school or college, etc. by full time students, students on day-release and part-time students following vocational courses.

Escort: used when the traveller has no purpose of his or her own, other than to escort or accompany another person; for example, taking a child to school. For example, escort commuting is escorting or accompanying someone from home to work or from work to home.

Shopping: all trips to shops or from shops to home, even if there was no intention to buy.

Personal business: visits to services eg hairdressers, launderettes, dry-cleaners, betting shops, solicitors, banks, estate agents, libraries, churches; or for medical consultations or treatment, or for eating and drinking unless the main purpose was entertainment or social.

Social or entertainment: visits to meet friends, relatives, or acquaintances, both at someone's home or at a pub, restaurant, etc; all types of entertainment or sport, clubs, and voluntary work, non-vocational evening classes, political meetings, etc.

Holidays or day trips: trips (within Great Britain) to or from any holiday (including stays of four nights or more with friends or relatives) or trips for pleasure (not otherwise classified as social or entertainment) within a single day.

Just walk: walking pleasure trips along public highways including taking the dog for a walk and jogging.

Real household income equivalent

Because of price inflation, and because household size and composition is not taken into account in the simple measure of household income, a measure of household affluence, known as real household income equivalent, is used. Household income equivalent scales are used to assign values to adults and children within a household – a technique used by the Department for Work and Pensions when assessing Housing Benefit Scales. Total household income is then divided by the sum of these values so that the household income relative to a household consisting of just one married couple can be obtained. These are then deflated to 1990 values using the Tax and Price Index (TPI). Households are then assigned to one of twenty groups in ascending order of affluence. These are usually grouped into five 'quintile' groups for analysis purposes.

The values assigned to individuals within a household were as follows:

Head of household single parent	0.71
Other head of household	0.61
Wife of other head of household	0.39
Adult dependant	0.36
Unrelated adult (depending on no. of adults in household)	0.38-0.43
Child aged under 2	0.09
Child aged 2-4 years	0.18
Child aged 5-7 years	0.21
Child aged 8-10 years	0.23
Child aged 11-12 years	0.25
Child aged 13-15 years	0.27

Car ownership

The figures for household ownership include four wheeled and three wheeled cars, off-road vehicles, minibuses, motorcaravans, dormobiles, and light vans. Company cars normally available for household use are also included.

Type of area

London borough – the 33 London boroughs;

Metropolitan built-up area – the built-up area of the administrative areas of the former metropolitan counties of Greater Manchester, Merseyside, the West Midlands, West Yorkshire, Tyne & Wear and Strathclyde;

Large urban – self-contained urban areas of more than 250,000 population in 1991;

Medium urban – self-contained urban areas of not more than 250,000 population in 1991, but more than 25,000;

Small urban – self-contained urban areas of not more than 25,000 population in 1991 but more than 3,000;

Rural – other areas are designated 'rural', including 'urban areas' under 3,000 population in 1991.

Transport expenditure

The Family Expenditure Survey and Expenditure and Food Survey data in Table 12.6 use unweighted data for adults.

Road Traffic

Figures for 1999 onwards have been produced on a new basis and are not directly comparable with earlier figures. In 2001/02, steps were taken to improve the quality of DTLR's major road network database. The net result of these improvements has been little change to the estimates of total motor vehicle traffic for Great Britain for after 1999, but some changes to the composition of the overall figure. In general, the new motorway traffic estimates are now higher than before, whilst those for other major roads are lower than before.

Public Performance Measure (PPM)

The PPM was introduced by the then Shadow Strategic Rail Authority (now the SRA) in June 2000 to give a better indication of the actual performance of Britain's passenger railways. It has now replaced the Passenger's Charter as the main means of measuring passenger train performance.

The PPM combines figures for punctuality and reliability into a single performance measure. It covers all scheduled services, seven days a week, and measures the performance of individual trains against their planned timetable.

Passenger death rates

Data in Table 12.22 have been revised from those previously published. The revisions are part of a review on comparisons of casualty rates by mode of transport.

Passenger fatality rates given in the table can

be interpreted as the risk a traveller runs of being killed, per billion kilometres travelled. The coverage varies for each mode of travel and care should be exercised in drawing comparisons between the rates for different modes.

The table provides information on passenger fatalities and where possible travel by drivers and other crew in the course of their work has been excluded. Exceptions are for private journeys and those in company owned cars and vans where drivers are included.

Figures for all modes of transport exclude confirmed suicides and deaths through natural causes. Figures for air, rail and water exclude trespassers and rail excludes attempted suicides. Accidents occurring in airports, seaports and railway stations that do not directly involve the mode of transport concerned are also excluded. For example, deaths sustained on escalators or falling over packages on platforms.

The figures are compiled by the Department for Transport. Further information is available in the annual publications *Road Accidents Great Britain: The Casualty Report and Transport Statistics Great Britain*. Both are published by the Stationery Office and are available at: www.transtat.dft.gov.uk.

The following definitions are used:

Air: accidents involving UK registered airline aircraft in UK and foreign airspace. Fixed wing and rotary wing aircraft are included but air taxis are excluded. Accidents cover UK airline aircraft around the world not just in the UK.

Rail: train accidents and accidents occurring through movement of railway vehicles in Great Britain. As well as national rail the figures include accidents on underground and tram systems, Eurotunnel and minor railways.

Water: figures for travel by water include both domestic and international passenger carrying services of UK registered merchant vessels.

Road: figures refer to Great Britain and include accidents occurring on the public highway (including footways) in which at least one road vehicle or a vehicle in collision with a pedestrian is involved and which becomes known to the police within 30 days of its occurrence. Figures include both public and private transport.

Bus or coach: figures for work buses are included. From 1 January 1994, the casualty definition was revised to include only those vehicles equipped to carry 17 or more passengers regardless of use. Prior to 1994 these vehicles were coded according to construction, whether or not they were being used for carrying passengers. Vehicles constructed as buses that were privately licensed were included under 'bus and coach' but PSV licensed minibuses were included under cars.

Car: includes taxis, invalid tricycles, three and four wheel cars and minibuses. Prior to 1999 motor caravans were also included.

Van: vans mainly include vehicles of the van type constructed on a car chassis. From 1 January 1994 these are defined as those vehicles not over 3.5 tonnes maximum permissible gross vehicle weight. Prior to 1994 the weight definition was not over 1.524 tonnes unladen.

Two-wheeled motor vehicle: mopeds, motor scooters and motor cycles (including motor cycle combinations).

Pedal cycle: includes tandems, tricycles and toy cycles ridden on the carriageway.

Pedestrian: includes persons riding toy cycles on the footway, persons pushing bicycles, pushing or pulling other vehicles or operating pedestrian controlled vehicles, those leading or herding animals, occupants of prams or wheelchairs, and people who alight safely from vehicles and are subsequently injured.

Part 13: Lifestyles and Social Participation

Cultural events

Data from 1986–1987 and 1991–1992 in Table 13.7 are taken from the Target Group Index, BMRB International, and data for subsequent years are taken from the Target Group Index Doublebase, BMRB International.

Parliamentary elections

A general election must be held at least every five years or sooner, if the Prime Minister of the day so decides. The United Kingdom is currently divided into 659 constituencies, each of which returns one member to the House of Commons. To ensure equitable representation, four permanent Boundary Commissions (for England, Wales, Scotland, and Northern Ireland) make periodic reviews of constituencies and recommend any change in the number or redistribution of seats that may seem necessary in the light of population movements or for some other reason.

Articles published in previous editions

No.1 1970

Some general developments in social statistics
Professor C A Moser, CSO

Public expenditure on the social services Professor B
Abel-Smith, London School of Economics and Political
Science

**The growth of the population to the end of the
century** Jean Thompson, OPCS

**A forecast of effective demand for housing in Great
Britain in the 1970s** A E Holmans, MHLG

No.2 1971

Social services manpower Dr S Rosenbaum, CSO

Trends in certificated sickness absence F E Whitehead,
DHSS

**Some aspects of model building in the social and
environmental fields** B Benjamin, CSC

Social indicators – health A J Culyer, R J Lavers and A
Williams, University of York

No.3 1972

Social commentary: change in social conditions CSO

**Statistics about immigrants: objectives, methods,
sources and problems** Professor C A Moser, CSO

**Central manpower planning in Scottish secondary
education** A W Brodie, SED

Social malaise research: a study in Liverpool M Flynn,
P Flynn and N Mellor, Liverpool City Planning Department

**Crimes of violence against the person in England
and Wales** S Klein, HO

No.4 1973

Social commentary: certain aspects of the life cycle
CSO

The elderly D C L Wroe, CSO

Subjective social indicators M Abrams, SSRC

Mental illness and the psychiatric services E R
Bransby, DHSS

Cultural accounting A Peacock and C Godfrey,
University of York

Road accidents and casualties in Great Britain J A
Rushbrook, DOE

No.5 1974

Social commentary: men and women CSO

Social security: the European experiment E James and
A Laurent, EC Commission

Time budgets B M Hedges, SCPR

Time budgets and models of urban activity patterns
N Bullock, P Dickens, M Shapcott and P Steadman,
Cambridge University of Architecture

Road traffic and the environment F D Sando and V
Batty, DOE

No.6 1975

Social commentary: social class CSO

**Areas of urban deprivation in Great Britain: an
analysis of 1971 Census data** S Holtermann, DOE

Note: Subjective social indicators Mark Abrams, SSRC

No.7 1976

Social commentary: social change in Britain
1970–1975 CSO

Crime in England and Wales Dr C Glennie, HO

Crime in Scotland Dr Bruce, SHHD

**Subjective measures of quality of life in Britain:
1971 to 1975** J Hall, SSRC

No.8 1977

**Social commentary: fifteen to twenty-five: a decade
of transition** CSO

The characteristics of low income households R Van
Slooten and A G Coverdale, DHSS

No.9 1979

**Housing tenure in England and Wales: the present
situation and recent trends** A E Holmans, DOE

Social forecasting in Lucas B R Jones, Lucas Industries

No.10 1980

**Social commentary: changes in living standards
since the 1950s** CSO

Inner cities in England D Allnutt and A Gelardi, DOE

Scotland's schools D Wishart, SED

No.14 1984

Changes in the life-styles of the elderly 1959 –1982
M Abrams

No.15 1985

British social attitudes R Jowell and C Airey, SCPR

No.16 1986

Income after retirement G C Fiegehen, DHSS

No.17 1987

Social Trends since World War II Professor A H Halsey,
University of Oxford

**Household formation and dissolution and housing
tenure: a longitudinal perspective** A E Holmans and S
Nandy, DOE; A C Brown, OPCS

No.18 1988

**Major epidemics of the 20th century: from coronary
thrombosis to AIDS** Sir Richard Doll, University of
Oxford

No.19 1989

Recent trends in social attitudes L Brook, R Jowell and
S Witherspoon, SCPR

No.20 1990

Social Trends, the next 20 years T Griffin, CSO

No.21 1991

**The 1991 Census of Great Britain: plans for content
and output** B Mahon and D Pearce, OPCS

No.22 1992

Crime statistics: their use and misuse C Lewis, HO

No.24 1994

**Characteristics of the bottom 20 per cent of the
income distribution** N Adkin, DSS

No.26 1996

The OPCS Longitudinal Study J Smith, OPCS

British Household Panel Survey J Gershuny, N Buck, O
Coker, S Dex, J Ermish, S Jenkins and A McCulloch, ESRC
Research Centre on Micro-social Change

No.27 1997

Projections: a look into the future T Harris, ONS

No.28 1998

French and British societies: a comparison P Lee and
P Midy, INSEE and A Smith and C Summerfield, ONS

No.29 1999

**Drugs in the United Kingdom – a jigsaw with
missing pieces** A Bradley and O Baker, Institute for the
Study of Drug Dependence

No.30 2000

A hundred years of social change A H Halsey, Emeritus
Fellow, Nuffield College, Oxford

No.31 2001

200 hundred years of the census of population M
Nissel

No.32 2002

Children B Botting, ONS

Index

The references in this index refer to table and chart numbers, or entries in the Appendix.

A

Abortions
conceptions, by outcome   2.14, 2.15
rates, by age   2.17
teenage conceptions, by age and outcome   2.15
Accidental deaths
childhood mortality   7.10
drug-related poisoning   7.14
Accidents
casualties from road accidents involving
illegal alcohol levels   12.23
childhood mortality, main causes   7.10
Accommodation type
by construction date   10.3
by tenure   10.6
by type of accommodation   10.12
dwelling prices   10.22
temporary   10.13, 10.14
used on holidays in the UK   13.19
without central heating, by tenure   10.15
Activity   13.1
Adoption   2.22, 8.23
by age of child   8.23
children looked after by local authorities   8.22
orders   2.22
Age
See also 'Children', 'Older people' and 'Young people'
abortion rates   2.17
at childbirth   2.19
at divorce   2.12
at marriage   2.12
breastfeeding, by age at which mother
completed full-time education   7.18
childhood mortality   7.10
childlessness   2.20
cinema attendance   13.9
cohabitation   2.9
economic activity rates   4.2
employees' receiving job-related training   3.18
enrolments on adult education courses
by subject and sex   3.13
expectation of life at age 65, by sex   7.1
GP consultations   8.16
household reference person, by tenure   10.10
immunisation of children by
their second birthday   7.22
living alone   2.3
multiple births   2.21
National Minimum Wage   5.23
neighbourliness   13.5
New Deal   4.25

new episodes
of asthma, by sex   7.5
of genital chlamydia, by sex   7.7
offenders found guilty of or cautioned
for indictable offences   9.13
one person households   2.3
overemployment   4.28
participation in education and training   3.10
pensioners' income, by source   5.4
plastic card holders   6.10
population   1.2
aged 65 and over, EU comparison   1.4
by ethnic group   1.5
dependent   1.3
prevalence of diagnosed diabetes, by sex   7.6
reasons for attending the arts   13.8
teenage conceptions   2.15
underemployment   4.29
unemployment   4.19
by ethnic group   4.20
victims of vehicle thefts and burglary   9.9
working towards a qualification   3.11
Agricultural land use   11.11
Aids
charitable expenditure on social protection   8.7
Air
household expenditure on air travel   12.6
international passenger movement, by air   12.21
international travel, by mode   12.19
passenger
death rates   12.22
transport   12.1, 12.5
pollution
by source   11.3
carbon dioxide, by end user   11.9
carbon dioxide, EU comparison   11.8
carbon monoxide   11.3
emissions   11.4
temperature   11.7
Alcohol
casualties from road accidents   12.23
consumption by sex and socio-economic group   7.15
draught lager, average price   6.15
percentage change in retail prices index   6.14
Ambulances   8.14
Anti-depressant drugs
prescriptions   7.9
Anxiety
prevalence of neurotic disorders, by sex   7.8
Asthma   7.5
Asylum Seekers

applications   1.14

Attitudes

area   10.17, 10.18

beliefs about change in the national crime rate   9.11

good things about nursery education providers   3.2

perception of local conditions, by sex   11.16

reasons for moving, by post-move tenure   10.20

road transport   12.16

satisfaction with NHS hospitals and GPs   8.17

to activities for the home   13.3

towards the environment   12.16

B

Bankruptcies

individual   6.12

Benefits   App Pt 8

by family type   8.5

child benefit   8.5

council tax benefit   8.5

expenditure   8.3

by recipient   8.4

EU comparison   8.2

on social protection   8.1

health and school exclusions   5.24

household income, composition of   5.2

incapacity and disability benefit

income support   8.5

jobseeker's allowance   8.5

pensioners' income, by age and source   5.4

recipients   8.5

pensioners   8.5

sick and disabled   App Pt 8, 8.18

state retirement pension   8.5

redistribution of income   5.17

social security benefit expenditure   8.4

working families tax credit   8.5

Bicycles

passenger death rates   12.22

passenger transport   12.1

Birds   11.15

Births   1.8

average age of mother   2.19

adoption orders   2.22

multiple births, by age of mother   2.21

outside marriage   2.18

as a percentage of all live births   2.18

population change   1.7

to teenage women, EU comparison   2.16

Body mass index   App Pt 7

by sex   7.20

Borrowing   6.11

Breast cancer screening   7.24

Breastfeeding   7.18

Burglary

crime, by area type   9.5

crime committed within last 12 months   9.2

detection rates for recorded crime   9.18

indictable offences, by type   9.15, 9.16

juvenile reconviction   9.14

offenders   9.9, 9.13, 9.14, 9.16

recorded crime   9.1

theft of mobile phones   9.7

worry about crime, by household income   9.10

victims of, by age   9.9

Buses

household expenditure   12.6

passenger

death rates   12.22

transport   12.1

transport prices   12.5

time to walk to nearest bus stop   12.11

travel, journeys and distance   12.15

C

Camping

type of accommodation   13.10

Cancer

cervical screening by age   7.23

charitable expenditure on social protection   8.7

breast cancer screening by region   7.24

death rates from selected   7.12

survival rates for major cancers, by sex   7.13

Cannabis

use among young adults, EU comparison   7.17

related poisoning deaths   7.14

Caravan

type of accommodation   13.10

Carbon dioxide

emissions of, by end user   11.9

emissions of, EU comparison   11.8

Carbon monoxide

air pollutants, by source   11.4

Carers   App Pt 8

home help and home care   8.9

informal

health symptoms   8.11

types of help given   8.10

Care homes

See 'Residential care homes'

Cars

See also 'Transport' and 'Travel'

attitudes to road transport and the environment   12.16

company car   5.11

crime   9.1, 9.2, 9.3, 9.9, 9.10, 9.14, 9.15, 9.16, 9.18

motoring offences   9.17

offenders cautioned, by type of offence   9.15

offenders sentenced, by type of
offence and type of sentence   9.16

expenditure   12.6, 6.14

households with regular use of car   12.9

households with access to one or more cars   12.10

licensed   12.8

passenger   12.1, 12.5

death rates   12.22

pollutants, by source   11.3

petrol

prices   6.15, 12.5, 12.7

household expenditure   6.7, 12.6

registrations   12.8

Cautions

offenders, by type of offence   9.15

Central heating

accommodation without central heating,
by tenure   10.15

Cervical screening   7.23

Channel Tunnel, international travel by mode   12.20

Charities

expenditure on social protection   8.7

volunteering, by type of activity   13.5

Cheques

non-cash transactions   6.9

Childlessness   2.20

Childminders

places for children   8.21

Children

See also 'Families'

adoptions   2.22, 8.22, 8.23

benefits, receipt by family type   8.3

clothing

household expenditure on selected items   6.7

day care places   3.2, 8.21

death rates, by age and sex   1.9, 7.10

dependent population   1.3

expenditure

charitable expenditure on social protection   8.7

on selected items, by family type   6.4

on social protection   8.1

local authority personal social
services expenditure   8.6

families with dependent children, by ethnic group   2.5

by family types   2.4, 2.5, 10.12

GP consultations, by age   8.16

health and school exclusions of
children by selected family types   5.24

immunisation   7.22

literacy of 15 year olds, EU comparison   3.8

looked after by local authorities   8.22

low income   5.23

mortality, main causes by sex and age   7.10

offenders, by sex, type of offence and age   9.13

population, by age   1.2, 1.3, 1.5

stepfamily couples   2.13

time taken to travel to school   12.13

under five in schools   3.1

Cigarette smoking

average price   6.15

by sex and socio-economic group   7.16

cessation by age and sex   7.25

tobacco, average change in retail prices index   6.14

Cinema

attendance   13.9

Citizenship   App Pt 1

international migration   1.12

Cohabitation   2.9

Community

indicators of neighbourliness, by age   13.4

trust, by age   A.4

Company directors fringe benefits, taxable   5.11

Conceptions   App Pt 2, 2.14, 2.15

by outcome   2.14, 2.15

to teenagers, by age and outcome   2.15

Consumers

net borrowing   6.11

Contraceptives

emergency number prescribed   7.21

Countryside

stewardship   11.12

Credit card

holders by age   6.10

non-cash transactions   6.9

Crime   App Pt 9, 9.2

beliefs about change in the national crime rate   9.11

by area type   9.5

by type of offence   9.1

committed within last 12 months,
by type of offence   9.2

detection rates   9.18

domestic violence   9.12

juvenile offenders

    reconviction within one year, by type of offence 9.14

legal aid   9.23

motoring   9.17

people convicted, See 'Offenders'

perception of local conditions   10.18

prison population   9.19

offenders cautioned for indictable offences   9.15

offenders sentenced for indictable offences   9.16

recorded

    by type   9.1

    in which firearms were used   9.8

    percentage change, EU comparison   9.4

repeat victimisation   9.12

reported, by type   9.1

seizures of selected drugs   9.6

theft of mobile phones, by type of offence   9.7

worry about   9.10

writs and summonses issued   9.21

Criminal damage

See also 'Vandalism'

detection rates, by type of offence   9.18

indictable offences   9.15, 9.16

juvenile reconviction, by type of offence   9.14

offenders, by sex, type of offence and age   9.13

recorded crime, by type of offence   9.1

D

Day care for children

children under five in school   3.1

good things about nursery education providers   3.2

places for children   8.21

Deaths   1.8, 1.9

cancer rates, by selected types and sex   7.12

casualties from road accidents involving alcohol   12.23

childhood mortality, main causes   7.10

drug related poisoning   7.14

infant mortality, by social class   7.3

life expectancy   7.1, 7.2

passenger death rates, by mode of transport   12.22

population change   1.7

rates   1.9, 7.11

road deaths, EU comparison   12.24

world demographic indicators   1.16

Debit cards

holders by age   6.10

non-cash transactions   6.9

Debt

individual insolvencies   6.12

net borrowing by consumers   6.11

Dentists, practitioners   8.15

Depression

anti-depressant drugs dispensed   7.9

prevalence of neurotic disorders, by sex   7.8

Deprivation   10.8

Diabetes   7.6

Diet

consumption of fresh fruit and vegetables,
by income group   7.19

Disability   App Pt 4, App Pt 5

See also 'Illness'

charitable expenditure on social protection   8.7

economic activity status   4.4

expenditure on social protection, by function 8.1

learning reported, by disability   3.20

local authority personal social services expenditure 8.6

recipients of benefits   8.5, 8.18

residential care homes, places available   8.8

types of help given by informal carers   8.10

Disposable income   5.1, 5.14

by ethnic group of head of household   5.15

Divorces   2.8, 2.10, 2.11, 2.12

average age   2.12

population, by marital status   2.8

rates, EU comparison   2.11

Doctors

See 'GPs'

Domestic violence

applications and orders   9.22

repeat victimisation   9.12

Drugs

alcohol consumption   7.15

use among young adults, EU comparisons   7.17

cigarette smoking   7.16

detection rates for recorded crime   9.18

drug-related poisoning deaths   7.14

juvenile reconviction, by type of offence   9.14

offences   9.6

offenders   9.13, 9.14, 9.15, 9.16

recorded crime, by type of offence   9.1

seizures   9.6

smoking cessation by age and sex   7.25

DVDs   13.15

Dwellings

See 'Housing'

E

Earnings
  average gross weekly earnings, by area 5.8
  composition of weekly pay, by type of work 5.10
  distribution of hourly earnings 5.9
  fringe benefits, taxable 5.11
  full-time employees 5.6
  hourly sex differential 5.7
  household income, composition of 5.2
  by industry 5.9
  pensioners' income, by age and source 5.4
EC budget
  contributions to and receipts from 5.32
Economic activity
  by employment status and sex 4.10
  by tenure 10.9
  household expenditure 6.2
    at constant prices 6.1
    by economic activity 6.3
    by region 6.6
    of retired households 6.5
    on selected items 6.4
    on selected items by place of purchase 6.7
  of disabled people, by sex 4.4
  of female lone parents 4.3
  low income 5.19
  rates 4.1, 4.2
  savings by economic status of benefit unit and amount 5.27
  working age households 4.6
Economic inactivity
  reasons for, by sex 4.5
Education
App Pt 3
  See also 'Schools'
  achievement
    by key stage 3.7
    GCE A level or equivalent 3.14
    GCSEs, by parents' socio-economic classification 3.9
  exclusions from school 3.5
    work/benefit status of selected family types 5.24
  expenditure 3.22
  graduates
    destinations of first degree graduates 3.16
  highest qualification
    by region 3.17
  languages
    pupils whose mother tongue is not English 3.6
  learning
    obstacles to, by sex 3.21
    reported, by disability 3.20
  literacy
    knowledge and skills of 15 year olds, EU comparison 3.8
  National Curriculum App Pt 3, 3.7
  nursery education
    good things about nursery education providers 3.2
  participation rates
    adult education, by subject, age and sex 3.13
    children under five in schools 3.1
    further and higher education 3.12
    16, 17 and 18 year olds in education and training 3.10
    people working towards qualifications 3.11
  pupils, by type of school 3.3
  students in further and higher education 3.12
  use of Information and Communications Technology (ICT) 3.25
  vocational
    NVQ awards, by area and level 3.15
Elderly
  See 'Older people'
Elections
  voting turnout A.2
Electricity
  proportion produced by renewable sources, EU comparison 11.10
Emergency calls 8.14
Emergency contraception
  number prescribed 7.21
Employees
  by sex and occupation 4.13
  composition of weekly pay, by sex and type of work 5.10
  fringe benefits, taxable 5.11
  hours worked 4.27
  jobs, by sex and industry 4.12
  length of service 4.22
  receiving job-related training 3.18
  second jobs, by industry 4.14
Employment
  distribution of weekly work hours 4.26
  job searching
    by sex and method 4.24
    reasons for looking for a new job 4.23
  length of service of employees 4.22
  overemployment, by age, sex and work pattern 4.28
  people entering through New Deal 4.25
  population of working age, by socio-economic classification 1.6
  rates App Pt 4, 4.7
  by area 4.9
  by ethnic group and highest qualification 4.11

reasons for economic inactivity	4.5
second jobs, by industry of main job	
self-employment	
by ethnic group	4.16
household expenditure	6.3
pension provision	8.19
second jobs	4.14
by sex, EU comparison	4.15
status	
EU comparison	4.8
National Minimum Wage	5.20
New Deal	4.25
pension provision, by sex and age	8.19
by sex	4.10
underemployment, by age, sex and work pattern	4.29
usual hours of work, by sex	4.26
working age households	4.6
Enrolments	
See 'Education, participation rates'	
Entertainment	
attendance at cultural events	13.7
CD, LP, cassette and single sales	13.17
cinema attendance, by age	13.9
DVD rentals and purchases	13.15
reasons for attending the arts	13.8
television viewing patterns	13.16
video rentals and purchases	13.15
visits to tourist attractions	13.11
Environment	
air pollution	
carbon dioxide, by end user	11.9
emissions	11.4
pollutants, by source	11.3
attitudes to road transport and the environment	12.6
bird populations	11.15
concerns	11.1
emissions	
carbon dioxide, EU comparison	11.8
carbon monoxide	11.4
energy produced by renewable sources, EU comparison	11.10
household impact	11.19
land use in environmental schemes	11.12
perception of local conditions, by sex	11.16
personal actions for positive impact	11.2
rainfall, regional comparison	11.20
reserves of oil and gas	11.22
residential use land change	11.13
schemes, land in environmental schemes	11.12
surface temperatures	11.7
waste management by method	11.17
water pollution	
incidents, by source	11.5
chemical quality of rivers and canals	11.6
woodland creation	11.14
Equivalisation	
distribution of equivalised income, by ethnic group	5.15
scales	App Pt 5
ESSPROS	8.2
Ethnic group	
classification	App Pt 1 1.5
distribution of income	5.15
employment rates	4.11
families with dependent children	2.5
of head of household, by tenure	10.11
population, by age	1.5
police officer strength, by sex	9.24
self-employment	4.16
unemployment rates by age	4.20
Europe	
EU expenditure	App Pt 5
holidays abroad, by destination	13.12
world demographic indicators	1.16
European Union comparisons	
asylum applications	1.14
drug use among young adults	7.17
comparative price levels	6.17
consumer prices	6.16
divorce rates	2.11
EC budget	5.32
electricity produced by renewable sources	11.10
emissions of carbon dioxide	11.8
employment status	4.8
expenditure	
education	3.22
social protection benefits	8.2
international migration	1.12
literacy of 15 year olds	3.8
live births to teenage women	2.16
marriage rates	2.11
population aged 65 and over	1.4
premium unleaded petrol prices	12.7
road deaths	12.24
self-employment, by sex	4.15
serious crimes recorded by the police	9.4
Exclusions from school	
by sex	3.5
work/benefit status of selected family types	5.24

Expenditure

  benefits

    by family type | 8.4

    social security | 8.3, 8.4

  comparative price levels, EU comparison | 6.17

  credit and debit cards | 6.9, 6.10

  education, EU comparison | 3.22

  government | 5.31

    National Health Service | 8.3

    social security benefits | 8.3, 8.4

  harmonised index of consumer prices, EU comparison | 6.16

  household | App Pt 6

    at constant prices | 6.1, 6.2

    by economic activity status | 6.3

    by family type | 6.4

    by region | 6.6

    retired households | 6.5

    on selected items, by place of purchase | 6.7

    on transport | 12.6

  motoring costs | 12.6

  non-cash transactions, by method of payment | 6.9

  retail prices index | 6.13

  retail sales, volume of | 6.8

  transactions

    non-cash, by method of payment | 6.9

F

Families | App Pt 2

  See also 'Children' and 'Households'

  adults Seeing grandchildren | 2.7

  adults Seeing relatives | 2.6, 2.7

  children living in different family types | 2.4, 2.5

  distribution of income for pensioners | 8.20

  GCSE achievement, by parents' socio-economic classification | 3.9

  expenditure on social protection, by function | 8.1

  health and school exclusions of children | 5.24

  household expenditure on selected items | 6.4

  household type | 2.2, 10.12

  income | 5.5

  lone parent | 2.2, 2.4, 2.5, 4.3, 10.12

  median individual net income, by sex | 5.5

  receipt of benefits | 8.5

  satisfactory networks, by length of residence | A.5

  stepfamily couples | 2.13

Farming

  land use | 11.11

  water pollution, by source | 11.5

Fertility rates

  world demographic indicators | 1.16

Financial assets/liabilities

  household sector

    income, composition of | 5.2

    net wealth, composition of | 5.25

Firearms

  recorded crimes involving | 9.8

Fostering | 8.22

Fraud and forgery

  detection rates for recorded crime | 9.1

  indictable offences | 9.13, 9.16

  juvenile reconviction, by type of offence | 9.14

  recorded crime, by type of offence | 9.1

Freight

  goods moved, by mode | 12.4

Friends

  frequency of adults Seeing | 2.6

  satisfactory networks, by length of residence | A.5

Fringe benefits, taxable | 5.11

Fuel

  petrol

    average price | 12.7, 6.15

    household expenditure by place of purchase | 6.7

    production of primary fuels | 11.21

    prices | 12.5

Further education

  students, by type of course | 3.12

G

Gas

  reserves | 11.22

GCE A level or equivalent

  achievement | 3.14

  highest qualification, by region | 3.17

  people working towards qualifications | 3.11

GCSEs

  achievement by parents' socio-economic classification | 3.9

  highest qualification, by region | 3.17

  people working towards qualifications | 3.11

Government

  See also 'Local authorities'

  expenditure

    by function | 5.31

    NHS | 8.3

    social security benefits | 8.3, 8.4

GPs

  consultations, by age | 8.16

  health symptoms felt by informal carers | 8.11

  people's satisfaction with | 8.17

  staff | 8.15

Gross domestic product

annual growth 5.28

expenditure on education, EU comparison 3.22

per head 5.1

EU comparison 5.29

Gross value added

by households 5.30

H

Harmonised index of consumer prices App Pt 6

EU comparison 6.16

Health

alcohol consumption, by sex and
socio-economic group 7.15

asthma, new episodes, by sex and age 7.5

body mass index, by sex 7.20

cancer screening

breast cancer, by region 7.24

cervical cancer, by age 7.23

children with long-standing illness or disability 5.24

cigarette smoking

by age and socio-economic group 7.16

cessation, by age and sex 7.25

contraception

emergency contraceptives prescribed 7.21

diabetes diagnosis, by sex and age 7.6

diet

consumption of fresh fruit and vegetables,
by income group 7.19

drugs

use among young adults 7.17

emergency calls 8.14

life expectancy

at age 65, by sex 7.1

at birth, by social class and sex 7.2

mental health

anti-depressant drugs dispensed 7.9

charitable expenditure, by function 8.7

local authority expenditure on social protection 8.6

NHS in-patient activity 8.14

places in residential care homes 8.8

prevalence of neurotic disorders, by sex 7.8

NHS

GP consultations, by age 8.16

notifications of selected infectious diseases 7.4

sexually transmitted diseases

genital chlamydia, by sex and age 7.7

staff 8.15

symptoms felt by informal carers 8.11

Health and personal social services staff App Pt 8

See also 'GPs', 'Health visitors' and 'Midwives'

Health visitors 8.15

Higher education

destinations of first degree graduates 3.16

expenditure, EU comparison 3.22

people working towards a qualification 3.11

students, by sex 3.12

students, by type of course 3.12

student standard maintenance grant and loan 3.26

Holidays

abroad, by destination 13.12

type of accommodation used in the UK 13.10

Home help and home care

households visited by 8.9

Homeless

households in temporary accommodation 10.13

reasons for 10.14

Hospitals

in-patients 8.12

people's satisfaction 8.17

staff 8.15

waiting lists, by region 8.13

Hotel

type of accommodation used on
holidays in the UK 13.10

Hours worked

by occupation 4.27

usual weekly hours 4.26

Housebuilding completions

by construction date 10.3

by number of bedrooms 10.5

rates, by sector 10.4

Households App Pt 2

by age of household reference person 10.10

below average income App Pt 5

cohabitation 2.9

composition of net wealth 5.25

crime, worry about 9.10

deprivation by tenure 10.8

economic status, working age households 4.6

by ethnic group of head 2.5, 10.11

expenditure

at constant prices 6.1, 6.2

by economic activity status 6.3

by region 6.6

on selected items

by family type 6.4

by place of purchase 6.7

of retired households 6.5

on transport 12.6

by family 2.2

gross value added 5.30

household sector   App Pt 5

by household type   2.2, 2.3, 10.12

income

  below median income   5.18

  children living in low income households   5.23

  composition   5.2

  disposable   5.1

    distribution of real household
    disposable income   5.14

    indirect taxes as a percentage of   5.13

  low income, by economic activity status   5.19

  low income, by region   5.21

  movements within the income distribution   5.16

  pensioners' gross income   5.4

  personal travel   12.3

  redistribution of, through taxes and benefits   5.17

  sources   5.2, 5.3

  worry about crime, by household income   9.10

one person households   2.1, 2.2, 2.3

resident under one year, by previous and current tenure
10.19

by size   2.1

by type of accommodation   10.12

visited by home help and home care   8.9

working age households   4.6

with access to one or more cars   12.10

with regular use of a car   12.9

Housing

average dwelling prices   10.22

by household type   10.12

by tenure   10.6

expenditure on social protection, by function   8.1

first time buyers

  average dwelling prices   10.23

moving house

  main reasons, by post-move tenure   10.20

mortgages

  by type   10.24

  loans in arrears and repossessions   10.25

percentage change in the retail prices index 6.13, 6.14

sales and transfers of local authority dwellings   10.21

satisfaction with area, by tenure   10.17

stock of dwellings   10.1, 10.2

type of, by construction date   10.3

I

Illness

benefits   8.1, 8.4, 8.5, 8.18

expenditure on social protection, by function   8.1

health symptoms felt by informal carers   8.11

NHS in-patient activity   8.12

work/benefit status of families   5.24

Immunisation   7.22

Income

See also 'Benefits' and 'Earnings'

consumption of fresh fruit and vegetables,
by income group   7.19

distribution

  by ethnic group   5.15

  number of movements   5.16

  of hourly earnings, by industry   5.9

  pensioners, by family type and pension scheme 8.20

disposable   5.1

  by ethnic group of head of household   5.15

  distribution of   5.14

  indirect taxes   5.13

by family type   5.5

fringe benefits, taxable   5.11

household, composition of   5.2

individual income   App Pt 5

  low incomes   5.18, 5.19, 5.21, 5.23

  number of movements within the
  income distribution   5.16

  persistent low income   5.22

  health and school exclusions of children   5.24

pensioners   5.4, 5.5

redistribution   5.17

sources of   5.3

trips per person per year, by household income 12.3

Industry

employee jobs   4.12

second jobs   4.14

Infant

incidence of breastfeeding   7.18

mortality, by social class   7.3

mortality, by world demographic indicators   1.16

Infectious diseases

notifications   7.4

Inflation   App Pt 6

harmonised index of consumer process,
EU comparison   6.16

retail price index   6.13, 6.14

Informal carers   App Pt 8

See 'Carers'

Insolvencies

individual   6.12

International comparison   1.15, 1.16

See also 'European Union comparisons'
and 'Migration'

asylum applications   1.14

International travel

  by mode   12.19

  passenger movement, by air   12.21

  UK residents visiting abroad, by month   12.20

J

Jobs

  See 'Employment'

  reasons for looking for a new job   4.23

  search methods   4.24

  second jobs   4.14

Juvenile offenders

  reconviction within one year, by type of offence   9.14

K

Key stages

  pupils reaching or exceeding expected standards, by sex   3.7

L

Labour force   App Pt 4

Land use

  agricultural   11.11

  changing to residential, by previous use   11.13

  in environmental schemes   11.12

Learning

  obstacles to, by sex   3.21

  reported, by disability   3.20

Library books issued   13.18

Life expectancy   App Pt 7

  at age 65, by sex   7.1

  at birth, by social class and sex   7.2

  world demographic indicators   1.16

Local authorities

  day care for children   8.21

  expenditure on personal social services   8.6

  housebuilding completions   10.3

  looked after children   8.22

  residential care homes, by sector   8.8

  sales and transfers of dwellings   10.21

Lone parents   2.2, 2.4, 2.5

  economic activity status   4.3, 4.6

Low income

  See 'Income'

M

Marriages   2.10

  average age at   2.12

  population, by marital status   2.8

  rates, EU comparison   2.11

Maternities

  conceptions, by outcome   2.14, 2.15

  with multiple births, by age of mother   2.21

  teenage conceptions, by age and outcome   2.15

Measles

  notifications of selected infectious diseases   7.4

Mental health

  anti-depressant drugs dispensed   7.9

  charitable expenditure, by function   8.7

  local authority expenditure on social protection   8.6

  places in residential care homes   8.8

  prevalence of neurotic disorders, by sex   7.8

Midwives   8.15

Migration   App Pt 1 1.7, 1.10, 1.11, 1.12

  international   1.12

  inter-regional   1.11

  population change   1.7, 1.10

  settlement grants   1.13

Minimum Wage

  See 'National Minimum Wage'

Minority ethnic group

  See 'Ethnic group'

MMR   7.22

Mobile phones

  theft of, by type of offence   9.7

Mortality

  See 'Deaths'

Mortgages

  by type   10.24

  loans in arrears and repossessions   10.25

Motorcycles

  currently licensed   12.8

  new registrations   12.8

  passenger

    death rates   12.22

    transport   12.1

    transport prices   12.5

Motorways

  motor vehicle flow   12.14

Music

  CD, LP, cassette and single sales   13.17

N

National Health Service

  activity for sick and disabled   8.12

  ambulance responses   8.14

  emergency calls   8.14

  expenditure   8.3

  GP consultations, by age   8.16

in-patients | 8.12, 8.13

people's satisfaction with hospitals and GPs | 8.17

staff | 8.15

waiting lists, by region | 8.13

National Minimum Wage

rates by age, sex and employment status | 5.20

Neighbourliness

indicators of neighbourliness, by age | 13.5

trust, by age | A.4

Neurotic disorders

anti-depressant drugs dispensed | 7.9

prevalence among adults, by sex | 7.8

New Deal | 4.25

Non-teaching staff, by type of school | 3.24

Nurses | 8.15

Nurseries

good things about nursery education providers | 3.2

places for children | 8.21

NVQ awards, by framework area | 3.15

O

Obesity

body mass index, by sex | 7.20

Obsessive compulsive disorder

prevalence of neurotic disorder, by sex | 7.8

Occupation

hours worked | 4.27

employees, by sex | 4.13

unemployment rates, by previous | 4.21

Offences

crime committed within last 12 months, by type of offence | 9.2

detection rates for recorded crime | 9.18

indictable offences

offenders, by sex, type of offence and age | 9.13

offenders cautioned for, by type of offence | 9.15

offenders sentenced for, by type of offence and type of sentence | 9.16

juvenile reconviction within one year, by type of offence | 9.14

motoring

by action taken | 9.17

recorded crime

by type of offence | 9.1

involving firearms | 9.8

sentenced for indictable offences, by sentence | 9.16

Oil

reserves | 11.22

Older people

See also 'Pensions'

benefits received | 8.5

death rates, by age and sex | 1.9, 7.11, 7.12

dependent population | 1.3

distribution of income by family type and pension provision | 8.20

expenditure

by whether or not dependant on state pension | 6.5

expenditure on social protection, by function | 8.1

charitable | 8.7

local authority personal social services expenditure | 8.6

social security benefit, by recipient group | 8.4

GP consultations, by age | 8.16

households visited by home help and home care | 8.9

income, by age and source | 5.4

life expectancy at age 65, by sex | 7.1

neighbourliness, indicators of | 13.5

population aged 65 and over, EU comparisons | 1.4

population, by age | 1.2, 1.3, 1.5

population by ethnic group and age | 1.5

residential care homes, places available | 8.8

victims of vehicle-related thefts and burglary | 9.9

Organic conversion | 11.12

Out of school clubs | 8.21

Overcrowding, by tenure | 10.16

Overemployment | 4.28

P

Passenger

bus travel | 12.15

death rates | 12.22

international passenger movements, by air | 12.21

transport, by mode | 12.1

transport prices | 12.5

Pay

See also 'Earnings'

below National Minimum Wage rates | 5.20

composition of weekly pay of employees, by type of work | 5.10

Pensions

See also 'Older people'

benefits received | 8.5

distribution of income for pensioners by family type | 8.20

expenditure

of retired households | 6.5

by economic activity status | 6.3

median individual net income, by sex

pensioners' income, by age and source | 5.4

provision, by selected employment status | 8.19

Personal social services | 8.15

households visited by home help and home care | 8.9

local authority expenditure 8.6

Petrol prices, EU comparison 12.7

Phobias

    prevalence of neurotic disorders, by sex 7.8

Plastic cards

    holders by age 6.10

    non-cash transactions 6.9

Playgroups

    places for children 8.21

Police officer strength, by sex, minority
ethnic group and rank 9.24

Pollution

    air pollution

        by source 11.3

        by type 11.4

    water pollution, incidents by source 11.5

Population App Pt 1, 1.1

    See also 'Migration'

    aged 65 and over, EU comparisons 1.4

    by ethnic group and age 1.5

    by sex 1.2

    change 1.7, 1.10

    density 1.15

    dependent, by age 1.3

    of the United Kingdom 1.1

    of working age

        EU comparison 1.4

        by socio-economic classification 1.6

    projections App pt1, 1.1, 1.2, 1.3, 1.7

    United Kingdom 1.1

    world 1.16

Prevention

    breast cancer screening 7.24

    cervical cancer screening 7.23

    immunisation 7.22

    smoking cessation 7.25

Prices

    average change in retail prices index 6.13, 6.14

    comparative price levels, EU comparison 6.16

    national rail fare price index 12.18

    of passenger transport 12.5

    premium unleaded petrol, EU comparison 12.7

    of selected items 6.15

Prison

    population 9.19

Psychiatric morbidity

    See 'Health, mental health'

Pupils

    by type of school 3.3

    whose mother tongue is not English 3.6

Q

Qualifications App Pt 3

    employment rates, by highest qualification 4.11

    GCE A level or equivalent, by sex 3.14

    GCSE achievement, by parents'
socio-economic classification 3.9

    highest, by region 3.17

    NVQ awards, by framework area 3.15

    people working towards, by age 3.11

R

Rail

    fares 12.5, 12.6, 12.18

    goods moved by domestic freight 12.4

    journeys, by operator 12.17

    household expenditure 12.6

    passenger

        death rates 12.22

        transport 12.1

        transport prices 12.5

Rainfall

    by region 11.20

Reading

    library books issued 13.18

Recorded crime App Pt 9

    by type of offence 9.1

    detection rates, by type of offence 9.18

    percentage change, EU comparison 9.4

    involving firearms 9.8

Reconviction

    juvenile 9.14

Recycling

    household waste recycling by area 11.18

    personal actions taken 11.2

    waste management 11.17

Redistribution of income App Pt 5

    through taxes and benefits 5.17

Regional comparisons 1.10, 1.11

    annual rainfall 11.20

    breast cancer screening 7.24

    dwelling prices 10.22

    earnings 5.8

    employment rates, by area 4.9

    highest qualification, by region 3.17

    hospital waiting lists 8.13

    housebuilding completion rates 10.4

    household waste recycling 11.18

    household weekly expenditure 6.6

    low income households 5.21

    time taken to walk to nearest bus stop 12.11

unemployment rates   4.18

    households with access to the Internet   13.14

    pupils whose mother tongue is not English   3.6

Relatives

    adults Seeing grandchildren   2.7

    frequency of contact   2.6, 2.7

    satisfactory networks, by length of residence   A.5

Residential care homes   8.8

Retail outlets

    household expenditure   6.7

Retail prices index   App Pt 6, 6.13

    change in average price of selected items   6.15

    national rail fare price index   12.18

    passenger transport prices   12.5

    percentage change   6.14

Retail sales volume   6.8

Retired households

    See 'Older people'

Retirement pension

    See 'Pensions'

Rivers and canals

    chemical quality   11.6

Roads

    attitudes to road transport   12.16

    casualties from road accidents involving alcohol 12.23

    deaths, EU comparison   12.24

    goods moved by domestic freight   12.4

    passenger transport   12.1

    passenger transport prices   12.5

    vehicle flow   12.14

Robbery   9.3

    detection rates for recorded crime   9.18

    indictable offences

        offenders, by sex, type of offence and age   9.13

        offenders cautioned for, by type of offence   9.15

        offenders sentenced for, by type of offence

        and type of sentence   9.16

    juvenile reconviction rates, by type of offence   9.14

    recorded crime, by type of offence   9.1

    theft of mobile phones, by type of offence   9.7

S

Savings

    by economic status of benefit unit   5.27

Schools

    children under five   3.1

    exclusions from school   3.5

        by work/benefit status of selected family types 5.24

    appeals launched against non-admission   3.4

    non-teaching staff   3.24

pupils

    by type of school   3.3

    whose mother tongue is not English   3.6

teachers   3.23

    who feel confident in the use of ICT   3.25

time taken to travel to   12.13

Sea

    international travel, by mode   12.20

Second jobs, by industry   4.14

Self-employment

    by ethnic group   4.16

    by sex, EU comparison   4.15

Sexual offences

    indictable offences

        offenders, by sex, type of offence and age   9.13

        offenders cautioned for, by type of offence   9.15

        offenders sentenced for, by type of offence

        and type of sentence   9.16

    juvenile reconviction, by type of offence   9.14

    recorded crime, by type of offence   9.1

    worry about crime, by household income   9.10

Sexually transmitted diseases

    new episodes of genital chlamydia by sex and age 7.7

Sickness

    See 'Illness'

Smoking

    See 'Cigarette smoking'

Social capital

    by characteristics of people   A.6

Social class

    See also 'Socio-economic group'

    infant mortality   7.3

    life expectancy at birth by sex   7.2

Social protection

    benefits   8.1

    EU comparison   8.2

Social security

    See 'Benefits'

Social services

    See 'Personal social services'

Socio-economic classification   App Pt 1

    alcohol consumption by sex   7.15

    cigarette smoking by sex   7.16

    GCSE achievement by parents' socio-economic

classification   3.9

    life expectancy at birth, by sex   7.2

    population of working age, by sex   1.6

    by tenure   10.7

Sport

    participation, by sex   13.6

Standard Occupational Classification   App Pt 4

Students

  destinations of first degree graduates   3.16

  in further and higher education

    by type of course   3.12

  standard maintenance grant and loan   3.26

Substance misuse

  See Drugs

Supermarkets

  household expenditure on selected items   6.7

T

Taxes

  household income, composition of   5.2

  income tax payable, by income   5.12

  indirect, as a percentage of disposable income   5.13

  redistribution of income through taxes and benefits   5.17

Teachers   3.23

  who feel confident in the use of ICT   3.25

Teenagers

  births, EU comparison   2.16

  fertility rates   App Pt 2

Telecommunications

  theft of mobile phones, by type of offence   9.7

Television

  viewing patterns   13.16

Tenure

  accommodation without central heating   10.15

  by age of household reference person   10.10

  by economic activity status   10.9

  by ethnic group of head of household   10.11

  household resident under one year, previous tenure, by current tenure   10.19

  households living in the most deprived wards and least deprived wards   10.8

  overcrowding   10.16

  reasons for moving, by post-move tenure   10.20

  satisfaction with area   10.17

  by socio-economic group   10.7

  stock of dwellings   10.2

  by type of accommodation   10.6

  under-occupation   10.16

Theft   App Pt 9

  crimes committed within last 12 months   9.2

  juvenile reconviction, by type of offence   9.14

  of mobile phones, by type of offence   9.7

  offenders   9.13, 9.14, 9.15, 9.16

  recorded crime, by type of offence   9.1

  reported and recorded crime, by type of offence   9.3

  victims of vehicle-related thefts and burglary, by age   9.9

Time use

  activities   13.2

  activities on weekdays   13.1

  television viewing patterns   13.16

Tourism

  tourist attractions   13.11

Training   App Pt 3

  employees receiving job-related training, by sex and age   3.18

  off-the-job, types of   3.19

  participation by 16, 17 and 18 year olds   3.10

Transactions, non-cash

  by method of payment   6.9

Transport

  air   12.19, 12.21

  attitudes to road transport   12.16

  bus   12.15

  by mode   12.1

  domestic freight   12.4

  expenditure   12.6, 6.2, 6.3, 6.5

  passenger

    death rates   12.22

    transport prices   12.5

  petrol prices, EU comparison   12.7

  rail   12.17

  sea   12.19

  traffic, average daily flow   12.14

Travel

  by mode   12.1

  by purpose   12.2

  fares and travel costs, average change in retail prices index   6.14, 12.5

  international

    by mode   12.19

    passenger movements, by air   12.21

    UK residents visiting abroad, by month   12.20

  personal

    by household income   12.3

    by mode   12.2

  time to school

    by age of child and area type   12.13

  traffic, average daily flow   12.14

  trips

    by household income   12.3

    by mode   12.2

  to work

    mean time taken, by sex and area type   12.12

Tuberculosis

  notifications   7.4

Twins

  See 'Births, multiple births'

U

Under-occupation

by tenure — 10.16

Underemployment — 4.29

Unemployment — App Pt 4

by age — 4.17

economic activity status of female lone parents — 4.3

expenditure by economic activity status — 6.3

expenditure on social protection, by function — 8.1

people entering employment through New Deal — 4.25

rates

by ethnic group and age — 4.20

by previous occupation — 4.21

by region — 4.18

by sex and age — 4.19

European comparison — 4.8

social security benefit expenditure, by function — 8.4

Urban land use, by previous use — 11.13

V

Vandalism — 10.18

Videos rentals and purchases — 13.15

Violent crimes

by area type — 9.5

committed within last 12 months — 9.2

detection rates for recorded crime — 9.18

indictable offences

offenders, by sex, type of offence and age — 9.13

offenders cautioned for, by type of offence — 9.15

offenders sentenced for, by type of offence
and type of sentence — 9.16

involving firearms — 9.8

juvenile reconviction rates, by type of offence — 9.14

recorded and reported crime, by type of offence — 9.1

repeat victimisation — 9.12

worry about crime, by household income — 9.10

Vehicles

See 'Cars'

Vocational

learning reported, by disability — 3.20

NVQ awards, by framework area — 3.15

Voluntary activities — 13.4

W

Waiting times — App Pt 8

Walking

time taken to walk to nearest bus stop — 12.11

Waste management

by method — 11.7

environmental concerns — 11.1

personal actions taken — 11.2

water pollution, by source — 11.5

Water

chemical quality of rivers and canals — 11.6

goods moved by domestic freight — 12.4

pollution incidents, by source — 11.5

Wealth

distribution of — App Pt 5, 5.26

household sector, composition of — 5.25

Whooping cough

notifications of selected infectious diseases — 7.4

Woodland

creation — 11.4

schemes — 11.12

World population density — 1.15

demographic indicators — 1.16

Work

See also 'Employment'

benefit status of family — 5.24

mean time taken to travel to — 12.12

population, by socio-economic classification — 1.6

composition of weekly pay of employees, by sex — 5.10

Working age population

by employment status and sex — 4.8

Working hours

distribution of usual working hours — 4.26

more than 50 hours a week — 4.27

Worry about crime, by household income — 9.10

Y

Young people

charitable expenditure, by function — 8.7

offenders, by sex, type of offence and age — 9.13

participation in education and training — 3.10

prevalence of recent use of drugs — 7.17